SO-DTQ-922

HISTORICAL PERSPECTIVES ON CANADIAN COMPETITION POLICY

Copyright by The Institute for Research on Public Policy 1991
All rights reserved

Printed in Canada

Legal Deposit Fourth Quarter
Bibliothèque nationale du Québec

Canadian Cataloguing in Publication Data

Main entry under title:

Historical Perspectives on Canadian Competition Policy

Prefatory material in English and French

ISBN 0-88645-136-1

1. Competition law and policy - Canada - historical perspectives
I. Khemani, R.S., 1946- II. Stanbury, W.T., 1943-
III. Institute for Research on Public Policy

The Institute for Research on Public Policy/
L'Institut de recherches politiques
P.O. Box 3670 South
Halifax, Nova Scotia B3J 3K6

HISTORICAL PERSPECTIVES ON CANADIAN COMPETITION POLICY

•A15045 911782

edited by

R.S. Khemani
and
W.T. Stanbury

KE
1639
.H57
1991
West

The Institute for Research on Public Policy
Halifax, N.S.
1991

Dedication

This volume is dedicated to the memory of
Bruce C. McDonald
He died tragically in an automobile accident
in 1991. His contributions to Canadian competition
law and policy will long be remembered.

Bruce was truly a scholar and a gentleman.

TABLE OF CONTENTS

Page

Acknowledgements

This volume and its companion volume, *Canadian Competition Law and Policy at the Centenary* (Halifax: The Institute for Research on Public Policy, 1991), which we also edited, originated at a lengthy dinner we had with Roy Davidson late in 1988. The issue we discussed was how to mark the centenary of Canada's first competition legislation which was enacted in 1889, a year before the much more famous *Sherman Act* in the U.S.. We agreed that the importance of the occasion merited a <u>national</u> conference and one or more volumes of papers analyzing Canadian competition policy in both historical and contemporary terms. Thus began the task of recruiting people to help organize the conference, prepare and deliver papers, to act as commentators on the conference presentations, and to contribute money to finance the deficit associated with the conference and the publications. The need for subsidies reflects the fact that competition policy is a public good and it is of direct and deep interest to only a fairly small number of people.

Yet, in fairly short order we were able to recruit three major sponsors who provided both financial and other resources. We are pleased to acknowledge the substantial support of the following organizations:

- Bureau of Competition Policy
  Department of Consumer and Corporate Affairs
  Ottawa

- Centre for International Business Studies
  Faculty of Commerce and Business Administration
  University of British Columbia

- The Institute for Research on Public Policy

The balance of the deficit was defrayed by generous contributions from nine major Canadian law firms:

- Bennett Jones (now Bennett Jones Verchere)
- Blake, Cassels & Graydon
- Davis & Company
- Fraser & Beatty Legal Publications,
  Canadian Competition Policy Record
- Freeman & Company
- Ladner Downs
- Lang Michener Lawrence & Shaw
- Ogilvy Renault

- Phillips & Vineberg

We gratefully record our sincere appreciation for their support. In addition, partners from each firm participated in the Conference in a number of ways.

Dr. David Conklin of the National Centre for Management Research and Development at the University of Western Ontario was IRPP's representative on the coordinating committee along with the editors. He had the onerous job of handling the logistics of the Conference, and ensuring that expenses did not exceed revenues from ticket sales plus donations from the sponsoring organizations. Furthermore, the Institute agreed to publish the two volumes of papers associated with the project.

Margaret Sanderson of the Bureau of Competition Policy did an outstanding job helping the coordinating committee with the myriad details involved in arranging for the two-day conference (held in Toronto on October 24-25, 1989), featuring scores of speakers, including a number from the U.S., Europe and Australia.

In organizing and presenting the Conference, a number of academics, lawyers, and public servants from both Canada and abroad gave generously of their time and talent. We are pleased to acknowledge the assistance of Donald Baker, Jeffrey Bernstein, Serge Bourque, Bill Brock, Charles Dalfen, Klaus Decker, Jonathan Faul, Christopher Green, Abraham Hollander, John L. Howard, Lawson Hunter, Hudson Janisch, Jean-Pierre LeGoff, Marilyn MacCrimmon, Don McFetridge, Frank P. Monteleone, Francois Rioux, Thomas Ross, J. William Rowley, David Rutenberg, Sandra Sutherland, Frederick Warren-Boulton, Leonard Waverman, and Howard Wetston.

Two people contributed a great deal to the production of the two volumes associated with this project. Meg Fellowes helped with the proofreading and checked many of the references. Sandra Carter did an outstanding job in "word processing" the manuscripts through several rounds of editing and revisions into camera-ready form.

Finally, we wish to thank our authors without whose efforts these volumes could not have been produced. They endured considerable delays while we were working on other projects, although we have tried to update the papers to reflect developments since the revised but not final versions of the papers were received in 1990. The usual caveat applies.

R.S. Khemani
W.T. Stanbury

Foreword

In 1889, Canada was the first western industrialized nation to enact legislation designed to prevent firms from forming agreements in restraint of trade. More than a century later, the conspiracy provisions remain at the core of competition legislation. The role of competition policy, however, has expanded significantly with the development of the Canadian economy. Along with monetary, fiscal and trade policy, competition policy in Canada, as well as in other countries, has become an integral part of the general framework of policies promoting structural adjustment, international competitiveness, economic growth, and price stability.

The importance of competition policy is heightened when considered in the context of an increasingly less regulated economic environment. It has been widely documented -- including in books published by the Institute -- that government intervention in the marketplace tends to induce distortions in economic performance. However, these distortions cannot be corrected simply by reducing regulatory constraints on business without simultaneously strengthening the forces of competition. It is worth noting that at the Toronto Economic Summit held in June 1988, the G-7 countries first explicitly enunciated the goal of intensifying both individual and collective efforts to remove unnecessary controls and barriers to the operation of competitive market forces, and to rely on increased competition to achieve economic efficiency and adaptability. These objectives have been re-affirmed in subsequent summit meetings. Moreover, as Michael Porter and others have emphasized, with the global scope of many markets for goods, services, and capital, a high level of domestic competition and inter-firm rivalry is essential for sustained advantage in international trade.

It may be recalled that shortly after the end of World War II, steps were taken to enact competition legislation in (West) Germany and Japan as part of the set of reconstruction measures. Competition policy has also been recognized as an important element in the economic and political reforms in Eastern Europe and even the Soviet Union. Czechoslovakia, Hungary, Poland and the Soviet Union have recently adopted or have pending "antimonopoly" legislation as they move toward a much more market-oriented economy. Simply privatizing state monopolies will not diffuse ownership and market power, foster competition and stimulate innovation. Effective competition law is necessary in order to provide a framework for business conduct, to protect consumer interests, and to maximize economic welfare.

Over the past 13 years the Institute for Research on Public Policy has published seven volumes on Canadian competition policy -- a list of relevant publications can be found at the end of this book. These span, as can be seen, a wide range of studies and commentaries on the functioning of markets and legislative or regulatory initiatives to discipline the exercise of market power, particularly in the protracted efforts of the federal government throughout the 1970s and 80s to adapt its competition policies to the needs of a more interdependent and technology-intensive economy.

The major reforms in Canadian competition legislation (e.g., those dealing with mergers and abuse of dominant position -- now enshrined in civil law) were not enacted until 1986 when the *Competition Act* replaced the venerable *Combines Investigation Act*. The new law immediately had to cope with the largest merger boom in Canadian history. The scores of very large and hundreds of smaller mergers -- together with the globalization of financial markets and efforts to reform federal and provincial regulations governing financial institutions -- prompted considerable concern about the implications of these developments. IRPP sponsored a national conference in March 1987 from which emerged a large proceedings volume entitled *Mergers, Corporate Concentration and Power in Canada*, published in 1988.

To mark the centenary of Canada's first anti-combines or competition legislation, the Institute, together with the Bureau of Competition Policy and the University of B.C., and with financial contributions -- gratefully acknowledged -- from nine major law firms, sponsored a national conference in October 1989. From the papers presented at the conference and commissioned for the occasion, R.S. Khemani and W.T. Stanbury have produced two volumes. The present volume and its companion volume, *Canadian Competition Law and Policy at the Centenary*, represent the culmination of the Institute's involvement in this area.

The centenary of competition law and policy in Canada provided an opportunity to trace the roots of this important public policy, analyze its evolution, assess its effects and speculate about its future. Readers will note from the diversity of views presented in these volumes that the debates and challenges confronting competition policy continue. The central role played by competitive forces in a free market economy means that competition policy needs to be reassessed and modified periodically in light of changing economic conditions.

In each of its publications on competition policy, the Institute has sought to stimulate and inform public debate on this important issue by presenting a variety of viewpoints. Even more vital than competition in the market for goods, services and capital, competition in the marketplace of ideas remains the key to effective public policy. The Institute hopes that these two volumes will help to illuminate the complex problems entailed in protecting individuals from the abuse of market power.

Rod Dobell
Victoria
August 1991

Avant-Propos

Le Canada a été le premier des pays occidentaux industrialisés à mettre en vigueur, dès 1889, une législation pour empêcher les entreprises de former des ententes visant à entraver le libre jeu de la concurrence. Plus d'un siècle après, les clauses relatives aux coalitions sont toujours à la base de la législation sur la concurrence. Toutefois, avec l'expansion de l'économie canadienne, le rôle de cette législation s'est accru d'une manière considérable. Que ce soit en matière de concurrence, de fiscalité ou dans le domaine monétaire, la politique du Canada, aussi bien d'ailleurs que celle d'autres pays, est devenue partie intégrante de toute une infrastructure réglementaire destinée à favoriser les ajustements structurels, la concurrence internationale, la croissance économique et la stabilité des prix.

L'importance de la politique en matière de concurrence se trouve renforcée quand on l'envisage dans un contexte économique de moins en moins réglementé. Il a été largement établi, y compris dans des études publiées par l'Institut, que l'intervention du gouvernement sur le marché tend à produire des distorsions dans les rendements de l'économie. Ces distorsions, cependant, ne peuvent pas être corrigées simplement par un assouplissement des contraintes réglementaires qui pèsent sur le monde des affaires, sans que soient simultanément renforcées les forces de la concurrence. Il est intéressant de remarquer que, lors du Sommet économique de Toronto de juin 1988, les pays du Groupe des sept ont expressément stipulé qu'il y avait lieu d'intensifier les efforts individuels aussi bien que collectifs afin de supprimer les contrôles et obstacles inutiles gênant le bon fonctionnement des forces concurrentielles du marché, et de s'appuyer sur une concurrence accrue, de manière à acquérir l'efficacité et la souplesse économiques qui s'imposent. Ces objectifs ont été de nouveau formulés lors des réunions au sommet ultérieures. En outre, comme Michael Porter et d'autres l'ont souligné, étant donné le caractère global de nombreux marchés dans les secteurs des biens, des services et des capitaux, un haut niveau de concurrence interne et de rivalité entre entreprises s'avère indispensable si l'on veut avoir des chances durables en matière de commerce international.

Il y a lieu de se rappeler que peu de temps après la Seconde Guerre mondiale, une législation sur la concurrence avait été instaurée en Allemagne (de l'Ouest) et au Japon, dans le cadre des mesures de reconstruction de l'époque. L'Europe de l'Est et même l'Union soviétique ont également reconnu l'importance d'une législation sur la concurrence pour les réformes économiques et politiques en cours. Dans leurs efforts d'orientation vers une économie de marché, la Tchécoslovaquie, la Hongrie, la Pologne et l'Union soviétique ont récemment adopté, ou sont en train de le faire, une législation «antimonopole». Mais la simple privatisation des monopoles d'État ne suffira pas pour établir la propriété privée et l'économie de marché, encourager la concurrence et stimuler l'innovation : une législation sur la concurrence est nécessaire si l'on veut aménager un cadre adéquat pour la conduite des affaires, la protection des intérêts des consommateurs et un rendement économique maximum.

Au cours des 13 dernières années, l'Institut de recherches politiques a publié sept ouvrages consacrés à la politique canadienne sur la concurrence (une liste de publications dans ce domaine figure à la fin du présent volume). On pourra constater que celles-ci comportent un grand nombre d'études et de commentaires, allant du fonctionnement des marchés et des initiatives législatives ou réglementaires jusqu'aux mesures de contrôle de l'exercice du pouvoir du marché, particulièrement en ce qui concerne les efforts poursuivis par le gouvernement fédéral, au cours des années 70 et 80, afin d'adapter ses politiques en matière de concurrence aux besoins d'une économie plus interdépendante et plus axée sur la technologie.

Les réformes majeures de la législation canadienne en matière de concurrence (comme par exemple celles portant sur les fusions d'entreprises et sur les abus dus à une situation dominante, qui sont maintenant inscrites dans le droit civil) ne sont pas entrées en vigueur avant 1986, quand la *Loi sur la concurrence* a remplacé la vénérable *Loi relative aux enquêtes sur les coalitions*. La nouvelle loi a eu immédiatement à faire face à la plus grande vague de fusions d'entreprises de l'histoire du Canada. Les vingtaines de fusions de grande envergure et les centaines de plus petites, venant s'ajouter à la globalisation des marchés financiers et aux efforts visant à réformer les réglementations fédérales et provinciales relatives aux institutions financières, ont suscité des inquiétudes considérables quant aux effets possibles que pouvait entraîner cette nouvelle situation. L'IRP a parrainé un colloque national, en mars 1987, dont les actes ont été publiés sous la forme d'un gros volume intitulé *Mergers, Corporate Concentration and Power in Canada*, qui a paru en 1988.

Pour marquer le centenaire de la première législation canadienne anticoalition, ou législation sur la concurrence, l'Institut, conjointement avec le Bureau de la politique sur la concurrence et avec l'Université de la Colombie-Britannique, et grâce au soutien financier de neuf cabinets juridiques importants, que nous remercions avec gratitude, a parrainé un congrès national en octobre 1989. À partir des communications présentées à ce congrès et qui avaient été commissionnées pour la circonstance, R.S. Khemani et W.T. Stanbury ont trouvé matière à la publication de deux volumes. Le présent volume et l'autre volume qui l'accompagne, *Canadian Competition Law and Policy at the Centenary*, représentent le point culminant des efforts de l'Institut en ce domaine.

Le centenaire de la législation et de la politique en matière de concurrence au Canada a fourni l'occasion de redécouvrir les origines de cet important aspect de notre politique générale, d'en analyser l'évolution, d'en évaluer les effets et de spéculer sur son avenir. Les lecteurs se rendront compte, d'après la diversité des points de vue exposés dans ces volumes, que les débats et les défis continuent pour la politique en matière de concurrence. Le rôle essentiel que jouent les forces de la concurrence dans une économie de marché oblige à réévaluer périodiquement la politique en matière de concurrence, afin de demeurer à même de la modifier en fonction des conditions économiques nouvelles.

Dans chacune de ses publications traitant de la politique en matière de concurrence, l'Institut a cherché à stimuler et à inspirer le débat public sur cette importante question, en présentant une grande diversité de points de vue. La concurrence sur le forum des idées est encore peut-être plus vitale que celle qui s'exerce sur le marché des biens, des services et des capitaux, car elle est la condition nécessaire à l'établissement de toute politique générale efficace. L'Institut espère que ces deux volumes aideront à faire la lumière sur les problèmes complexes que soulève la protection des particuliers contre les excès de l'économie de marché.

A.R. Dobell
Président

Introduction

EDITORS' OVERVIEW

R.S. Khemani
Visiting Professor
Faculty of Commerce & Business Administration
University of British Columbia

W.T. Stanbury
UPS Foundation Professor of Regulation
and Competition Policy
Faculty of Commerce & Business Administration
University of British Columbia

The papers in this volume are part of a major project to mark the centenary of Canada's competition legislation which originated in 1889. The project, described in more detail in the "Acknowledgements," consisted of a national conference in October 1989 and two volumes of papers published by the Institute for Research on Public Policy.[1]

In this volume, we have brought together eight papers which provide new insights into the history of competition law in Canada and its administration. We believe there is much value in George Santayana's (1863-1952) observation that "those who do not remember the past are condemned to relive it." Even Regis Debray, apostle of revolution, acknowledged the influence of history on the present:

> We are never completely contemporaneous with our present. History advances in disguise; it appears on stage wearing the mask of the preceding scene, and we tend to lose the meaning of the play.

---

1. The companion volume, R.S. Khemani and W.T. Stanbury (eds.) *Canadian Competition Law and Policy at the Centenary* (Halifax: The Institute for Research on Public Policy, 1991).

J.K. Galbraith, with more diffidence than usual, has said that "perhaps it is a good sense of history that divides good economics from bad." These papers should add to our sense of the history of competition policy with a view to seeing that future legislation reflects sound economic analysis.

In Chapter 1, Carman D. Baggaley re-examines the origins of Canadian competition law and policy by concentrating on the period 1888 to 1900. In 1988, a Parliamentary Committee was appointed to examine allegations that numerous cartels were bilking consumers. In 1900, the original enactment of 1889 was made enforceable by the elimination of the word "unlawfully."[2] Baggaley's approach is to put the 1889 legislation in the context of prevailing economic conditions, political pressures and the state of the common law. The lesson to be learned from studying Canada's original anti-combines legislation is that "legislators are too often directed by 'the clamorous opportunity of partial interests'."

In Chapter 2, Paul K. Gorecki and W.T. Stanbury extend their previous work on the administration and enforcement of competition policy in Canada back to cover the period 1889 to 1952. They trace in some detail the evolution of the administrative machinery which changed several times during that period. In addition, they examine enforcement activity and the outcomes of prosecutions which grew in frequency over the half century. Gorecki and Stanbury conclude that the weaknesses in the administration and enforcement of competition policy "was an accurate reflection of the set of values that dominated the nation's economy and public policy. Only some of the most severe forms of anti-competitive behaviour were addressed, the tools were faulty, and the remedies largely ineffective."[3]

Brian R. Cheffins, in Chapter 3, offers an assessment of two failed experiments with the use of civil law in Canadian competition policy in 1919 and 1935.[4] The experiments foundered on the shoals of constitutionality, but he concludes that "the government was taking a step forward when it dismantled the legislation." Cheffins states that the *Board of Commerce Act* and *Combines and Fair Prices Act* of 1919, and the *Dominion Trade and Industry Commission Act* of 1935 and amendments to the *Combines Investigation Act* and *Criminal Code* in 1935 were "not the result of a long-term shift in attitudes toward competition." Rather, they were "components

---

2. However, the word "unduly" was retained and remains in the conspiracy provisions to this day. See S.45 of the *Competition Act*.

3. Their conclusion reminds us of George Santayana's (1863-1953) dyspeptic assessment of "the working of great institutions" which he said "is mainly the result of a vast mass of routine, petty malice, self interest, carelessness and sheer mistake. Only a residual fraction is thought."

4. The first successful civil law provisions came into effect on January 1, 1976. Others were added in 1986.

in larger legislative packages which were enacted quickly to alleviate political pressure arising from distressed economic conditions." These legislative initiatives "focused more on controlling competitive forces than enhancing the operation of the market."

Although it is clear that resale price maintenance (RPM) existed in Canada since at least the 1880s, the federal government did not prohibit RPM and its frequent means of achieving this restraint (refusal to supply) until 1951. In Chapter 4, Tamara Hunter traces the background of the price maintenance legislation, emphasizing the role of the MacQuarrie Committee which was appointed in 1950. Hunter also describes the evolution of the statutory provision, particularly the loss leader defences enacted in 1960, and the broadening of the provisions in the 1976 amendments. Next to the misleading advertising provisions, the price maintenance provisions, now in S.61 of the *Competition Act* of 1986, account for the largest number of prosecutions under Canada's competition legislation.

In Chapter 5, W. Chris Martin describes and analyzes the evolution of the legislation governing misleading advertising and other deceptive marketing practices and its administration. While the *Criminal Code* contained a section dealing with misleading advertising between 1914 and 1960, few cases were prosecuted. In 1960, the *Combines Investigation Act* was amended to prohibit misrepresentations about prices. In 1969 the *Criminal Code* provisions were transferred to the Act, and were thereby made the administrative responsibility of the Director of Investigation and Research. As a result of these two changes, the number of cases soon grew to exceed the number under all other sections of the Act combined. While a number of other deceptive marketing practices were enacted in 1976, they have not resulted in a large number of cases. Martin also examines the jurisprudence, including the effect of the 1982 *Charter of Rights and Freedoms*, and the application of the recently-developed compliance-oriented approach to deceptive marketing practices.

As emphasized by Baggaley, Gorecki and Stanbury, and Cheffins, political forces have long shaped Canadian competition policy. Yet in Chapter 6, Ian D. Clark suggests that the *Competition Act* of 1986 was "a policy thrust supported by successive Governments over two decades which anticipated the Canadian economy would become increasingly integrated with a global economic system." Clark reviews the complicated policy process out of which the Stage I amendments were enacted in late 1975 while the passage of the *Competition Act* occurred in mid-1986. Clark identifies three lessons that can be learned from this process. First, the lengthy and loud debate that occurred reflects the "fundamental role played by competition in our society." Policy makers underestimated the need for consultation, particularly with the business community. Second, "competition policy represents an extremely important piece of legislation" which is designed to advance several objectives, although in recent years the allocative and dynamic efficiency objective has been emphasized. Third, the civil law approach, proposed by the Economic

Council in 1969, "represented a definitive break from the past." It is not surprising, therefore, that there was a vigorous debate, particularly about the test to be applied to mergers and the appropriate forum for adjudication of cases.

In Chapter 7, historian Michael Bliss provides a comparison of the competitive environment in Canada in 1889, when the first anti-combines legislation was enacted, and that which prevailed a century later. He begins by reviewing the role of N. Clarke Wallace - the Conservative MP considered the father of the 1889 legislation. Bliss notes that the supporters of the legislation were concerned about the proliferation of combines which sought to "prevent unprofitable competition." He contrasts this situation to that of 1989 when "the invisible hands of the marketplace... challenge the collectivist order put in place by big business, big labour, and, above all, big government." Deregulation, privatization and trade liberalization have all increased the importance of market forces. Yet, Bliss contends, it is easy to find examples of government-induced restraints of trade - for example supply management marketing boards which he describes as "a gouging monopoly." Such forms of government intervention reflect - as they did in 1889 - the ambivalence Canadians feel about the role of competition. Bliss goes so far as to say that 1989 marked the "centenary of a non-event, at best the centenary of a symbol, certainly not the commencement of serious anti-combines legislation in North America." He gives the pride of place to the United States' *Sherman Act* of 1890. Bliss concludes by suggesting that "trustbusting institutions" should focus on "the proclivities of government and politicians to limit competition, equality of opportunity, efficiency and economic growth."

Finally, in Chapter 8, Douglas Rutherford and J.S. Tyhurst trace the battles over the constitutionality of competition law in Canada over the period 1889-1989. They begin by noting that it was not until April 1989 that the Supreme Court of Canada "confirmed that such legislation as a whole is a valid exercise of a head of legislative authority other than the criminal law, namely, the trade and commerce power." The importance of this decision cannot be underestimated given the extensive use of civil law in the *Competition Act* of 1986. Rutherford and Tyhurst review the successful challenges to the constitutionality of the civil law provisions embodied in new legislation in 1919 and 1935 (described by Cheffins in Chapter 3), and they discuss the famous *Proprietary Articles* case which "finally confirmed [in 1931] a criminal law constitutional foundation for both the administrative structure and substantive aspects of competition law."

Constitutional issues have not been laid to rest by the Supreme Court's decisions in 1989. The constitutionality of the merger and conspiracy provisions of the *Competition Act* have been challenged as being inconsistent with the *Charter of Rights and Freedoms* embodied in the Canadian constitution in 1982.[5] Should the Crown not ultimately prevail, new legislation will be necessary.

In conclusion, with the publication of these papers we hope to contribute in a modest way to the refutation of Hegel's (1770-1831) assertion that "what experience and history teach is this - that people and governments have never learnt anything from history, or acted on the principles deduced from it."

---

5. See *Alex Couture v. Attorney-General of Canada* (1990), 30 C.P.R. (3d) 486; *L'Association quebecoise des pharmaciens proprietaires v. R.* (Quebec Superior Court, Unreported December 6, 1990); *R. v. Nova Scotia Pharmaceutical Society (No. 2)* (1990), 98 N.S.R. (2d) 296 (NSSC) and Nova Scotia Court of Appeal, Unreported, April 24, 1991.

Chapter 1

TARIFFS, COMBINES AND POLITICS: THE BEGINNING OF CANADIAN COMPETITION POLICY, 1888-1900

*Carman D. Baggaley**
Price Waterhouse Management Consultants

> The legislature, were it possible that its deliberations could be always directed, not by the clamorous importunity of partial interests, but by an extensive view of the general good, ought upon this very account, perhaps, to be particularly careful neither to establish any new monopolies of this kind, nor to extend further those which are already established. Every such regulation introduces some degree of real disorder into the constitution of the state, which it will be difficult afterwards to cure without occasioning another disorder.

> Adam Smith, *The Wealth of Nations*,
> (Book IV, Chapter 11)

1.0 INTRODUCTION

It has generally been accepted that Canada's first competition legislation, *An Act for the Prevention and Suppression of Combinations formed in restraint of Trade*;[1] was "a political sham"; or, at best, a well-intended but ineffectual gesture.[2] The first successful prosecution under the Act did not take place until more than a dozen years after it was passed and that would not have been possible if the Act had not been amended in 1900. One could

---

*. The paper was originally prepared for the Institute for Research on Public Policy in 1982.

1. Statutes of Canada, (hereinafter S.C.), 1889, 52 Vic., c. 41.

2. See Bliss (1973), Reynolds (1940), Ball (1934) and Gosse (1962). Bliss (1973, p. 182) refers to the passing of the Act as "a political sham" while Reynolds, Ball and Gosse tend to the latter view. The issue will be discussed below.

suggest that this was an appropriate beginning for our competition policy; in the wake of the wave of mergers in the late 1980s, some people might suggest that little has changed, that our present legislation is still a political sham.[3] Granted, we are in the midst of another attempt to amend our competition laws, but, as we know from recent experience and as we shall see below, proposing amendments is much easier than getting them passed.

The purpose of this study is not to try to overturn the conventional wisdom about the 1889 Act. Its purpose will be served if it manages to shed light on some dark corners. The study examines the introduction of the Act against various backdrops. The introduction of the Act will be viewed in the context of the economic background, the political background, and the common law background. As well, contemporary opinions on competition and combinations will be surveyed and, partly for the purposes of comparison, modern theories about the benefits of competition and the costs of restricting competition will be set out. The study also examines the various attempts to amend the legislation culminating in the successful attempt in 1900.

2.0   THE ECONOMIC BACKGROUND

During the last twenty years of the nineteenth century, the economic development of Canada was dominated by two events: the introduction of the National Policy tariff in 1879; and the construction of the Canadian Pacific Railway between 1881 and 1885. For the purposes of this study, the former was the more important. The National Policy was the result of a number of factors: a prolonged economic down-turn that began in 1873; charges that American companies were dumping their products in Canada; the growing influence of manufacturers; and the Conservatives' need for a platform with which to fight the 1878 election.[4]

Tariff levels were increased substantially; but, because there was a shift away from *ad valorem* tariffs to a combination of *ad valorem* and specific tariffs, it is not possible to provide a simple comparison of pre- and post-National Policy levels. There is no doubt that the main purpose of the upward revision was to encourage domestic manufacturing, which meant inducing American companies to set up branch plants in Canada.[5] Certain industries were particularly favoured with the highest tariff levels reserved for consumer goods. Duties on textiles were raised from approximately 15 per cent to what

---

3.   For a useful list of the more important mergers and takeovers during the 1970s and 1980s see Newman (1981, Appendix) and Stanbury (1988).

4.   See McDiarmid (1946) and Forster (1979) for useful accounts of the introduction of the National Policy.

5.   See Bliss (1970). It has been argued recently that Canada's first protective tariff had been introduced two decades earlier. See Barnett (1976) and Otter (1982).

worked out to be about 30 per cent. The rate on shoes and boots went up to 25 per cent. The duty on refined sugar was raised to encourage domestic refining while the duty on raw sugar was retained for revenue purposes (McDiarmid, 1946, pp. 162-163).[6]

In the case of textiles, footwear, and refined sugar, the tariff changes were designed to protect and encourage existing industries.[7] Sugar had been refined in Canada since the 1850s. By the 1870s the industry was in trouble and George Drummond, the president of the Redpath refinery, threatened to abandon the business if the duty on refined sugar was not increased substantially (Naylor, 1975, p. 45).[8] The 1879 tariff provided for a one cent a pound specific duty and a 35 per cent *ad valorem* duty. This was one of the most controversial changes. During the debate in the House, one Liberal member estimated that it would cost the people of Canada more than one million dollars annually to promote the refining interest (*Debates*, 1897, p. 1486).[9] Another Liberal argued, "No increased employment given to our population would compensate for the amount of money deliberately taken out of the pockets of the people, for the benefit of two or three refiners, by this tax on an article of universal consumption" (*Debates*, 1879, p. 1490).

At first glance it might appear that the impact of the National Policy was slight. Although the gross value of manufacturing output did increase by 4.8 per cent per year during the 1880s, it had increased by 4.4 per cent per year during the previous decade. Furthermore, the growth of secondary manufacturing actually declined during the 1880s (Bertram, 1967, p. 82). However, these aggregate figures mask important changes in output. Much of the growth that occurred in the 1880s took place in the first few years of the decade. Second, some of the industries that received particular attention in 1879 grew rapidly. In 1878 slightly more than 100 million pounds of sugar were consumed in Canada, only six per cent of which was refined domestically. By 1883, consumption had increased by almost 50 per cent and 94 per cent of the sugar consumed was refined in Canada (*Debates*, 1891, pp. 1215-1216). Five new refineries were built to take advantage of the new market (Naylor,

---

6. Nominal rates understate the actual rate of protection, "the effective rate." See Melvin and Wilkinson (1968).

7. According to the 1871 Census, 85 per cent of the woollens consumed in Canada were domestically produced, 24 per cent of cottons and denims, 99 per cent of the footwear, and 60 per cent of the refined sugar (p. 148).

8. See also Public Archives of Canada, *Sir John A. Macdonald Papers*, (M.G. 26 A), Vol. 349, George Dustan to Macdonald, 7 May 1878, pp. 160560-160561. Dustan wanted Macdonald to do something for the sugar refiners. He concluded his letter with, "I am indeed sick at heart and it largely depends on your reply to this letter, whether I will give up the fight and abandon this misruled unfortunate young country."

9. The citation "Debates" refers to House of Commons, *Debates*. (*Debates of the Senate* are referred to as *Senate Debates*.)

1975, pp. 45-46). Growth in the cotton industry was just as spectacular. Capital investment increased from $3.5 million to $13.2 million as the number of mills more than quadrupled. Most of this growth took place early in the decade; imports of raw cotton doubled between 1879 and 1883 and then increased by about 50 per cent during the rest of the decade (McDiarmid, 1946, p. 200).[10]

The introduction of the National Policy coincided with, and no doubt contributed to, a rising business cycle that peaked in mid-1882. The downward cycle that followed was both longer (it lasted almost three years) and more serious than average (Chambers, 1964, pp. 399-400). The succeeding expansion was limited. Despite the impetus provided by the National Policy, business conditions for most of the 1880s were somewhat discouraging. In every year from 1883 to 1890 over one thousand business failures were reported. The average number of failures increased from 771 per year for the first three years of the decade to over 1700 per year for the last two years. In 1883, 1884, 1887, and again in 1890, liabilities exceeded $15 million (*Debates*, 1891, p. 4894). Seven of the businesses that failed in the 1880s were banks. Equally serious in the eyes of many contemporaries was the modest increase in Canada's population. The country experienced a net migration loss during the 1880s. A further characteristic of Canada's economic condition that merits attention was the declining price level. The wholesale price index (1935-39 = 100) fell from 71.8 in 1880 to 67.1 in 1890 to 62.4 in 1900 (Bertram, 1967, p. 81).

It is not surprising that the most heavily protected industries were among the first to experience difficulties. As early as 1883 there were indications that the cotton industry was in trouble. The manufacturers' initial response was an unsuccessful attempt to set up a combine. The Canadian Cotton Manufactures' Association, created in 1886, enjoyed some success in limiting production and fixing prices until it collapsed in the late 1880s. In the early 1890s the number of firms was decreased as a result of a series of mergers (Acheson, 1971, pp. 88, 146). By the mid-1880s the sugar refiners faced similar problems (*Monetary Times*, 1883, pp. 912-913).[11] They too tried to solve their problems by fixing prices. In both cases the Conservative Government tried to help by raising import duties, but competition from imports was the least of the industries' problems.

Although the unfavourable economic conditions after 1882 no doubt contributed to the difficulties encountered by these industries, their main

---

10. Between 1878 and 1884 the number of cotton mills increased from five to twenty-three (Naylor, 1975, p. 50). In addition to the tariff, many of the mill owners benefited from bonuses and tax concessions granted by the towns in which the mills were located. See DeLottinville (1980, pp. 100-115) for an interesting account of one town's experience.

11. The industry was suffering from excess capacity and the Dartmouth refinery was not yet open.

problem was the one that had been predicted by the Liberal MP, Sir Richard Cartwright in 1879:

> This tariff assuredly cannot stand. Manufacturers will obtain no permanent relief from it. For one, two or three years they may succeed in making considerable profit out of the operations of the tariff, but in the end they will find that it was the greatest misfortune to encourage the undue home competition which will inevitably take the place of foreign competition of which they may complain (*Debates*, 1879, p. 446).

As Cartwright argued, many of the difficulties faced by domestic manufacturers were the result of the protective tariff they had lobbied so hard to get.

Unfortunately, the falling price level, which was common to the whole North-Atlantic economy, masked the impact of the tariff. The Conservatives could point to the falling prices as evidence that the tariff not only did not raise prices as the Liberal critics had predicted, it actually produced a drop in prices. The Government could even use the difficulties experienced by the sugar refiners and cotton manufacturers to refute the charges that the tariff increases had unfairly benefited certain manufacturers. During the 1884 budget debate, the Minister of Finance offered the following defence of the Government's tariff policy:

> ...the very moment a few hundred operatives in a cotton mill were out of employment for a month, there was a cry through the country that the National Policy was a failure, that this pampered industry was in a desperate condition, and was in this condition as a result of the protection that had been given. I am prepared to say here to-day that these industries, though they are in difficulty for want of capital - and that is the main cause - are placing themselves in such a position that an occurrence such as took place last summer will not take place again. They are arranging to have diversified manufactures....the point I want to bring out is this, that the consumer is obtaining his goods, the clothing that he requires, the cotton necessary for himself and his family at a price less than he would have had it under the Tariff of the hon. gentleman opposite. Now, the next pet industry was the sugar industry. It was said that large fortunes were being made out of that. I should not wonder now if we were told by the gentlemen opposite that the protection we gave them has encouraged the construction of so many refineries, that there is ruin before them as well....I think I am in a position to state that, at no period in the history of Canada, has the consumer of sugar had it as low a price as he has obtained it during the past year....(*Debates*, 1884, p. 578).

3.0 THE IMPACT OF TARIFFS AND MONOPOLY

Without specific studies of the industries in question, it is impossible to measure the effect of the tariff. However, there is little reason to assume that the expected income transfers and welfare losses did not occur. In the first place, tariff barriers raise the price of the commodity in question as firms engage in what is known as "tariff-limit pricing." Second, consumption drops as a result of the price increase. According to one Member of Parliament, per capita consumption of sugar in Canada was about half that in England and about 25 per cent less than in the United States (*Debates*, 1882, p. 762). Third, government revenues increase unless the tariff is completely prohibitory. In 1878, $12.8 million in duties were collected; the figure rose to $18.5 million in 1881 and $23.2 million in 1883 (McLean, 1895, p. 47). Customs revenues accounted for about three-quarters of the federal government's income during this period. Fourth, existing firms, those able to compete without tariff protection, or with the lower tariff, will earn "economic rent" as will new firms unless the tariff is set just high enough to induce them to enter the industry. The effect of a tariff is to transfer income from consumers to producers and the government. In the process though there is a deadweight loss, i.e., the consumers' loss is greater than the government's and producers' gains.

With the exception of the income transfer to the government, monopolies can have the same impact as tariff barriers. In both cases there is an income transfer and a deadweight loss due to misallocation, i.e., restriction of output. Attempts to measure the deadweight loss, or welfare loss, resulting from monopolies and tariffs have produced consistently small estimates ranging from .0075 per cent of GNP to a maximum of one per cent (Leibenstein, 1966, p. 393).[12] These figures could easily lead one to conclude that the economic costs of tariff and monopolies are not worth worrying about. However, these estimates take into account only the costs resulting from allocative inefficiency. There are additional costs that should be considered.

First, there are the costs stemming from technical inefficiency. As Gordon Tullock has suggested, a tariff that results in import substitution can be thought of as "a governmental requirement that the goods be obtained in an inefficient manner...." (Tullock, 1980, p. 42). It allows domestic firms to compete with foreign firms even though they are technically less efficient. Similarly, a monopolist is not forced to produce at the least cost nor does a monopolist have the same incentive as a competitive firm to search for ways to lower costs. The term "X-inefficiency" is used to refer to the technical inefficiency that occurs when monopolists do not produce at least cost. While allocative inefficiency leads directly to welfare losses because it raises prices, X-inefficiency leads to welfare losses by raising costs.[13]

Second, there are the costs involved in obtaining tariff protection or monopoly privileges:

> Generally governments do not impose protective tariffs on their own. They have to be lobbied or pressured into doing so by the expenditure of resources in political activity. One would anticipate that the domestic producers would invest resources

---

12. See also West (1978).

13. On the issue of "X-inefficiency" see Leibenstein (1966) and Comanor and Leibenstein (1969). More generally, see Reynolds (1940, pp. 128-130). For a skeptical view, see Stigler (1976).

> in lobbying for the tariff until the marginal return on the last dollar so spent was
> equal to its likely return, which would produce the transfer. There might also be
> other interests trying to prevent the transfer and putting resources into influencing
> the government in the other direction. These expenditures, which may simply offset
> each other to some extent, are purely wasteful from the standpoint of society as a
> whole; they are spent not in increasing wealth, but in attempting to transfer or resist
> transfer of wealth (Tullock, 1980, p. 44).

The argument here is that potential monopolists, or potential beneficiaries of a protective tariff, will dissipate anticipated rents in an attempt to secure monopoly privileges or a favourable tariff. This means that the income transfer from the consumers to the producers has to be added to the deadweight loss as an additional cost. As well, the costs sustained by the unsuccessful bidders and those opposed to the income transfer have to be considered as part of the welfare loss resulting from tariffs and monopolies. When the additional costs produced by x-inefficiency and rent-seeking are added to the costs resulting from allocative inefficiency (caused by the reduction in output and the increase in prices) it is apparent that the losses resulting from tariffs and monopolies are worth worrying about.[14]

Although these arguments must seem rather removed from reality, they do bear some resemblance to what happened in Canada during the last quarter of the nineteenth century. As expected, some existing firms flourished behind the protective wall of the National Policy (Naylor, 1975, p. 56).[15] However, the period of prosperity was short-lived as new firms, seeking a share of the increased profits, rushed into production. Soon, some industries were plagued by excess capacity. The problems experienced by the sugar refining and cotton industries suggest that a misallocation of resources did occur. Consumers might have received some temporary benefits from the overexpansion if competitive forces had been allowed to operate. Instead, the federal government provided the industries with still further protection and the firms in the industries attempted to reach agreements to counteract competitive forces.

There is also reason to believe that considerable resources were used convincing the Conservatives to adopt a high tariff policy, getting them elected in 1878, and keeping them in office. In 1903, a well-informed Canadian journalist commented that "every Dominion election since 1887 had been controlled by manufacturers" (J.S. Willison, quoted by Waite, 1974, p. 103). This may have been an exaggeration, and it certainly suggests more unanimity among manufacturers then ever existed; it does, however, point out that

---

14.   See Hunter (1979, pp. 111-112) for a summary of attempts to measure the impact of tariffs on Canada.

15.   Acheson (1971, p. 128) says that "the tariff of 1879 provided a temporary bonanza for the existing cotton firms, most of which declared dividends of eight to ten per cent the following year."

elections in late nineteenth century Canada were notoriously corrupt affairs. Following the 1874 and the 1891 elections, 49 and 40 members, respectively, were unseated as a result of election petitions (English, 1977, pp. 23, 18-30). Elections were costly, perhaps more so than contemporary elections in constant dollars, and the money must have come from somewhere. Some of it was raised during meetings with manufacturers in the infamous "Red Parlor" of a Toronto hotel.[16] Ultimately, it was Canadian consumers who paid the costs - not just the higher prices and the cost of financing elections, but also the cost of a lower level of political morality.

4.0 TRADE COMBINATIONS IN THE 1880s

It would be both naive and simplistic to argue, as did many Liberals, that the National Policy was the sole cause of the trade combinations that appeared in the 1880s. Combinations existed in mercantilist Tudor England, and they existed in free-trade Victorian England (Mathias, 1969, pp. 386-395); they existed in protected manufacturing industries such as textiles, and they existed in service industries such as undertaking; they existed during depressions and they existed during booms; and they have survived almost all attempts to destroy them. Adam Smith's famous observation has become trite; but nonetheless, it bears repeating: "People of the same trade seldom meet together, even for merriment and diversion, but the conversation ends in a conspiracy against the public, or in some contrivance to raise prices." Despite their ubiquitousness, it is reasonable to suggest that businessmen were given a special impetus to attempt to restrict competition as a result of the circumstances in which they found themselves in the 1880s. The impact of the tariff has already been mentioned; by encouraging overexpansion, it led to combinations designed to limit production and stabilize prices. Equally important, it protected combinations from foreign competition. Improvements in transportation and communications were another factor. Between 1870 and 1890 the number of railway track miles in operation increased fivefold, from 2,617 to 13,151 (Urquhart and Buckley, 1965, p. 528). Businesses which previously had enjoyed some degree of local monopoly as a result of distance now found themselves facing competition.

Increasing specialization in the marketing of goods also encouraged combinations. The wholesale grocers organized to prevent retailers from

---

16. See Bliss (1974, pp. 111-112): "The Liberals were substantially correct in the 1880s in charging that the manufacturers subsidized the Conservative party in elections in return for government subsidies through the tariff schedules.... There is no doubt that campaign contributions were pledged at the Red Parlor meetings. These must have been substantial; manufacturers present in 1887 were reported to represent invested capital worth $35,000,000. The manufacturers' contributions on top of the $1,000,000 the C.P.R. poured into Conservative coffers between 1882 and 1890, might well mean that the National Policy and the transcontinental railway survived not on their merits but because the electorate was bought and paid for."

buying directly from manufacturers as well as to fix prices. Similarly, retailers tried to prevent wholesalers from selling directly to the public (Bliss, 1974, pp. 37-39). The generally depressed economic conditions after 1882 may have provided the most immediate impetus. Another important factor was the declining price level. It is understandable that businessmen would have attributed falling prices to increasing competition and price-cutting rather than to exogenous factors. For the reasons just mentioned, competition may have increased during the 1880s; or, at least, they help explain the feeling among businessmen that competition was particularly fierce and destructive.

Throughout most of the decade the combinations and rings that existed attracted relatively little attention and even less criticism. During the seemingly endless House of Commons debates on tariff policy, Liberal members occasionally referred to combinations or rings while denouncing the National Policy. Their comments were usually very general. One of the few explicit references to trade combinations took place in 1881 when Dr. Orton, a Government back-bencher, moved that a Select Committee be appointed to investigate an alleged coal-oil ring (*Debates*, 1881, pp. 861-862). The motion was withdrawn. The two leading business periodicals of the day, the *Monetary Times* and the *Canadian Journal of Commerce*, reported regularly on trade combinations, without arousing public interest.[17]

As the decade passed, agreements to limit production and/or fix prices began to receive more critical attention. It is possible to suggest some reasons why this occurred. Events in the United States were an important factor. The 1880s were the decade when the "trusts" first appeared in the United States. Standard Oil was the first company to make use of the trust arrangement. It was also the most famous. A cotton oil trust and a linseed oil trust were soon formed and in 1887 they were joined by the whisky trust, the lead trust and the sugar trust (Chandler, 1977, pp. 320-321). The formation of the last three trusts seems to have spurred public and political interest. President Cleveland referred to the trusts in his annual message to Congress at the end of 1887. In January 1888 the first of several antitrust bills was introduced in Congress (Letwin, 1965, pp. 86-87). These events did not go unnoticed in Canada. Commenting on the formation of the whisky trust, the *Monetary Times* prophesied: "These combinations will one day bring their own remedy; and we almost shudder to think of the form in which, other measures failing, it may possibly make its appearance" (December 9, 1887, p. 727).[18]

---

17. See, for example, the reports of meetings of the Canadian Fire Underwriters' Association, the Grocers' Guild and the Cotton Manufacturers' Association in the *Monetary Times*, April 9, 1886, p. 1153; May 7, 1886, p. 1265; August 13, 1886, p. 180. The *Journal of Commerce* reported on the recently formed Oatmeal Millers' Association on July 3, 1887, p. 113; August 26, 1887, p. 364.

18. The *Globe*, January 31, 1888, contained a brief item on the introduction in Congress of a resolution dealing with combines and trusts.

Although many Canadians must have been aware that combinations existed in Canada, two events during the fall and winter of 1887/88 increased public awareness. The first, surprisingly, was the Toronto mayoralty elections. Three men contested the election, but it was a two-man race between Elias Rogers, a coal merchant and city alderman, and E.F. Clarke, a Conservative member of the provincial legislature.[19] Rogers, the reform candidate, was able to get good mileage out of the accusation that Clarke was the representative of the liquor interest until it was revealed that he was a member of a "coal ring" that fixed prices. Rogers spent much of the subsequent campaign denying the charge:

> It has been said that enormous profits are made out of the coal business. To this I want to give a distinct contradiction...we do not make over 25 cents per ton. I say, if any one disbelieves that statement or questions it, I will give to the charitable institutions of the city any amount that may be made in my business over that figure (*World* (Toronto) December 27, 1887, p. 1).

Although Rogers' involvement in the coal ring may have cost him the election, its existence did not seem to cause too much concern. The newspaper that reported the speech just quoted did not bother to investigate the matter. It was later revealed that similar rings existed in other cities, most notably Ottawa, but during the winter of 1887/88 the Ottawa *Evening Journal* never once mentioned the possibility that such a ring might exist. It is possible that the Toronto election was important not so much because the coal ring was uncovered, but because of the participation of Nathaniel Clarke Wallace. Wallace, the Conservative MP for West York (a Toronto suburban riding) campaigned on behalf of Clarke. Wallace was also the person responsible for the appointment of the Select Committee that investigated combinations in the spring of 1888. It was later charged that Wallace had raised the issue of combines in an attempt to get Rogers.[20]

It is more likely that it was the Dominion Wholesale Grocers' Guild rather than Elias Rogers' participation in the Toronto coal ring that motivated Wallace. The Grocers' Guild was formed in 1884. In 1887 the members of the Guild agreed to sell sugar to retailers at fixed prices and they managed to get the refiners to agree to charge wholesalers who did not participate a

---

19.   See Morton (1973, pp. 86-102) for an account of the campaign.

20.   In a speech delivered before the Toronto Board of Trade, Mr. Hugh Blain, a Toronto wholesaler, made the following accusation: "In opposing Mr. Rogers the question of coal and its prices came up for discussion. Mr. Wallace thought he had discovered a system of robbery by the Coal Merchants' Agreement, and when disconcerted by Mr. Rogers, who knew more about the matter than he did, threatened to bring it up in the House. He did so, but when he found that the price of coal was controlled by a foreign Company, over which he had no jurisdiction, he at once directed all his energies against the Wholesale Grocers' Association." Blain's speech, along with some related material, can be found in the Public Archives of Canada, *Macdonald Papers* (M.G. 26A, Vol. 334, pp. 150847-150862).

higher price for sugar.[21] The sugar combination, as it was commonly called, received far more attention than the Toronto coal ring or any other combination. During January and February 1888 the Toronto *Globe* had several stories on combines in general, and the sugar combine in particular. Like the good Liberal paper that it was, the *Globe* blamed the tariff: "of course the increase in sugar prices that the refiners have gained by bulldosing [sic] the grocers is a bagatelle to the whole sugar robbery promoted by the tariff" (January 12, 1888, p. 4). In the same issue, the paper quoted the advice of a rival: "If such a nefarious combination cannot be destroyed by existing law, the law certainly needs amendment." The Ottawa *Evening Journal* was much less interested; the one article it ran on the subject was reprinted from the Montreal *Star*, "There is but one way to bring these wealthy monopolists to a sense of the impropriety of their conduct and that is by withdrawing the protection they are abusing. Kill the sugar combine with free sugar and the cotton combine with free cotton" (March 14, 1888, p. 2). Newspapers that supported the National Policy, such as the Toronto *World*, denied that the tariff was to blame (February 4, 1888, p. 4; March 3, 1888, p. 4).

One reason why the sugar combine received more attention was because it operated throughout Ontario and part of Quebec. Unlike the Toronto coal ring, it was not a local phenomenon. The way in which it functioned also caused concern; in particular its impact on non-combiners. This was what bothered the *Monetary Times*: "But when it interferes with the rights of grocers who are not of the guild, and undertakes to dictate to them the way in which they shall do their business, under a penalty for non-compliance, objection comes in" (March 16, 1888, p. 1159). Much of the publicity concerning the combine was a result of the efforts of J.A. Matthewson, the only wholesale grocer who refused to participate. Matthewson seems to have supplied the Montreal press with information about the combine, and in February 1888, he sent a detailed, four-page petition to the Governor-General.[22]

While it is true that interest in trade combinations increased during 1887 and the first two months of 1888, it would be misleading to suggest that there was widespread public demand for their suppression. Matthewson's petition seems to be the only one that the Governor-General received on the subject. The *Globe* did urge action, but it was at least partially motivated by a desire to attack the tariff:

---

21. Wholesale grocers' associations were prosecuted unsuccessfully in 1909-1910 and 1922-1923. *R. v. Beckett* (1910), 20 O.L.R. 401, 15 C.C.C. 408 and *A.G. Ont. v. Canadian Wholesale Grocers' Association* 1923, 53 O.L.R. 627, 39 C.C.C. 272, 1923 2 D.L.R. 617 (C.A.).

22. Public Archives of Canada, *Privy Council Records* (R.G. 2-3), Vol. 47, P.C. 367, J.A. Mathewson Petition, February 22, 1888.

> Legislation against combines would meet with almost universal approval, and we hope to see it proposed by the opposition. The people are tired of the whole array of evils that have their root in the Protectionist tariff.... The N.P. National Policy is exploded. The people now understand perfectly that it never was anything but a humbug (February 22, 1888, p. 4).

Perhaps one reason why the *Globe* wanted to see legislation proposed was because of the confusion that existed concerning the status of the combines under the common law. The day before the above appeared, the paper cited the opinion of a Mr. G.W. Stephens (a Montreal lawyer?) who doubted that criminal proceedings could be taken against the combiners. Stephens did think Matthewson could launch a civil suit (*Globe*, February 21, 1888, p. 1). The other two newspapers surveyed had almost nothing to say on the subject and *Saturday Night*, a Toronto weekly that commented occasionally on similar issues, made only one brief reference to trusts and combines prior to the appointment of the Select Committee.

5.0 THE SELECT COMMITTEE INQUIRY

The 1888 Session of Parliament opened on February 23. Combines were first mentioned five days later when an Opposition member complained that a Montreal newspaper had announced there would be no change in the tariff. Another member inquired whether this was "an assurance to the sugar combine of Montreal." This led to another member's comment, "In Montreal we have a cotton combine, a flour combine, a sugar combine, a rubber combine, a shirtmakers' combine, and an undertakers' combine. We cannot even get buried on moderate terms now, though, no doubt, the Government would like to bury some of us" (*Debates*, 1888, p. 24). On the following day, Nathaniel Clarke Wallace moved that a Select Committee be appointed, "to examine into the nature, extent and effect of certain combinations said to exist with reference to the purchase and sale in Canada of any foreign or Canadian products...." (*Debates*, 1888, p. 28). Wallace went on to refer to the Wholesale Grocers' Guild, the coal ring and he suggested that oatmeal, biscuits, confectionery and coal oil were subject to combines.

While condemning the combines, Wallace was quick to defend the National Policy. This brought forth a predictable response from James Edgar, a member of the Opposition:

> When I saw this motion, I concluded that we had arrived at the third and last stage of the system of protection. The first stage, we know, was very pleasant for the manufacturers, at least. They had the market to themselves, and they made money, of course, at the expense of the consumers.... Then everybody rushed in who could get a chance, and what the result was before long, in this country, is a matter of history. These highly protected industries were nearly all overdone, and the manufacturers in their turn suffered loss. Well, for a short time the consumers reaped the benefit of that, and the advocates of a high tariff told the country: "There you see, you are getting competition, that is what we promised you, you are getting competition, and you are getting cheap goods." As a result of this

competition among the manufacturers the third stage of the protective system at last
came on, namely, combines among the manufacturers to protect themselves against
the public (*Debates*, 1888, p. 29).

Edgar's claim that combines were a result of the protective tariff was
predictable, but the way in which he reached that conclusion demonstrated a
good deal of insight. He successfully proposed that Wallace's motion be
amended by the inclusion of the words "or manufacturer and sale" (*Debates*,
1888, p. 31) so that the investigation would include manufacturing combines.
(The powers of the Committee were later extended to include an alleged
combination of fire insurance companies (*Debates*, 1888, p. 103).) Only about
half a dozen members spoke on the motion, all of whom agreed that such an
investigation was necessary.

Wallace's motives in proposing the Select Committee have never been
explained satisfactorily. Except for his brief career as a combines-buster,
Wallace is remembered primarily as a somewhat independently-minded
Conservative whose main interests were promoting the Orange Order (he was
the Grand Master for British North America) and resisting the advances of
the Papacy. He was one of the so-called "Devil's Dozen" or "Noble Thirteen"
who, in 1888, voted for the disallowance of a Quebec act compensating the
Jesuits for property that had been taken over by the state when the Order was
temporarily dissolved.

One possible motive has already been mentioned, his desire to embarrass
Elias Rogers, the Toronto coal merchant, who had run unsuccessfully for
mayor. It is also possible that, in attacking combines, Wallace, who was a
small businessman, was simply expressing the hostility shared by many small
businessmen towards combines that interfered with their right to do business
as they pleased. *Saturday Night* suggested that his motion was looked upon
"as a trick by which he could get some campaign material by which he could
find favor among the workingmen whose votes are numerous in the suburbs
which form an important part of his constituency."[23] This is certainly a
plausible motive; combines were not a burning issue, but they had received
enough attention to suggest that someone could benefit politically by attacking
them. In commenting on Wallace's plan to move for the appointment of a
House Committee, the *Globe* claimed, "A dozen or more members of the
House were ready to occupy the ground which Mr. Wallace has pre-empted...."
(February 27, 1888, p. 1). Two days after Wallace's motion was accepted, a
Liberal member withdrew his motion from the Order Paper (*Debates*, 1888,
pp. 60-61).

The Select Committee met 26 times between March 6 and May 8 and
examined 63 witnesses. The Committee produced an eight-page Report,

23. *Saturday Night*, March 24, 1888, p. 1. To be fair to Wallace, the article admitted that he had
established his sincerity.

almost 500 pages of testimony and almost 250 pages of additional evidence (Report of the Select Committee, 1888). Of the 13 businesses examined, the Wholesale Grocers' sugar combine and the local coal rings received the most attention - more than half of the testimony. At the other extreme, the Committee's investigation of an alleged combination among agricultural implements manufacturers consisted of asking two different manufacturers if there was a combination. When they replied in the negative, the subject was dropped (Report, 1888, pp. 356, 392). Surprisingly, the Committee did not even raise the possibility that a combine existed among cotton manufacturers.

The testimony of the various witnesses revealed that the Grocers' combine operated primarily as a resale price maintenance scheme. (Such schemes were common at the time and remained so until well into this century. They were not made illegal *per se* until 1951.) Members of the Guild agreed to sell sugar to retail merchants at fixed advances on the price they paid the refiners. The refiners, in turn, agreed to charge wholesalers who refused to cooperate one eighth of a cent per pound more, without benefit of the 2.5 per cent discount allowed to the combiners. The Guild had asked the refiners to refuse to sell to the non-combiners. Those wholesalers who also operated as retailers were forced to pay the higher price even if they were willing to join the combine. According to George Drummond, the President of the largest refinery in Canada, the refiners agreed to the scheme because the wholesale trade was being demoralized by some wholesalers who sold sugar at or below cost and the wholesalers suggested that they might have to get out of the sugar business (Report, 1888, p. 36). The effect of the combine was to ensure the wholesalers a mark-up of about one half cent per pound on sugar they purchased for seven cents (less 2.5 per cent) (Report, 1888, pp. 49-50). The retail price for granulated sugar was eight cents. One wholesaler, who claimed that his expenses were lower than normal, suggested that his net profit on sugar was 1.25 per cent. However, his sales were between $275,000 and $300,000 which meant that his profits were approximately $3,500 (Report, 1888, p. 109).

The wholesalers may not have been making exorbitant profits, but this did not mean that the consumers were enjoying cheap sugar. In 1888 just over 200 million pounds of sugar were imported into Canada, 92 per cent of this was raw. Its value was $5.2 million and the duty paid was $3.4 million (or 61.5 per cent) (*Debates*, 1891, pp. 1215-1216). In other words, the refiners paid 2.55 cents per pound for their raw sugar and the federal government received another 1.7 cents per pound. It cost the refiner just over four cents a pound for raw sugar and they received almost seven cents a pound for the sugar they sold. Obviously, there was some loss in the refining process, but to put this in perspective, refined sugar could be purchased in Glasgow for 3.5 cents per pound (presumably, a wholesale price) (Report of the Select Committee, 1888,

p. 27).[24] Compared to the tariff, the impact of the combine on prices was almost insignificant, or, to put it another way, it was one more burden on the already overburdened consumer.

The local coal rings were more tightly organized than the Grocers' combine. In Toronto, four or five dealers imported all the coal that came into the city (Report, 1888, p. 202). In order for the other dealers to get coal they had to buy it from the importers, at an increased price, and agree to sell it at a fixed price. The importers were able to impose these conditions because the American mining companies, which were also organized, refused to sell coal to anyone except the importers. In addition, the importers agreed on the price at which they would supply coal to local institutions. The dealer who received the contract, by tendering at the agreed upon price, paid the others a premium (Report, 1888, pp. 166-167).

The Ottawa combination was more interesting. All of the Ottawa dealers seem to have been able to import coal provided they sold it to the Coal Cartage Company at cost price upon its arrival in Ottawa. The Company then delivered the coal to the dealers' customers and charged prices fixed by the Company's six directors (Report, 1888, p. 260). As in Toronto, tenders were fixed. The Cartage Company's profits were shared by the six shareholders with a portion of the profits going to the dealers who participated in the scheme but were not members of the Company (Report, 1888, pp. 176-177). The Ottawa combine is intriguing because it seemingly offered a better way of distributing coal. As one of the combiners argued, it was a more efficient way of doing things (Report, 1888, pp. 192-193). Since the coal was delivered to Ottawa by as many as four different railway companies at four different stations, a merchant had to have employees at all the stations. The coal then had to be transported to the merchant's shed and then delivered anywhere in the city. The Cartage Company made it possible to reduce the number of employees at the train stations and it also allowed deliveries to be made from the most convenient coal supply. Unfortunately, these savings went into the pockets of the merchants rather than into the pockets of the consumers.

The Committee members were not very successful in determining the combiners' profits or in determining the amount by which the price of coal was enhanced. One of the Ottawa dealers claimed that his net profit was between 50 and 60 cents a ton, on sales of about 3,000 tons (Report, 1888, p. 201). A year later, while moving Second Reading of his bill to deal with combinations, Wallace summarized the evidence concerning the Ottawa ring as follows:

> We found that three men, with an aggregate capital of $15,000, after paying enormous bonuses to those who were not in the ring - $10,000 to one man, $5,000

---

24. The low price of sugar in Europe was, in part, a result of the bounties paid by countries such as Germany to encourage the sugar beet industry.

to another, and to others less or greater sums than these - divided amongst themselves, on a capital of $15,000, after paying all expenses of management, and all the expenses of the combination, $33,000 (*Debates*, 1889, p. 1111).

The Committee had less success with Elias Rogers, the major Toronto dealer. Some indication of the effect of the coal rings can be gained by comparing retail prices in Toronto and Ottawa with prices in Cobourg where there was no collusion. During the winter of 1887/88 stove coal, the highest grade, sold for a high of $6.75 per ton in Toronto, $8.00 in Ottawa and $6.00 in Cobourg (Report of the Select Committee, 1888, pp. 198, 209, 230). It is difficult to believe that the profits of the Toronto importers such as Rogers, who handled 600,000 tons of coal, were not substantial (Report, 1888, p. 153). They enhanced the prices of the coal they sold to other dealers, the coal they sold to consumers and the coal they sold on contract to the city and the provincial government (*Ibid.*).[25]

The biscuit manufacturers' combine was basically a straightforward price-fixing scheme. However, according to the one manufacturer questioned, the principal object was to maintain quality. Unfortunately, the only example he could come up with was a Toronto manufacturer who was asked to raise his prices because his biscuits were too good (Report of the Select Committee, 1888, p. 140). Even with a duty of 20 per cent on unsweetened biscuits and 35 per cent plus 1.5 cents per pound on sweetened biscuits (what we would call cookies) one grocer claimed that he could import American biscuits for slightly less than he could buy Canadian ones (Report, 1888, p. 128). Obviously, the combine could never have survived without the protective tariff.

The undertakers' combine was able to survive because of the cooperation of the coffin and basket manufacturers. The manufacturers would not sell to anyone who was not a member of the Undertakers' Association of Ontario and the only way one could become a member was by getting the approval of at least three of the four closest members (*Ibid.*).[26] The undertakers, to repay the favour, purchased their supplies from members of the manufacturers' combine. The stated object of the Undertakers' Association was "to secure harmony in business, cultivate a more friendly spirit socially, to elevate and bring to a higher state of perfection our profession...and to promote the interests of all recognized legitimate undertakers doing business in the Province of Ontario" (Report, p. 706). Like most professional associations, its primary goal was to restrict entry.

The Oatmeal Millers' Association operated more like a cartel than the other combines. The industry's main problem was excess capacity. The 60 mills in Ontario had a capacity of 900,000 barrels a year while the domestic

---

25. The first successful prosecution under the 1889 Act was against an association of coal dealers. *R. v. Elliott* (1905), 9. O.L.R. 648, 9 C.C.C. 505.

26. See the By-laws of the Undertaker's Association of Ontario (Report, 1888, pp. 707-710).

demand was only 158,000 barrels, an amount that could be supplied by the four largest mills (Report, 1888, p. 376). Although the Association fixed prices, its primary goal was to regulate production. Ten mills were paid amounts ranging from $300 to $800 a year not to operate (Report, 1888, p. 380). The 24 millers who were members were given production quotas. Most of the non-members were small millers who supplied local markets and the two or three larger non-members adopted the Association's price list. For an industry that should have been competitive, profits were large. The miller who testified before the Committee accepted Wallace's calculation that he made a profit of 80 cents on a barrel of oatmeal that sold for $5.45. His quota was 2,800 barrels a year which meant that by operating for as few as 30 or 40 days a year he made over $2,000 profit with a mill that could have been built for $10,000 to $12,000 (Report, 1888, pp. 386-388).

During the hearings, those who were involved in the combines offered a variety of ingenious justifications for their existence. The arguments that combinations were necessary to avoid "ruinous competition" or because "business had become demoralized and unprofitable" were used frequently (Report, 1888, p. 88). One Montreal wholesaler argued: "before this sugar agreement was entered into, this article was sold at ruinous competition, and since it is sold at a fair living profit" (Report, 1888, p. 109). Maintaining uniform standards of quality was another popular rationale. A member of the Undertakers' Association of Ontario claimed that its purpose was "to keep out men who are not fit for the business and to do it respectably" (Report, 1888, p. 408). Elias Rogers actually suggested that the coal merchants were helping the low-income consumer: "the effect has been that it has increased the price of the rich man's trade and reduced the price of the poor man's trade, that is, it has equalized the summer and winter trade" (Report, 1888, pp. 163-164).

These complaints about ruinous competition and demoralized trade and the claims that combinations improved quality and benefited the consumer could be written off as predictable rationalizations. They can also be seen as part of what Michael Bliss has called "the flight from competition." Bliss suggests that price-fixing agreements, early-closing movements, demands that peddlers be licensed and attempts to restrict the granting of credit were products of "a climate of business opinion that attacked open competition as being destructive of profits, security and business morality" (Bliss, 1974, p. 43).[27] Although Bliss suggests elsewhere that this "protective impulse" was not limited to the business community, but was operative among other sectors of

---

27. An interesting example of this type of thinking can be found in a short article entitled "The Waste of Competition," written by Erastus Wiman. Wiman, a well-known businessman and advocate of closer economic ties between Canada and the United States, favoured "the universal regulation of competition." A copy can be found in the Public Archives of Canada, *Macdonald Papers*, Vol. 334, pp. 150863-870. It was apparently sent to him by the Toronto Board of Trade.

society, such as the working class (Bliss, 1972, pp. 174-188), it is not clear to what extent it was a new response to changing economic conditions. In other words, was "the flight from competition" simply the late-nineteenth century manifestation of the centuries-old attempt to subvert the forces of competition, or, was it a result of a unique set of circumstances?

It was suggested above that competitive pressures may have been increasing in the last half of the nineteenth century, or at least, it is understandable why they were perceived to be increasing.   Although combinations are as old as trade itself, it is clear that they proliferated during the period being studied. All of the combinations investigated by the Select Committee were of recent origin. The tendency of such arrangements to have a short life span is not a sufficient explanation, nor is the introduction of the tariff. The evidence suggests that the resale price maintenance schemes, the price-fixing arrangements, and the attempts to limit production and restrict entry uncovered by the Select Committee were part of a new assault on competition.

6.0   ATTITUDES TOWARDS COMPETITION AND COMBINATIONS

As is often the case, economic thought mirrored economic reality. By the 1880s businessmen who argued that competition was often wasteful and that combinations were necessary to prevent ruinous competition were beginning to get some support from professional economists. Many American economists began to question the reigning orthodox view that competition was necessarily good while interference with competition was almost always harmful. This questioning of one of the central tenets of classical economics was the result of a variety of causes. One of the more important influences was that of the German "historical school." Several of the leading American economists had gone to university in Germany where they had encountered an approach to economics that put little faith in Adam Smith's "invisible hand" and a good deal of faith in the interventionist state.

As well, many economists, impressed by benefits of large-scale production and misled by the discovery of the concept of natural monopoly (industries characterized by decreasing unit costs as output increases), seemed to believe that large concentrations of capital were necessarily more efficient. This was essentially the position taken by David Wells, an American economist:

> Society has practically abandoned - and from the very necessity of the case has got to abandon, unless it proposes to war against progress and civilization - the prohibition of industrial concentrations and combinations. The world demands abundance of commodities and demands them cheaply; and experience shows that it can have them only by the employment of great capital upon the most extensive scale (quoted by Thorelli, 1955, p. 111).

Social Darwinism also had an impact on the thinking of economists. Although it suggested that competition was ultimately beneficial, it also implicitly gave its approval to the product of the competitive struggle. The notion that combinations were the natural result of an economic struggle of the fittest can be detected in an article written by John Bates Clark entitled, "The Limits of Competition":

> Combinations have their roots in the nature of social industry and are normal in their origin, their development, and their practical working. They are neither to be deprecated by scientists nor suppressed by legislators. They are the result of an evolution, and are the happy outcome of a competition so abnormal that the continuance of it would have meant wide-spread ruin (Clark, 1887, p. 55).

The comment made by Edwin Seligman at the first meeting of the American Economic Association, which was modelled on the German Association for Social Policy, sums up neatly the attitude of many American economists: "Competition is not in itself bad. It is a neutral force which has already produced immense benefits, but which may under certain conditions, bring in its train sharply defined evils" (quoted by Thorelli, 1955, p. 120).[28]

Unfortunately, it is not easy to determine the extent to which these views were shared by the few Canadian economists.[29] W.J. Ashley, of the University of Toronto, was the only economist who seems to have written explicitly on the subject. In an article on the sugar combine, published in 1890, Ashley echoed Seligman's sentiments arguing that, to the economist, competition is "in itself neither good nor bad." He then went on to contrast this point of view to that held by the classical economists:

> But economists did not always hold this view....Adam Smith and most of his successors down to about 1848, believed not only that free competition was the best way to arrive at certain ends, not only that if there was free competition certain results would follow, but also that there <u>ought to be</u> free competition. Not only that if there were free competition, wages and prices would be so and so, but that they ought not to be regulated by anything else....With all reasonable economists this feeling has long ago passed away. But the result of all this insistence for almost a century upon the idea of free competition has been to create an impression in the public mind that any interference with competition is itself wicked (Ashley, 1890, p. 36).

Working on the premise that competition can only be judged by its effects, Ashley turned his attention to the sugar combine. He concluded that it was not all that bad. He estimated that it increased the cost of living of a skilled artisan family by only one quarter of one per cent. (However, if Ashley

---

28. On this subject see also Letwin (1965, pp. 71-77) and Gordon (1963).

29. The standard text on the subject of economic thought in Canada, Goodwin (1961), has little to say on this issue.

had summed the total effect by multiplying the added cost per pound by the number of pounds sold, the figure would have been significant.) Balancing this, he suggested that it may have protected the small wholesaler and retailer against "the big man" and that it "has introduced greater steadiness in the business of wholesaler and retailer, with the result of lessening jealousy and suspicion all round." In concluding that "it is impossible wholly to condemn or wholly to praise the sugar combine," Ashley was implicitly defending the combine (Ashley, 1890, pp. 37-39).

Ashley's position, and that of many of his fellow economists, could be summarized as, "Combinations are not necessarily bad; competition is not necessarily good." This position is based on two fundamental misconceptions. The first, which is found in the Wells quotation above, is that there is a direct relationship between concentrations of capital and economic efficiency. In some cases large firms are more efficient, but when they are they will emerge from the competitive process. Agreements to restrain competition will have one of two effects: they will either produce concentrations that are inefficient, or they will prevent the competitive process from producing larger, more efficient firms. The second misconception stems from a failure to appreciate the role and importance of "destructive competition." It is understandable why businessmen abhorred this aspect of competition; it is more difficult to understand why so many economists agreed with them. To simplify, the competitive process performs two different, but closely interrelated functions.[30] The first is that it works to ensure that existing firms will employ the available resources to produce an optimal output at competitive prices. This is what is known as static efficiency. The second function involves dynamic efficiency. This is where so-called "destructive competition" comes in, or what Joseph Schumpeter called, in a beautifully evocative phrase, "the perennial gale of creative destruction" (Schumpeter, 1950, p. 84). It is this second type of efficiency that leads to innovation and the introduction of new technology and ensures continued economic growth. If the combines investigated by the Select Committee had only struck at price competition it would be possible to agree with Ashley that the sugar combine was not all that onerous and with Bliss' comment that the Committee "had not in fact uncovered a particularly alarming situation" (Bliss, 1973, p. 179). What made the combines dangerous, and this was even more true of the protective tariff, was that they struck at this second aspect of competition.

This digression on economists' views on the role of competition is not directly relevant. The era of the economist as policy advisor was still many years in the future. It is relevant in that the ambiguity towards trade restrictions and unfettered competition found among economists was found elsewhere in society. Sentiments similar to those discussed above can be

---

30.   On the role of competition and the various ways in which the concept has been viewed see McNultly (1968) and Stigler (1965).

found in contemporary newspapers and business periodicals. The *Journal of Commerce* denied that the tariff had anything whatever to do with the formation of combines although it did concede that it may have made their maintenance easier (May 11, 1888, p. 901). It suggested that combines were somehow a natural development: "This is emphatically an age of combinations. Nothing is more marked among the tendencies of modern times than this increasing effort to merge a comparatively feeble individuality into a powerful combination...." (November 25, 1887, p. 1041). The Ottawa *Evening Journal* presented a similar point of view:

> Combinations are largely the outcome of the many inventions of the age. The invention of labor-saving machinery has greatly cheapened production but it made capital a necessity of production and so reduced the number of competitors, while the telegraph, the railways and the fast ocean steamships have brought the capitalists of the world into close communication (March 7, 1888, p. 2).

Neither the *Evening Journal* nor the *Journal of Commerce* proposed any solutions. The former questioned whether it was possible to devise legislation to check combinations (March 29, 1888, p. 2); the latter doubted that any harm had yet been done - prices were lower than before - and suggested that before the harmful stage was reached their growth would be checked, "The laws of supply and demand are too powerful and comprehensive in their character for any effort at combined action to even swerve them from their course...."[31]

Publications that blamed the tariff for the combines were convinced that the solution was a lower tariff. The *Monetary Times* was one of the few business journals to urge such a policy:

> The public is at all times entitled to relief against monopoly. People inclined to monopoly and exaction should be given to understand that if they artificially raise the price of domestic products, to the injury of general public, the corrective will be applied by lowering the tariff. The promise of the National Policy was at least the benefit of domestic competition, when this is denied, foreign competition must be allowed to take its place (March 2, 1888, p. 1097).

The *Globe* shared this conviction that lower duties were the solution although it was dismayed by the oatmeal millers' combination. It did not think that the tariff was a factor (although there was an import duty of one dollar a barrel on oatmeal) and it was not sure what type of legislation would be effective against it (April 19, 1888, p. 4).

---

31. *Journal of Commerce*, Vol. 25, No. 21, November 25, 1887, pp. 1001-1002.

7.0   THE WALLACE ACT OF 1889

The Select Committee did not propose any solutions; its brief Report was little more than a disapproving summary of the testimony it had heard. It suggested that legislative action was justified, but stopped short of recommending any action. Thus, when Wallace, the Committee chairman, rose in the House of Commons on May 18 to introduce Bill (No. 138) for the prevention and suppression of combinations formed in restraint of trade, he was acting on his own initiative (*Debates*, 1888, p. 1544). His reasons for introducing the Bill were a bit unclear. At one point he said that the "extent of combination...constitutes a serious evil which calls for legislation," but then he went on to suggest that the coal combines' actions were "entirely illegal" and "in many ways violating the laws." A moment later he argued, "I think the influence of this investigation has done a good deal to remove the evils of combinations by acquainting people with the acts of these companies; but I think a more severe and permanent remedy is required...." (*Debates*, 1888, pp. 1544-1545). In his short speech, Wallace managed to convey three different, and somewhat contradictory ideas: first, that publicity was a useful means of suppressing combinations; second, that the combinations were already illegal (under the common law); and third, that a more severe legislative remedy was required. In short, his speech was an indication of the confusion that was to follow.

Wallace's Bill consisted of three clauses. The first set out the activities that were declared illegal and specified the punishment; the second declared that any federally incorporated company found guilty of these activities shall forfeit its charter; and the third stated that the Bill was not intended to interfere with *The Trades Union Act* passed in 1872. A curious feature of the Bill was the reference to agreements "with any railway, steamship, or steamboat or transportation company." Nothing had been said during the Select Committee hearings to suggest that any of the combines involved a transportation company. Apparently this reference was a carry-over from the New York State Bill that formed the basis for Wallace's Bill.

Wallace urged "prompt and decisive action" on the grounds that the combines should be strangled in their infancy (*Debates*, 1888, p. 1545). Both Sir John A. Macdonald and Sir Richard Cartwright urged delay (*Ibid.*). Macdonald thanked Wallace for instituting the inquiry and expressed his belief that the Committee's Report and the introduction of the Bill would have a beneficial effect, but questioned whether the House should proceed any further during the present session. Wallace's failure to protest suggests that he had not expected his Bill to pass.

Wallace introduced the same Bill early in the 1889 session (*Debates*, 1889, p. 19). His brief speech was simply a summary of the Bill. The Bill was introduced on February 6; on February 28, the Minister of Justice asked that Second Reading be delayed. For reasons that were not explained, it did not receive Second Reading until April 8. One possible reason was revealed while Wallace was moving Second Reading:

> The Bill I proposed at first was the one of which I gave notice at the end of last Session. I have gone over it carefully and I intend to ask the House to permit its substitution by the second Bill which I have the honour to submit. The objection made to the old Bill was that it created a new offence, and the judges might perhaps interpret the Bill more severely than was intended. This new Bill does not create a new offence. It simply states what the law of England and Canada to-day is and has been for years past, and fixes a penalty for offences against the law and warns them not to break it (*Debates*, 1889, p. 1113).

It is reasonable to assume that the two-month interval between the First and Second Readings and Wallace's decision to replace his original Bill with a new one were related.

The Bill passed Second Reading and then, despite the objections of Wallace and two of his fellow Conservative back-benchers, it was sent to the Committee on Banking and Commerce. About two weeks later, the Bill passed Third Reading and was sent to the Senate. This Bill was substantially different from the one that had been introduced two and a half months earlier. The most controversial change was the inclusion of the word "unlawfully" (the word "conspires" was also added). The reference to arrangements that discriminated against third parties, for example, noncombining businessmen, was dropped. The other four clauses in the original Bill were rearranged with the qualifying adverbs "unreasonably" and "unduly" being omitted. Finally, the phrase "trade and commerce" was inserted, presumably in an attempt to deflect criticism on constitutional grounds. The first section of the Bill that was sent to the Senate read as follows:

1.   Every person who <u>conspires</u>, combines, agrees or arranges with any other person, or with any railway, steamship, steamboat or transportation company, <u>unlawfully</u> (emphasis added)
 (a)   to limit the facilities for transporting, producing, manufacturing, supplying, storing or dealing in any article or commodity which may be a subject of trade and commerce; or
 (b)   to restrain or injure trade or commerce in relation to any such article or commodity; or
 (c)   to prevent, limit, or lessen the manufacture or production of any such article or commodity, or to enhance the price thereof; or
 (d)   to prevent or lessen competition in the production manufacture, purchase, barter, sale, transportation or supply of any such article or commodity, or in the price of insurance upon person or property;

Is guilty of a misdemeanour and liable on conviction, to a penalty not exceeding four thousand dollars and not less than two hundred dollars, or to imprisonment for any term not exceeding two years; and if a corporation, is liable on conviction to a penalty not exceeding ten thousand dollars and not less than one thousand dollars.

Two different explanations have been offered for the alteration of the Bill. The first is that it was altered because of business pressure. Lloyd Reynolds offers the following explanation:

> Opponents of the measure moved that it be referred to the Committee on Banking and Commerce. Large lobbies of manufacturers and traders descended on Ottawa to oppose the bill, and were heard by the Committee. Apparently as a result of this business pressure, the original measure was withdrawn while still in Committee and a startlingly different bill was substituted. The clause which forbade the securing of special concessions was dropped, as was also the provision concerning forfeiture of the corporate charter..... Mr. Wallace reluctantly adopted the new act which passed the House and went to the Senate.[32]

As Bliss and Gorecki and Stanbury point out, and as the excerpt from Wallace's speech quoted above indicates, Wallace altered the Bill himself (in effect, substituting a new bill) before it went to the Committee (Bliss, 1973, p. 182 and Gorecki and Stanbury, 1981, p. 3). Although it is not entirely clear, it would seem that the Committee did not amend the Bill.[33] Bliss' explanation denies Wallace the good intentions with which Reynolds and others credit him. He says that Wallace "deliberately watered down his own bill until it was ineffectual," and describes the passing of the legislation as "no more than a political sham" (Bliss, 1973, p. 182). Bliss (1973, p. 182) leaves the impression that business pressure had little to do with Wallace's actions.

> There is a third possible explanation for the alteration of the Bill: that Wallace was responding to both business pressure and political pressure when he substituted a new Bill for the original one at Second Reading. It is clear that neither Macdonald nor any of his Ministers were very enthusiastic about the legislation. Macdonald gave it his lukewarm support in 1888, in 1889 he was even more reserved in his brief comments on the Bill. Sir John Thompson, the Minister of Justice, was the only other Minister who spoke during the debates. His comments were designed more to explain the common law background of the legislation than to muster support for its passage. The Macdonald government was clearly in a difficult position; it was obvious that legislation was necessary, but it could neither afford to admit that its tariff policy contributed to trade combinations nor run the risk of alienating the businessmen who filled the party's coffers at election time. Wallace's original Bill was much too harsh for most of the business community and, one suspects, for the Conservative hierarchy. In mid-February, Sir John Thompson received twelve telegrams within the space of two days with comments ranging from: "Please use

---

32. Reynolds (1940, p. 134). Ball (1934, p. 7) and Gosse (1962, p. 71) also suggest that the Bill was altered in Committee.

33. The comments of Mr. Guillet, a Conservative MP, suggests that the Bill was not changed in Committee: "That hon. gentleman attended the Banking and Commerce Committee on the occasion when large deputations, representing the combines, appeared before it to oppose this Bill. They came to oppose, not the old Bill, but the present Bill, and they opposed it because they know it will deal effectively with the combines and punish such associations severely. These deputations went away very much disappointed and loudly declaring their indignation" (*Debates*, 1889, p. 1446).

your influence against adoption of Wallace bill"; to, "an almost fatal blow to the entire cotton industry" (*Department of Justice Records*, 1889).[34] Second Reading of the Bill was postponed at the request of the Government, probably as a concession to business interests.[35]

Although the Bill was not formally taken over as a Government Bill until after Second Reading there is evidence to suggest that the Government assumed responsibility somewhat earlier (*Debates*, 1889, p. 1328). During Second Reading, one of the supporters of the legislation suggested that it was on the Orders of the day as a Government Order. Macdonald did not deny this, but rather replied, "Oh yes, so it was, but if you choose to take it out of the hands of the Government, you must manage it after your own fashion" (*Debates*, 1889, p. 1116). As well as suggesting that the Government would only accept the Bill on their own terms, this also suggests that the Government may have had a hand in its alteration. Admittedly it is speculation, but it is plausible to suggest that during the two-month interval between First and Second Readings the Government bowed to business lobbying and managed to convince Wallace to make certain changes in return for assistance during the Bill's passage.

It is also possible that Wallace changed the Bill because he really did believe that the original was too harsh and all that was needed was a measure to declare the common law. This interpretation is suggested in a recent study by Gorecki and Stanbury. They point out that it was Wallace who was responsible for inserting the word "unlawfully," "apparently because he believed, or had been persuaded, that this word would make it clear that the purpose of the new Act was simply to declare the existing common law on restraint of trade as indicated in the preamble" (Gorecki and Stanbury, 1981, p. 5). This is a plausible explanation because, as we shall see, many people believed that combinations were already illegal under the common law.

The already weakened Bill was further altered in the Senate. The words "unduly" and "unreasonably," which had been dropped from the original when unlawfully was added, were reinserted.[36] The Senate also added a section pertaining to appeal procedure and amended the final section, the purpose of which was to exclude trade unions from conviction as combinations in restraint of trade. The amended Bill was returned to the House two days before the end of the session. The supporters of the measure were faced with the choice

---

34. Six of the telegrams came from cotton manufacturers, three were from sugar refiners, one was from a coal company, another came from the wholesale grocers of Montreal and the other was from the secretary of the biscuit manufacturers and wholesale confectioners (Public Archives of Canada, *Department of Justice Records* (R.G. 13A2), Vol. 72, Item 164 (1889)).

35. See the letter from Wallace to Macdonald March 22, 1889 (*Macdonald Papers*, Vol. 471, pp. 234378-79).

36. The Senate amendments are discussed in greater detail below.

of either concurring in the amendments, thereby accepting a weaker act, or rejecting the amendments and having no act at all. Wallace agreed to accept the amendments (*Debates*, 1889, p. 1689).

Before discussing the Act any further, it is necessary to determine what the Members of the House and the Senate thought they were doing when they passed it. The supporters of the measure objected to trade combinations for two main reasons: they interfered with the rights of businessmen who chose not to combine, and they increased the prices of consumer goods. Wallace raised both issues, describing the Grocers' Guild's agreement with the refiners "as objectionable and illegal in two directions." He then went on to say:

> in the first place, those members of the wholesale trade who did not choose to become members of the Wholesale Grocers' Guild, were almost debarred from entering into the sale of sugar at all; they were placed at an immense disadvantage, and illegal and improper disadvantage, while sure and certain profits were secured to all those who were members of the Wholesale Grocers' Guild, because the price at which they were to sell to retailers was a fixed profit regulated by the guild (*Ibid.*, p. 1112).

Other MPs were more explicit about the connection between combinations and higher prices. As Mr. Guillet, a Conservative MP from Ontario, argued:

> Competition safeguards the prosperity of the country; it is the life of trade; and all classes have to meet it....Why, then, should there be combinations in a few lines of manufacture to oppress others? I say it is a condition essential to the prosperity of the country that there should be free competition, and no monopoly to compel people to pay excessive prices (*Ibid.*, p. 1114).

The same argument was used by another Conservative member, Mr. Sproule: "Now competition is the only guarantee we have that the article produced will be given to the people at least possible price" (*Debates*, 1889, p. 1442).[37] Sproule was the only MP who referred to a recognized authority in the field. He quoted several excerpts from a book on trusts written by William W. Cook, a prominent American lawyer. Cook is interesting because, unlike many of the economists of the day, he was strongly antimonopolistic and he favoured legislative action to suppress combinations.

The members who opposed the Bill did not necessarily believe that combinations were harmless; some of them opposed it because they thought it took the wrong approach or because it was ineffectual. Most Liberals maintained that the only way to get rid of combinations was by lowering the tariff. One Liberal introduced a bill providing that articles manufactured by

---

37. For a more extended discussion of the arguments used by the supporters of the legislation and, more generally, of the change in the objectives of Canadian competition policy over time, see Gorecki and Stanbury (1984).

a combine were to be placed on the (duty) free list (*Debates*, 1889, p. 248).[38]
Mr. Davies, a Liberal MP from Prince Edward Island, called the revised Bill
a fraud for "ostensibly holding up to the public the proposition that it is
dealing with the evils which the first Bill was designed to prevent" (*Debates*,
1889, p. 1440). The most damning criticism was that the Bill left the law
exactly as it was, but, by lessening the penalties, it actually made it less of a
deterrent. The same critics charged that the Senate amendments made the
law even weaker than it was before. This was the argument used by Mr.
Mills:

> The Bill did approve when it left this House for the punishment of acts that were
> unlawful for it left the law just as it was except that in certain cases it modified the
> punishment that was attached to this particular offence. It made nothing unlawful
> that was lawful before, so that in every respect the Bill was absolutely colorless. The
> hon. gentleman accepts of an amendment by the Senate which modifies and
> weakens the law as it before stood and the law after it receives the royal sanction
> will be more favourable to combinations than it was before (*Debates*, 1889, p. 1689).

This argument was based on the premise that existing law, based on the
unwritten common law, was opposed to trade restrictions. Most of the MPs
and Senators who spoke on the subject, supporters and critics alike, agreed
that the legislation was declaratory, that is, that it simply asserted what the law
already was. The issue debated was whether there was any purpose in doing
so: the supporters of the measure insisted that a declaratory act would serve
a useful purpose, the critics of the measure argued that it was essentially a
fraud.

8.0   A DIGRESSION ON THE COMMON LAW

The notion that the common law was opposed to trade restraints was a
widely held belief. Thus we find William Cook, the American author of a
book on trusts, declaring:

> And, indeed, ever since the days of Lord Coke, who, in the great and leading "Case
> of the Monopolies," declared that a monopoly was illegal and void, there has been
> a continuous line of cases which have protected trade and the public against any and
> all schemes and devices of competitors to unite and regulate prices. Even the few
> cases which may seem to vary this principle of law are found, on close examination,
> to sustain and uphold it (Cook, 1888, p. 27).

As we have seen, both Wallace and the *Monetary Times* believed that some
of the actions of the combines uncovered during the Select Committee
hearings were clearly illegal. In truth, the common law was much less clear

---

38.   Bill (No. 56) to provide for placing on the free list articles of merchandise the production
of which may be controlled by trusts or combinations. The Bill was introduced by James Edgar.

cut although one could almost turn the last portion of Cook's argument on its head - some cases that seemed to declare monopolies void did not necessarily do so. An obvious example was the very case mentioned by Cook.

The "Case of the Monopolies," or *Darcy v. Allen*, hinged on the legality of a monopoly to manufacture playing cards granted to Darcy by Queen Elizabeth 1. When Darcy tried to secure a judgement against Allen for manufacturing cards, the Court of King's Bench ruled the patent void. The usual explanation is that the ruling was based on the common law principle that every man had a right to pursue his trade and Darcy's monopoly prevented Allen from doing so. More recently, it has been argued that the decision was not an attack on monopoly as much as it was an attack on the monarch's right to grant a monopoly. According to this argument, the decision was part of a struggle between Parliament and the Crown to see who would become the sole supplier of monopoly rights (Ekelund and Tollison, 1980). This is worth considering because, a few years after this decision, Parliament granted the same monopoly to someone else under the recently enacted Statute of Monopolies.

By the nineteenth century, the monarch's right to grant monopolies was no longer a contentious issue. Parliament had long since replaced the Crown as the supplier of certain types of monopoly privileges, for example, patents of inventions, and its authority was not subject to the common law. The types of restraint of trade to which the common law did apply, in theory at least, can be considered under three headings: (i) individual attempts to corner markets; (ii) loose agreements, i.e. combinations, to fix prices or limit production; and (iii) contracts under which one or more parties agreed not to compete. Restraints of the first type were subject to both the common law and statute law from the thirteenth century to the mid-nineteenth century when the last of the laws against forestalling, regrating and engrossing (related activities involving the purchase of commodities, usually foodstuffs, by middlemen in order to enhance prices) were repealed.

With respect to the status under the common law of the other two types of restraints, there are some important points to be kept in mind. The first is that their status changed over time; or, to be more accurate, the terms by which they were judged changed. An important step was taken early in the eighteenth century in *Mitchell v. Reynolds* when the test of reasonableness was explicitly introduced. In this case a restraint was held to be valid because it was limited in extent (in terms of both time and place) and because it was considered to be a reasonable one for both parties. This "test" was broadened until, by the end of the nineteenth century, general restraints were being upheld. Second, one has to distinguish between the enforceability of agreements to restrain trade and their legality. Thus, an agreement that was ruled to be unreasonable and hence unenforceable would not necessarily be unlawful. Third, during the eighteenth and nineteenth centuries, combinations of workers were more likely than combinations of businessmen to be considered criminal conspiracies at common law.[39] It is ironic, but the one type of combination to which Wallace's bill in 1889 might have applied was specifically exempted from prosecution.

Cook's belief that trade and the public were protected against all schemes and devices to regulate prices, if it was ever justified, was certainly not justified by the late nineteenth century. Two famous cases from the period illustrate the point. The first was the *Mogul Steamship* case. The Mogul Steamship Company had been a member of a shipping combine that monopolized tea shipments from Chinese ports. The combining companies divided the trade among themselves and used various tactics to exclude competitors. When the Mogul Company tried to operate independently, the other companies undercut rates in an attempt to drive it out of business. Mogul sued for damages. The suit failed because, in the words of one of the Justices, the defendants had done nothing more than "pursue to the bitter end a war of competition waged in the interest of their own trade."[40]

The other important case, *Nordenfelt v. Maxim Nordenfelt Co.*[41] involved a contract in restraint of trade. The plaintiff had agreed to a contract not to manufacture or sell armaments in competition with the defendant. When a dispute arose, the contract was ruled to be invalid by a lower court. On appeal, the contract was upheld. The reasoning used was that, "the community has a material interest in maintaining the rules of fair dealing between man and man. It suffers far greater injury from the infraction of these rules than from contracts in restraint of trade."[42] The Nordenfelt case is important because it raised one of the central issues of competition policy; the need to balance the freedom of trade against the freedom of contract. Thus at the same time that Canadian parliamentarians were invoking the common law to protect freedom of trade, English courts were using it to uphold freedom of contract.

Canadian politicians might have realized that the common law was a shadowy weapon with which to combat restraints of trade if they had been familiar with an Ontario case heard about twenty years earlier. It involved the Canadian Salt Association, which had been formed,

> for the purpose of selling on such terms as to secure as far as possible a fair share for their capital invested in such operations, and generally for the purpose of

---

39. The above is based on Gosse (1962, pp. 11-67) and Gorecki and Stanbury (1981, pp. 16-19).

40. *Mogul Steamship Co. v. McGregor* (1889), 23 Q.B.D. 598 at 614. See Thorelli (955, pp. 49-50) for more details.

41. *Nordenfelt v. Maxim Nordenfelt Co.* (1894) A.C. 535. See Thorelli (1955, p. 20) and Letwin (1965, pp. 44-45).

42. (1894) A.C. 535 at p. 552.

combined action and mutual protection in all matters relating to the manufacture and sale of salt in Canada.[43]

The counsel for the Merchants Salt Company, which had been a member of the Association, argued that the agreement should not be enforced because, among other things, it was contrary to public policy as tending to a monopoly and that it was void because it constituted an undue restraint of trade. At one point, Strong, V.C., gave his view of the state of the law:

> The law on the subject is now well settled, though there is sometimes much difficulty in applying it. *Prima facie* every contract in restraint of trade is void; but if an agreement appears to be for a partial restraint for valuable consideration and reasonable, the law sanctions it.[44]

He applied these two tests - the extent of the restraint and its reasonableness - and concluded that the agreement was not an undue restraint of trade. He then went on to suggest that even if the agreement had been unreasonable he would have hesitated to rule it void:

> Did I even think otherwise than I do, that this arrangement was injurious to the public interest, I should hesitate much before I acted on such an opinion, for I feel that I was called on to relieve parties from a solemn contract, not by the mere application of some well established rule of law, but upon my own notions of what the public good required - in effect to arbitrarily make the law for the occasion.[45]

The common law with respect to restraints of trade was not as simple or as clear-cut as this summary would suggest.[46] Because the common law is unwritten, because it is based on custom and usage, it is evolving constantly. To a degree then, the misunderstanding among Canadian politicians about the state of the law was understandable. Richard Gosse suggests that they were misled by the manner in which combinations of workers were treated at common law (Gosse, 1962, p. 38). American politicians operated under a similar misapprehension. John Sherman, the American Senator who gave his name to the antitrust act of 1890, argued that the legislation "does not announce a new principle of law, but applies old and well-recognized principles of the common law" (quoted by Thorelli, 1955, p. 9). Whatever the reason for their confusion, both the supporters and critics of Wallace's Bill

---

43. *Ontario Salt Co. v. Merchants Salt Co.* (1871) 18 Grants Ch. 540, at p. 541.

44. *Ibid.*, at p. 544.

45. *Ibid.*, at p. 549.

46. For example, in another case heard at approximately the same time as the *Mogul* and *Nordenfelt* cases, *Urmston v. Whitelegg* (1891) 7 T.L.R. 295, the Court of Appeal refused to enforce the rules of an association of mineral water manufacturers. The association was suing Whitelegg for selling at a price below the association price. The suit was unsuccessful.

were operating under a false assumption. The common law that Wallace thought he was declaring, and the common law that his critics thought was being weakened, did not exist.

If possible, the confusion was even greater in the Senate. Several Senators were concerned that what they thought were legitimate combinations would become unlawful as a result of the proposed legislation. Two different Senators used the example of competing steamboat companies agreeing to limit competition and fix prices to prevent ruinous competition (*Senate Debates*, 1889, p. 639). Their fears were almost certainly groundless. About seventy-five years earlier such an agreement between two stage coach companies was held to be valid as "merely a convenient mode of arranging two concerns that might otherwise ruin each other."[47] In order to protect such agreements, the Senate accepted an amendment to include the words "unduly" and "unreasonably" so that only those agreements that "unduly" limited production, "unduly" lessened competition or "unreasonably" enhanced prices would be punishable. As we have seen, this was unnecessary since the test of reasonableness was already an important element of the common law.

Senator Power seemed to have the best grasp of what the Bill entailed. He argued that the amendment was unnecessary and suggested that if any amendment was made, "unlawfully" should be struck out (*Senate Debates*, 1889, p. 632). Power was in a distinct minority; the majority of the Senators favoured the amendment and several opposed the Bill on principle. One of those who argued that it was unnecessary and even harmful was Senator Clemow, one of the people who had been accused of profiteering in the Ottawa coal-ring (*Senate Debates*, 1889, p. 635).

To summarize, the Bill introduced by Wallace in 1888 and again in 1889 went beyond the common law. It would have made certain activities punishable that were not punishable at common law. At Second Reading, Wallace replaced this Bill with the revised Bill containing the words "unlawfully" and "conspires." In doing so, he drastically changed the meaning of the proposed legislation. Now the activities listed were punishable only if they were the result of a conspiracy , a conspiracy being an agreement between two or more persons to commit an unlawful act or a lawful act by unlawful means. Wallace, the Minister of Justice, and several other MPs and Senators thought that, by including the word "unlawfully," they had made the Bill declaratory of the common law. This belief is reflected in the preamble to the Act: "whereas it is expedient to declare the law relating to conspiracies and combinations formed in restraint of trade and to provide penalties for the violation of the same...." However, as one authority has noted: "Since there was no conspiracy in restraint of trade at common law along the lines imagined by the legislators, the Bill at this point had become meaningless"

---

47. *Hearn v. Griffin* (1815) 2 Chitty 407 at p. 408.

(Gosse, 1962, p. 72). By the time the Senate was finished with the Bill it had become, if possible, even more meaningless. As a result of the Senate's amendments, "not only did a criminal offense have to be committed, it had to be committed 'unduly'" (Gosse, 1962, p. 73).

9.0   ATTEMPTS AT AMENDMENT, 1890-1896

As has already been mentioned, Wallace was unhappy with the Senate amendments but agreed to accept them in order to get legislation on the books. In 1890, Wallace introduced Bill (No. 77) to amend the Act by removing the words "unreasonably" and "unduly" (*Debates*, 1890, p. 504).[48] According to Bliss, this was an attempt "to squeeze more political mileage out of the issue" rather than a serious attempt to improve the Act since "it was well understood that the word 'unlawfully' made it ineffectual" (Bliss, 1973, p. 183). It is certainly possible that Wallace was motivated primarily by political considerations; however, the motives of his supporters should not automatically be questioned on the basis of guilt by association. A reading of the Parliamentary Debates suggests that several of the MPs and Senators who supported Wallace in 1888,1889 and 1890 and who continued to press for the amendment of the Act during the next ten years were genuinely interested in improving the legislation. Nor should their motives be questioned just because they favoured removing the words "unduly" and "unreasonably." It was not well understood that it was the word "unreasonably" that made the Act ineffectual. In fact, there was a great deal of confusion on this point.

Wallace's 1890 Bill passed the House with little debate. In the Senate it received a much less favourable reception. It was sent to the Committee on Banking and Commerce, which recommended that it should not be passed (*Senate Debates*, 1890, p. 712). A Conservative Senator, Mr. Read, moved non-concurrence in the Committee's recommendation. The strongest defence of the Bill was offered by Mr. McCallum, another Conservative Senator:

> The word unreasonable sic ought to be struck out, because any combination to raise the price of an article must be unreasonable, since it is contrary to the natural state of the market. The prices of articles are already reasonably protected by the tariff. To allow of a further protection by private tariffs is to allow private individuals to assume the powers of Parliament and tax the people without the legal right to do so (*Senate Debates*, 1890, p. 725).

McCallum went on to remind some of his fellow Senators - Lord Undertaker, Lord Coal, Lord Sugar and others - that if they had a direct interest in the issue they should not vote.

---

48.   Bill (No. 77) to amend the Act for the prevention and suppression of combinations in restraint of trade (*Debates*, 1890, p. 504).

His arguments were to no avail. Trade combinations were defended ably by Senators Drummond, the President of Canada Sugar, Thibaudeau and Clemow. The latter suggested the Bill was misnamed, "I rather think that the proper term would have been: Bill for the purpose of preventing persons from protecting themselves in a legitimate way in their trade" (*Senate Debates*, 1890, p. 752). Read's motion of nonconcurrence was lost 27 to 14. The Government leader in the Senate and future Prime Minister, John J. Abbott, was one of the 22 Conservative who opposed the motion. (Six Conservatives supported it.) This suggests that the Government's attitude towards the Bill was, at best, one of ambivalence.

Wallace reintroduced his Bill to amend the 1889 Act in 1891 and again it was passed by the House (*Debates*, 1891, p. 142).[49] This time there was more debate. Wallace was somewhat contradictory in his assessment of the impact of the Act.   He stressed the need to remove "unduly" and "unreasonably" and yet he maintained that, "Combinations have been broken up by the Act as it was passed, and warnings have been given to other combinations which have had the effect of compelling them to dissolve their organizations." He blamed the Attorneys-General of the provinces for not enforcing the law (*Debates*, 1891, p. 2552). The Liberal opposition held a variety of conflicting opinions: one member wanted Wallace to make the act of combining itself illegal by removing the word "unlawfully"; another member thought that they were trying to regulate things better left alone; the Liberal member who had previously called the legislation a fraud now wanted it left as it was; and a fourth argued in favour of lowering tariffs to combat combines (*Debates*, 1891, pp. 2560, 2561, 2577 and 2555). Thompson, the Minister of Justice, gave the Bill his cautious support.

The Senate passed the Bill, but not without amending it. Senator Vidal, who had first suggested adding the words "unduly" and "unreasonably" in 1889, agreed to their removal, but moved that the phrase "provided that nothing in the said Act shall apply to business arrangements or transactions which are not to the detriment of the public interest" be added (*Senate Debates*, 1891, p. 432).[50] This proposal met with the approval of Abbott, who had succeeded John A. Macdonald as Prime Minister, and McCallum, who had introduced the Bill in the Senate. Abbott's support is understandable since he was never very enthusiastic about the legislation. McCallum's support is more difficult to understand since Vidal's amendment with the nebulous phrase, "the public interest," was open to the same criticism as the words it was designed to replace, i.e., how do you define "unduly," or "the public interest"? For some

---

49. Bill (No. 15) to amend the Act for the prevention and suppression of combinations in restraint of trade (*Debates*, 1891, p. 142).

50. In urging the adoption of his amendment, Vidal (*Senate Debates*, 1891, p. 434) quoted the opinions of two of Canada's most prominent lawyers. Both men thought the proposed phrase was necessary if the two words were removed.

reason the Bill never received Royal Assent even though it had been passed by both the House and the Senate. This is all the more puzzling since Prime Minister Abbott seemingly gave it his support. The explanation cannot be found in the lateness of the session; the House sat for some time after the Senate passed the Bill and it had ample time to consider the Senate amendment.

Two somewhat related measures did become law in 1891. The first involved tariff changes. In his budget speech, the Minister of Finance announced that the duty on raw sugar was to be removed and the duty on refined sugar lowered (*Debates*, 1891, p. 1209).[51] This was a significant step since sugar duties were the most important single source of customs revenue. The Minister planned to recover $1.5 million of the $4.5 million that was going to be lost from tobacco and alcohol. (There are certain constants in budget-making.) As well, the duty on salt was cut in half. The reason given is interesting:

> This we have been impelled to do because we considered that, owing to the protection which was given and certain combinations which have been entered into, a monopoly has been created, and it is a wise and prudent for us to meet that state of things by reducing the duty one-half (*Debates*, 1891, p. 1220).[52]

Having moved tentatively in the direction of freer trade with the tariff changes, the Conservative Government then proceeded to retreat back into protectionism. In the same session, the Government passed an act granting bounties to encourage the production of sugar beets.[53] The rationale was that the bounty was supposed to replace the protection the industry had previously enjoyed from the duty on raw sugar. Although at the time the Minister of Finance emphasized that the bounty was only for one year, it was renewed in subsequent sessions.

The Government's actions - removing the duty on raw sugar, lowering the duty on salt, and granting bonuses to encourage the production of sugar beets were an acknowledgement that trade combinations were a problem. Lowering the duty on salt was an explicit acknowledgement that the tariff contributed to combinations. However, rather than striking at the root of the problem, the Government resorted to half-measures. The Liberals were quick to point this

---

51. The tariff changes were contained in *An Act to Amend the Acts Respecting the Duties of Customs*, S.C. 1891, 54-55 Vic., c. 45.

52. Perhaps it was a coincidence, but Sir John A. Macdonald had received a letter from a Mr. F. Culham about three and a half months earlier complaining about the salt combine. It was Culhams' understanding that the combine was composed principally of Grits (Liberals). Culham to Macdonald, March 11, 1889 (*Macdonald Papers*, 1888, Vol. 12, pp. 28346-48).

53. *An Act to encourage the production of Beet Root Sugar*, S.C. 1891, 54-55 Vic., c. 31. For details on the success of this scheme see Naylor (1975, pp. 121-124).

out. Their criticisms were damning and to the point. Commenting on the removal of the duty on raw sugar, Cartwright suggested, "Thus we have the maximum of loss to the revenue, the minimum of advantage to the people, the maximum of advantage to these monopolists, the refiners and their friends opposite" (*Debates*, 1891, p. 1234). David Mills' criticism of the proposed bounty was more sweeping:

> Now, if the production of beets for the purpose of being manufactured into sugar is a profitable branch of agriculture, there is no more propriety in giving the producers of beets a bounty, than there is in giving it to the producers of cabbage, of barley, or of oats.... We have misdirected an immense amount of capital in this country; we have misdirected capital in the manufacture of cotton, until if all the cotton mills were run to-day they would produce twice the amount of cotton for which we could find a market in the country. That is one of the effects you produced. Then, also, you have combines for the purpose of keeping up the prices and for closing certain establishments, and dividing the profits of those who labour with those who do nothing... you have taken from certain industries of the country millions of dollars and turned them in other directions in which no market can be found, and the result is that you have a fitful pursuit of those industries; you have thousands of people left at times without employment and sustained at the expense of the rest of the population; you have industries called into existence to a large extent that would have otherwise existed to a very small extent, and you have denuded the rural districts of their population, to remove them into towns where they are less profitably employed, either for themselves or the country at large. You diminish enormously the value of real estate by the policy which you have pursued, and if you continue that policy you will bring still greater calamities upon the people (*Debates*, 1891, pp. 3961-3963).

In 1892 the Wallace Act became sections 517 and 520 of the *Criminal Code*.[54] Section 1 became section 520, with the wording slightly rearranged. The meaning stayed the same. The section referring to trade unions was likewise reworded. As well, a definition of conspiracy was added, (section 516), "A conspiracy in restraint of trade is an agreement between two or more persons to do or procure to be done any unlawful act in restraint of trade." During the debate on the *Criminal Code*, there was no attempt by Wallace or anyone else to remove "unduly," "unreasonably" or "unlawfully."

The next attempt to amend the legislation came in 1894. It originated in the Senate with Mr. Read, one of the most consistent supporters of stronger anti-combines legislation (*Senate Debates*, 1894, p. 289).[55] Read's approach was curious; at Second Reading he spent as much time defending the Senate and urging the Senators to pass the Bill to restore the Senate's reputation as he did discussing the merits of the issue. His main argument in favour of removing the words "unduly" and "unreasonably" was that, as the law

---

54. The *Criminal Code*, 1892, S.C. 1892, 55-56 Vic., c. 29.

55. Bill (AA) An Act to amend the law relative to conspiracies and combinations formed in restraint of trade.

stood, "the best lawyers in the country will not advise their clients to bring an action" (*Senate Debates*, 1894, p. 351). There was no opposition to the Bill until Third Reading and then only one Senator spoke against it. He claimed that he thought it was "a sort of burlesque" rather than a serious measure (*Senate Debates*, 1894, p. 460). The Bill was introduced in the House by T.S. Sproule about a month before it was prorogued (*Debates*, 1894, p. 4393).[56] The Bill never got as far as Second Reading. The same thing happened to a Bill introduced by Sproule in 1895 (*Debates*, 1895, p. 2259).[57] In 1896 Sproule tried again (*Debates*, 1896, p. 30).[58] This time the Bill died on the Order paper after Second Reading.

In the nine sessions of Parliament between 1888 and the general election of 1896, eight separate attempts were made to pass legislation dealing with combinations in restraint of trade. The only successful attempt was the Wallace Bill that became the Act of 1889. In two cases bills passed the House and were either rejected by the Senate (1890) or passed with an amendment but not given Royal Assent (1891). In 1894 the Senate passed a Bill that failed to get the House's approval and in three instances (1888, 1895 and 1896) the proposed legislation failed to pass either House. The eighth attempt was Edgar's 1889 Bill that proposed to use the tariff to fight combines. The most obvious reason for the failure of these Bills was the lack of Government support. It is implausible to argue that this was because they knew that removing "unduly" and "unreasonably" would do little to strengthen the law; it is more likely that if they had been convinced of this they would have passed the legislation.

Following the death of Sir John A. Macdonald in 1891, the office of the Prime Minister was occupied, in quick succession, by four men: John J. Abbott, John Thompson, Mackenzie Bowell and Charles Tupper (Clark, 1961). As we have seen, Macdonald's attitude towards the legislation was one of ambivalence. His successor, Abbott, who led the Government from the Senate, had, in effect, voted in favour of rejecting Wallace's 1890 amending Bill. Thompson, the former Minister of Justice, was probably better informed on the issue than any other Government member. His speeches on the subject were usually of a legalistic nature. It was he, more than anyone else, who insisted that the Act was merely declaratory. In 1891 he argued that there was no harm in removing the words "unduly" and "unreasonably," at the same time he left the impression that it would do little good:

---

56. Bill (No. 140) to amend the law relating to conspiracies and combinations in restraint of trade.

57. Bill (No. 112) to amend the law relating to conspiracies and combinations formed in restraint of trade.

58. Bill (No. 1) to amend the law relating to conspiracies and combinations formed in restraint of trade.

> Let us leave the offence as it is stated at common law. Let us only declare what penalties shall attach to the common law offence, and if we do that we omit these words in the Bill, which may amount to nothing but which are only surplusage and will not weaken the Act by their removal (*Debates*, 1891, p. 2579).

On the basis of his comments in the House, Mackenzie Bowell's interest in the issue was limited to defending the National Policy against the accusation that it led to trade combinations (*Debates*, 1891, pp. 2566-2567). His successor, Charles Tupper was Prime Minister for only two months and he never had an opportunity to address the issue. As well as being personally disinterested in the legislation, there was no obvious political reason to risk alienating the business community by strengthening the legislation. Thorelli suggests that after the *Sherman Act* was passed in 1890 interest in the issue declined in the United States (Thorelli, 1955, p. 342). Since much of the Canadian interest was stimulated by American events, it is reasonable to assume that interest in Canada declined as well. Members of Parliament were certainly less interested. No Bills were introduced in 1892 or 1893 while the Bills introduced in 1894, 1895 and 1896 were not debated at any length in the House. T.S. Sproule, a Conservative back-bencher, was the only MP who maintained an active commitment to the issue. Wallace's silence after 1891 can be explained, in part, as a result of his appointment as Controller of Customs in 1892 (a Ministerial but non-Cabinet position). Wallace's appointment speaks volumes about the nature of Canadian politics. It is generally accepted that Wallace, who was as staunch a Protestant as it was possible to find, was appointed to the position to balance the elevation of John Thompson, a convert to Catholicism, to the Prime Ministership (Clark, 1961, p. 63).

This was exactly the type of problem with which the Conservative leadership was concerned after the election of 1891. Keeping the crumbling party united in the face of religious and "racial" tensions that threatened to rip the party and the country apart occupied much of the energy of the men who succeeded Macdonald. Not only did they not have time for anti-combines legislation, they had little time for anything except trying to find a way out of the political morass created by the Manitoba School Question.

10.0 ANTI-COMBINES LEGISLATION UNDER THE LIBERALS, 1896-1900

The election of the Liberals in the general election of 1896 did not bring about the dramatic changes that one could reasonably have expected. Despite the party's commitment to a "tariff for revenue only" and its conviction that combinations were a product of high tariffs, the Conservative's tariff wall was not dismantled (McDiarmid, 1946, p. 204).[59] For all practical purposes, the Liberals accepted the National Policy; however, they did propose their own legislation to deal with combines. This measure, like Edgar's unsuccessful 1889 Bill, provided that the Governor in Council (the Cabinet) could place any article on the free list or reduce the duty on it when a combination existed among the manufacturers who produced it or the dealers who sold it.[60]

This proposal prompted the first significant debate on trade combinations since 1891. The Conservatives opposed the provision. They talked about terrorizing manufacturers, sacrificing the innocent with the guilty, and they made frequent references to the Star Chamber (*Debates*, 1891, pp. 3248-50, 3334). There was even an accusation that the Government would be able to use the legislation to threaten manufacturers into contributing election funds (*Senate Debates*, 1897, p. 872). Some MPs and Senators continued to maintain that there were no combinations in Canada, or, if there were, that they were harmless. A Conservative Senator argued: "I believe that where there is a combination as a general thing among manufacturers in this country, it is only brought about from absolute necessity and to prevent bankruptcy" (*Senate Debates*, 1897, p. 871). The Liberals defended the legislation by claiming it was preventive rather than punitive, "There are some laws which are valuable by reason of what they prevent rather than what they punish...my expectation is that under this law combines will soon dissolve and that we shall have fair and legitimate competition, which the people are entitled to have" (*Debates*, 1897, p. 3251).

The combines clause in *The Customs Tariff, 1897* contains many of the qualifications that were in the Wallace Act. For example, it refers to "any trust, combination, association or agreement...to <u>unduly</u> enhance the price of such article or in any other way to <u>unduly</u> promote the advantage of the manufacturers...." (emphasis added). To pacify the Opposition, a provision was added that the Governor in Council had to refer the question of whether a combination existed to a Superior Court judge, and if he reported that it did exist, and if it appeared that the disadvantage to the consumer was facilitated by the duty, the Governor in Council could "place such article on the free list or so reduce the duty on it as to give to the public the benefit of reasonable

---

59. The Liberal platform, which had been declared at an 1893 convention, listed a series of charges against the government's tariff policy, among them: "That the existing tariff, founded upon an unsound principle, and used, as it has been by the Government, as a corrupting agency wherewith to keep themselves in office has developed monopolies, trusts and combines" (Carrigan, 1968, p. 34).

60. *The Customs Tariff, 1897*, S.C. 1897, 60-61 Vic., c. 16, s. 18. It also contained a provision (s. 17) concerning preferential tariff arrangements.

competition in such article." With these qualifications, it is not surprising that the legislation was employed only once.[61]

In the same session a Government Bill to amend the *Criminal Code* was introduced in the Senate (*Senate Debates*, 1897, p. 297).[62] The debate on the Bill makes fascinating reading because many of its clauses were attempts to legislate morality. One finds Senators discussing how many days horse-racing could be permitted before the moral fabric of society started to crumble. (They settled on twelve days (*Senate Debates*, 1897, pp. 552-555).) Changes were proposed to Section 520. One Senator wanted to strengthen the legislation while the Liberal leader wanted to add a subsection making it clear that the section was not to apply to trade unions (*Senate Debates*, 1897, pp. 559, 565-571). Neither proposal was accepted. The Bill passed the Senate, but the House did not give it serious consideration.

In 1898 Sproule renewed his attempt to remove the words "unduly" and "unreasonably" from the legislation (*Debates*, 1898, p. 2241).[63] The Bill never came up for Second Reading. In the following year Sproule's persistence paid off. He offered the same justification in 1899 that he had used several times before:

> The law has been on the Statute-book many years, and efforts have been made from time to time, to get the Attorney-General of the province to prosecute under the Act, and several times applications have been made to private individuals to do so; and they all raised the same objection - that it would be almost impossible to secure a conviction under the law as it reads (*Debates*, 1899, p. 1937).[64]

He also gave some evidence about a combination in the leather trade. Only two Ministers spoke during the debate on the Bill: Richard Cartwright, the Minister of Trade and Commerce, was noncommittal; W.S. Fielding, the Minister of Finance, was more encouraging. He suggested that he was "disposed to look upon it with favour." Although these comments reveal little about the Government's thinking, the obvious reason that the Bill passed was because the Government wanted it to pass.

The discussion in the Senate was typically confused, it was as if the subject had never been discussed. Mackenzie Bowell, the ex-Prime Minister

---

61. In 1901, following a complaint by the Canadian Press Association, an alleged combination of Canadian paper manufacturers was investigated. When it was determined that a combination did exist, the duties on some types of paper were reduced by 40 per cent (Reynolds, 1940, p. 135).

62. Bill (H) An Act further to amend the Criminal Code.

63. Bill (No. 89) to amend the Act for the prevention and suppression of combinations formed in restraint of trade.

64. The Bill under discussion was Bill (No. 40) to amend the Criminal Code 1892, with respect to combinations in restraint of trade.

and the Conservative leader in the Senate, actually argued that examples of combinations from the Select Committee referred to by Senator Power, "were covered by the law as it stands upon the statute-book at the present time," (*Senate Debates*, 1899, p. 778) demonstrating once again the confusion that existed concerning the state of the law. Senator Allan thought that it would be "hardly fair" if the law was to apply to owners of salt wells who agreed to limit production in order to maintain prices (*Ibid.*, p. 781). Despite Senator Power's insistence that innocent arrangements would not be affected, several Senators were worried about removing the two words (*Ibid.*, pp. 782-783). In the end, the Bill passed.[65]

At the same time that it was considering the above Bill, the Senate was again considering a general Bill, similar to the one passed by the Senate in 1897, to amend the *Criminal Code*.[66] During the debate on this Bill, a motion was passed to remove the word "unlawfully" from section 520. Michael Bliss has suggested that "this happened by accident when a Senator who prided himself on his drafting ability suggested omitting the word in order to get rid of the 'surplusage' in the section" (Bliss, 1973,. p. 183). The Senator in question, David Mills, the Minister of Justice, was not responsible for removing the word. Mills did think that the wording of the section was inadequate; however, it is not clear that he thought it should be changed, "Those are anomalies in the section which might be corrected, but which I did not think it worthwhile to interfere with....They are a surplusage and, as a matter of art, ought not to prevail." A moment later Mills suggested, "if 'unlawfully' is left in 'unduly' should be struck out" and then, following an interjection by Bowell, he suggested, "The word 'unlawfully' should come out, or the other word" (*Senate Debates*, 1899, p. 492). Mills was uncertain about whether any change should be made and about which word should be removed. (At this point the Bill discussed above had only received First Reading.)

It was Senator Power, not Mills as Bliss suggests, who moved that the word "unlawfully" be omitted and Power knew exactly what he was doing.[67] Power, a graduate of Harvard Law School, had been advocating such a change since 1889. In that year, when the Senate first considered the legislation, he had argued, "If we want to make a good and effective Bill we should strike out the word 'unlawfully'" (*Senate Debates*, 1889, p. 632). In 1899, during the debate on the Bill to remove unduly and unreasonably, he argued, "in any

---

65. *An Act to amend the Criminal Code, 1892, with respect to Combinations in restraint of trade*, S.C. 1899, 62-63 Vic., c. 46.

66. Bill (Q) An Act further to amend the Criminal Code (*Senate Debates*, 1899, p. 321).

67. "The word 'unlawfully' in the first subsection is clearly unnecessary. When we pass this clause forbidding a thing, we make it unlawful.... The word 'unlawfully' has no use here at all and I move to strike it out" (*Senate Debates*, 1899, p. 494).

case the word 'unlawfully' is unnecessary and objectionable here, and it is better to have it out in any case, and if we can strike out the word 'unduly' also we shall still further improve the law" (*Ibid.*, 1899, p. 782). Power's motion was accepted and the Bill to amend the *Criminal Code* passed the Senate. The Bill was sent to the House, but it was not passed (*Debates*, 1899, p. 7893); perhaps because, with only five weeks left in the session, there was not enough time to give it the consideration it warranted.

Thus, largely as a result of Senator Power's efforts, the usually cautious Senate agreed to delete all three of the crucial qualifying words from section 520. At the time, it may have appeared that the Bill removing unduly and unreasonably was the more important because it was the one that became law. However, section 520 remained in this form for only one year. When yet another comprehensive *Criminal Code* Bill was introduced in the Senate in 1900, the words unduly and reasonably were back in while the word unlawfully was omitted. The Minister of Justice's explanation was brief and ambiguous, "instead of retaining the word 'unlawful', sic I have retained the word 'unduly'. The reason is that the word 'unlawful' does not mean anything unless you declare what is unlawful, but the word 'unduly' refers to a question of fact" (*Senate Debates*, 1900, p. 417). There was almost no debate on this change although the Senators did go on to argue about a proposed subsection dealing with combinations of workers. The House passed the Bill without raising the question of the change in wording.[68] Again there was debate on the proposed clause dealing with workers. Despite the Senate's objections, the House insisted on adding a subsection that read, "Nothing in this section shall be construed to apply to combinations of workmen or employees." The Bill became law with the subsection intact and the word unlawfully removed.

The passage of *The Criminal Code Amendment Act, 1900*, marked an obvious stage in the development of Canada's anti-combines legislation. With the removal of the word "unlawfully" the decade-long attempt to amend the legislation came to an end. The 1889 legislation had finally been put in a workable form. During the next ten years, nine prosecutions were started, seven of which were successful (Stanbury, 1991). Despite the successful prosecutions, the passage of the 1900 Act marked an end rather than a beginning. Ten years later, when Canadian politicians again turned their attention to the issue, it was apparent that a new approach was needed.

11.0 CONCLUSION

A number of factors led to the introduction and eventual amendment of Canada's competition policy legislation of 1889. The structure of the economy in the 1880s and 1890s, the politics of late nineteenth century regulation;

---

68. *The Criminal Code Amendment Act, 1900*, S.C. 1900, 63-34 Vic., c. 46.

contemporary attitudes towards competition; beliefs about the status of restraints of trade under the common law; party politics; and the influence of American events were the more important. The purpose of this conclusion is simply to summarize the role played by some of these factors. In the process, comparisons will be drawn with the *Sherman Act* as a means of highlighting the Canadian Act.

11.1 The Structure of the Economy

One feature of the late nineteenth century Canadian economy was the downward trend of prices. This has already been mentioned, but it merits further comment. Prices fell in Great Britain and the United States as well and it is reasonable to conclude that the appearance of trusts, cartels and combinations in all three countries was, in part, a result of this phenomenon. But, if the decline of prices contributed to the appearance of these schemes to limit competition, it also dampened their impact and helps to explain why the public outcry was not greater. One reason that the wave of mergers that began in 1909 received so much attention was because it occurred during a period of rising prices.[69] Mackenzie King specifically raised this point when he introduced new anti-combines legislation in 1910:

> It is this question of the cost of living which has helped to make the question of combines, trusts and mergers and the possible effect they have on prices so important. In the popular mind there has come to be a gradual association between these two phenomena (*Debates*, 1910, p. 6803).[70]

The National Policy was important in an obvious sense because it contributed to the misallocation of resources and overexpansion. Manufacturers were often right when they complained about cutthroat competition. However, instead of seeing the high tariffs as part of the problem they lobbied for a higher wall behind which they could form combinations. Although all combinations were not a result of high tariffs, the Wallace Act can be seen as the corollary of the National Policy. It was the cure that was administered to minimize the disorder created by the protective tariffs. The cure was mild because it was supposed to reduce the symptoms, not attack the disease.

11.2 The Politics of Regulation

The National Policy was also important because it helps explain the emergence of modern regulation. Some economic historians have suggested

---

69. The wholesale price index rose from 62.4 in 1900 to 78.5 in 1910 (1935-39 = 100) (Bertram, 1967, p. 81).

70. Competition policy as a means of fighting inflation is discussed in Gorecki and Stanbury (1984, Ch. 5).

that the victory of Parliament over the monarchy as the sole supplier of regulatory legislation was one of the reasons for the decline of mercantilist regulation in England (Ekelund and Tollison, 1980, pp. 593-595). With Parliament's victory, the cost of supplying regulatory legislation increased and deregulation occurred. Using this insight, one can hypothesize that the reappearance of regulation in its modern form may have been caused, in part, by a fall in the cost of supplying regulatory legislation.[71] One factor that made regulation "cheaper" was the emergence of relatively stable parliamentary majorities based on party politics. For those seeking legislative favours it became easier to identify and influence the suppliers of such favours. Contributions could be made to the party rather than to specific individuals and, in the process, they were made to appear more legitimate. For the Cabinet, the strengthening of party loyalty made it easier to get controversial legislation passed. To those who think that regulation is used to transfer wealth rather than to protect the public, the National Policy stands out as one of the landmarks in the growth of regulation in Canada. (Although nominally a taxation measure, to the extent that it was protective, the National Policy was a means of transferring wealth rather than a means of raising revenue.)

The existence of identifiable political parties provided focal points for those opposed to such transfer schemes as well as for those who sought them. In the late nineteenth century, groups opposed to the tariff, or in favour of stronger anti-combines legislation, were much weaker than the groups whose interests they opposed.[72] As Lloyd Reynolds has pointed out, it is significant that the only time section 18 of the *Customs Tariff Act* was used to lower a tariff, "this case involved a well-organized group of consumers the Canadian Press Association able to spend the sums necessary for adequate defence of their interests" (Reynolds, 1940, p. 135).[73] With no powerful groups supporting such a measure, the Conservatives had much to lose and little to gain by

---

71.   I would emphasize that this was only one factor among many that contributed to the growth of modern regulation. The introduction of new technologies, the emergence of a class of middle-class experts; the organization of interest groups; the growth of "big-business"; and the widening of the franchise were some of the other factors. See Baggaley (1981).

72.   Both labour and farmers' groups supported stronger anti-combines legislation. *Journals of the House of Commons* (1891, p. XXVII) lists 15 petitions that were received from labour organizations praying for amendments to the 1889 Act. However, all the petitions were the same and they were all accompanied by petitions dealing with other matters, such as the immigration of Oriental labourers. This suggests that they may not have been an accurate reflection of labour opinion. Both the Dominion Grange and the Patrons of Industry (a farmers' organization) urged the federal government to strengthen the Act. They seemed to be more interested in using the tariff to fight combines. In 1891 the Patrons of Industry sent the federal government a 25,000 name petition asking that twine, salt and iron be placed on the free list. See Wood (1975, pp. 97-98; 143-44).

73.   The Liberals apparently by-passed the legislation when they put binder twine on the free list in 1898. See Wood (1975, p. 98).

passing an effective anticombines act. It was not a big enough issue to risk alienating the business interests who supported the party.

11.3 Combines and the Common Law

Another reason for the weakness of the Act was the confusion about the state of the common law with respect to restraints of trade. If the common law had been as hostile to trade combinations as some MPs and Senators believed it was, then a statute that merely declared the common law would not necessarily have been ineffective. The truth of the matter was that during the nineteenth century the courts had become more tolerant of restraints of trade. As has been pointed out, American politicians were similarly confused about the common law. As one American Senator put it, "I suppose no lawyer needs to have argument made to him that these combinations and trusts are illegal without statute" (quoted by Letwin, 1965, p. 96).[74]

Nevertheless, the *Sherman Act* proved to be a more effective act than its Canadian counterpart. The maximum fine for corporations was actually less in the American statute - $10,000 as compared to $5,000. The American statute also had the disadvantage of being limited to interstate commerce. The first case to reach the Supreme Court was decided on this point. The American Sugar Refining Company, after purchasing four Pennsylvania companies giving it control over more than 95 per cent of the sugar refined in the United States, was acquitted:

> The fact that an article is manufactured for export to another State does not of itself make it an article of interstate commerce, and the intent of the manufacturer does not determine the time when the article or product passes from the control of the State and belongs to commerce (Thorelli, 1955, p. 447).

The *Sherman Act* was set out in general terms without the qualifying adverbs of the Canadian Statute. Section 1 begins: "Every contract, combination in the form of trust or otherwise, or conspiracy in restraint of trade or commerce among the several States, or with foreign nations, is hereby declared to be illegal." The idea behind the American legislation seems to have been to frame a general act and leave its interpretation to the courts; in contrast, the Canadian legislation was more specific as if there was a feeling that the courts could not be trusted to interpret it correctly. This is a characteristic that often distinguishes Canadian regulatory legislation from similar American legislation. The latter relies more heavily on the judiciary for interpretation and enforcement. It is also worth noting that the *Sherman Act* contained provisions for triple damages to be awarded in private actions. It provided that anyone whose business or property was damaged as a result of any action

---

74. The common law as it had evolved in the United States was less tolerant of restraints of trade, but not to the extent suggested by this comment.

declared unlawful could sue for triple the damages plus legal fees. There was no similar provision in the Canadian Act.

11.4 The Enforcement Issue

Both statutes have been criticized because no provisions were made for enforcement. In the Canadian case the difficulty was partly constitutional; it was left to the provincial Attorneys-General to initiate proceedings. Their unwillingness to prosecute has been usually attributed to the weakness of the legislation, although it is plausible that part of their reluctance to prosecute stemmed from the realization that they had little to gain by doing so. The issue was seen as a federal problem and while trying to enforce a weak act would have cost the provinces both time and money, any credit for a successful prosecution would have gone to the federal government. This argument has added force when one realizes that both Ontario and Quebec, where most of the prosecutions would have occurred, were governed by the Liberals who had no desire to aid the federal Conservatives (generally, see Gorecki and Stanbury, 1991).

On this question, it has to be kept in mind that the notion of enforcement, or policing, by means of boards or agencies, was still something of a novelty in 1889. In trying to explain why Congress failed to vote funds or create an agency to enforce the *Sherman Act*, Thorelli (1955, p. 369) suggests that "the idea that once a prohibitory statute is enacted general observance of its provisions will follow as a matter of course influenced many congressmen...." One can suggest that the same idea influenced Canadian politicians. This can be seen not only in the 1889 Act but in several other pieces of legislation as well. The *Railway Act*, the *Bank Act* and the *Insurance Act* are other examples of nineteenth century legislation in which certain activities were prohibited with little or no attention paid to enforcement. It was not until after 1900 (the creation of the Board of Railway Commissioners in 1903 was an important milestone) that enforcement became a major concern.

11.5 The Effectiveness of the 1889 Act

The question of the Act's effectiveness has thus far been begged. Probably the main reason why it has been judged to have been ineffective is that no convictions were secured under it until after it was amended in 1900. The only case tried under the Act prior to 1900 resulted in an acquittal. The case in question, *R. v. American Tobacco Company of Canada*,[75] hinged on the legality of an agreement that the Company required its dealers to sign. Under the agreement the dealers sold the Company's cigarettes on consignment at fixed prices. They were paid a commission provided that they

---

75. *R. v. The American Tobacco Company of Canada* (1897), 3 Rev. de Jur. 453.

refrained from selling the cigarettes of any other manufacturer and satisfied all of the other terms of the agreement. The court held that:

> It is not <u>unlawful</u> for the proprietor of certain manufactured goods, (in this case <u>cigarettes</u>), in order to secure the greatest circulation for his goods, to agree with as many parties as he can find, that they consent to sell only such <u>cigarettes</u> exclusively to those of other proprietors.[76]

Although the judge made several references to the word "unlawfully" the decision did not depend on its inclusion in the Act:

> And even if the word "unlawfully" were not in the article 520, of the *Criminal Code* I do not see that the same agreement would bring the company under the law, for the same reason that I can only see in the doings of the Company a way of theirs of disposing of their own goods in the way that they think fit, which is a right which pertains to any citizen or legal persons existing under our laws.[77]

The case is significant because it demonstrates that the problem with the 1889 Act went deeper than the presence of the word "unlawfully."

Insofar as it failed to punish any of the trade combinations examined by the 1888 Select Committee, the Act could be considered to have been ineffective prior to its amendment in 1900. However, this does not necessarily mean that it did not have any impact. The Act was aimed at horizontal combinations; it was apparently not intended to deal with the problems posed by mergers, trusts, or individual attempts to monopolize. If we accept that the businessmen of the day were not as convinced as modern commentators that the law was toothless, it is possible that it may have discouraged combinations or, conversely, it may have contributed to the mergers that became more commonplace after 1890. One of the first and most important consolidations occurred in the troubled cotton industry. By 1892 almost all the mills in Canada had been absorbed by either the Dominion Cotton Mills Company or the Dominion Coloured Cotton Mills Company.[78] (Both were under the same management.) A dozen years later these companies and a few others, were merged to form Dominion Textiles. The early 1890s also saw the merger of the Massey and the Harris farm implement companies. During the next few years the new company proceeded to absorb several smaller firms (Denison, 1948, pp. 119 ff). These mergers were dwarfed by the wave of mergers that began in 1909. During the five years between 1909 and 1913, 221 enterprises were reduced to 97 with gross assets in excess of $200 million (Weldon, 1966,

---

76. *Ibid.*, at p. 453.

77. *Ibid.*, at p. 463.

78. See the speech by J. Edgar (*Debates*, 1893, pp. 807-819).

p. 233). The Liberal government responded by passing the *Combines Investigation Act* in 1910.[79]

Even though it was passed with greater deliberation and was significantly more detailed, this new Act did not prove to be any more effective than the one it replaced. (Between 1910 and 1923, when the legislation was again amended, only one prosecution was started and it resulted in the acquittal of the Canadian Wholesale Grocers' Association.)[80] This raises a larger issue about our competition policy in general. Canada was the first country in the world to pass modern legislation designed to prevent abuses arising from restraints of trade. Since 1910 this legislation has undergone significant amendment almost every decade. Still, our economy has remained one of the most highly concentrated in the world. One popular answer to this apparent paradox is "we've never been all that keen on competition in Canada,"[81] or, as Herschel Hardin puts it more positively, "We have an aptitude for monopoly" (Hardin, 1974, p. 174).

While it is true that Canada has never experienced an "anti-trust movement" comparable to those of the United States, it is not apparent that we are less keen on competition than anyone else. Nor is it apparent that we are more adept at managing monopolies. For every successful monopoly in Canada one can think of at least one that is inefficient - the Post Office comes to mind rather quickly. It is more to the point that, at least for some people, monopoly offers more tangible rewards. Competition, in contrast, increases the general welfare but the benefits accruing to any individual or group are not necessarily that large. Thus we find more groups or individuals lobbying for monopoly privileges or for legislation that will redistribute wealth in their favour than for effective competition legislation and, as the quotation from Adam Smith that prefaces this study suggests, legislators are too often directed by "the clamorous importunity of partial interests." This is what happened in 1889 and, for those who believe that history should teach lessons, this is the lesson to be learned from that experience.

---

79. *Combines Investigation Act*, S.C. 1910, 9-10 Edw. VII, c.9. More generally, see Gorecki and Stanbury (1991).

80. See note 21.

81. Robert Bertrand, quoted by *Maclean's*, November 17, 1980, p. 246.

REFERENCES

Acheson, T.W. (1971) "The Social Origins of Canadian Industrialism: A Study in the Structure of Entrepreneurship" (Unpublished Ph.D. Thesis, University of Toronto).

Ashley, W.J. (1890) "The Canadian Sugar Combine," *University Quarterly Review*, Vol. 1, February, pp. 24-39.

Baggaley, Carman D. (1981) *The Emergence of the Regulatory State in Canada, 1867-1939* (Ottawa: Economic Council of Canada).

Ball, John A. (1934) *Canadian Anti-Trust Legislation* (Baltimore: The Williams & Wilkins Company).

Barnett, D.F. (1976) "The Galt Tariff: Incidental or Effective Protection?" *Canadian Journal of Economics*, Vol. 9(3), pp. 389-407.

Bertram, G.W. (1967) "Economic Growth in Canadian Industry, 1870-1915: The Staple Model" in W.T. Easterbrooke and M.H. Watkins (eds.) *Approaches to Canadian Economic History* (Toronto: McClelland and Stewart Limited).

Bliss, Michael (1970) "Canadianizing American Business: the Roots of the Branch Plant" in Ian Lumsden (ed.) *Close the 49th Parallel, etc.: the Americanization of Canada* (Toronto: University of Toronto Press).

Bliss, Michael (1972) "The Protective Impulse: An Approach to the Social History of Oliver Mowatt's Ontario" in Donald Swainson (ed.) *Oliver Mowat's Ontario* (Toronto: Macmillan of Canada), pp. 174-188.

Bliss, Michael (1973) "Another Anti-Trust Tradition: Canadian Anti-Combines Policy, 1889-1910," *Business History Review*, Vol. XLVII(2), Summer, pp. 177-188.

Bliss, Michael (1974) *A Living Profit: Studies in the Social History of Canadian Business, 1883-1911* (Toronto: McClelland and Stewart Limited).

Carrigan, Owen D., ed. (1968) *Canadian Party Platforms, 1867-1968* (Toronto: Copp Clark).

Chambers, Edward J. (1964) "Late Nineteenth Century Business Cycles in Canada," *Canadian Journal of Economics and Political Science*, Vol. 30(3), pp. 399-400.

Chandler, Alfred D. (1977) *The Visible Hand: The Managerial Revolution in American Business* (Cambridge, Mass.: Harvard University Press).

Clark, John Bates (1887) "The Limits of Competition," *Political Science Quarterly*, Vol. II(1).

Clark, Lowell C. (1961) "The Conservative Party in the 1890s," *Canadian Historical Association Report*, pp. 58-74.

Comanor, William S. and Harvey Leibenstein (1969) "Allocative Efficiency, X-Efficiency and the Measurement of Welfare Losses," *Economica*, Vol. 36(143), pp. 304-309.

Cook, William W. (1888) *"Trusts": The Recent Combinations in Trade* 2nd ed. (New York: L.K. Strouse & Co.).

DeLottinville, Peter (1980) "Trouble in the Hives of Industry: The Cotton Industry Comes to Milltown, New Brunswick, 1879-1892," *Canadian Historical Association, Historical Papers*, pp. 100-115.

Denison, Merrill (1948) *Harvest Triumphant: The Story of Massey-Harris* (Toronto: McClelland and Stewart Limited).

Ekelund, Robert B., Jr. and Robert D. Tollison (1980) "Economic Regulation in Mercantile England: Heckscher Revisited," *Economic Inquiry*, Vol. 43(4), pp. 588-593.

English, John (1977) *The Decline of Politics: The Conservatives and the Party System, 1901-1920* (Toronto: University of Toronto Press).

Forster, Ben (1979) "The Coming of the National Policy: Business, Government and the Tariff, 1876-1879," *Journal of Canadian Studies*, Vol. 14(3), pp. 39-49.

Goodwin, Crauford D.W. (1961) *Canadian Economic Thought: The Political Economy of a Developing Nation, 1814-1914* (Durham, N.C.: Duke University Press).

Gorecki, Paul K. and W.T. Stanbury (1981) "Declaring the Common Law: The Genesis of Canadian Competition Policy" (Faculty of Commerce and Business Administration, University of B.C., unpublished paper).

Gorecki, Paul K. and W.T. Stanbury (1984) *The Objectives of Canadian Competition Policy, 1888-1983* (Montreal: The Institute for Research on Public Policy).

Gorecki, Paul K. and W.T. Stanbury (1991) "The Administration and Enforcement of Competition Policy in Canada, 1889-1952" in R.S. Khemani and W.T. Stanbury (eds.) *Canadian Competition Law and Policy at the Centenary* (Halifax: The Institute for Research on Public Policy).

Gordon, Sanford D. (1963) "Attitudes towards Trusts Prior to the Sherman Act," *The Southern Economic Journal*, Vol. 30(2), pp. 156-167.

Gosse, Richard (1962) *The Law on Competition in Canada* (Toronto: The Carswell Company Limited).

Hardin, Herschel (1974) *A Nation Unaware: The Canadian Economic Culture* (Vancouver: J.J. Douglas Ltd.).

Hunter, W.T. (1979) "The Decline of the Tariff - but not of Protection," *Journal of Canadian Studies*, Vol. 14(3), pp. 111-112.

Leibenstein, Harvey (1966) "Allocative Efficiency v. 'X-Efficiency'," *American Economic Review*, Vol. 56(3).

Letwin, William (1965) *Law and Economic Policy in America: The Evolution of the Sherman Antitrust Act* (New York: Random House).

Mathias, Peter (1969) *The First Industrial Nation: An Economic History of Britain, 1700-1914* (New York: Charles Scribner's Sons).

McDiarmid, Orville John (1946) *Commercial Policy in the Canadian Economy* (Cambridge, Mass.: Harvard University Press).

McLean, Simon J. (1895) *The Tariff History of Canada* (Toronto: Warwick Bros. & Rutler).

McNultly, Paul J. (1968) "Economic Theory and the Meaning of Competition," *Quarterly Journal of Economics*, Vol. 83(4), pp. 639-656.

Melvin, James R. and Bruce C. Wilkinson (1968) *Effective Protection in the Canadian Economy* (Ottawa: Economic Council of Canada).

Morton, Desmond (1973) *Mayor Howland: The Citizens' Candidate* (Toronto: Hakkert).

Naylor, Tom (1975) *The History of Canadian Business, 1867-1914* Vol. 1 (Toronto: James Lorimer).

Newman, Peter C. (1981) *The Acquisitors: The Canadian Establishment*, Volume Two (Toronto: McClelland and Stewart).

Otter, A.A. Den (1982) "Alexander Galt, the 1859 Tariff, and Canadian Economic Nationalism," *Canadian Historical Review*, Vol. 63(2), pp. 151-178.

Report of the Select Committee to Investigate and Report upon Alleged Combinations in Manufactures, Trade and Insurance in Canada (1888) *Journals of the House of Commons*, 18888, Appendix No. 3.

Reynolds, Lloyd C. (1940) *The Control of Competition in Canada* (Cambridge, Mass.: Harvard University Press).

Schumpeter, Joseph A. (1950) *Capitalism, Socialism and Democracy* 3rd ed. (New York: Harper and Brothers).

Stanbury, W.T. (1988) "List of Large Mergers and Acquisitions in Canada, 1978 to 1987" in R.S. Khemani et al. (eds.) *Mergers, Corporate Concentration and Power in Canada* (Halifax: The Institute for Research on Public Policy), pp. 583-601.

Stanbury, W.T. (1991) "Legislation to Control Agreements in Restraint of Trade in Canada: Review of the Historical Record and Proposals for Reform" in R.S. Khemani and W.T. Stanbury (eds.) *Canadian Competition Law and Policy at the Centenary* (Halifax: The Institute for Research on Public Policy).

Stigler, George (1965) "Perfect Competition, Historically Contemplated" in George Stigler, *Essays in the History of Economics* (Chicago: University of Chicago Press), pp. 234-267.

Stigler, George (1976) "The Xistence of X-efficiency," *The American Economic Review*, Vol. 66(1), pp. 213-216.

Thorelli, Hans B. (1955) *The Federal Anti-Trust Policy: Origination of an American Tradition* (Baltimore: The John Hopkins Press).

Tullock, Gordon (1980) "The Welfare Costs of Tariffs, Monopolies and Theft" in James M. Buchanan, Robert D. Tollison and Gordon Tullock (eds.) *Toward a Theory of the Rent-Seeking Society* (College Station: Texas A&M University Press).

Urquhart, M.C. and K.A.H. Buckley (1965) *Historical Statistics of Canada* (Toronto: Macmillan of Canada).

Waite, P.B. (1974) *Canada, 1874-1896: Arduous Destiny* (Toronto: McClelland and Stewart Limited).

Weldon, J.C. (1966) "Consolidations in Canadian Industry, 1900-1948" in L.A. Skeoch (ed.) *Restrictive Trade Practices in Canada* (Toronto: McClelland and Stewart Limited).

West, E.G. (1978) "The Burdens of Monopoly: Classical Versus Neoclassical," *Southern Economic Journal*, Vol. 44(4), pp. 829-845.

Wilkinson, Bruce W. (1968) *Effective Protection in the Canadian Economy* (Ottawa: Economic Council of Canada).

Wood, Louis A. (1975) *A History of Farmers' Movement in Canada* (Toronto: University of Toronto Press, first published in 1924).

Chapter 2

THE ADMINISTRATION AND ENFORCEMENT OF COMPETITION POLICY IN CANADA, 1889 to 1952

Paul K. Gorecki
Economic Council of Canada
and Statistics Canada

W.T. Stanbury
UPS Foundation Professor of Regulation
and Competition Policy
Faculty of Commerce &
Business Administration
University of B.C.

In his book and in many of his speeches Mr. [W.L. Mackenzie] King pats himself on the back for two of his pre-1914 legislative achievements, the Industrial Disputes Investigation Act and the Combines Investigation Act. They have not been useless, but how little have they accomplished in dealing with labour disputes and with concentration of control in modern mass industry! When we look around at the monopolies and near-monopolies in Canada which dominate so much of our economy, the Combines Act resembles nothing so much as the bleating of a pathetic vegetarian lamb in the midst of a carnivorous jungle. That is just it. Mr. King never quite got it that our civilization is dominated by carnivorous animals. He was meant to be a professor safe in the study, not a statesman out in the jungle. For sooner or later the statesman must clear out the jungle and make it habitable (Frank Underhill, 1944, pp. 114-115).

1.0 INTRODUCTION

The objective of this study is to provide a general account of the administration and enforcement of competition policy legislation over the first six decades of its history. We pay particular attention to the development of the administrative machinery as the federal government sought a practicable set of institutional arrangements to deal with a variety of restraints of trade ranging from price fixing to mergers to predatory pricing.

We have focused our efforts on the period 1889-1952 for several reasons. First, detailed studies already exist for the periods 1952-1960 (Rosenbluth and Thorburn, 1963), and for 1960-1975 (Gorecki and Stanbury, 1979; Gorecki, 1981). With this study, Canadians will have a detailed and systematic analysis of the first 86 years of its competition policy. Second, while various authors have addressed parts of the period before 1952,[1] there has been no single treatment of the entire period. Because the period was characterized by several quite different approaches to administration and enforcement, it is useful to examine it using common analytic techniques. Third, our work on the period 1960-1975 indicated that a better understanding of the administration and enforcement of competition legislation in the modern era requires a deeper appreciation of its roots, some of which go back several decades. Some of the important elements of present day administration of the *Competition Act*[2] have not always been part of the machinery (e.g., the high degree of independence of the Director of Investigation and Research, and prosecution of criminal cases exclusively by the federal Department of Justice).

There are several justifications for an examination of the historical antecedents of a public policy and administrative process that continues to be the source of considerable controversy and debate. First, complex policy institutions such as competition policy do <u>not</u> arrive in one fell swoop. Rather, they evolve through a process of collective learning and adaptation to changing circumstances. This study shows that the present law and administrative apparatus for competition policy is the result of experience with a number of less satisfactory alternatives tried in the past. It also shows that this process can take decades.

Second, to know where we are - let alone know where we are going - it is useful to know where we have been. Many of the elements of the present legislation and enforcement process were shaped in the forge of the past. To understand what they were intended to do and how they got there requires one to look backward and to appreciate the forces and circumstances when the legislation or administrative machinery was changed. Such an understanding may result in useful lessons for the present administration and enforcement of competition policy in Canada. Those who ignore history are destined to repeat its mistakes.

Third, a knowledge of its history helps to explain why Canadian competition policy (like that in the U.S.) has a number of objectives and why they can be in conflict. While we have pursued the evolution of the policy's

---

1. See Ball (1934) who covers the period 1889-1934; Reynolds (1940), who covers the period 1889-1939; Bladen (1956), who covers the period 1889-1956; the MacQuarrie Committee (Canada, 1952) which briefly covers the period 1889-1952; and Stanbury (1981) who provides a survey of the changes in Canada's <u>legislative</u> history from 1888 to May 1981.

2. Effective June 19, 1986 the *Combines Investigation Act* was amended and renamed the *Competition Act* R.S.C., 1985, c. C-34. See Stanbury (1986).

objectives elsewhere (Gorecki and Stanbury, 1984), in this study we are able to more closely link these to changes in administration and enforcement over the first six decades.

Fourth, a study of the administration and enforcement of competition policy reminds us that public policy, government institutions and administrative behaviour all reflect the pulling and hauling of the political process (Dunlop et al., 1987, p. 8). Both law and administrative processes are in large part responses to the real politik of competing interest groups and the discretionary power of the cabinet in the Westminster model of democratic government. The decisions of the cabinet in changing competition policy is necessarily a value judgment which - like all policies - must meet the ultimate test of contemporary political support. This requires, in the words of Rosenbluth and Thorburn (1963, p. 96), that the cabinet walk a "political tightrope" between mass support and business support. Some indication of how this was done between 1889 and 1952 is provided by this study.

Since this study concentrates exclusively on administration and enforcement, changes in the substantive sections of the legislation, judicial interpretation of the law, major changes in the political environment, and the intent of the law are addressed only in so far as they relate and explain the form of administrative machinery created and the vigour of its enforcement.[3]

For the purposes of description and analysis, the development of the administrative machinery and the record of enforcement over the first 64 years can usefully be divided into two periods: 1889 to 1923, and 1923 to 1952. This division is based on the nature of major developments in the administrative machinery. The first period marks the rather lengthy search to find and establish a viable administrative structure. From 1889, when the first legislation was enacted, to 1910, enforcement was left entirely up to the attorneys general of the provinces (see Section 2). While a number of public prosecutions occurred between 1900 and 1910, there were more private civil actions which sought to rely on the amended provisions regarding combines in the *Criminal Code* (see Appendix B). Prior to 1900 the original legislation was unenforceable because it rested on a total misconception of the common law on restraint of trade. Although the *Combines Investigation Act* of 1910 did provide for an enforcement process within the federal government, it proved ineffective for several reasons and no prosecutions occurred before it was replaced by the *Board of Commerce Act* and the *Combines and Fair Prices Act* in 1919. The civil provisions were soon held to be unconstitutional (see Section 4). Shortly thereafter the *Combines Investigation Act* of 1923

---

3. The legislative history is summarized in Stanbury (1981); the evolution of the objectives of Canadian competition policy is discussed in Gorecki and Stanbury (1984); the politics of amending the legislation is discussed in Forster (1962) and the changing interpretation of the law is analyzed in Sommerfeld (1948), Dunlop et al. (1987), and Quinlan (1966a), (1966b).

was enacted. It was designed chiefly by Mackenzie King, then the Prime Minister (see Section 5).

The second period involves the application of the administrative machinery created in the 1923 Act (see Section 6). Again, the federal government tried to use civil law to administer restrictive agreements through the Dominion Trade and Industry Commission beginning in 1935 (see Cheffins, 1991). These were held to be unconstitutional in 1937 and the federal government returned to the enforcement techniques, with minor modifications, established in the 1923 *Combines Investigation Act*. With the exception of W.W.II, this machinery held sway until 1952. The amendments in 1952 were prompted by the crisis precipitated by the delay in publication of the *Flour Milling Report* in the late 1940s and the consequent resignation of Canada's chief anti-combines official.[4] This in turn led to the establishment of the MacQuarrie Committee (Canada, 1952) and further changes in the administrative machinery, notably the creation of the Restrictive Trade Practices Commission to take over the appraisal and report functions formerly performed by the Commissioner, the chief enforcement official.[5]

In analysing and describing the administrative machinery particular attention is paid to the following topics: the method(s) by which an investigation can be started; the responsibility for conducting an investigation; and the decision as to what remedy, if any, should be sought.

Enforcement activity varied considerably over the period 1889 to 1952. In some periods, such as 1889-1900, 1914-1918, 1930-35 and 1939-45 there is virtually no enforcement activity at all, while in others, such as 1900-1905 marked increases in activity occurred.[6] These changes are related to a wide variety of factors including wars, inflation, depressions, and changes in the law and/or administrative machinery. Rather than create a whole new set of periods relating specifically to enforcement, enforcement activity will be analysed within each of the two long periods, 1889-1923 (see Sections 2-4) and 1923-1952 (see Sections 5 and 6). This can be justified, in part, on the grounds that changes in the administrative machinery were an important influence on enforcement activity. In other words, a set of common forces may have caused changes in both administrative machinery and enforcement activity.

---

4. See Rosenbluth and Thorburn (1963, Ch. 2, 3) and Winnipeg Free Press (1949).

5. Even with the 1952 and 1960 amendments, the fundamental elements of the structure put in place in 1923 remained in place. See Rosenbluth and Thorburn (1963), Gorecki and Stanbury (1979) and Gorecki (1981).

6. We measure enforcement activity by number of investigations or prosecutions started during each period. In Tables 1 and 11 prosecutions are dated by the trial court's decision in each case. The lag between investigation and final appeal can be several years. See Section 6 below.

2.0 THE FIRST LEGISLATION, 1889

2.1 Background

In the 1880s and the 1890s, following the introduction of the National Policy of 1879 which created substantial tariff barriers against imports, there was a "massive flight from competition" which took a wide variety of forms (Bliss, 1974, p. 34). The *Journal of Commerce* commented in 1887 that "there are few branches of trade in this or any other country which are not represented by associations which seek to prevent unprofitable competition." In the period 1883-1911, "an exhaustive list of combinations mentioned in trade journals or claimed to exist by newspapers would extend into every nook and cranny of the Canadian business world" (Bliss, 1974, p. 40). Further, "sporadic complaints by businessmen subjected to the prices charged by combinations and monopolies and the objections to combinations by a few principled free traders were almost totally submerged in a climate of business opinion that attacked open competition as being destructive of profits, security, and business morality" (Bliss, 1974, p. 43).

Concern over the activity of trusts supplying coal, salt, binder twine, and other necessities had been heard in Parliament during the 1870s and 1880s (Reynolds, 1940, p. 131). For example,

> Dr. G.T. Orton, Conservative member for Centre Wellington, raised the question of a coal-oil ring in Parliament in 1881. He claimed the ring sold coal oil at thirty-five cents a gallon when it ought to have been eighteen cents (Waite, 1971, p. 180).

However, "the existence of pools and combines was easy to allege, harder to prove" (Waite, 1971, p. 180).

In examining the "diverse species of joint undertakings [which] are popularly stigmatized as 'trusts'" revealed by three official investigations which reported in 1888 (two U.S. and one Canadian), Andrews (1889, p. 119) distinguished at least eight different categories. These ranged from "amorphous enterprises involving plurality of interest..." to "agreements as to prices or production lived up to with more or less fidelity" (Andrews, 1889, p. 119). Judged by the number of examples given, Canadian trusts seemed most prevalent in the category, "contracts, with or without... sanctions, to grant special favors or rates in return for exclusive patronage" (Andrews, 1889, p. 119). The Wholesale Grocers' Guild of Ontario and Quebec, the Coal Section of the Toronto Board of Trade and the Coffin-Makers' and Undertakers' Trust all fell into this category.

The Dominion Wholesale Grocers' Guild was formed in 1884 and that it quickly set up price-fixing agreements with the manufacturers of tobacco, starch, baking powder, pickles and other items (Bliss, 1974, p. 33). In this vertical combine, prices were enforced by manufacturers who refused to sell to wholesalers who cut their prices to retailers. In the summer of 1887, the

Guild reached an agreement with refiners to obtain a lower price for sugar for its members who agreed to limit their profit margin. Price cutting, which had been universal, was eliminated on this item which accounted for about 40% of the grocery trade in the late 1880s. The Guild's actions, according to Bliss (1974, pp. 33-34) were a major cause of the creation of the Select Committee of 1888 described below.

The protection afforded the public against the activities of the trusts by the common law was negligible. Dunlop et al. (1987, pp. 30-31) explain that

> With few exceptions, beginning early in the 19th century, cartel agreements were fairly routinely enforced. Many of these were transparently and, to modern sensibilities, outrageously antithetical to consumer welfare, and involved price and output-fixing agreements, market and profit division agreements, bid-rigging agreements on tenders, and no-bid agreements at auctions. The courts typically rationalized their enforcement of these agreements on the grounds that they were the product of free consent amongst mature parties and therefore presumptively reasonable with respect to their interests. The public's interest in freedom of trade (as opposed to freedom of contract), to the extent that it was considered at all, was inverted into an interest in avoiding "ruinous" competition [notes omitted].

Gosse (1962, p. 39) states that in 1889 the common law did not condemn agreements to fix prices, although it did so a century earlier. Agreements to fix prices or restrict output "were quite respectable [and were] continually becoming more deeply embedded in the minds of the judiciary." Reynolds (1940, p. 131) comments that, "Canadian courts followed the British common law dealing with restraint of trade. British common law has been and continues to be very lenient toward trade combinations" (see also Trebilcock, 1986). In fact, the common law may have facilitated the effectiveness of trusts. For example, in 1871 a combine to fix the price of salt, which was held to be an acceptable restraint of trade, was able to gain injunction enforcing the rules of the combine against a rule breaker.[7] Hence if the public was to be protected against the deleterious effects of trusts and combinations a change in the law was necessary.

In February 1888 a Select Committee of the House of Commons was appointed "to examine into and report upon the nature, extent and effect of certain combinations said to exist with reference to the purchase and sale, or manufacture and sale, in Canada, of any foreign or Canadian products" (Quoted in Bliss, 1973, p. 178). The chairman of the committee, N. Clarke Wallace, had been active in drawing public attention to the activities of trusts.[8]

---

7. This is referred to in Bliss (1973, p. 178) and Reynolds (1940, p. 132). *Ontario Salt* v. *Merchants Salt Co.* [(1871) 18 Gr. 540] was the leading Canadian case prior to the 1889 legislation.

8. See Bliss (1973, p. 178) and Baggaley (1991).

The report of the Committee was submitted to the House of Commons with commendable dispatch on May 16, 1888.[9] The Select Committee found combinations to the detriment of the public existing in all but one of the commodities it studied: sugar and groceries, coal, watch cases, binder twine, stoves, coffin makers and undertakers, oatmeal milling, egg dealers, fire insurance. "Price-fixing was common, the agreements being accompanied by the issuing of favored lists and even employment of detectives to spy upon those breaking the agreement... In nearly every case the association controlling the particular industry ruled with an iron hand" (Ball, 1934, p. 4). The Committee concluded that

> ... the evils produced by combinations such as have been inquired into, have not by any means been fully developed as yet in this country, but sufficient evidence of their injurious tendencies and effects is given to justify legislative action for suppressing the evils arising from these and similar combinations and monopolies (Quoted in Ball, 1934, p. 6).

2.2 The Act of 1889

In 1888 Mr. Wallace introduced a private member's bill which was not enacted before the House adjourned. He introduced another bill in February 1889 and its sponsorship was taken over by the Conservative Government of Sir John A. Macdonald.[10] After some important changes which weakened it greatly, *An Act for the Prevention and Suppression of Combinations in Restraint of Trade*, became law on May 2, 1889.[11] In 1892 the substantive provisions of this *Act* were incorporated into the first *Criminal Code* of Canada.[12]

The substantive section of the 1889 Act was as follows.

> 1. Every person who conspires, combines, agrees or arranges with any other person, or with any railway, steamship, steamboat or transportation company, unlawfully,
>   (a) to unduly limit the facilities for transporting, producing, manufacturing, supplying, storing or dealing in any article or commodity which may be a subject of trade or commerce; or -
>   (b) to restrain or injure trade or commerce in relation to any such article or commodity; or -

---

9. See Canada (1888). The select committee's findings are summarised in Ball (1934, pp. 3-6); Goodwin (1961, pp. 138-140); and Baggaley (1991).

10. See Ball (1934, Ch. 2), Gosse (1962, Ch. 3).

11. Chapter 41 of S.C. 1889. For details of how this came about, see Gorecki and Stanbury (1984, pp. 14-20, 108-112), Gosse (1962, pp. 68-75) and Ball (1934, Ch. 2). Salt combines had existed on and off in Canada since at least 1871. When the Act of 1889 was before the House of Commons, a new syndicate raised the price to consumers from 55 cents to $1.05 per barrel.

12. S.C. 1892, c. 29, Section 520.

    (c)   to <u>unduly</u> prevent, limit, or lessen the manufacture or production of any such article or commodity, or to <u>unreasonably</u> enhance the price thereof;or -

    (d)   to <u>unduly</u> prevent or lessen competition in the production, manufacture, purchase, barter, sale, transportation or supply of any such article or commodity, or in the price of insurance upon person or property.

Is guilty of a misdemeanour and liable, on conviction, to a penalty not exceeding four thousand dollars and not less than two hundred dollars, or to imprisonment for any term not exceeding two years; and if a corporation, is liable on conviction to a penalty not exceeding ten thousand dollars and not less than one thousand dollars (from Ball, 1934, pp. 8-9; his emphasis).

In terms of offences, the Act was concerned with combinations or conspiracies in restraint of trade. In other words, mergers, monopolies, resale price maintenance and other forms of anticompetitive behaviour were not included under the *Act*.[13] This reflected the focus of concern of the Select Committee of 1888. The Act was not meant to be a comprehensive statement on competition policy, but rather solve the problem of combines or conspiracies in restraint of trade to fix prices or restrict output by declaring what the government (incorrectly) believed to be the common law at the time.

The penalty for breaking the law for a corporation was a fine between $1,000 and $10,000; for an individual $200-$4000 or imprisonment for up to two years. Other possible penalties such as the removal of tariff protection were not included.[14] This partly reflected the fact that the Conservatives under Macdonald had introduced the National Policy of 1879. To admit that tariff reduction was an appropriate remedy was tantamount to an admission of the Liberal charge that "the tariff was the mother of trusts" (see Baggaley, 1991).

The extraordinary weakness in the original legislation created by the modifiers "unlawfully" and "unduly" was recognized during the debates in Parliament in 1889 (see Gorecki and Stanbury, 1984, pp. 108-111).[15] As Lloyd Reynolds (1940, pp. 134-135) pointed out, between 1889 and 1900, "members of a combine could not be convicted unless the Crown proved that they were 'unduly' doing something which was [said to be] already unlawful at common law." Gosse (1962, p. 72) notes that the word "unlawfully" effectively vitiated the legislation "since there was no conspiracy in restraint of trade at common law along the lines imagined by the legislators..." According to a prominent business historian,

---

13. The U.S. *Sherman Act* of 1890 dealt specifically with conspiracies in restraint of trade as well as monopoly and monopolization.

14. This was changed in 1897. See Appendix A and Baggaley (1991).

15. In 1890 the U.S. *Sherman Act* condemned "every contract, combination in the form of a trust or otherwise, or conspiracy, in restraint of trade or commerce..."

> The 1889 law was pious anti-monopoly posturing that had no effect on anything. As the Liberal opposition pointed out, a government whose National Policy was to restrict imports was not likely to be enthusiastically committed to free competition in the domestic market" (Bliss, 1987, p. 362).

He has also described the Act of 1889 as "utterly useless" (Bliss, 1974, p. 39).[16]

Only two years after the legislation was enacted, the Minister of Justice, Sir John Thompson, who had insisted that the word "unlawfully" was necessary for its proper application as being declaratory of the common law,[17] indicated that the law was unenforceable.

> Those who have undertaken to administer the law have told me, or those who desire its execution have declared from time to time, that the multiplication of these words upon the Statute-book has led to confusion in the interpretation of the Act; and I believe they have had legal opinions on the subject to the effect that it is not sufficient in a prosecution under the Act to establish that a combination was distinctly unlawful at common law, but that in addition the burden of proof lies upon the prosecutor to show that the price has been unduly and unreasonably enhanced thereby (Quoted in Ball, 1934, p. 11).

Parliament provided for no federal official to enforce the Act of 1889. Enforcement was left up to the Attorneys General of the provinces. (In contrast, enforcement of the *Sherman Act* of 1890 was assigned to the federal Attorney General.) In the period 1889 until 1900 there was only one prosecution.[18] It was unsuccessful on the grounds that the American Tobacco Company's "dealer contracts, which forbade the dealer to sell tobacco of any other manufacturer, were not illegal under common law" (Reynolds, 1940, p. 135). Ball (1934, p. 19) points out that in this case "there was no conspiracy with other manufacturers to limit trade; nor was any other manufacturer prevented from entering into competition. Rather, the case involved resale price maintenance and exclusive dealing." Given wording of the original legislation, a conviction would have been extremely surprising.

The evidence of the pervasiveness of various restraints of trade, including conspiracies to fix prices and/or restrict output, suggests that the number of public prosecutions should have been much greater, although the word "unlawfully" almost certainly made success very, very slight. It is useful to recall the words of a Liberal member of the opposition summarised the legislation in 1889 when he said, "It need not be opposed; it will die from sheer inanition" (Quoted in Bliss, 1973, p. 179).

---

16. Professor Bliss' re-examination of the origins of the law can be found in Chapter 7.

17. See House of Commons *Debates*, April 22, 1889, p. 1446. Gosse (1962, p. 73) notes that "for a Minister of Justice, who must have had some staff to advise him [Thompson] showed an appalling lack of knowledge of the common law."

18. See *R. v. American Tobacco Co. of Canada* (1897) 3 Rev. de Jur. 453. More generally, see Ball (1934, pp. 17-20).

2.3   1900 Amendment Leads to More Prosecutions

In 1900, S. 520 of the *Criminal Code* was amended to delete the critical word "unlawfully."[19] However, both "unduly" and "unreasonably" were restored to the legislation after being deleted in 1899 (see Appendix A). After the word "unlawfully" was removed, nine prosecutions were undertaken in the next decade and convictions were obtained in seven cases. See Table 1. In addition, there was a larger number of private civil actions under the Act of 1889 and in about one-half of these the plaintiffs relied successfully on the anti-combines legislation - see Appendix B. Therefore, with the same administrative structure significant changes in enforcement activity occurred because of a change in the wording of the law.

Several points should be noted about these prosecutions. First, five of them (#3, 4, 5, 6, 7 in Table 1) arose out of the nefarious activities of the Master Plumbers and Steam Fitters Cooperative Association which sought to fix the price of plumbing work (including the mark-up on fixtures) in the Montreal area over several years.[20] Second, the provincial attorneys general initiated very few of the investigations that led to prosecutions. Third, compared to the 1950s to mid-1960s, in few of the cases did the accused plead guilty (Stanbury, 1991). It is not surprising that with an untested law defendants should seek to have the courts indicate exactly where the line of illegality was to be drawn. Fourth, because so many of the accused were owners of unincorporated businesses, the Crown charged them as individuals.[21] From the 1920s on, almost all of the accused were corporations.

Fifth, the largest single fine imposed was $5,000 on the Master Plumbers and Steam Fitters Association. This was one-half the maximum for corporations at the time.[22] Individuals were never fined more than $500 each, with the exception of Clarke, president of the Ontario Coal Association, who was fined $4000. This was the maximum for individuals at the time. It should be appreciated, however, that in terms of 1989 dollars these amounts would have to be multiplied by eight or nine times.[23]

---

19. Bliss (1973, p. 183) claims it was removed by accident. Baggaley (1982) indicates that this was not the case.

20. See Ball (1934, pp. 28-29); Edgar (1906, pp. 428-30).

21. For example, in *R. v. Armstrong* (1905) seven individuals were charged; in *McKittrick* (1905), five were charged; in *McGuire*, 38 individuals were charged. See Stanbury (1991).

22. From 1952 to 1976 the maximum fine for a corporation was entirely at the discretion of the court (Stanbury, 1976). Then it was set at $1 million and in 1986 it was raised to $10 million (Stanbury, 1986).

23. For example, the Wholesale Price Index (1935-39 = 100) increased from 62.1 in 1900 to 484 in mid-1975 (Stanbury, 1976, p. 631).

The legislation of 1889 (which became S. 520 of the *Criminal Code* in 1892) did not deter the price-fixing arrangements of the Dominion Wholesale Grocers' Guild: new agreements on woodenware, rice, starch and molasses were reached in 1890 and 1891. While the Guild effectively collapsed after the sugar agreement fell apart in 1892, beginning in 1898 it began to establish itself by insisting that grocery manufacturers practice resale price maintenance "under the covert threat of a boycott (illegal after 1900) by the Guild members." The Guild was acquitted of operating a combine in 1910[24] and "went on into World War I stabilizing the trade in its usual way" (Bliss, 1974, p. 34). The *Retail Merchants' Journal* in 1907 stated that "notwithstanding... the Statute books... it is well known to most businessmen in Canada that agreements are now made and entered into in many lines of trade, with a view of preventing ruinous and unfair competition... and to act as a pendulum to regulate and steady trade" (quoted in Bliss, 1974, p. 40).

2.4 Problems With Enforcement Prior to 1910

In addition to the problems attributable to the word "unlawfully," the original legislation suffered from the method Parliament chose to have it enforced. Enforcement of the 1889 legislation was delegated to the attorney general of the province in which the offence was alleged to have occurred. The Act of 1889, which was put into the *Criminal Code* in 1892, was apparently seen as just another criminal law statute. It was believed at the time that constitutional authority dictated that enforcement be done by provincial authorities. Therefore, the police were responsible for detecting conspiracies in restraint of trade. Such an arrangement had two notable disadvantages. First, the typical criminal case investigated by the police is usually started with the knowledge that an offence has taken place (e.g., a robbery, a murder). The problem then is to find out the identity of those responsible. In contrast, in a conspiracy case there is no "dead body" for the police to find, but rather allegations, suspicions and rumour. This requires very different investigatory skills. Further, the police did not have the investigatory tools to examine alleged combines. Later, the power to compel the testimony of witnesses under oath and to require written returns of information from companies under investigation were deemed essential to deal with price-fixing conspiracies.

This defect was recognized in 1907 when the *Customs Tariff Act* was amended to provide that the Cabinet could appoint a judge to inquire into combine or conspiracy alleged to exist "among manufacturers or dealers in any article of commerce to unduly promote the advantage of the manufacturers or dealers in such article [protected by tariffs] at the expense of the consumers..." The judge was to make his report to the Cabinet which

---

24. See *R.* v. *Beckett et al.* (1910) 15 C.C.C. 408. It was also acquitted again in 1923. See *A-G of Ontario* v. *Canadian Wholesale Grocers* (1923) 52 O.L.R. 536 (Trial) 53 O.L.R. 627 (Appeal).

could reduce the tariffs on such articles "to give the public the benefit of reasonable competition in the article..." The judge was given the power to "compel the attendance of witnesses and examine them under oath and require the production of books and papers." The Cabinet could also give him other "necessary powers." Similar powers were to be given to Boards of Investigation appointed under the *Combines Investigation Act* three years later - see Section 3.

Second, the individuals responsible for actually bringing the prosecution were the provincial attorneys general. Those prosecuted were likely to be members of the local elite. Given the fact that there was even more reluctance then than now to see combines as inimical to the public interest, there was likely to be little enthusiasm to bring prosecutions of such white collar individuals. This reluctance was commented upon by the father of the 1889 Bill, Mr. Wallace, in 1891, "I think that we have some reason to find fault with the Attorneys General of the various provinces for not having seen fit to enforce the law as it stands against those who are breaking it" (Quoted in Ball, 1934, p. 11). In addition, problems arose over which provincial attorney general would deal with conspiracies which spanned several provinces.

An analysis of the origins of the cases prosecuted under the 1889 Act indicates the weakness of relying on provincial attorneys-general to investigate and prosecute combines cases. Two of the ten prosecutions started between 1889 and 1910 were the result of official investigations conducted by the federal government in order to gather evidence concerning an alleged combine.[25] In at least three of the ten cases, the prosecution was launched by a private citizen laying an Information.[26] The cases were then prosecuted by the Crown. Clearly, if the administrative structure had been adequate such methods of gathering evidence and starting prosecutions would not have been employed.[27]

Bliss (1974, p. 39) argues that the several prosecutions between 1903 and 1910 "heightened public awareness of and opposition to combines" and "forced" the government to introduce the *Combines Investigation Act* of 1910. But it

---

25. *R.* vs. *Clarke* arose of *Proceedings of the Select Committee appointed for the purpose of inquiring into the prices charged for lumber in the Provinces of Manitoba, Alberta and Saskatchewan, Journal of the House of Commons*, 1906-7, vol. XLII, part II, Appendix 6, pp. xi, 734. This case is discussed in Bladen (1932, pp. 70-71), Ball (1934, pp. 29-30). Concerning *R.* vs. *Beckett et al.*, Edgar (1906, p. 430) says, "Proceedings were... instituted as a result of statement made before the Tariff Commission which had been holding sessions..."

26. *R.* vs. *Master Plumbers and Central Supply* (1907) 12 C.C.C. 37 (Trial and Appeal). For details see Edgar (1906, pp. 428-430), Ball (1934, pp. 28-29). This also led to the case *R.* vs. *McMichael* (1907) 18 C.C.C. 185 and two others which were unreported - see Table 1. The first case under the 1889 Act was also apparently instituted by a private individual. See Gosse (1962, p. 75, footnote 26) re *R.* v. *American Tobacco* (1897) 3 *Rev. de Jur.* 453.

27. On the other hand, many price-fixing agreeemnts in Canada at that time were quite overt, therefore, easier to detect and prosecute.

"too, was a largely ceremonial attack on combinations and did not represent a serious legislative attempt to restore open competition in business." We now examine this assertion in some detail.

3.0 MACKENZIE KING'S COMBINES INVESTIGATION ACT OF 1910

3.1 Origins of the 1910 Act

The previous section demonstrated the inadequacy of the administrative structure created to enforce the Act of 1889. The need for reform had been amply demonstrated by 1900. The fact that there were nine prosecutions between 1903 and 1910,[28] with seven convictions, may have been interpreted as evidence that the enforcement machinery was adequate.[29] However, reform had to wait until 1910. The timing of new legislation reflected a number of more immediate factors which forced the Liberal Government to take some kind of action. This lack of enthusiasm for the anti-combines legislation is consistent with the view of Bliss (1973, p. 177) that Canadian legislation "did not reflect a serious desire by legislators to resist economic consolidation or to restore the forces of the free market."

The factors immediately responsible for the 1910 legislation were a merger boom and the advent of sharply rising prices.[30] One of the major merger movements in Canadian history took place over the period 1909 to 1913, peaking in 1910-1911 (Weldon, 1966, pp. 233-234). It established oligopolies and monopolies in many industries such as cement, steel, and flour milling. The existing legislation was concerned only with price-fixing and market sharing agreements. It was felt that the "new and colossal forces [i.e., mergers] operating in our industrial life require to be controlled by a systematic scheme of government supervision in the direct interests of the people" (Swanson, 1910, p. 354). The second factor was the "rapidly rising prices after 1907" (Brown and Cook, 1974, p. 92).[31]

These factors, together with the traditional disaffection over the relationship between tariffs and monopoly power brought about new legislation (Baggaley, 1991). Bladen (1932, p. 71) summarises the interaction of forces in the following manner,

---

28. *R. v. Beckett et al.* (1910) 20 O.L.R. 410 was prosecuted under S. 520 of the *Criminal Code* before the *Combines Investigation Act* of 1910 became law. Generally, see Stanbury (1991).

29. Mackenzie King himself thought it was not. See Ball (1934, p. 38).

30. King (1911, p. 102), author of the 1910 Act, wrote that, "We find an increase in the cost of living went on simultaneously with the organisation of capital on a large scale, the formation of trusts, mergers, and combines of one kind or another."

31. The period of inflation is documented in Epp (1973, particularly Part II). See also Stapells (1922).

> An agrarian revolt was developing against the policy of protection and against the monopolies [that] were supposed to flourish under such protection. The cost of living was rising and was attributed to these two factors, protection and monopoly. A deputation led by Mr. E.C. Drury, then a high official in the Grange, waited on the government in Ottawa in 1909 to ask that a special officer be appointed to investigate monopolies and that the tariff reduced on such articles as were found to be monopolised. Then in 1909 the "merger movement" got underway and created new anxiety; though ministers had probably more reason for anxiety than consumers.

Ferns and Ostry (1955, p. 103) stress that the aforementioned factors were destroying the farmers' and small businessmens' folk-dreams about the competitive system. Such a constituency was then more politically significant.

Mackenzie King (1912, pp. 153-154), who as Minister of Labour introduced the Act of 1910,[32] stated that it had been shaped by "three important considerations":

- "It is the possible inimical effects of combination and not combination as such that is to be aimed at in legislation... [Combination, meaning large scale industrial enterprises including those resulting from mergers] is an inevitable and necessary development."
- "It is the duty of government to secure to the community some of the advantages which the community itself makes possible... it becomes the duty of government to see that the interests of the many who compose the state, are not sacrificed to the interest of the few whose powers and opportunities they have helped to create."
- "There are certain evils in the prevention and removal of which publicity is more effective than penalty and that no single remedy can be found for all the possible abuses that may arise... Where public confidence and approval is essential to business, the fear of exposure is the real deterrent of wrong."

According to King (1912, p. 153), anti-combines prosecutions under the *Criminal Code* were "the subject to constant complaint that proceedings were slow, uncertain, and expensive which made it extremely difficult to secure convictions." The *Code* provisions were left in place, according to King, "so that the penalties there provided might the more easily be enforced should they be deemed to be, after investigation of conditions, the most suitable and effective form of punishment of offenders" (King, 1912, p. 153). (The result was that Canada had parallel provisions in the *Criminal Code* and the *Combines Investigation Act* which condemned combines in restraint of trade.)

The administrative reforms introduced in the *Combines Investigation Act* of 1910 were "the outcome of the successful working of the policy of investigation as applied to industrial disputes in the *Industrial Disputes*

---

32. Note that King had a PhD in economics from Harvard University and considered himself something of a social reformer. He was also extraordinarily cautious and politically wily, two factors that contributed to his political longevity.

Investigation Act" (King, 1912, p. 149).[33] As Minister of Labour, King was responsible for introducing the *Industrial Disputes Investigation Act* in 1907. The 1910 Act, as its title made clear, *An Act to Provide for the Investigation of Combines, Monopolies and Mergers,* provided a means by which citizens could initiate the investigation process into alleged combines, monopolies or mergers.   The Act also made the federal government responsible for administering the new law but it did not establish a permanent official with responsibility for enforcement.

The Act was greeted with considerable enthusiasm by some contemporary commentators. For example, Boyle (1913, p. 167) wrote that "the procedure is simple, swift, and free from technicalities." Swanson (1910, p. 351), stated that "It was nothing if not novel and progressive; and indicates a real desire on the part of the government to aid the people in their struggle against the continually mounting cost of living." However, inspection of the procedures in the legislation and the use of the Act over the period 1910 to 1919 do not seem to confirm such enthusiasm.

3.2 New Enforcement Machinery

Under S. 5 of the 1910 Act, any "six or more persons, British subjects residents in Canada and of full age" could start the investigatory process. They were required to "make an application to a judge for an order directing an investigation into [the]... alleged combine." In order to convince a judge to order an inquiry, the six citizens had to establish a *prima facie* case that an offence had been committed. Section 5(3) of the Act required that the application "shall be accompanied by a statement setting forth:

> (a)   the nature of the alleged Combine and the persons believed to be concerned therein;
> (b)   the manner in which the alleged combine affects prices or restricts competition, and the extent to which the alleged combine is believed to operate to the detriment of consumers or producers;[34]...

In addition each of the six or more applicants had to submit a "statutory declaration... declaring that the alleged combine operates to [his or her]... detriment as a consumer or producer..."

---

33. King (1912) claimed that his *Industrial Disputes Investigation Act* of 1907 had "demonstrated publicity to be a real factor in furthering justice, and public opinion, intelligently formed, an effective instrument in the protection of innocent third parties against public wrongs arising out of a conflict of private interests." He noted that many of the clauses in the 1907 Act were put into the first *Combines Investigation Act* "respecting the methods and procedure of investigation..."

34. At this time, as the *Debates* in the House of Commons make clear, the word "producers" referred to farmers, although in some prosecutions the defendants interpreted it as manufacturers, retailers, etc..

Upon receiving the application, the judge had to set a time and place for a hearing within 30 days of receiving the application. At the hearing both the applicants and those complained about and their counsel could appear. The judge had powers of the court in which he normally presided to "...summon before him and enforce the attendance to witnesses, to administer oaths, and require witnesses to give evidence on oath, and to produce such books, papers or other documents or things as the judge deems requisite" (S. 7(2)). At the conclusion of the hearing, the judge could order that an inquiry be conducted if he was "satisfied that there is reasonable ground for believing that a combine exists which is injurious..." (S. 7(1)).

In those instances in which the judge ordered that an inquiry be started, the Minister of Labour[35] was required to establish an *ad hoc* Board of Investigation. A Board consisted of three members: one nominated by the applicants; one nominated by the companies/individuals accused of infringing the law; one, the chairman, nominated jointly by the applicants and those to be investigated (see Sections 10-12 of the Act). If they failed to agree on a chairman, the Minister of Labour nominated the chairman. No qualifications were made concerning those appointed.[36]

The Board was required under Section 18 to "expeditiously, fully and carefully inquire into the matters referred to it and all matters affecting the merits thereof, including the question of whether or not the price or rental of any article concerned has been unreasonably enhanced, or competition in the supply thereof unduly restricted, in consequence of a combine..."

Under S. 32 of the 1910 Act, a Board of Investigation had all the powers vested in any court of record in civil cases, that is to say, the right to summon and examine witnesses under oath, and the right to require production of such books, papers or other documents or things as the board deems requisite to the full investigation of the matters into which it is inquiring. Further, the Minister could have the Minister of Justice "instruct counsel to conduct the investigation before a board." The Board had discretion in deciding whether to hold its hearings in public or not.

The Board had wide powers of report. It could make a finding as to whether the provisions of the law had been broken. S. 18 provided that the Board was to make "such findings and recommendations as, in the opinion of the board, are in accordance with the merits and requirements of the case."

---

35. From 1910 to 1934 the administration of competition policy was the responsibility of the Minister of Labour, although all prosecutions had to be approved by the Department of Justice. Then it was transferred to the Department of Justice where it stayed until 1966 when it was transferred to the predecessor of the Department of Consumer and Corporate Affairs.

36. The members of a Board were, however, to be British subjects and should not be applicants for the Board nor persons having any direct pecuniary interest in the alleged combine (Ball, 1934, p. 41).

A Board had no permanent status and was dissolved immediately after it submitted its report to the Minister of Labour. The report, which had to be signed by at least two members, was to be published in the *Canada Gazette*. Any minority report was also to be published. If the Board concluded that an offence had taken place then the corporations/individuals concerned had to cease and desist ten days after the Board's report was published in the *Canada Gazette*.[37] Failure to discontinue the combine as found by a Board of Investigation was an indictable offence under S. 23 for which the penalty was a maximum fine of $1,000 per day, after the expiration of the ten days following the publication of the Board's report.

For the small minority of potential businessmen who wished to form combines and did not find the power of public opinion "irresistible" (Boyle, 1913, p. 168), the *Combines Investigation Act* of 1910 had certain additional penalties:

(a) The tariff could be reduced or eliminated by an order of the Governor-in-Council under S.21 of the *Act*. This provision was originally introduced in the 1897 *Tariff Act* and had been used once since its inception, in 1902 when the *ad valorem* duty on newsprint was reduced from 25% to 15% (see Ball, 1934, pp. 13-17 and Gorecki, 1981, pp. 185-192).

(b) If a combine was unduly limiting competition by the abuse of its patent rights then, by an order of the court the patent could be cancelled under S. 22 of the Act.

Outside the Act were two other possible penalties:

(d) The 1889 Act, amended in 1900, still remained in force as sections 516, 517 and 520 of the *Criminal Code*.[38] Convictions could result in the imposition of a fine (or imprisonment for individuals).

(e) Finally, an amendment to the *Inland Revenue Act* in 1904 was passed "so as to prevent [a contract system] gaining a monopoly in any product which necessitated a license and paid an excise duty" (Ball, 1934, p. 19). Complete discretion was given to the Minister of Inland Revenue in abolishing licensing and excise duty. This provision had been used in the contract systems of the American Tobacco Co. and the Empire Tobacco Co. (see Ball, 1934, pp. 17-20).

3.3 Results of the 1910 Act

The provisions of the 1910 *Combines Investigation Act* were used only once before the Act was repealed in 1919 (see below). The practices of the

---

37. A Board could grant an exemption. In the United Shoe Machinery case, the board recommended a six-month extension. See Combines Investigation Board (1912, p. 474).

38. Although these sections were subsequently amended several times, and also renumbered, they remained as parallel (but not identical) provisions dealing with conspiracies in restraint of trade until 1960 when they were incorporated into S. 32 of the *Combines Investigation Act*. Indeed, most prosecutions for price fixing, etc. were conducted under the *Criminal Code*.

United Shoe Machinery Co.[39] were examined by a Board of Investigation, but no prosecution resulted despite the fact that the Board concluded that

> The United Shoe Machinery Company of Canada is a combine, and by the operation of the clauses of the leases, quoted in the foregoing, which restrict the use of the leased machines... competition in the manufacture, production... and supply of shoe machinery in Canada has been and is unduly restricted and prevented (Combines Investigation Board, 1912, p. 474).

Such a record (one investigation in nine years), it could be claimed, was confirmation of the view that publicity and the power of intelligent public opinion was indeed sufficient deterrence to prevent the formation of combines.[40] However, such a view seems in conflict with most of the available evidence, which suggests that the 1910 Act had little, if any, impact. Bliss (1973, p. 185) cites the example of the Dominion Wholesale Grocers' Guild which in 1910, "twenty-two years after its methods had first been exposed... was still recording its price-fixing arrangements in its minute books." R.J. McFall (1922, p. 178), had an opportunity to examine business behaviour at first hand while serving as Cost of Living Commissioner in 1918-1919, concluded that many examples of price fixing arrangements "exist in defiance of the letter of the law and yet many of them exist openly." The more traditional sources on Canadian combines policy also conclude that the 1910 Act had little effect (e.g., Canada, 1952, pp. 10-11).

3.4 Assessment of the 1910 Act

The enforcement mechanisms embodied in the 1910 Act reflected the belief of Mackenzie King in the value of publicity as a deterrent to potential wrongdoers. King stated this belief on numerous occasions both inside and outside Parliament,[41] for example,

> The one end and purpose of this legislation is to prevent the mean man from profiting in virtue of his meanness, and I know of no way by which that can be more effectively done than by providing some kind of machinery which will enable an intelligent public opinion to be formed and focussed upon the particular evil which you are endeavoring to stamp out. Penalties are frequently of no service towards that end, but publicity is all important and essential, and it is for that reason that in dealing with this particular class of cases we have to endeavour to devise an instrument which would bring into play that most potent force in society, namely,

---

39. See also the private case which preceded the public inquiry: *United Shoe Machinery Co.* v. *Brunet et al.* (1905) Que S.C. 200-217; (1909) A.C. 330. Generally, see Ball (1934, pp. 44-48).

40. In the 1910 legislation, a combine had been defined to include mergers and monopolies. Although the word monopoly was used, it was not defined until 1935.

41. A good sampling of Mackenzie King's views as expressed in Parliament can be found in Winnipeg Free Press (1949, pp. 30-31). See also Skeoch (1966b).

an intelligently formed public opinion which is so effective a factor in the regulation of commercial and industrial affairs (King, 1911, p. 105).

Publicity, he said, "is an honest endeavour to grapple in a fearless, practical and thorough manner with what is, undoubtedly, the most complicated, intricate and far reaching of these problems to which our present social, industrial, and commercial life have given rise..." (King, 1911, p. 106). King's view as to the value of publicity was shared by some commentators. Boyle (1913, p. 168), for example, wrote that "publicity, and fear of publicity is doubtless the strongest remedy." Vincent Bladen (1932, p. 71) felt that Mr. King "rightly believed in the value of publicity." Such a view is correct if the mere fact of exposure earns those committing the offence sufficient social approbation and ostracization to serve as an effective punishment or deterrent. However, there is no evidence to such that combines offences were held in that much odium. Thus it is not clear how far the legislation through publicity could rely "on the moral sense of the community as a 'compelling force'" (King, House of Commons, *Debates*, April 12, 1910, p. 6860).

The reasons for the failure of the 1910 Act seem clear. First, those initiating an application had to bear the costs of preparing sufficient evidence so as to convince a judge that a *prima facie* case existed. Then they had to make representations to the Board of Investigation if one was appointed. There was a possibility that the applicants could be reimbursed for their expenses, but that was at the discretion of the court. At the Board's hearings, "if the parties have their own counsel they must bear their expenses, unless the board orders differently" (King, 1912, p. 203).

Second, the identity of those people complaining were known at the hearing before the judge and at the Board of Investigation by those they accused. Therefore, there was a possibility of retaliation by the accused.[42] In the words of McFall (1922, p. 182), "to anyone who is an injured party under an alleged combine to lay information is to court reprisals, whether or not the case is successful." Hence, only well organized groups were likely to use the mechanism of the Board, not consumers or competitors trying to break into a market.

Third, after the board made its report it ceased to exist. Therefore, no public official was responsible for implementing the Board's report and for determining that the combine had ceased to function. Recall that a fine would be imposed only if the combine did not promptly cease its nefarious activities. Bladen (1932, p. 73) commented that "If there is to be any regulation of combines it would seem desirable to entrust such regulation to a permanent board..."

---

42. Complainants would typically be victims of a price-fixing conspiracy, or rivals who had been invited to participate but chose not to do so. Indeed, the policy objective of "maintaining free competition" was as much concerned with protecting businessmen outside cartels from the restraints effected by those in them. See Gorecki and Stanbury (1984, pp. 52-62).

Fourth, the enforcement process was likely to be long and cumbersome as the case involving the United Shoe Machinery Co. illustrates. It started late in 1910[43] with an application by a shoe manufacturer and concluded with a Board of Investigation report dated October 18, 1912. The report, however, gave the United Shoe Machinery Co. until April 1913 to comply with its order. The process was "long, expensive and resulted in only a paper victory for the applicants" (Ball, 1934, p. 139). The Company fought the investigation every step of the way (see Ball, 1934, pp. 45-46). While the majority of the Board found a combine, no prosecution resulted. The Company, however, apparently made some changes to its leasing practices (Ball, 1934, pp. 46-48). In any event, this case was hardly one to encourage other applicants under the 1910 Act.

4.0   EXPERIMENTING WITH ANOTHER INSTITUTION

The inflation engendered by World War I[44] and the obvious limitations of the administrative process in the 1910 Act resulted in the first attempt at using civil procedures to deal with combines.[45]

> The reliance on criminal remedies in early attempts to deal with combines clearly reflected the view that what was wrong was not the existence of the combine but its bad behaviour. In 1919, however, a short-lived attempt was made to introduce more sophisticated remedies of a regulatory nature. These were part of a broader attempt to regulate prices in response to public concerns over post-war inflation. This seems to have been the first recognition of the fact that the criminal law was too blunt an instrument to deal with some of the more intricate problems of combines. If they were to be allowed to exist but their behaviour controlled, then orders that would mould or modify the behaviour would do a more effective job than criminal prosecutions in many circumstances.   So, too, would a continuing expert administrative body.   The Board of Commerce was established by the *Board of Commerce Act* [S.C. 1919, c. 37] to administer the *Combines and Fair Prices Act*, and it was given extensive powers to permit or to restrain and prohibit the formation and operation of combines and to influence the production and price of goods. These remedies were in addition to the criminal remedies (Dunlop et al., 1987, pp. 46-47).

The *Combines Investigation Act* of 1910 was repealed and replaced by the *Board of Commerce Act* and the *Combines and Fair Prices Act* effective

---

43.   The case actually began with a private civil action. See *United Shoe Machinery* v. *Brunet* (1905) Que S.C., 200-217; (1909) A.C. 330 (Privy Council). See Appendix B.

44.   Traves (1974a, p. 87, n, 4) indicates the cost-of-living index remained virtually unchanged until the end of 1915. Then, in 1916, it increased by 8 per cent; in 1917 it increased by more than 18 per cent, and in 1918 prices rose an average of 13.5 per cent. A Parliamentary Special Committee on the High Cost of Living was established. See its report in House of Commons, *Journals*, Vol. 55, 1919 Part II, Appendix 7.

45.   For a more detailed analysis, see Cheffins (1989), (1991).

July 7, 1919. The former Act set up a <u>permanent</u> three-person board to supervise the administration and enforcement of the latter Act.[46]

Thomas Traves (1974a, p. 86) describes the price control aspects of the *Combines and Fair Prices Act* as follows:

> ...the Board of Commerce was instructed to control or prevent hoarding and to limit undue and unscrupulous increases in the price of necessaries of life. This latter term was taken to include food, fuel, and clothing, and any products necessary to their production or derived from them. The powers given to the board to achieve this aim were quite extensive. In cases involving the taking of unfair profits, the board was authorized to determine exact figures as to a fair return and to compel businesses to sell at those figures. This provision involved the right to control the output, price, and, to some extent, distribution policies of individual firms. To ensure compliance with such regulations, violation of board orders was made an indictable offence punishable by fines and prison sentences.

With respect to the administration of competition policy, the Board of Commerce could initiate an inquiry of its own accord or at the request of a citizen. The Board, which was "empowered and directed to restrain and prohibit the formation and operation of combines," was provided with extensive powers of investigation:

- It could hold hearings and compel the attendance of persons whose actions had been impugned and require them to show cause why a cease and desist order should not be made against them.
- For the purpose of a hearing before a member of the Board, the member had the power to "summon before him and enforce the attendance of witnesses, to hear evidence on oath or solemn affirmation and compel the production of such books, papers, and other documents and things as he deems requisite."
- The Board could "whether or not it makes or could lawfully make or issue with respect to any particular subject matter and consequential order of a binding character, it may make findings and declarations concerning such matter if, in the course of investigation, such matter comes properly before it and is relevant generally to the inquiry being made."

After its inquiry, the Board of Commerce could issue an order against a combine to cease and desist "from any practices complained of or discovered during the investigation which were contrary to the Act" (Ball, 1934, p. 44). For example, "The French-speaking bakers of Montreal were found to have combined for the purpose of reducing competition and in January 1920 they were ordered to dissolve their illegal combination" (Traves, 1974a, p. 90). The Board's findings of fact were final. Penalties for breaking the Board's ruling

---

46. This description is taken from Ball (1934, Chapter 7, pp. 54-60), unless otherwise stated.

were substantial.[47] Finally, "no prosecution could commence for violations of either the [Combines and Fair Prices] Act or section 498 of the Criminal Code without the written authority of the Board of Commerce" (Ball, 1934, p. 55). Hence, the two Acts passed in July 1919 placed all the stages of the conduct of inquiry into the hands of one body. Mackenzie King called this arrangement in 1923 "an extraordinary court, a court of record with powers of inquisition, accusation and judgment, all excisable by the same body" (quoted in Ball, 1934, p. 56). Nevertheless, despite these extraordinary powers, the Board of Commerce was ineffective for two reasons. Two of the three commissioners were appointed because they were largely out of sympathy with the Act. Problems arose over staffing and the way the Board should be organized.[48]

Although the 1919 legislation met many of the criticisms of the administrative machinery of the 1910 legislation, in one respect the 1919 legislation marked a radical departure from the earlier legislation. The 1910 legislation had been based on the theory of publicity enunciated by Mackenzie King (see Skeoch, 1966b, pp. 24-26). In 1919 publicity was no longer the main thrust of the legislation. The reasons for this change were twofold. First, the Board of Commerce not only had to administer the control of combines, but it also had to examine rising prices and make orders as to their appropriate level. The legislation was passed in 1919, amid considerable labour unrest as a result of rising prices. Clearly the cumbersome 1910 legislation was inappropriate if prompt results were required. Labour leaders were hardly likely to be impressed with Mackenzie King's adoption of Justice Brandeis' view that "sunlight is the best possible disinfectant." Second, the committee of the House of Commons which looked into the high cost of living following the World War I recommended a structure similar to that in the 1919 Acts.[49]

Not surprisingly, the constitutionality of the new legislation was challenged.

---

47. These were similar to the 1910 *Combines Investigation Act* - a maximum fine of $1000 per day or a maximum of a two year jail sentence for failing to cease acting as a combine within 10 days of the publication of the report of a Board of Investigation. The tariff and patent remedies of the 1910 Act also survived. But these were enforced by the Governor-in-Council and the Minister of Justice, respectively, and not by the Board of Commerce.

48. These are detailed in Traves (1974a, 1974b) and Ball (1934, Ch. 7). See also letter of resignation of one of the members of the Board of Commerce (House of Commons, *Debates*, Fifth Session, 13th Parliament, Vol. IV, May 19, 1921, pp. 3603-3608); and Cheffins (1991).

49. See Reynolds (1940, pp. 141-142) and Cheffins (1991) for the background on the 1919 legislation.

The matter was referred to the Supreme Court of Canada. The six judges who sat on the case were equally divided and no judgment was rendered.[50] The issue was taken to the Judicial Committee of the Privy Council which concluded that Parliament could not validly enact such a law.[51] The legislation dealt with property and civil rights of the inhabitants of the provinces and this was a subject over which provincial legislatures possessed "quasi-sovereign authority." Neither the general power of the Dominion nor its power over trade and commerce justified the action by Parliament. It thus became necessary to revise the approach to combines and to fall back on criminal remedies, inadequate as they might be, at the same time retaining a permanent administrative structure (Dunlop et al., 1987, p. 47).

On November 11, 1921 the Judicial Committee of the Privy Council held that the two 1919 acts, which had replaced the 1910 *Combines Investigation Act*, were "*ultra vires* of the Dominion Parliament as interfering with the property and civil rights of the provinces" (Ball, 1934, p. 59). Therefore, new legislation was needed and Mackenzie King, now Prime Minister, responded some 18 months later.

5.0 MACKENZIE KING'S SECOND ATTEMPT: THE 1923 COMBINES INVESTIGATION ACT

The second *Combines Investigation Act* came into force on June 13, 1923. Like its predecessor in 1910, it was designed by Mackenzie King and closely reflected his values and beliefs regarding combines and how to control them. It reaffirmed the theory of publicity as the main force for obtaining compliance with competition policy legislation in Canada. For example, in introducing the 1923 legislation, King said,

I think powers of investigation, rightly, legitimately and carefully exercised will go far toward curing ills, with respect to which penalties would be found wholly ineffective... there are certain classes of offences, those particularly which relate to social and economic conditions, which publicity is infinitely more effective to prevent and to redress than penalty. Once the public has the facts before it... the public may be expected to find some means, through its parliament and in other ways, to provide the necessary remedy or cure for any particular situation (quoted in Winnipeg Free Press, 1949, pp. 30-31).

King drew an analogy with the sun to illustrate the power of publicity:

In other words, it seeks to do for the social system in the matter of its moral health what the light of day or the sun does for the physical body in the matter of its health. Exclude the sun and its power from the physical universe, and very soon you find disease setting in where there shold be health and vigour. Prevent the light of day from penetrating the secret recesses of various business devices, and very

---

50. Re *Board of Commerce Act* and *Combines and Fair Prices Act* of 1919 (1920) 60 S.C.R. 456; 54 D.L.R. 354.

51. [1922] 1 A.C. 191; 60 D.L.R. 513.

> soon industry, instead of being the great servant of humanity which it should be, comes to be an instrument to be used against the well-being of the people themselves (House of Commons, *Debates*, May 8, 1923, p. 2604).

The 1923 Act can therefore be seen as the logical development of King's ideas on the value of publicity as the major instrument by which to control combines which since 1910 had been defined to include mergers, but did not include monopolies (except in name) until 1935. Indeed, King stated quite explicitly, "The remedies that are proposed are first of all... the remedy of publicity" (House of Commons, *Debates*, March 9, 1923, p. 989). Therefore, the 1919-1923 period can be viewed as an interregnum forced on the government by the exigencies of rising prices and labour unrest.

Mackenzie King could claim in 1923 that his theory as to the efficacy of publicity had never been tested under the 1910 legislation because of the difficulties of initiating investigations. Like Christianity, publicity was an instrument of policy that had not really been tried. While introducing the 1923 Act, King said

> It was found under the Combines Investigation Act [of 1910] that obliging individuals in the first instance to associate themselves together and make out a *prima facie* case before a judge discouraged in large measure any investigation. The parties seemed to be under the impression - although the law did not give ground for it - that they would necessarily have to bear the expense of the preliminary investigation and might have to bear the expense of the investigation before the board that was subsequently appointed. For that reason, and possibly others as well, the Combines Investigation Act of 1910 was not used to the extent expected at the time that that measure was passed (quoted in Ball, 1934, pp. 67-68).

As a result, the 1923 Act attempted to facilitate the investigatory process by reducing the cost to potential applicants.

Nevertheless, King did not ignore criminal sanctions when reforming the Act in 1923. For example, at First reading, King stated:

> Now, it is recognized that there are distinct limitations in the matter of the protection of the public under the provisions of the Criminal Code. The legislation which the government is introducing proceeds on the theory that the reason why section 498 of the Criminal Code is of so little effect is not that there are no combinations that are detrimental to the public or that such combinations are rare, but rather that the existence of these combinations, and their method of operation is difficult to discover; that what is needed is effective machinery of investigation which will disclose the existence of combines operating to the detriment of the public, and afford the information whereby proceedings under the Criminal Code can be made really effective in the case of individuals who are violating its provisions, or who are associated with combines that are operating to the detriment of the public. The legislation to be introduced provides machinery for investigation which it is hoped and believed will be effective toward this end. I will describe the proposed method of investigation a little more in detail when I refer to that particular phase of the subject (House of Commons, *Debates*, March 9, 1923, p. 988).

Thus improving the machinery of investigation would facilitate both publicity and enforcement of the Criminal Code.

5.1 Investigatory Process

An investigation under the 1923 Act could be initiated in one of three ways. First, any six persons, provided they were British subjects resident in Canada of at least 21 years of age, could write to the Registrar (a permanent official responsible for the administration of the Act) complaining that an alleged infringement of the Act had occurred. The applicants were required to do no more than lay their evidence and allegations before the Registrar. Their names were not revealed to those who were the subject of the allegations and if any inquiry took place the applicants were not required to shoulder any of the cost.[52] This contrasted sharply with the 1910 Act under which the applicants had to bear the cost of making a *prima facie* case before a judge and having their identity revealed. The second way an inquiry was commenced was whenever the Registrar had reason to believe an offence had been or was about to be committed. Finally, the Minister (of Labour, later Minister of Justice) could order the Registrar to carry out an inquiry.

Under the 1923 Act, the federal government appointed, for the first time in the 34 years that Canada had anti-combines legislation, a permanent official responsible for the administration and enforcement of the Act: the Registrar.[53] The Registrar's primary role was to conduct <u>preliminary</u> inquiries which could be started in any of the three ways listed in the previous paragraph. Bladen (1932, p. 74) considered the preliminary hearing by the Registrar to be a substitute for the hearing before a judge under the 1910 legislation. The Registrar could conclude that either a full investigation was required, or that the preliminary investigation revealed nothing untoward. On the other hand the Minister could order a full investigation.

Investigations were undertaken in one of two ways. Either the Registrar could conduct the inquiry or he could request that the Minister appoint a Special Commissioner to do so. Under the *Combines Investigation Act* of 1923, the Registrar or a Special Commissioner had the power to summon and examine witnesses under oath, and to require the production of documents. The use of a Special Commissioner could be seen as a continuation of the Board of Investigation under the 1910 legislation. Certainly King in 1923 felt that "effective investigations will be conducted by the different commissioners who will be appointed to deal with cases which the registrar thinks are deserving of more careful attention" (House of Commons, *Debates*, May 8, 1923, p. 2604).

---

52. The cost of some of the investigations is reported in Stanbury (1976, pp. 623-625).

53. In 1937 the Registrar was renamed as the Commissioner. In 1952 he became the Director of Investigation and Research, which title was retained under the *Competition Act* of 1986.

The final report usually contained opinions as to the guilt or innocence of those whose conduct was the subject of investigation. All reports written by the Special Commissioners had to be published 15 days after they had been transmitted to the Minister.[54] On the other hand, a report written by the Registrar had to be transmitted to the Minister, but the Minister had complete discretion in deciding whether the report would be published. This is a surprising provision, given Mackenzie King's theory of the benefits of publicity. However, since in the 1920s and early 1930s most investigations were carried out by Special Commissioners, the latter provision had virtually no effect.

5.2 Criminal Offence

Under the 1910 Act it had been an offence to <u>continue</u> the operation of a combine more than 10 days after the report of the three-person Board of Investigation had been published. Only if the combine continued its activities could a fine be imposed. Further, the findings of fact by the Board were final and not subject to review by the courts. However, no official existed to verify whether the Board's recommendations were implemented. Under the 1923 legislation, all this changed. The offence provision was as follows:

> Every one is guilty of an indictable offence and liable to a penalty not exceeding ten thousand dollars or two years imprisonment, or if a corporation to a penalty not exceeding twenty-five thousand dollars, who is a party or privy to or knowingly assists in the formation or operation of a combine within the meaning of this Act (quoted in Ball, 1934, p. 65).[55]

In other words those who were party to or assisted in the formation or operation of an illegal combine (see the definition in Appendix A) were guilty of an indictable offence whether their actions took place before or after the report of the Commissioner is published. Further, the determination whether an offence had occurred was assigned to the courts and not to the Registrar or Special Commissioner writing a report following his investigation. Finally, although the Minister transmitted a report to a provincial Attorney General for possible prosecution, the matter did not necessarily end there if he failed to prosecute. (Recall that one of the criticisms of the administration of the 1889 Act between 1889 and 1910 had been the reluctance of provincial Attorneys General to prosecute.) If the provincial Attorney General decided not to take any action, then,

> ...any citizen over twenty-one years of age may lay any information against the combine before the Solicitor General [of Canada]; and if the Governor in Council

---

54. The Commissioner could recommend that part of all of the report not be published. It was up to the Minister in such instances to decide what part(s) of the report should be published.

55. The provision concerning the tariff and patent remedies which were in the 1910 Act also appeared in the 1923 Act.

deems the case sufficient in the public interest the Minister of Justice may appoint counsel to prosecute the offender on behalf of the Dominion. This specific statement is important because it had been frequently alleged that many of the enforcement bodies had not been overly anxious to prosecute. Now, even if there is extreme reluctance on the part of the Attorney General, the complaint of any citizen may initiate the machinery for prosecution (Ball, 1934, p. 66).

Note that an important political "filter" - Cabinet approval - was placed over the decision whether the citizen's Information would result in a prosecution. The decision was not to be left to the senior officials in the Department of Justice who would normally make the decision to prosecute on the substantive merits of the case. The Cabinet's discretion, however, was probably somewhat constrained by the fact that the report of the Registrar or Special Commissioner, together with their recommendation, had been made public.

To a considerable degree, the shortcomings of both the 1889 and 1910 legislation had been overcome by the 1923 legislation. Bladen (1932, p. 74), however, was skeptical: "This seems to be an improvement, assuming the dominion government is sincere in its legislative aims."

The 1923 Act survived with few amendments until major legislative changes were introduced in 1952 (see Appendix A). There were, however, two periods 1935-37 (when the Dominion Trade and Industry Act was in force - see Cheffins, 1991) and 1941-45 (when the enforcement of the Act was effectively suspended and the Registrar became the enforcement administrator for the Wartime Prices and Trade Board) when the 1923 Act was of little consequence. Most commentators tend to ignore these periods. For example, in reviewing antitrust developments in Canada, the MacQuarrie Committee (Canada, 1952, p. 12) remarked that the 1923 Act "was basically the Act as it stands to-day" (i.e, 1952) while Reynolds (1940, p. 146) wrote twelve years earlier that "The Combines Investigation Act of 1923, with certain amendments, is still in effect..." Changes did take place in the administrative machinery of the 1923 Act before 1952. These were largely minor or ephemeral, however. See Appendix A.

6.0 THE APPLICATION OF A VIABLE ADMINISTRATIVE STRUCTURE, 1923 to 1952

This section is divided into two major subsections. The first is concerned with an empirical study of the administrative procedures employed under the 1923 Act and how they varied over time. As can be observed from the previous section, some choice existed concerning the manner in which the *Act* could be administered (e.g., who initiated an inquiry; who conducted an inquiry; who undertook a prosecution). The second major sub-section (6.2) attempts to assess the effectiveness of the administrative machinery in responding to alleged infringements of the *Combines Investigation Act*. Were the procedures operated without undue delay? Were the penalties imposed adequate? Did the administration of the Act direct its attention to relatively insignificant local industries or were large national industries the primary area of interest?

In this section we use the term preliminary inquiry to refer to the period from the receipt of an informal complaint from an individual or a formal six-citizen complaint to the decision that the situation required a formal investigation. Section 21 of the 1923 *Combines Investigation Act* read, in part, "at the conclusion of every [formal] investigation the Registrar and every Commissioner shall make a report in writing..." L.A. Skeoch (1966b, pp. 97-116) provides a list of 41 reports made to the Minister under the authority of the 1923 Act and subsequent amendments. In those instances where the Minister ordered an investigation, the formal investigation is assumed to start on the date of the receipt of the letter from the Minister.

6.1 The Process of Investigation and Prosecution 1923 to 1952

Initiating an Investigation: Under the 1923 *Combines Investigation Act*, the Registrar[56] could conduct a formal investigation on his own initiative. As with the period after 1952,[57] the initial source of information which led the Registrar to institute a formal inquiry could be divided into three categories.

(1) Informal complaints from members of the public in their role as consumers, producers, competitors, suppliers, employees or purchasers.

(2) The Registrar himself on the basis of his surveillance of the economic landscape. Such devices as the close monitoring of the trade and daily newspapers and reading government inquiries into industry were employed (e.g., Report of the Royal Commission on Price Spreads, 1935).

(3) A formal application for an inquiry signed by "six persons, British subjects, resident in Canada." The application is a statutory declaration which contains the names of those who constituted the applicants, the "nature of the alleged combine and the names of the persons believed to be concerned... the manner in which... the alleged combine is believed to operate... to the detriment of the public" (1923, *Combines Investigation Act*, section 5). This section of the Act remained substantially unchanged between 1923 and 1952 and a similar one can be found in the *Competition Act* of 1986.

We have been unable to determine precisely the number of preliminary inquiries in each of these three categories over the period 1923/24 to 1951/52.

---

56. His title was changed to Commissioner when the Act was amended in 1937. Unless specifically indicated the term Registrar is taken to refer to the permanent official in charge of Canada's antitrust policy between 1923-1935 and 1937-1952. In the period 1935-37 the administration was delegated to the Dominion Trade and Industry Commission. See Appendix A and Cheffins (1991).

57. See Rosenbluth and Thorburn (1963) for the period 1952-1960, and Gorecki and Stanbury (1979) and Gorecki (1981) for 1960-1975.

We have obtained information on the number of <u>files opened</u> by the Registrar and have reviewed the *Annual Reports* of the Registrar over the period. Table 2 provides data on case files opened, while Table 3 provides, from a different and perhaps not entirely comparable data source, figures on the sources of preliminary inquiries. It appears that more than 90% of case files opened also resulted in a preliminary inquiry. In other words, it would appear that some case files opened resulted in no more than the communication received being placed in a new file and nothing else occurring, except a letter of acknowledgement. This may have been because there was already an inquiry underway on the issue or the complaint referred to something clearly outside the scope of the Act.

In our work on the period 1960-1975 (Gorecki and Stanbury, 1979), we defined a preliminary or informal inquiry as one that does not require the use of one or more of the investigatory powers provided under the Act (e.g., to compel witnesses to attend or to compel the production of documents from those under investigation). An informal inquiry is likely to involve discussions with the complainant, review of information in the Registrar's files, and gathering of information from trade journals and other public sources (i.e., library research). It may even involve telephone calls to and interviews with people in the industry that is the subject of the complaint. An inquiry becomes formal when the Registrar or Special Commissioner makes use of one or more of the formal investigatory powers provided for in the *Combines Investigation Act*.

Informal complaints from members of the public were more significant than instances in which the Registrar himself noticed a situation worthy of a preliminary investigation. See Table 3. This partly reflects the concentration on conspiracy cases and the absence of any serious attempt to attack single firm monopolies or mergers (Reynolds, 1940, p. 154).[58] The latter were likely to come to the Registrar's attention through public media, but not so the former. Certainly in the period 1960/61 to 1974/75 a high proportion of preliminary inquiries instituted by the Director were concerned with mergers reported in the newspapers (see Gorecki, 1981). In the early annual reports of the Registrar[59] little mention is made of the Registrar taking the initiative in starting investigations. Table 2, however, indicates that from 1923/24 to 1932/33 he initiated from one to seven case files opened per year out of a total of 19 to 47 per year. Complaints seemed to trigger most preliminary inquiries. Immediately after W.W. II, the Registrar began initiating more

---

58. Recall, however, that monopoly was not defined properly as a separate offence until 1935. See Stanbury (1978). From 1923 to 1952 only two cases involving a merger and one involving a monopoly were prosecuted. See Table 11.

59. See, for example, *Annual Report 1923/24* to *Annual Report 1928/29*. Mackenzie King's former personal secretary, Fred McGregor, was appointed as Registrar in 1925. See McGregor (1962).

investigations as Table 2 makes clear. This continued with the ratio of preliminary inquiries started by the Registrar and those started by the informal complaint was 46:70 in 1950/51[60] and 16:122 in 1951/52.[61] The increased importance of the Registrar in the latter part of the period no doubt reflects the increase in the staff of the office of the Registrar as well as their increased experience and awareness of the industrial landscape (1.5 person-years in 1923/24, eight in 1940, 34 in 1950/51).[62]

Six citizen applications were small both in absolute numbers and in relation to the number of complaints received over the period. Their number ranged from zero to six annually from 1923/24 to 1940/41 - see Table 2. From 1923/24 to 1947/48, they accounted for 57 of 723 case investigations. As note 2 to Table 2 indicates, only 10 of these six citizen applications came from consumers. The rest came from competitors, other businesses or farmers. From the beginning of W.W. II to 1952, however, the number of inquiries based on six citizen complaints fell to one.[63] The changing relative importance of six citizen inquiries reflected a greater willingness on the part of the Registrar to institute a full investigation without the backing of a six citizen complaint. Earlier he had been more reluctant. For example, in the Registrar's *1924/25 Annual Report* (p. 2) the following appears,

> Included in the representations received in the department during the first seven months of the operation of the Act,... was a complaint regarding conditions said to exist in connection with the marketing of British Columbia fruit and vegetables. This matter was being investigated by the registrar at the close of the fiscal year 1923-24, and in July, 1924, an application for an investigation, signed by six residents of British Columbia, led to the appointment of Mr. Lewis Duncan, barrister of Toronto, as commissioner by an Order in Council, which named various parties to the alleged combine, these parties being for the most part members of the Nash organization in Canada, or shareholders in the Growers' Sales Agency, Limited.

This reluctance may have reflected the feeling for continuity with the 1910 legislation in which the applicants had to make *prima facie* case before a judge before an investigation could begin. Second, the Registrar had a small staff and this may have been one way of selecting cases for investigation. As his staff expanded, he apparently grew more confident for he was much more willing to undertake investigations based on informal complaints so six citizen inquiries became less important.

In sum, if we consider the whole of the period 1923/24 to 1951/52, the evidence contained in Tables 2, 3 and a reading of the *Annual Reports* of the

---

60. See *Annual Report 1950/51*, p. 3.

61. See *Annual Report 1951/52*, p. 27.

62. See Bladen (1956, p. 230, footnote 23), and *Annual Report 1950/51*, p. 12.

63. See Table 4 and *Annual Report 1950-51* (p. 3) and *Annual Report 1951/52* (p. 27).

Registrar indicates that informal complaints were by far the most important source of preliminary inquiries: 526 of 723 case files opened from 1923/24 to 1947/48. Although the evidence suggests that informal complaints were always the most significant source of preliminary inquiries, the latter two sources changed in relative significance. Six citizen applications for an inquiry were of greater significance in the pre-1946 period, while converse was the fact in the post-war period.

Following a Preliminary Inquiry: A preliminary inquiry could result in several outcomes. First, the complaint[64] could be "frivolous or vexatious" under the 1923 *Combines Investigation Act* in which case no further action was required. The first annual report of the Registrar records one such example," Bread. - Complainant refused to make formal application for investigation and informal investigation... disclosed... that complainant was mainly concerned in embarrassing a firm from whose employ he had been discharged" (*Annual Report 1923/24*, p. 1).

Second, although the complaint was in good faith and neither vexatious or frivolous, it could have been outside the scope of the *Combines Investigation Act*. One example was recorded in the *1931/32 Annual Report* of the Registrar:

> Complaint by a representative of a Canadian organisation of producers that three foreign-owned companies in Canada, controlling over half the Canadian output, would not assist in developing the Oriental market. No action was taken because the question was considered beyond the jurisdiction of the *Combines Investigation Act* (*Annual Report, 1932/32*, p. 16).

Third, the complaint, although in good faith and referred to actions within the purview of the Act, did not reveal that an offence had been committed. This would seem to be the most numerous result of a preliminary inquiry. Many examples can be found in most annual reports. One example will suffice to illustrate the point: "Complaint that a stove company refused to supply complainant with any more stoves on the ground that he was failing to maintain the resale price[65] set by them. Result: Complaint found to be unjustified (*Annual Report, 1924/25*, p. 8).

Fourth, the Registrar could negotiate a solution to the complaint. For example, in the *1931/32 Annual Report* (p. 15), the Registrar managed to successfully restore the source of supply to a dealer who had previously been cut-off. In some instances, as indicated in Table 2, firms would come to the Registrar specifically for guidance. However, unlike some of his successors

---

64. We use this term as a convenient short-hand for a complaint from an individual, a six-citizen application for an inquiry, or the initiation of an inquiry by the Registrar of his own volition or at the request of the Minister.

65. Recall that resale price maintenance and refusal to deal did not become criminal offences until December 29, 1951 (see Stanbury, 1981). More generally, see Hunter (1991).

McGregor (1932) was not too enthusiastic about what he called an "advice in advance" policy: "The Government has not the facilities, for one thing, to make a thorough check-up or any check-up of the plans innumerable, which would be submitted to it if such a policy were adopted." Moreover, "the consequent shifting of responsibility from the public to the state, more paternalism, would not be good for either the public or the state" (quoted in Ball, 1934, p. 103).

The fifth outcome of the preliminary inquiry was a full-scale formal investigation undertaken either by the Registrar or a specially appointed Commissioner. The evidence suggests that only a small percentage of complaints resulted in a formal inquiry. For example, between 1923 and 1946 there were 585 informal complaints, but only about five per cent led to a full scale investigation.[66]

From the available data it is not possible to quantify with which sections of the Act most complaints were concerned. However, the Registrar remarks on several occasions on the importance of refusal to sell complaints. For example, in the *Annual Report 1938/39* (p. 7) the following observation appears: "As in previous years, the most numerous complaints were those involving the refusal of manufacturers to sell to particular dealers." Reynolds (1941, pp. 153-154) has remarked on the policy of the Registrar of generally not getting involved in refusal to supply cases as follows:

> Disputes between business men which do not to any extent involve the public interest will usually not be investigated. There has been no attempt, for example, to regulate "unfair" trade practices as such. Only in cases which appear to affect directly or indirectly the interests of consumers or primary producers has action been taken.

Skeoch (1966a) notes that in 1941 some 425 food items were subject to some form of RPM. By 1947 the number had increased to about 600, mainly in the high mark-up items. In the late 1940s RPM was common in jewellery, watches, silverware, equipment sold to barbers and beauty salons, proprietary articles sold to drug stores and hardware items. The two unsuccessful prosecutions of the Dominion Wholesale Grocers Guild and related organizations in 1910 and 1922 make it clear that food wholesalers practiced RPM as far back as 1884 (see Bliss, 1974). The inquiry into the distribution of tobacco products in 1938 showed that RPM was widespread in that area (Corry, 1938; Curtis, 1938). Yet it was not until December 1951 that Parliament made RPM and refusal to deal illegal *per se* under the *Combines Investigation Act* (see Rosenbluth and Thorburn, 1963, Ch. 2; Hunter, 1991). **Formal Investigations:** Table 4 shows which source was responsible for instituting a <u>formal</u> investigation, i.e., one that resulted in a report by the Registrar or a Special Commissioner: six citizen applications; the Registrar

---

66. See Tables 2, 3 and 15.

either on his own initiative or on the basis of an informal complaint; or the Minister responsible to Parliament for the *Combines Investigation Act*. A word or two on each is necessary before discussion of the table commences. Six citizen applications for an inquiry need no comment. With respect to the Registrar it was not possible always to distinguish whether an investigation was based on his own initiative or that of a complaint, and hence the following breakdown of the data in Table 4 should be viewed with some caution:

- On Own Initiative   2
- On Basis of Informal Complaint   9
- Not Possible to Infer Source of Registrar's Action 3

Both of the instances in which the Registrar initiated any inquiry led to formal investigations which commenced in the post-war period.[67] In two instances,[68] although the Minister formally ordered the inquiry, the evidence contained in the Annual Reports and the final report indicated the primary source was the Registrar (and are so recorded in Table 4). Under the *1923 Act*, the Minister responsible to Parliament for the administration of the Act could order a formal investigation. Between 1923 and October 1, 1945, the relevant minister was the Minister of Labour, and thereafter the Minister of Justice.[69] Finally, some formal inquiries, the evidence indicates at least five,[70] were started from a series of different sources. In such instances, the source which played the greatest part in commencing a formal inquiry is listed. For example, report #1 was started by complaints and then a six-citizen application was received, but the six-citizen application was clearly the catalyst that commenced the formal inquiry.

Over the whole of the period 1923/24 to 1951/52 the primary source of formal inquiries was six-citizen applications, accounting for 46% of the total, followed by the Registrar (34%) and the Minister (10%). In four instances (10%) the available data did not permit assigning the source of the formal inquiry. These data, taken together with the information in Table 5 indicate that a six citizen-application had a one in three chance of leading to a formal inquiry, while for an informal complaint the probability was less than .015, for the Registrar the probability was less than .03.

Further examination of Table 4 reveals some interesting variation over time in the source of initiation of the formal inquiries. From 1923/24 to 1939/40, 75% of all formal investigations were started by six-citizen applications. Earlier it was suggested that a six-citizen application was virtually the only way the Registrar could start a formal inquiry in the 1920s.

---

67. See Reports #30 and #37 in Table 5.

68. See Reports #9 and #10 in Table 5.

69. See the Registrar's *Annual Report 1945/46* (p. 1).

70. Reports #1, 3, 6, 11, 14 - see Table 5.

At least one citation was produced to support this inference. In contrast, after World War II six-citizen applications dropped to virtually zero and the Registrar initiated virtually all inquiries. This change may have been attributable to the expansion of the staff of the Registrar after the war, or Parliament's endorsement of the fine job that the Registrar was doing.[71] It may have been attributable to the experience of the Registrar as the Enforcement Administrator of the Wartime Prices and Trade Board between December 1941 and the end of the war.[72] There he saw which industries had formal price-fixing arrangements sanctioned by the State and some of these continued unofficially after the war. McGregor became a more activist enforcer of the legislation after the war.

> After the World War II control period, competition policy was seen as an integral part of the establishment of normal peacetime free market conditions. In his *Annual Report* for 1944/45 (p. 6), the Commissioner commented, "Attention is being given to adapting the organization and nature of operations under the Combines Investigation Act to the need for providing further safeguards against the development and exercise of monopolistic restraints of trade in the post-war period" (Gorecki and Stanbury, 1984, pp. 118-119).

McGregor instituted nine formal inquiries between 1945/46 and 1948/49. These were often in major industries. This flourish of activity may have been the real reason for his removal in 1949[73] and not the resignation over the publication of the *Flour Milling Report*.[74] After all McGregor had already published portions of the *Flour Milling Report* in his annual report for the fiscal year ending March 31, 1949 (pp. 5-7), months before it was officially released.

McGregor's approach to the enforcement of the Act has been described as follows:

---

71. See House of Commons *Debates*, Vol. III, 1946, pp. 3049-3102.

72. In September 1939 the Wartime Prices and Trade Board was established. The Maximum Prices Regulations came into effect on 1 December 1941. McGregor became Enforcement Administrator of the Board. The price ceilings were not suspended until January 1947. See Magwood (1981) and *Annual Report 1941/42* (p. 1). Sources do not indicate when he terminated employment with Board, but it must have been near end of the war.

73. Rosenbluth and Thorburn (1963, Chapter 2) discuss the existence of a group within the Cabinet which wanted to weaken the powers of the Registrar. Given the endorsement of the fine work of the Registrar in the House of Commons in 1946, this change in attitude almost certainly must have come from the activist approach of McGregor.

74. The Minister of Justice received the first version of the report on December 29, 1948. He received the final version on February 23, 1949. It should, therefore, have been released before March 10th. When McGregor resigned on October 29, 1949 the release of the *Flour Milling Report* was some 10 months overdue. It was published on November 2, 1949. More generally, see Rosenbluth and Thorburn (1963, Ch. 2) and Winnipeg Free Press (1949).

Commissioner McGregor... repeatedly emphasized in his speeches that the Act was not designed to regulate business, rather it was designed to be "anti-monkey-business." He saw the Combines Branch as "neither gestapo nor bureaucracy nor a body of snoopers; it is made up of a group of Canadian citizens who have been assigned the job of assisting in keeping the channels of trade clear of artificial obstructions that are bad for business itself as well as bad for the public; a group of men who are taking their work seriously without taking themselves too seriously."

McGregor saw himself as a "traffic cop in congested areas, not telling businessmen and others where to go, but preventing traffic jams, restraining road hogs and speeders, reckless drivers and other offenders who may disregard the rules of the road" (McGregor, 1946c, pp. 3-4).

In a speech to the Standard-Imperial Oil Conference McGregor used a railway analogy to describe the anti-combines organization in the Department of Justice: "a maintenance-of-way organization to see that the tracks are kept clear of obstructions, that the whole roadbed on which the nation's business travels is maintained on a sound and safe and solid basis" (McGregor, 1945, p. 9).

McGregor (1946a, p. 13) did, however, have a clear vision of what he meant by a system of private enterprise: "freedom must exist for buyers as well as sellers; public benefits, as well as private benefits, must be abundantly apparent; and real enterprise, individual initiative, must not be curbed by all kinds of restrictive agreements designed to prevent the active competition of active competitors. Competition is still the life of trade" (Gorecki and Stanbury, 1984, p. 159, n. 86).

Registrar or Special Commissioner? A formal inquiry under the 1923 *Combines Investigation Act* could be conducted by two different officials: the Registrar, the permanent official appointed to administer the Act; and a Special Commissioner, appointed solely for the task of carrying out an investigation. Table 6 provides data on the use of each method.[75] In two instances, the reports were written by a special assistant to the Registrar (#13 in Table 5), and on behalf of the Registrar (#16). However, the person responsible was not formally designated by the title Special Commissioner. Nevertheless, in both of these instances the author was treated as though he was a Special Commissioner since he did not appear to be a permanent member of the staff of the Registrar.

Over the period 1923/24 to 1951/52, the vast majority of formal inquiries were conducted by the Registrar (30 compared to 10), with one formal inquiry leading to a report (#6) by both the Registrar and a Special Commissioner. The chief factor which determined whether the Registrar or a Special Commissioner would be employed was the availability of staff in the office of the Registrar. For example, Bladen (1956, p. 230, footnote 23) comments that "with the increase in the staff the use of special commissioners declined..." while the Registrar commented in one case that the "appointment of a special commissioner, as authorised under section 7 of the Combines Investigation Act, was necessary because of the pressure of other inquiries on which the

---

75. Skeoch (1966b, p. 100) lists #9 as consisting of a report by both the Registrar and a Special Commissioner. However, the Registrar carried out only a preliminary investigation. Hence #9 is treated here as a report only by the Special Commissioner.

permanent staff of the Commission was engaged" (Commissioner's *Annual Report 1947/48*, p. 6). The professional staff of the office of the Registrar grew very slowly. Yet as Table 6 shows, the use of Special Commissioners virtually fell to zero after the period 1929/30 to 1933/34. The much more important role of Special Commissioners in the 1920s and early 1930s reflected King's desire to rely on such commissioners, noted above.

The Special Commissioners were appointed by the Governor-in-Council, i.e., by the Cabinet of the day. Given the absence of evidence, it is not possible to say whether the selection process was chiefly one of political patronage or whether the choices were largely determined by the Registrar on the basis of the person's expertise. Nevertheless, the evidence shows lawyers were usually appointed as Special Commissioners. With two exceptions, each Special Commissioner was responsible for only one report.[76] The use of Special Commissioners to conduct inquiries on an *ad hoc* basis did not help accumulate expertise in the area of antitrust as Bladen (1956, p. 227) notes. "Unfortunately, however, the further investigations [i.e., formal investigations leading to a published report] were usually [1923-1931] conducted by commissioners, appointed *ad hoc* and generally selected from the legal profession." Similar feelings were voiced earlier by Swanson (1910, p. 355) with respect to the 1910 *Combines Investigation Act*.

The formal inquiry conducted by either the Special Commissioner or the Registrar usually involved extensive hearings and the procurement of information either on a voluntary basis or using the formal powers provided for in the Act: written returns of information and/or the power to search for documents.[77] The *1923 Act* was the first competition policy legislation in Canada to provide investigatory tools specifically fashioned to deal with the nature of the offences involved.[78] The inquiry was conducted in private as required under the Act. At the conclusion of the hearings there was usually a summing up by counsel on behalf of those who had been accused of committing an offence under the Act. This procedure is described in the report concerning the importation and distribution of British anthracite coal as follows:

> In the course of the inquiry seventy-one witnesses were examined under oath in sessions held in Montreal, Toronto, Quebec and Ottawa, the chief centres of

---

76. Lewis Duncan wrote two reports on fruit and vegetables, #1 and #5 (Table 5), while Carl Goldenberg was responsible for the last two reports written by a Special Commissioner, #31 and 41.

77. The information in this paragraph is largely taken from reading the introduction to the reports of the Registrar or Special Commissioner.

78. Recall the powers given to a judge to conduct an inquiry under the Customs Tariff Act in 1907 and to the Board of Investigation under the 1910 *Combines Investigation Act*. See Sections 2 and 3 above.

> distribution of British anthracite coal. At the conclusion of the hearings arguments were made by counsel representing the principal importers and wholesale distributors. In all, forty-four days were occupied in the hearing of evidence and argument. The hearings were conducted in private, in accordance with the provisions of Section 25 of the Combines Investigation Act (Report #33, p. 7).

This description refers to the procedure which operated during the period 1923/24 to 1947/48 (i.e., reports #1 to #31). After the final argument, the Registrar or Special Commissioner would write a report on the basis of the available documentary evidence and the transcript of the hearings. The report was then submitted to the Minister.

From 1948/49 until 1951/52 a slight change was made in the procedure in conducting a formal inquiry. After the final argument, the Registrar or Special Commissioner would prepare a summary and commentary on the evidence presented which was then forwarded to the persons and companies who had appeared at the hearings. These persons or companies were then given an opportunity to comment on the summary. Further hearings could be held. The report was then written and forwarded to the Minister. In the words of the *Flour Milling Report*, the procedure was as follows:

> At my [i.e., the Registrar's] request counsel for the Commission prepared a detailed summary of the commentary on the evidence which I then sent to the companies and persons involved as notice of the matters alleged. At the same time they were invited to supplement in any way they wished the representations and evidence already given during the hearings in regard to the same matters. Full opportunity was then given for those involved to present such further representations and evidence. Written or oral argument was then presented by or on behalf of all to whom notice had been given. In some instances the argument was directed primarily to a claim that the Commissioner had acted without jurisdiction and without giving them adequate notice. On June 4, 1948, further hearings were held before me in Ottawa during which argument was heard from an officer of one company and its counsel (Report #32, p. 5).

No indication was given for this change in procedure.

Reports: The reports of the Registrar and Special Commissioner varied considerably in length and complexity. For example, the one concerning Rubber Goods (Report #36) was 433 pages in length while that relating to the Electrical Estimators Association (#10) was only 12 pages long. (Both, it might be added, led to successful prosecutions despite their disparate size - see Table 5.) It is beyond the scope of this study to deal with the competency of the reports. However, the opinion of those who have reviewed all the reports might be briefly cited. For example, L.A. Skeoch (1966b, p. 94), in reviewing reports issued between 1923/24 and 1964/65, remarked that

> One of the major impressions left by a review of the combines reports is of their highly uneven quality; another is of their failure to display, over time, any consistent improvement in the level of economic analysis. Some of the most effective reports were written by the permanent Commissioners [i.e., the Registrar]; some of the least competent by Special Commissioners.

This last remark would seem to confirm the misgivings that Bladen (1956, p. 227) and Swanson (1910, p. 355) had about the appointment of Special Commissioner - usually lawyers - to conduct only one inquiry each.

The reports themselves usually contained a detailed description of the industry, the practices complained of, and the Registrar's or Special Commissioner's opinion as to the legality or illegality of the alleged practices.[79] The last page of most reports sounded like a judge rendering his verdict except that the penalties were not specified. For example, the final paragraph of the report on dental supplies reads as follows:

> It is my [i.e., Registrar's] opinion, therefore, that a combine exists in the distribution and sale of dental supplies in Canada, within the meaning of the Combines Investigation Act, and that all members of the Canadian Dental Trade Association have been parties and privy to this combine and have knowingly assisted in its formation or operation (Report #29, p. 88).

In most cases, as will be discussed further below, the courts agreed with the Registrar's or Special Commissioner's finding of the existence or absence of a combine.

Publicity and the Publication of Reports: Section 22 of the 1923 *Combines Investigation Act* laid down that all reports written by the Special Commissioner be made public promptly:

> Within fifteen days after its receipt by the Minister... shall be made public, unless the Commissioner is of the opinion that the public interest would be best served by withholding the publication and so states in the report itself, in which case the Minister may exercise his discretion as to the publicity to be given to the report in whole or in part.

A similar section appeared in the 1937 and 1949 *Combines Investigation Acts*. The evidence indicates that all reports by a Special Commissioner were published, typically within 15 days of its transmission to the Minister and that they were published in full.

However, between 1923 and 1937, the *Combines Investigation Act* was silent on the subject of whether the reports of the Registrar should be published or not. This was generally interpreted by the appropriate Minister that publication was at his discretion. However, in 1937 the Act was amended to state that reports of the Registrar were treated in the same fashion as those of a Special Commissioner (i.e., they had to be published by the Minister within 15 days of receipt unless the Registrar indicated otherwise, in which case publication was at the discretion of the Minister).

---

79.   Brief summaries of all the reports are to be found in Skeoch (1966b, pp. 97-116). Somewhat more detailed summaries/discussions are to be found in Bladen (1956, pp. 235-253) for at least some of the reports written during the 1923/24 - 1951/52 period.

The record of publication or non-publication of the reports of the Registrar is summarised in Table 7. It indicates that the period 1923/24 to 1936/37, when the reports of the Registrar (or Commissioner) were published at the Minister's discretion, can be divided into several sub-periods. In the years immediately following the passage of the 1923 *Combines Investigation Act* (1923/24 to 1926/27) all of the reports of the Registrar (or Commissioner) were published. However, in the period 1928/29 to 1934/35, only three of the ten reports submitted by the Registrar to the Minister were published. In two instances, the reports were published only reluctantly. According to J.L. Ilsley, a Liberal MP then in opposition,[80]

> ...the report of the registrar on the alleged combine of tobacco manufacturers and buyers of raw leaf tobacco in Ontario, which the minister at first refused to produce and did produce only under pressure of the house and because of the circumstances that a by-election was pending in one of the counties in Ontario (House of Commons *Debates*, June 11, 1935, p. 3525).

In Report #17 of the distribution of anthracite coal in eastern Canada, the delay between the report being transmitted to the Minister by the Registrar (the basis of Table 6) and the actual publication of the report was nearly three years (April 21, 1933 and March 10, 1936 respectively). In those instances in which the Minister decided not to publish the Registrar's report, perhaps the most bizarre instance is Report #15 regarding the Canadian Fruit Basket Pool. In his report, the Registrar concluded combine existed, a successful prosecution was instituted, and yet the report was not published! (see Skeoch, 1966b, pp. 104-105).

Subsequent to 1936/37 all reports of the Registrar (now Commissioner) were supposed to be published. However, as Table 7 shows, this practice was introduced but slowly over the period 1938/39 to 1952/53. Indeed, the delay in publication of the *Flour Milling Report* from December 29, 1948 to November 7, 1949 led to the resignation of the long-serving Registrar then Commissioner, F.A. McGregor.

The question which naturally arises is what explanation can be found for the behaviour of successive Ministers in their attitude toward publication of reports by the Registrar. Separate explanations will be offered for the period 1923/24 to 1936/37 and 1937/38 to 1952/53. First, in the period 1923/24 to 1926/27, after the legislation of 1923 had been introduced and Mackenzie King's views of publicity still echoed in the House of Commons, the reports of the Registrar were published. In the period 1928/29 to 1934/35, however, with Great Depression, the prevailing attitude toward conspiracies changed. Industry self-government because of the destructive competition of the market system became a feasible policy option. Indeed, the *Dominion Trade and*

---

80. Ilsley became Minister of Finance and Receiver General between July 8, 1940 and December 9, 1946 in Mackenzie King's government.

Industry Commission Act of 1935 allowed price and production agreements to prevent "wasteful or demoralizing competition" - see Cheffins (1991). Similar policies were also instituted in the U.S.[81]

In the period 1937/38 to 1952/53 two questions require explanation. First, why were some reports of the Registrar published and others not? Second, why did F.A. McGregor wait until 1949 to resign when some of his previous reports had not been published? One explanation is that after 1937/38 the Registrar (now Commissioner) developed the following policy: reports which found a combine should be published; reports which did not find a combine should not be published. Where no combine was found, the Registrar would recommend to the Minister that the report not be published. Table 8 attempts to provide information to test this hypothesis. The evidence is largely consistent with this hypothesis: reports of the Registrar which were published between 1937/38 and 1952/53, with one exception, found a contravention of the Act. Reports of the Registrar which were not published usually found no contravention. In contrast, in the period 1923/24 to 1934/35 the pattern is quite different for both published and unpublished reports. For example, of the seven unpublished Registrar's reports between 1928/29 and 1934/35, five found an infringement of the Act. The resignation of McGregor in 1949 over the failure to publish the *Flour Milling Report*, which found very strong evidence of conspiracy, is consistent with this hypothesis.[82] No evidence was at hand to directly test the above explanation.

Prosecution: The next strategic decision in the enforcement of the *Combines Investigation Act* concerns prosecution. Should a prosecution take place? If the answer is yes, who should undertake the prosecution, the Attorney General of the province in which the offence was committed, or the federal Attorney General? The two decisions were not entirely independent. The procedure between 1923 and 1949 was outlined in S. 25 of the 1923 *Combines Investigation Act* as follows:

> Whenever, <u>in the opinion of the Minister an offence has been committed</u> against any of the provisions of this Act, the Minister <u>may</u> remit to the Attorney General of any province within which such alleged offence shall have been committed, for such action as such Attorney General may be pleased to institute because of the conditions appearing, (1) any return or returns which may have been made or rendered pursuant to this Act and are in the possession of the Minister and relevant to such alleged offence; and (2) the evidence taken on any investigation by the

---

81. For a comparison of R.B. Bennett's and Roosevelt's "New Deals," see McConnell (1971) and Cheffins (1989). See also Forster and Read (1979) and Weaver (1977).

82. The one report in the 1938/39 - 1940/41 period which found an offence but was not published (#27), does not seem inconsistent with this hypothesis because the outbreak of war prevented the successful completion of the report (see Skeoch, 1966b, p. 109). This also occurred with the publication of report #30 on April 24, 1948 (optical goods). Report #27 can be treated as a separate report since it led to an action to impeach certain patents, which commenced in 1945, prior to the publication of report #30.

Registrar or a Commissioner, and the report of the Registrar or Commissioner. If within three months after remission aforesaid, or within such shorter period as the Governor in Council shall decide, no action shall have been taken by or at the instance of the Attorney General of the Province as to the Governor in Council the case seems in the public interest to warrant, the Solicitor General may on the relation of any person who is resident in Canada and of the full age of twenty-one years permit an information to be laid against such person or persons as in the opinion of the Solicitor General shall have been guilty of an offence against any of the provisions of this Act; and the Solicitor General may apply to the Minister of Justice to instruct counsel to attend on behalf of the Minister at all proceedings consequent on the information so laid, and upon such application the Minister of Justice may instruct counsel accordingly (emphasis added).

In 1949 an amendment to this procedure was introduced in the *Combines Investigation Act* because

Under the *Criminal Code* only the attorney general of a province has status to present an indictment. Since for some time the practice has been for the Attorney General of Canada to take responsibility in major combines prosecutions, this amendment is designed to give him equal status with an attorney general of a province without excluding the latter. The subsection to be repealed reads:
"31.(2) The Minister of Justice may instruct counsel to attend on behalf of the Minister at all proceedings consequent on any information being laid for an offence under this Act."[83]

The new amendment, passed in 1949, stated that,

The Attorney General of Canada may institute and conduct any prosecution or other proceedings under this Act, or under section four hundred and ninety-eight or section four hundred and ninety-eight A of the *Criminal Code* and for such purposes he may exercise all the powers and functions conferred by the *Criminal Code* on the attorney general of a province.

Prosecutions for conspiracy usually took place under the Criminal Code rather than the *Combines Investigation Act*.[84]

Table 9 provides data on the number of prosecutions undertaken by the federal and provincial authorities, either separately or together. It shows that the federal presence was important in prosecutions from 1923/24 onwards, although from fiscal year 1949/50 all prosecutions were undertaken by the federal authorities, probably reflecting the aforementioned amendment passed in 1949.

---

83. Explanatory notes to accompany Bill 144, 1st Session, 21st Parliament 13 George VI, 1949.

84. It was not until 1960 that conspiracy provisions in the *Criminal Code* and the *Combines Investigation Act* were combined into S.32 of revised *Combines Investigations Act*. Of the 34 conspiracy cases successfully prosecuted between 1910 and 1960, only two were brought under the *Combines Investigation Act* and two others were brought under both the Act and the *Criminal Code*. The rest were brought under the *Criminal Code* (see Stanbury, 1976, pp. 623-624). For more details, see Stanbury (1991).

No hard and fast rules seem to have developed in the period 1923/24 to 1948/49 concerning the division of responsibility for prosecution between federal and provincial authorities. According to Reynolds (1940, p. 160), there was often a considerable amount of negotiation between the two levels of government before a prosecution was undertaken. For example,

> The Western Fruit case was turned over to the Dominion by British Columbia; there was some ground for this, as the case involved the four western provinces. Ontario handed the A.B.C. [Amalgamated Builders' Council] case to the Dominion, on the ground that the province was at the time contesting the constitutionality of the Combines Act. The anthracite coal case was passed back and forth between Quebec and Ottawa several times before the province finally began the prosecution (Reynolds, 1940, p. 160, fn. 36).

In the case of *R.* vs. *Container Materials et al.*[85] and *R.* vs. *Bathurst Power and Paper*[86] the provinces failed to institute a prosecution so "the Dominion undertook prosecution" (Skeoch, 1966b, p. 108). Argument as to who was responsible for prosecution was more likely to occur when the report of the Registrar or Special Commissioner referred to the whole of Canada or at least several provinces. Table 9 shows that this was often the case, even in the pre-1949/50 period.

Unfavorable Report But No Prosecution: Table 9 only informs us of those cases in which a report was made and in which a prosecution actually took place. In all instances the prosecution followed a finding that a combine existed by the report of the Registrar or Special Commissioner.[87] What Table 9 does not deal with are the eight instances in which the Registrar or Special Commissioner's report concluded that a combine existed within the meaning of the Act, but in which neither the provincial or federal governments decided to institute a prosecution. These are described in Table 10. In some instances prosecution was not forthcoming because of inaction by the province (Reports #3, #14), while in others a deliberate decision was taken by the federal government, because of a difference in assessment of the evidence (#37), an alternative form of action seemed feasible (#6), or there was a deep philosophical difference about the administration and application of the Act (#32). Also of note is the fact that most cases of inaction took place in the period 1931/32 to 1934/35, which as noted above, was a period in which the Minister generally tended not to publish reports of the Registrar, but it was also the period of severe disillusion with the efficacy of competitive markets

---

85. (1940) 74 C.C.C. 113 (Trial); (1941) 76 C.C.C. 18 (Appeal); (1942) 77 C.C.C. 129 (SCC).

86. Quebec Court of Queen's Bench, November 12, 1958, Unreported judgment, copy of which may be obtained from the Bureau of Competition Policy.

87. With the exception of *R.* vs. *Stinson-Reeb et al.*, [1929] S.C.R. 276; which the Province of Quebec undertook of its own volition, with no prior investigation by the federal authorities under the *Combines Investigation Act*.

after the Great Depression. Consistent with this is the indication in Table 9 that some of the Registrar's reports were not forwarded to the relevant provincial Attorney General since the *1923 Act* said the Minister "may remit" such reports at his discretion.

Outcome of Prosecutions: Under the *Combines Investigation Act* of 1923 as well as the *Criminal Code*, the final decision as to whether the participants of an alleged combine, monopoly or merger are guilty of a criminal offence rested with the courts. The finding of the Registrar or Special Commissioner had no force in law.[88] Table 11 provides details of the outcomes of the 24 prosecutions undertaken as a result of investigations instituted in the period 1923/24 to 1951/52.[89] The data indicate that the Crown was highly successful in gaining convictions in 20 out of 24 cases. In seven instances, however, a plea of guilty was entered. (See Stanbury, 1991 for the guilty plea rate in later cases.) In the 22 cases in which a conspiracy charge was preferred (including the one in which a merger charge was also laid), the Crown won 19 cases. In the subsequent twenty years this success in conspiracy cases continued; with the Crown winning, over the period 1950/51 - 1969/70, 95% of a growing number of conspiracy cases, with a guilty plea rate of 60%. However, the success rate fell dramatically to 58% between 1975/76 and 1984/85 (Stanbury, 1991).

However, the Crown lost both cases involving mergers, while a conviction was obtained in the only monopoly case prosecuted. In the subsequent twenty to thirty years the Crown did no better, losing the few contested merger and monopoly cases that occurred. The upshot of the jurisprudence was that the merger and monopoly provisions became a virtual dead letter.

In sum, the Crown concentrated almost exclusively on conspiracy cases, with little or no attention to mergers and monopolies which became offences in 1910 and 1935 respectively (see Stanbury, 1978). The 1935 amendments outlawing price discrimination and predatory pricing was never enforced by way of a prosecution prior to 1952, and only to a limited extent thereafter.[90] This lack of attention to mergers and monopolies is surprising, given the

---

88.   However, where the Registrar or Special Commissioner decided that no offence has been committed it was very unlikely that a prosecution would be instituted. Hence the Registrar and Special Commissioners acted as an important initial filter in deciding whether alleged combines had violated the law.

89.   It excludes one patent case taken to the Exchequer Court. See Skeoch (1966b, pp. 110-111).

90.   The first prosecutions were *R.* v. *Ray et al.* (unreported decision, Police Court, South Burnaby, B.C., 1957) and *R.* v. *Howard et al.* (unreported decision, Police Court, South Burnaby, B.C., 1958). See Dunlop (1979).

significance of the merger movement in the late 1920s (Weldon, 1966, pp. 232-235).[91]

The most usual penalty upon conviction was a fine. Indeed, as Table 11 shows, every successful prosecution led to a fine. In the period 1923 to 1952, the minimum and maximum fines and prison terms for merger, monopoly and conspiracy offence were as follows:

- **Criminal Code S. 498**: Individual: $200 - $4000 or 2 years imprisonment; Corporation: $1,000 - $10,000
- **Combines Investigation Act**: Individual: Less than $10,000 or 2 years; Corporation: Less than $25,000[92]

However, since virtually all prosecutions were under the *Criminal Code* (except *R. vs. Singer et al.*, *R. vs. White et al.*, *R. vs. Imperial Tobacco of Canada Ltd. et al.*)[93], and were usually against corporations the relevant maximum becomes $10,000. In the 16 successful prosecutions under Section 498 of the *Criminal Code* in only nine cases was the maximum fine levied; in the four prosecutions under the *Combines Investigation Act* the maximum of $25,000 was levied only once, although in one other instance a fine of $15,000 was levied.[94] Whether these fines were too "high" or too "low" is another question (see Stanbury, 1976). However, it should be noted that although individuals were charged in some cases,[95] they were never jailed if convicted. In one case, a year's suspended sentence was imposed. Tariffs were not reduced with the possible exception of flat glass, and patents were revoked in only one case.

---

91. The first merger prosecution did not take place until the early 1930s. See *R. v. Canadian Imports Co. et al.* (1933) 61 C.C.C. 114 (Trial); (1935) 62 C.C.C. 342 (Appeal). Leave to appeal refused [1935] A.C. 500. The case involved both a conspiracy and a merger and resulted in a conviction for conspiracy and acquittal on the merger. The second merger case, also an acquittal, was *R. v. Staples et al.* (1940) 74 C.C.C. 178. No other mergers were prosecuted before 1960. The only monopoly prosecution prior to 1962 occurred after the Second World War. See *R. v. Eddy Match Co. Ltd. et al.* (1952) 104 C.C.C. 39 (Trial); (1954) 109 C.C.C. 1 (Appeal). See Stanbury (1978).

92. From Stanbury (1976, p. 621).

93. See [1931] O.R. 202 (Trial), O.R. 699 (Appeal); Supreme Court of Ontario, 1932, unreported; (1942) 77 C.C.C. 316, respectively.

94. For details see Stanbury (1976, Table 3, pp. 623-625 and Table 4, p. 626).

95. Of the 19 conspiracy cases in which a conviction was obtained, in three only individuals were charged, in 10 only firms were charged, and in six both were charged (Stanbury, 1976, pp. 623-624). With the exception of heads of trade associations, individuals were charged because they were the owners of unincorporated businesses. Thirty years later, there is some evidence to suggest that the Director is taking a harder line regarding executives involved in conspiracy cases - see Stanbury (1991).

Other Actions: In several instances, either in addition or as a substitute for a prosecution, action was taken outside the purview of the *Combines Investigation Act*. There are three such instances:

Report #	Date Transmitted to Minister	Action
#1 Fruits, Vegetables, Western Canada	Feb. 18, 1925	"A new Sales on Consignment Bill, drafted by the Special Commissioner, was enacted into law by a number of the Western provinces" (Skeoch, 1966b, p. 97). The charges were dropped in the case *R.* vs. *Symington et al.* A conviction was obtained under the *Secret Commissions Act* (1926) 45 C.C.C. 249.
#5 Fruits, Vegetables Ontario	July 31, 1926	"The Minister of Agriculture for Ontario introduced a bill to regulate the sale of fruit and vegetables on consignment, which became law in 1927" (Skeoch, 1966b, p. 99). No prosecution was undertaken although the Special Commissioner found certain practices which inhibited exports.
#28 Ammunition, CIL Ltd.	Sept. 3, 1946	As a result of the report, Canadian Industries Ltd., the subject of the inquiry, agreed to change certain marketing practices (*Annual Report* 1946/47, p. 5). However CIL was the subject of a report ten years later by the RTPC and it was not prosecuted then either.

Such action clearly provides a useful supplement to the enforcement of competition policy in Canada.

6.2 Effectiveness of the Administration and Enforcement, 1923/24 to 1951/52

In the period 1889 to 1923 there were a number of criticisms of the adequacy of the administrative machinery to enforce the competition laws of Canada. Therefore, in evaluating the effectiveness of the administrative machinery over the period 1923/24 to 1951/52, we focus first on the extent to which earlier shortcomings were remedied by the 1923 Act. The administration and enforcement of competition policy in Canada cannot be viewed in a historical vacuum. The shortcomings of the period prior to the second *Combines Investigation Act* were as follows:

- The openness of the inquiry process discouraged complaints except by large, powerful firms or trade associations.
- The cost of convincing a judge that there was a *prima facie* case against a combine was high for would-be complainants and hence discouraged complaints which are necessarily an important element in the enforcement process.

- There was no permanent official with responsibility to oversee the process of investigation and prosecution (and to build up expertise on combines problems).
- The process was cumbersome; it involved long delays and hence discouraged the use of the *Act*.

Each of these shortcomings will be considered in turn in order to assess the adequacy of the 1923 *Combines Investigation Act* in addressing them. In general, it appears that the 1923 legislation ameliorated most of the problems encountered in the earlier period. However, there were still a number of minor shortcomings as we shall discuss below.

The second aspect of anti-combines policy is the effectiveness of its administration and enforcement. Effectiveness will be looked at in terms of:

- The industries investigated, their size and geographical coverage, i.e., did the administrators focus on cases likely to have a larger impact on economic welfare?.
- The speed with which a complaint is acted upon. This has a double effect: the faster the reaction the more incentive to complain and less incentive to break the law.
- The effectiveness of the investigations and prosecutions in terms of success in court, effects on prices, publication of reports, and "ripple effects" of inquiries. Most of the evidence on these matters is likely to be of a qualitative nature rather than quantitative.

The effectiveness will, of course, have to be judged by the exogenous constraints within which competition policy was administered. Two such constraints are of particular significance: the relatively small size of the permanent staff of the office of the Registrar (later Commissioner), and variations in the degree of political support for competition policy (ranging from indifference to outright hostility). Of course the small number of people in the office of the Registrar is, in part, an indication of the political weight given to competition policy by the government of the day.

Responding to the Defects in the 1910 Act: We now assess the adequacy of the 1923 *Combines Investigation Act* in meeting the limitations and problems of the 1910 Act of the same name. Section 19 of the 1923 *Combines Investigation Act* stated that "The proceedings of the Registrar and every Commissioner shall be conducted in private, but the Minister may order that any portion of the proceedings before the Registrar or any Commissioner shall be conducted in public." An examination of the *Annual Reports* of the Registrar and the *Reports* of the Registrar and Special Commissioner verify that the proceedings under the Act were conducted in private[96] and that the

---

96.   We could find no cases in which the Minister ordered the proceedings to be held in public.

identity of the individual complaining to the Registrar was not revealed. The policy of the Registrar was stated to be as follows:

> It has been departmental policy in the administration of the Combines Investigation Act, in dealing with inquiries in the preliminary stage, to give no publicity to the complaint or to the fact that an inquiry has been asked for. Occasionally the applicants themselves have disclosed such information, as was the case with respect to the inquiries into the motion picture industry and into the alleged combine of Montreal milk producers (*Annual Report 1929/30*, p. 14).[97]

This was an undoubted improvement on the 1910 *Combines Investigation Act* and rectified one of the shortcomings listed above.

Under the 1910 legislation a complainant had to make a *prima facie* case, at his own cost, before a judge, in order to start an inquiry into an alleged violation of the antitrust laws of Canada. (The judge had to decide whether a Board of Investigation should be set up to investigate the matter more thoroughly.) In contrast, under the 1923 legislation a complaint to the Registrar was sufficient to put the investigation and enforcement machinery in gear. The Registrar first conducted a preliminary inquiry to see whether a full inquiry using formal investigatory powers (e.g., search) was warranted. The cost was borne entirely by the federal government, although the complainant(s) might be interviewed by the Registrar. On the basis of this preliminary inquiry a decision was taken regarding future action. This stage of the investigatory process was analogous to the appearance before a judge under the 1910 Act. This change in responsibility and cost substantially met the second shortcoming listed above.

One of the criticisms of the 1910 *Combines Investigation Act* was that after a Board of Investigation completed its report it was disbanded. Each Board was an *ad hoc* procedure. Therefore no permanent institution existed to ensure compliance with the findings of the Board. More generally, no official body was created to monitor competitive developments and thereby create expertise in competition policy matters. This problem was resolved in the 1923 legislation by the creation of the post of Registrar, who was a permanent official responsible for the administration of the *Combines Investigation Act*. During most of the period under consideration the Registrar (called Commissioner in 1937) had the power to conduct an inquiry upon his own initiative. This authority is crucial to the effectiveness of the policy as current and earlier experience indicates.

---

97. However, in two inquiries based on six citizen complaints, the Report of the Commissioner not only listed the identity of the complainants but also printed, in full, their formal application. It is not clear why this unusual course of action was followed (see Reports #2, #16 listed in Table 5).

In the period 1923/24 - 1951/52 there were three Registrars or Commissioners. Their respective periods of tenure[98] were as follows:

Aug. 25, 1923 to Sept. 7, 1925[99]	Harry Hereford[100]
Sept. 8, 1925 to Sept. 30, 1935	F.A. McGregor
April 10, 1937 to Dec. 31, 1949	F.A. McGregor
Feb. 23, 1950 to Sept. 1, 1960	T.D. MacDonald[101]

For the period Oct. 1, 1935 to April 1937 responsibility for the administration of the Act rested with the Dominion Trade and Industry Commission (see Cheffins, 1991 and Appendix A). Therefore, during most of the period under consideration F.A. McGregor was the Registrar. He had been the personal secretary of Mackenzie King. The evidence suggests that McGregor was a strong believer in competition policy.[102] When the government refused to publish the *Flour Milling Report* in the late 1940s, contrary to the Act, McGregor resigned. He said, in part,

> There is greater need now for strong action under the combines act than there has been at any time in the past twenty-five years. To an alarming degree price-fixing activities... have been developing in the post war years... (Quoted in House of Commons *Debates*, November 7, 1949, p. 1512).

Hence, the third criticism of the 1910 legislation was met with the appointment of a permanent official, responsible for administration and enforcement. For the most part, the men who held the post were not pliant tools of the politicians.[103]

Timing of Steps in the Process: The fourth criticism of the process of investigation under the 1910 legislation concerned its cumbersome and slow nature. To test whether a similar charge could be laid against the 1923 legislation we have attempted to measure the speed with which a complaint was processed after its receipt by the Registrar. For the purpose of statistical

---

98.   The dates were taken from the *Annual Reports* of the Registrar, Commissioner, Dominion Trade and Industry Commission and Director of Investigation and Research.

99.   We assumed that Hereford's period of tenure ended when McGregor was appointed Registrar. A similar assumption is made concerning the end of McGregor's first period of tenure as Registrar.

100.   He had been an industrial engineer in the Department of Labour (Ball, 1934, p. 70).

101.   From 1940 to 1949 MacDonald was Deputy Attorney-General of Nova Scotia; he became Superintendent of Bankruptcy for the federal government (Rosenbluth and Thorburn, 1963, p. 28, n. 2). See also *Canadian Competition Policy Record*, Vol. 10(4), 1989, p. 1.

102.   See McGregor (1932) (1944) (1945a) (1945b) (1946a) (1946b) (1946c) (1954) and his *Annual Reports* as Registrar.

103.   The relative importance of the Registrar increased as after 1937 all his reports had to be published and gradually the use of Special Commissioners for individual formal investigations declined.

analysis the investigation and prosecution process has been divided into the following periods:

T1 = the time from the opening of a file upon receipt of a complaint until the date at which the report (either the Registrar's or Commissioner's) is transmitted to the Minister. [Responsibility of the Registrar and/or Special Commissioner.]

T2 = the time period between the Minister receiving the report and legal action being instituted. [Responsibility of federal and/or provincial attorney general.]

T3 = the interval between the institution of legal proceedings and the trial judgment.[104] [Responsibility of the judicial system.]

T4 = the interval between the institution of legal proceedings and the final disposition. [Responsibility of the judicial system.]

T5 = the time between the opening of the file upon receipt of a complaint to the completion of the case. In those instances in which legal proceedings did <u>not</u> take place the completion of the inquiry is assumed to take place when the Minister received the report of the Registrar or Special Commissioner.[105]

Table 12 presents the relevant data. It should be noted that the table refers only to the 41 reports of the Registrar and Special Commissioner and the 23 prosecutions to which they gave rise (i.e., all those listed in Table 9 less *R.* vs. *Stinson-Reeb*). The availability of data restricted analysis to this sample of 41 inquiries out of 1125 files opened in the period 1923/24 to 1951/52, or slightly less than four per cent.

The data in Table 12 are subdivided by reports which were completed prior to World War II, and those which were completed after the war. This division was introduced after inspection of the raw data (see Table 15) indicated that cases seemed to be taking longer as between these two sub-periods.

The basic question to be answered is whether the process of administering the *Combines Investigation Act* was swift or slow over the period 1923/24 to 1951/52. Table 12 indicates that the time from the opening of a file to the writing of the report to the Minister was quite short in the

---

104. Obviously, the timing depends upon a combination of the volume of other cases, judges, the Crown and defence counsel.

105. This assumption is made for lack of data. In those cases where the report found no offence then this is quite a reasonable assumption. However, for those eight instances, recorded in Table 9, where the report found a contravention but no action was taken, then this assumption is less reliable.

period 1923/24 to 1939/40 (13.2 months). However, in the post-war period, the time for completion of the average report more than doubled (to 33.8 months). This large difference is partly spurious. Report #30 began in February 1941 and was completed in April 1948. No work was done on the report during the war at all. Report #36, which dealt with the rubber industry, took five years and one month to complete. It was, however, really three reports rolled into one (and resulted in three successful prosecutions).

Reports which did not result in a prosecution were usually carried out quite quickly in both the pre- and post-war period (about 13 and 15 months respectively). However, reports which led to a prosecution took a considerable time to complete in the post-war period compared to the pre-war period (14 versus 36 months respectively).

The period under the control of the federal and/or provincial Attorney General (T2) more than doubled between the pre- and post-war eras. This is somewhat surprising because in the post-1945 period the federal government had virtual monopoly on the prosecution process whereas in the period 1923/24 to 1939/40 authority to prosecute was split between the two. Indeed, only the Attorney General of a province had authority to prefer an indictment under the *Criminal Code* and the great majority of cases were brought under the *Code*. Nevertheless, in both periods, the absolute time-period between receipt of report and decision to prosecute (i.e., institution of legal proceedings) was quite short (4.3 and 10.7 months respectively).

The proceedings in court took approximately the same time (T4) for both pre- and post-war cases (about 17 months), although the trial period (T3) was shorter for post-war cases (8.2 versus 13.2 months). It is not possible to say whether this is quick or slow except by reference to other court cases.

For reports which led to prosecutions in the pre- and post-war periods the length of time from file open to final disposition more than doubled. No such change was noticed for reports which led to no prosecution. Table 12 indicates that the main agencies responsible for the increasing length of the cases were the Registrar and, to a lesser extent, the federal Department of Justice. It is difficult to explain the increasing length of reports after World War II. Several factors would appear to be responsible: a greater number of complaints had to be dealt with in the post-war period; the average annual number of inquiries undertaken in the period 1945/46 to 1951/52 (14) was proportionally greater than in the period 1923/24 to 1939/40 (25); and several of the inquiries were of major proportions (especially rubber, fine papers, and electrical wire and cable) which were atypical of the period 1923/24 to 1951/52. No matter what the reasons, the process of investigation and prosecution slowed considerably in the period after World War II. However, for most of the period the process of investigation and prosecution was relatively expeditious.

The 1923 legislation apparently solved most of the important administrative problems of the 1910 *Combines Investigation Act*. One test of this conclusion (or perhaps more accurately a corollary) concerns the flow of complaints to the Registrar. If there were few complaints to the Registrar one must doubt the efficacy of the administrative procedures.[106] The data, however, indicate that a substantial number of complaints were received and that the number grew over the period 1923/24 to 1931/32, from 19 to 47 annually - see Table 2. Whether this number is too "high" or too "low" is impossible to say. However, the inference can be drawn that there was a body of perceived antitrust violations and the 1923 *Combines Investigation Act* provided a means by which people could and did complain to the Registrar. The growing number of prosecutions, a high percentage of which were successful, indicates that violations did occur. Moreover, the publicity surrounding prosecutions may well have stimulated more complaints (see Gorecki and Stanbury, 1979).

Shortcomings of the 1923 Act: Having shown how the 1923 *Combines Investigation Act* alleviated the major administrative problems of its 1910 predecessor, we now turn to those that were associated with the *1923 Act*. First, responsibility for prosecution was divided between the federal and provincial authorities. This resulted in delay in some prosecutions, as arguments over who was responsible took place. It appears that federal authorities often had to try to persuade the provincial attorney general to prosecute. In other words, there was seldom a competition as to who could prefer an indictment first. In some cases, a passive provincial government meant no prosecution was undertaken (e.g., Report #3). This problem was gradually resolved over the period 1923/24 to 1951/52 as the federal government gained primary responsibility for prosecutions (see Appendix A). By the end of the period it had a monopoly.

Second, the reports of the Registrar and Special Commissioner, as the MacQuarrie Committee suggested in 1952, became a prelude to prosecution. Given Mackenzie King's belief in publicity as the primary remedy, a report's publication was an integral part of the government's efforts to gain compliance with the law. What was called for then was a change in the nature of the reports. This was one of the recommendations of the MacQuarrie Committee (Canada, 1952).

The fact that prosecution followed in such a high percentage of cases where a report concluded that a combine existed is evidence that the federal government believed that the publicity attendant to the publication of an adverse report was not enough to ensure an effective competition policy. Recall that it was King himself who in 1923 redesigned his earlier attempt in

---

106. Except, of course, in the unlikely event that there were no violations of the *Combines Investigation Act*. Such a situation seems highly unlikely. It is also inconsistent with the perceptions of contemporary commentators.

1910 after admitting it had been ineffective. While the rhetoric of publicity as a means of deterring combines remained - since few public men take delight in repudiating their own ideas - King himself changed the enforcement techniques. He no longer relied on the imposition of fines only if a combine did not end its nefarious activities within days of the publication of the report by the *ad hoc* Board of Investigation. Rather, the 1923 Act clearly contemplated prosecution of the members of a combine even if it had ceased to function. As Ball (1934, p. 65) points out,

> in the former legislation [Act of 1910] the crime was to continue to do something which had been adjudged contrary to or in violation of the law. Here the crime was in agreeing or assisting in the formation of a combine and a prosecution could take place even if the combine after investigation ceased its unlawful activities.

He concludes - and this is the crucial point - "this provision undoubtedly gave to the new legislation teeth which had been lacking under the former laws." The Act of 1923 gave a much more important role for the courts: they ascertained whether an offence had been committed and what the penalty would be (subject to the upper limits specified in the Act). In summary terms, the Prime Minister himself demonstrated that he believed that the formal disclosure of business conduct contrary to the public interest alone was not enough. Fines and imprisonment were necessary. No wonder the reports of the Registrar and Special Commissioners began to read like legal briefs. While they may have lacked in popular appeal,[107] their authors were evidently intent on seeing that a successful prosecution resulted where they felt that the evidence disclosed a combine contrary to the *Act* or *Criminal Code*.

Third, at several strategic points in the period 1923/24 to 1951/52 there was political interference with the administration of the Act. For example, the Minister failed to publish reports of the Registrar in the early 1930s especially #13 which "reached the definite conclusion that a combine did exist" (Skeoch, 1966b, p. 103). There was also the refusal to publish[108] the *Flour Milling Report* in the late 1940s which led to McGregor's resignation as Registrar (see Winnipeg Free Press, 1949). This suggests that stronger safeguards were needed to assure the independence of the officials responsible for enforcement from political influence. Yet, just as war is too important to be left entirely to the generals, so perhaps competition policy is too politically

---

107. Rosenbluth and Thorburn (1963) point out that the government downplayed the publicity attendant to the publication of the reports by the RTPC between 1952 and 1960.

108. The report was published (10 months late) a few days after McGregor resigned and after intense questioning of the Government in the House of Commons by both opposition parties. See Winnipeg Free Press (1949).

sensitive to be left entirely to an independent official, no matter how trustworthy.[109]

Effectiveness of Enforcement: We now focus on the effectiveness of the enforcement of the 1923 *Combines Investigation Act*. There were several ways in which compliance with the Act may be secured: by private negotiations between the Registrar and those whose conduct has been called into question; publicity following the report of an investigation; prosecution leading to appropriate penalties and remedies. Each will be analysed and discussed in turn.

The available data does not permit us to determine the frequency with which private negotiations between the Registrar and companies subject to a complaint were used to secure compliance with the *Combines Investigation Act*. Reference to the *Annual Reports* of the Registrar, however, does permit us to make a number of qualitative statements. The use of private negotiations typically seems to have taken place when a firm refused to supply a customer (which did not become an offence until the end of 1951).[110] For example,

> In another case, a co-operative organisation which had purchased a business as a going concern complained that manufacturers of one commodity who had long supplied the business under its previous owners refused supplies when it came under co-operative ownership. Inquiry into the circumstances was followed by the acceptance of the co-operative as a direct buyer on the same basis as had previously applied (Commissioner's *Annual Report 1948/49*, p. 12).

On the general subject to negotiations the Registrar once remarked that "In some instances adjustments in the public interest have been secured without recourse to publicity or prosecution" (Registrar's *Annual Report 1932/33*, p. 7).

---

109. In practice, the official responsible for enforcement is subject to more bureaucratic counterweights than political ones. For example, the decision to prosecute lies with senior officials in the Department of Justice. Because combines cases usually involve considerable resources, are often highly technical, requiring some knowledge of economics, and the defendants are members of at least the upper middle class, the Department of Justice are unlikely to be enthusiastic about them. Given the usual budget constraints, it is easier to deal with crimes to which the public evidently attaches more importance. The Justice Department's "filter" on the chief anti-combines official was modified in the case of civil reviewable matters under the *Competition Act* of 1986. The Director of Investigation and Research has independent authority to bring merger, abuse of dominant position and other civil matters before the quasi-judicial Competition Tribunal (see Stanbury, 1986; Sanderson and Stanbury, 1989).

110. See, for example, Registrar's *Annual Report 1929/30* (p. 15), *Annual Report 1932/32* (p. 15), and *Annual Report 1940/41* (pp. 1-2). See also the report concerned with the sale of ammunition (#28) which was resolved because "The main cause of complaint was removed; a new sales policy was announced by the manufacturer" (Skeoch, 1966b, p. 110). One indication of the importance of negotiations, where individuals approached the Registrar for advice, is presented in Table 2. However, as noted above, the Registrar was not authorized to provide such policy advice in advance.

It is difficult to conclude how extensive or effective such private negotiations were in encouraging less restrictive distribution policies by manufacturers and wholesalers. It is obvious that methods of distribution must have been somewhat less restrictive, and the fact that only one of the 41 reports of the Registrar or Special Commissioners between 1923 and 1952 was primarily concerned with the distribution policies (i.e., refusal to sell) of a firm (report #28) may reflect considerable effectiveness.[111] Note, however, that Report #22 on the distribution of tobacco products contained an appendix reviewing the law on resale price maintenance by J.A. Corry (1938). Skeoch (1964) argued that RPM was important, in varying degrees, in only six products: books, confectionery and tobacco, hardware, radio and electrical equipment, and jewellery. He found evidence to indicate that the ban on RPM (and refusal to deal) in December 1951 had released competitive pressures in previously price-maintained products. Not only did retail margins fall in real terms, but he found that wholesale gross margins also fell between 1951 and 1957 on items which had been subject to RPM arrangements.

In introducing both the 1910 and 1923 *Combines Investigation Act* Mackenzie King had stressed the value of publicity as a means of eliminating or deterring combines in restraint of trade. Publicity, in the sense it was meant by King, referred to the moral disapprobation and perhaps social stigma that would be incurred by those breaking the law or said to have done so by independent authorities. It is clearly difficult, if not impossible, to evaluate the usefulness of this enforcement tool. (No doubt this was a political advantage of which Mackenzie King was not aware.) The Registrar commented, in a similar vein that "It is impossible to estimate the effectiveness, as preventive factors,... of the publicity given to the Act through different investigations which have been held" (Registrar's *Annual Report 1929/30*, p. 15). However, the suppression of reports by Ministers in the 1930s and the long delay in publishing the *Flour Milling Report* in the late 1940s suggests that at least some ministers, at least, felt that the publicity given to firms which appeared to have broken the law was not to be encouraged or that it embarrassed the government in some way. Perhaps the minister succumbed to intense lobbying by those whose conduct had been impugned. Mackenzie King's approach to combines and other restraints of trade was based on the "abuse theory of detriment." For example, in introducing the 1910 Act King stated that it was "in no way aimed against trusts, combines and mergers as such, but rather only at the possible wrongful use or abuse of their power, of which certain of these combinations may be guilty."[112] As

---

111. Of course it may also reflect the fact that potential complainants were worried that the firm complained of may take retaliatory action which the Registrar would be powerless to stop (e.g., orders go missing, the wrong orders are sent, etc.).

112. House of Commons, *Debates*, April 12, 1910, p. 6823.

Skeoch (1966b, p. viii) notes, "since... detriment was assumed to be due to deliberate wrong-doing on the part of businessmen, [then] the cure was to publish far and wide the nature of such unconscionable or misguided conduct..." Although the issue was construed largely in terms of morality, there has been no broad public support for competition as the most desirable means by which to allocate scarce resources.[113] Rather, the public has been prepared to tolerate a wide range of public and private restraints on trade - so long as they don't go "too far." How far is "too far" is, of course, not well defined. It is largely a product of contemporary attitudes. Public opinion, which moves politicians (particularly those in power), is in turn shaped by economic conditions (e.g., inflation, unemployment, recession, the rate of growth).[114] Moreover, competition policy is an issue which lends itself to the practice of symbolic politics which focuses on the public's perceptions of the efficacy of a policy rather than its substantive effects.

The number and other characteristics of prosecutions under the *Combines Investigation Act*, the third method of enforcing the Act, is described in Table 11. There was a total of 24 prosecutions <u>started</u> in the period 1923/24 to 1951/52,[115] of which convictions were obtained in all but four instances. In contrast in the period 1889 to 1922/23 there were only 11 prosecutions in seven of which the Crown was successful in securing a conviction. Therefore, measured by their number and success, prosecutions in the period 1923/24 to 1951/52 showed a considerable improvement over the earlier period.

It should be noted, however, that enforcement activity was mainly directed against price-fixing offences. The only two cases involving a merger charge were unsuccessful, mainly for technical reasons.[116] Only one monopoly case was brought,[117] and that was so blatant it was difficult to see how a conviction could have been avoided,[118] although the accused were acquitted at the trial level.

Resources for Enforcement: In any evaluation consideration must be made not only of outputs (i.e., the enforcement activity), but also the inputs. As has

---

113. The problem is more than the fact that competition policy is a public good. It lies in Canada's economic culture.

114. The linkages between the changing stated objectives of Canadian competition policy and contemporary economic conditions are discussed in Gorecki and Stanbury (1984).

115. This excludes one patent case taken to the Exchequer Court. See Skeoch (1966b, pp. 110-111).

116. See *R. v. Canadian Import Co. et al.* (1933) 61 C.C.C. 114 (Trial); (1935) 62 C.C.C. 342; and *R. v. Staples et al.* (1940) 74 C.C.C. 178.

117. *R. v. Eddy Match Co. et al.* (1952) 104 C.C.C. 39 (Trial); (1954) 109 C.C.C. (Appeal).

118. But see the analysis of Waverman (1985).

been remarked before the office of the Registrar was quite small: 1.5 person-years in 1923; three in 1925; eight in 1941; 34 in 1951/52 (of which only 13 were professional staff).[119] Ball (1934, p. 99) states that

> the policy of the Registrar has been to administer the law with as small a staff as possible... in ordinary times the staff consists of the Registrar, one male assistant and two or three competent women secretaries.... when the situation demands additional aid, temporary help is procured.

The total annual cost (in nominal dollars) of administering the 1923 Act in its first eight years ranged from $22,000 to $90,000 p.a. See Table 13. The costs of individual inquiries ranged from $7217 (Report #3) to $41,591 (Report #1). Even the two reports (#6a, 6b) on the Proprietary Articles Trade Association cost only $36,543 (Ball, 1934, p. 100). No wonder that Ball (1934, p. 100) was able to state that "with the economical record already compiled in administration the taxpayer have little to fear in the future, even if necessity demands a somewhat more complex organization."

Rosenbluth and Thorburn (1963, p. 3) point out that it was not until 1948 that total expenditures for investigation and enforcement exceeded $100,000. They described the resources devoted to competition policy prior to the early 1950s as "prolonged privation." As Table 13 indicates, expenditures were a trivial $3400 in 1935/36, they rose to $61,800 in 1940/41 then fell during World War II, even in nominal dollars. By 1946/47, they had increased to $77,600. Then they more than doubled in two years (in nominal dollars), rising to $267,000 in 1952/53. In constant (1949) dollars, expenditures on administration and enforcement doubled from 1945/46 to 1946/47 and then doubled again by 1950/51.

Importance of Industries Investigated: The effectiveness of the way in which these people administered the Act can be examined by reference to the size and scope of industries investigated and prosecuted, and any evidence as to whether a successful prosecution resulted in lower prices or cessation of similar schemes by other industries.[120] The evidence in Tables 9 and 14 suggests that the activities of the Registrar were directed toward large industries which were regional or national in scope. Reynolds (1940, p. 154) comes to a similar conclusion when he remarks that, "The commodity must be of considerable importance in commerce, and the agreement in question must cover a considerable area." The post-war prosecutions of the rubber industry, fine papers, matches and electrical wire and cable would support and strengthen Reynold's conclusion.

---

119. See Bladen (1956, p. 230, footnote 23) and Rosenbluth and Thornburn (1963, p. 55). The number of professionals rose to 21 in 1952/53 (Rosenbluth and Thorburn, 1963, p. 55).

120. For a careful study of more recent years, see Shorthill and Jones (1990).

For 10 reports between 1948 and 1953 which resulted in as many prosecutions, we can draw upon Rosenbluth and Thorburn's assessment - see Table 14. They found that seven industries that were investigated involved a rather small amount of economic activity, under $2.50 per $1000 of GNP. Rubber products was the largest industry investigated, with $11.90 per $1000 of GNP. They rated four of the 10 investigations as "not effectively handled," even though in two of the four cases convictions were obtained. The bases for their conclusions can be summarized as follows:

- Dental supplies: The report found a combine among members of the Canadian Dental Trade Association, acquitted because it was not proven that the actions of corporate officers had been authorized by their corporations (this resulted in an amendment in 1949); dentists report that the agreement is still in existence.
- Matches: The fines were low in relation to the company's profits; the monopoly was not dissolved; no prohibition order was issued (but the provision was not enacted until after the conviction); "it may therefore be assumed that monopoly control continues."
- Flour milling: The report found an elaborate price fixing agreement; no steps were taken to prosecute.
- Fine papers: Although the firms were convicted, fined and made subject to a prohibition order, "the record suggests that, nevertheless, competition in the sale of fine papers has not [been] restored" (Rosenbluth and Thorburn, 1963, pp. 68, 69).

Effect on Prices: It is not possible to say that anti-combines prosecutions were successful in terms of the fact that prices fell, there was no repetition of the offence, and that other firms were deterred from undertaking illegal price conspiracies. An authoritative answer would require an extraordinary amount of research. There is, however, sufficient fragmentary evidence available to suggest that in some instances the investigations (with their public report) and the prosecution of some cases was an effective method of enforcement.

First, there is the direct impact of a successful prosecution or investigation on prices. (Presumably if the conspiracy has any effect at all prices would be higher than in its absence.) There are three recorded instances where an investigation/prosecution led to a lowering of prices: radio tubes, anthracite coal, and tobacco products.[121]

Second, a successful prosecution should deter the firms from repeating the offence (as well as deterring other firms considering violating the law in this area). The evidence indicates that no firm was a recidivist with respect

---

121.   Reports #14, 17, 22 per Skeoch (1966b, pp. 104, 105, 107).

to *Combines Investigation Act* offences in the period 1923/24 to 1951/52.[122] In this sense, enforcement of the Act deterred repetition. However, this conclusion needs several important qualifications. First, in one instance (Report #28) the company which was the subject of the report, Canadian Industries Ltd., avoided any court action by agreeing to change its distribution policy. In an identical situation a decade later, CIL again avoided any punitive action by agreeing to change its distribution policy following a negative report by the RTPC in 1959 (RTPC, 1959). Second, Report #10 (October 4, 1930) led to a successful prosecution of the members of the Electrical Estimators Association. Thirty years later a similar organisation was prosecuted *R.* vs. *Electrical Contractors of Ontario*.[123] Third, some companies were the subject of a report in which the Registrar or Special Commissioner found no combination, but recommended continued government monitoring of the industry. In two instances there was a subsequent report and successful prosecution.[124] A corollary of this discussion is that instances in which the Registrar found a combine but the federal Minister of Labour decided not to publish the report or send it to provincial authorities, despite a strong finding of an illegal combine, can but result in that industry coming up for a subsequent investigation. This occurred with the flour milling reports of December 1931 (Report #13) and the subsequent report in December 29, 1948 (Report #32). In summary, investigations/prosecutions seem to have had some deterrent effect, but there are important exceptions that have to be borne in mind.

Deterrence: The final dimension to effectiveness is the deterrent effect of the legislation on other than those actually under investigation. King clearly understood this when in 1923, concerning the *Combines Investigation Act*, he stated:

> The value of a measure of this kind is not to be estimated by the number of prosecutions that take place, nor by the number of investigations. Rather is it to be estimated by the power of prevention which lies in the fact that it is known that a certain course of procedure will inevitably lead to an investigation and disclosure of conduct that is contrary to the public interest. Is it not desirable to have upon the statute books of this country a power of that kind which stands at all times as a safeguard of the interest of the public? (House of Commons, *Debates*, May 8, 1923, p. 2605).

---

122. Excluded from this statement are cases where a firm was prosecuted several times as the result of one report. Perhaps the best example is the three prosecutions which took place as a result of report #36 dealing with the rubber industry.

123. *R. v. Electrical Contractors Association of Ontario and Dent* (1960) 127 C.C.C. 273 (Trial); (1961) 131 C.C.C. 145.

124. For the first case (*R. v. McGavin Bakeries et al.* (1948)) see reports #11 and 31 and for the second case (*R. v. Eddy Match Co. et al.*), see reports #8 and 35 as listed in Table 5.

Again data are difficult to obtain and generally impressionistic. In the case of the Proprietary Articles Trade Association which dissolved as a result of Report #6, the Registrar commented,

> There are many evidences that the findings in the case of the Proprietary Articles Trade Association have been taken into consideration by manufacturers and others in deciding sales policies, and that they have had weight in their decisions. More than one scheme similar in aim to that of the Proprietary Articles Trade Association, if not similar in methods, and possessed of possibilities of injury to the public, has been abandoned or has become ineffective partly, if not largely, through the influence of the findings in the P.A.T.A. case. It is impossible to estimate the effectiveness, as preventive factors, of that decision and others and of the publicity given to the Act through the different investigations which have been held. The public hearings in the recent A.B.C. [Amalgamated Builders' Council] case have served a highly useful purpose in this respect, in creating greater public interest in the Combines Investigation Act and in making its provisions more widely known, better understood, and therefore more generally observed (*Annual Report*, 1929/30, p. 15).

Again no doubt such a ripple effect existed but it is difficult to be precise about its magnitude and variance over time.

To summarize, the administration and enforcement of the *Combines Investigation Act* very likely increased the effectiveness of competition policy in Canada by a noticeable amount between 1923/24 and 1951/52 compared to the period 1889 to 1922/23. Administration and enforcement in both periods, however, was handicapped by inadequate resources[125] and a political environment which did little more than tolerate competition policy as a necessary evil. In other words, things got better, but, as our school report cards used to say, there is much room for improvement.

7.0 CONCLUSIONS

7.1 Long Search for a Viable Method of Enforcement

Canada, at least compared to the U.S., was very slow to find practicable machinery to enforce its competition policy legislation. While the first legislation was enacted in 1889 - a year before the more famous *Sherman Act* in the U.S. - Canada did not put in place viable methods of investigating and prosecuting illegal restraints of trade until 1923. As noted in Figure 1, responsibility for enforcement was shifted several times:

- 1889-1910   Provincial attorneys-general
- 1910-1919   Individual applications to a judge to establish a *prima facie* case, then an *ad hoc* Board of Investigation made a report to the Minister.

---

125. But Rosenbluth and Thorburn (1963, p. 31) state that "McGregor apparently felt that (except during the Conservative regime) he was getting all the funds and staff that he needed. See *Hansard*, 1946, p. 3088."

Fines imposed only if the combine did not cease its operations.

- 1919-1921   Board of Commerce
- 1923-1935   Registrar (and Special Commissioners)

While there were nine prosecutions in the decade after the vitiating word "unlawfully" was removed in 1900, the provincial attorneys general played a very modest role in <u>initiating</u> (as opposed to prosecuting) such cases.

While the *Combines Investigation Act* of 1910 created an additional investigatory apparatus, it was so cumbersome that it was used only once in its nine year history.[126] Despite the fact that the Board of Investigation found a combine existed, the case was not prosecuted. Therefore, by 1919, when rising inflation pushed the federal government to both create the Board of Commerce to try to grapple with rising prices and to investigate combines, there had been only 10 combines prosecutions in Canada. In other words, over the first three decades of Canadian anti-combines law, the average number of prosecutions was only 0.33 cases per year. Yet, there are plenty of accounts suggesting that horizontal and vertical restraints of trade (such as RPM) were widespread.[127]

The contrast between the Canadian fumbling to find a viable enforcement process and the simplicity and directness of the U.S. approach is enormous. In the U.S. responsibility from the beginning lay with the federal Attorney General reflecting the U.S. law's focus on interstate commerce. While a special antitrust division was not set up until 1905, the number of prosecutions was at first several times the Canadian level and by 1905 to 1914 from four to 30 times the Canadian level. Furthermore, there is nothing to suggest that Canada should have less of a problem with respect to conspiracies and other offences. Canda was a much smaller market than the U.S. with high tariffs which greatly facilitated trust formation. However, the tariff has rarely been used as an appropriate remedy despite the fact that, in some instances, it clearly helped support cartels and that since 1897 legislated authority existed to reduce tariffs in relation to competition policy (Gorecki, 1981, pp. 185-192).

In the U.S. between 1890 and 1904 the government brought an average of less than 1.5 cases per year (Weaver, 1977, p. 27). The reasons given for this initial low level of activity include the following: some of the federal

---

126. It may be that the onset of W.W.I in 1914 effectively forestalled enforcement although there was much concern about profiteering. Ball (1934, p. 51) points out that under the *War Measures Act* of 1914 an Order in Council (PC 2777) was passed on November 10, 1916 designed to "prevent undue enhancement of the cost of living." Section 498 of the *Criminal Code* was amended to delete the words "unduly" and "unreasonably" in cases involving the "necessaries of life" (staple foods, clothing, and fuel). Excess stocks of necessaries were prohibited and people were required to sell any excess "at prices no higher than are reasonable and just." In 1919, S. 498 was amended to return it to its original language. More generally, see Cheffins (1991).

127. See, for example, *Wampole v. Karn* (1906) 11 O.L.R. 619, and *R. v. Beckett* (1910) 15 C.C.C. 408.

attorneys general were antagonistic to the *Sherman Act*; there was uncertainty about the Act's constitutionality; there was no special appropriation granted to the Department of Justice for antitrust purposes and the entire department had only 18 lawyers during the period (Weaver, 1977, p. 27). However, in 1904 an appropriation of $500,000 (this is equivalent to about $4 million in 1989) for antitrust work permitted the Department to hire five full-time lawyers to work on antitrust matters. From 1905 through 1909 the average number of cases prosecuted was almost eight per year. In Canada, this was a period of high activity, but the average was less than two prosecutions per year. In the U.S., the average for 1910 to 1914 was 31 prosecutions p.a., a level that was not reached again until the late 1930s (Weaver, 1977, p. 28). In Canada, there was only one case brought in this period. In 1915, despite an increase in the number of antitrust staff lawyers to 18, prosecutions in the U.S. fell to an average of seven per year. During W.W.I, President Wilson "simply gave orders that certain antitrust cases were not to be brought."

While the U.S. had a clearly designated federal official responsible for antitrust since 1905 (and added the Federal Trade Commission in 1914), by 1923, when the second *Combines Investigation Act* was introduced, Canada had "experimented" with three quite different administrative processes, all of which could only be described as unsuccessful.[128] Moreover, the *Sherman Act* of 1890 provided strong incentives for private civil actions to enforce the law, namely treble damages. It was not until 1976 that Canada amended its legislation to provide for private, civil actions for single damages (Strekaf, 1991). Recall, however, that between 1889 and 1910 at least nine private civil actions were brought in which the plaintiff relied upon the anti-combines provisions of the Criminal Code. In about one-half the actions, plaintiffs successfully relied on the *Criminal Code* (see Appendix B).

7.2 Slow to Expand Substantive Provisions

Canada was slow to create statutory provisions to address restraints of trade beyond price-fixing and market-sharing agreements. While S.2 of the *Sherman Act* condemned monopoly and monopolization in 1890, Canada did not do so until 1935 (Stanbury, 1978). While the U.S. used their law to actually attack monopoly in less than a decade after it was enacted, Canada's first monopoly case (*Eddy Match*) was not prosecuted until the early 1950s (Waverman, 1985). More importantly, the U.S. brought many times more monopoly cases over the years as did Canada and with much more effect.

Despite the very general language of S. 1 of the *Sherman Act* of 1890, it was used to attack single-firm RPM cases shortly after the turn of the

---

128. Recall that the flurry of prosecutions between 1903 and 1910 had nothing to do with any change in the method of enforcement.

century.[129] In Canada, RPM and refusal to deal by a single firm were made illegal *per se* in December 1951 (Hunter, 1991). Yet there is plenty of evidence that both single firm and collective versions of these restraints were quite widespread before the turn of the century (recall the Dominion Grocers Guild which began collective RPM in 1884!). The membership of the Proprietary Articles Trade Association in the mid-1920s included 157 manufacturers, 28 wholesale druggists and 2732 retail druggists (Ball, 1934, p. 78). Its stated objective was to maintain fixed mark ups of 33.3% for retailers and 16.7% for jobbers. Petitions containing over 4000 names resulted in a formal inquiry by the Registrar in 1926. He found there was an illegal combine that fixed resale prices, limited competition and enhanced prices (Ball, 1934, p. 80). Lobbying by PATA resulted in a report by a Special Commissioner. He reached the same conclusion. "Following the publication of this report the P.A.T.A. withdrew its stop list and ceased operations" (Ball, 1934, p. 82). The Association, however, did challenge the constitutionality of both the Criminal code and the 1923 Act. Both were upheld.[130] But the federal government did not prosecute P.A.T.A. RPM continued to be used in a number of product lines for years prior to the 1951 legislation (see Skeoch, 1964; 1966a).

In 1935, Canada enacted S. 498A of the *Criminal Code* to deal with price discrimination and predatory pricing, apparently in response to the plethora of evidence adduced before the Royal Commission on Price Spreads (see Forster, 1962). Yet, the first prosecutions did not take place until 1957 (see Dunlop, 1979).. In the U.S. the *Robinson-Patman Act* was passed in 1936 to deal with price discrimination. A substantial number of prosecutions followed quite quickly. Although some economists have been sharply critical of this legislation (see Posner, 1976), we must question why it took so long in Canada to attempt to use S. 498A. Perhaps there was no real problem, and the enactment was very largely a <u>symbolic</u> gesture to appease a temporarily aroused public opinion shaped by the unusual period of the Great Depression.

7.3 Failure to Condemn "Bare" Cartels

From the beginning, Canada has psychologically, legally and administratively failed to come to grips with the evils of simple price-fixing,

---

129. RPM was first condemned in the U.S. in two cases decided in 1908 (*Bobbs-Merrill* v. *Strauss* (1908) 210 U.S. 399; (1908) *Scribner* v. *Strauss* (1908) 210 U.S. 352). In *J.D. Park and Sons* v. *Hartman* (1907) 153 Fed. 24, a lower court ruled for the first time that a system of RPM contracts was illegal under common law and the *Sherman Act* in the absence of proof showing the necessity for such a system. In *Dr. Miles Medical Co.* v. *J.D. Park and Sons* (1911) 220 U.S. 373, the Supreme Court held that RPM contracts were illegal, citing the *Hartman* case as precedent. Despite this decision, the legality of RPM was still uncertain until the early 1920s. In the 1920s decisions of the courts and the Federal Trade Commission narrowed the scope of permissible RPM to virtual *per se* illegality. See Seligman and Love (1932).

130. (1929) D.L.R. 802 (Supreme Court of Canada); (1931) 2 D.L.R. 1 (Privy Council).

market-sharing or entry-barring cartels among direct competitors. Section 1 of the *Sherman Act* stated that

> Every contract, combination in the form of trust or otherwise, or conspiracy, in restraint of trade or commerce among the several States, or with foreign nations, is declared to be illegal. Every person who shall make any contract or engage in any combination or conspiracy hereby declared illegal shall be deemed guilty of a felony...

In contrast, the Canadian legislation of 1889 condemned only "unlawful" agreements that lessened competition "unduly" or enhanced prices "unreasonably."[131] Although the vitiating word "unlawfully" was removed in 1900, "unduly" remains in the law to this day! The Canadian Bar Association, not to mention every business trade association, supports the retention of this critical qualifying word - even for bare cartel agreements - i.e., those whose only objective and effect was to fix prices, allocate market shares, agree on mark-ups and so on. While "unduly" was the cause of few acquittals in conspiracy cases before the mid-1960s, after that time it was the cause of more than one-half the acquittals in conspiracy cases (see Stanbury, 1991).

The central problem is that in framing legislation so as to try to preserve what we would now call the efficiency benefits of mergers, Mackenzie King greatly muddied the waters with respect to garden variety cartels. This confusion was rife in the U.S. in 1890 when the *Sherman Act* was passed (see Weaver, 1977, Ch. 2). However, by 1910 (and certainly by 1923) King should have been able to distinguish horizontal mergers (which may be good, bad, indifferent or both good and bad from a policy perspective) from horizontal agreements to fix prices. In the case of mergers it makes sense (if one has to use the criminal law) to condemn them only if they operate to the detriment of the public. For "bare cartels," such a requirement (or qualifying word such as "unduly") is both unnecessary and undesirable. King had an intense desire to differentiate Canada's approach from the U.S. in 1910 (see Ball, 1934, p. 39) before the U.S. Supreme Court distinguished between agreements that were to be held to be illegal *per se* and others to be judged by the rule of reason in the *Standard Oil* case of 1911.[132] In any event, King and his legislation did not distinguish between price fixing agreements which undermine the very foundation of a capitalist market economy and mergers

---

131. Under the Act of 1889 and its successors in the *Criminal Code*, it was illegal to enhance unreasonably the price of an article. This provision was carried over when the Code sections were incorporated (with modifications) into S. 32 of the *Combines Investigation Act* in 1960. It can now be found in S. 45 of the *Competition Act* of 1986 (as renumbered under the Revised Statutes, effective December 12, 1988).

132. *United States* v. *Standard Oil* (1911) 221 U.S. 1. See also the earlier case *United States* v. *Addyston Pipe and Steel* (1897) 175 U.S. 211.

which may strengthen competition, increase efficiency, or severely reduce competition.

In 1889, 1910, 1919, 1923, 1935 and 1937 when the legislation was amended, Canadian federal legislators failed to appreciate the wider and serious consequences of not condemning cartels in an unqualified manner. The fact is that policy makers - and certainly judges in some of the early cases - were as much concerned with the effects of conspiracies on rivals excluded from the cartel or punished by it for failing to join, as they were about the effects of high prices on consumers until well into the 1920s. It is not by chance that the first and all sequent *Combines Investigation Acts* (until 1960) condemned price fixing conspiracies in terms of their detriment to consumers or producers.[133]   In 1910, the term producers was taken to refer to both farmers and to businesses (manufacturers, wholesalers, retailers, etc.). Several judges followed the Privy Council where the "public" was held to include those engaged in the production and distribution of articles of consumption, as well as the consumers.[134]

7.4   Immediate Pressures Largely Explained Changes in Competition Law and Its Enforcement

Our review of the first six decades of Canadian competition policy make it clear that changes in the substantive law and machinery for administration and enforcement were largely the result of two types of highly contemporary factors: current economic conditions, notably inflation, depression, and widespread evidence of cartels, and clear evidence of the failure of existing legislation, including enforcement procedures.

The Act of 1889 was largely attributable to the public's appreciation that cartels and many other forms of restraint were widespread in Canada. The amendment in 1900 was necessary to remove a fatal flaw in the original legislation deliberately inserted because of the putative ignorance of the common law on restraints of trade. The 1910 legislation was remedial in at least two senses. It was to provide better machinery to enforce the Act of 1889 (which had been put into the *Criminal Code*) and it was a political response to public and political agitation over a current large wave of

---

133.   The 1910 Act used the phrase "to the detriment of consumers or producers." In the 1923 Act this was changed to "to the detriment of or against the interest of the public, whether consumers, producers or others..." This language was also used in the *Combines and Fair Prices Act* of 1919.

134.   (1913) A.C. 781 at p. 801. See also Hodgins, J.A. in *Canadian Wholesale Grocers* (1922) 53 O.L.R. 627 where he cites the Privy Council's interpretation. More generally, see Rutherford and Tyhurst, Chapter 8 in this volume.

consolidations and rising prices.[135] (At the same time, King created another combines offence which included both conspiracies to fix prices, etc. and mergers which operated to the detriment of consumers or producers.)

In 1919, a combination of rapidly rising prices and the obvious failure of the slow and cumbersome machinery created in 1910, prompted passage of the *Combines and Fair Prices Act* and *Board of Commerce Act*. Its (predictable?) failure on constitutional grounds created a legal and administrative vacuum[136] together with the failure of the 1910 Act resulted in the second *Combines Investigation Act* of 1923.

The short-lived *Dominion Trade and Industry Commission Act* of 1935 which gave the Commission the power to approve cartel agreements to deal with "wasteful or demoralizing competition," was clearly a response to the changed attitudes engendered by the Great Depression and a recognition of some of the weaknesses of the 1923 Act (see Cheffins, 1991). The enactment of S. 498A re price discrimination and predatory pricing was the direct result of Stevens Commission which was another child of the Depression (see Cheffins, 1991).

The 1951 legislation to address RPM and refusal to deal finally addressed a long-standing gap in Canadian competition legislation. The MacQuarrie Committee, which recommended the legislation, was created as a means of diffusing a political crisis associated with the resignation of Fred McGregor in October 1949 because the Minister refused to publish a report as required by law (see Rosenbluth and Thorburn, 1963; Hunter, 1991).

In summary, therefore, the evidence is clear that over the first six decades of its life, changes in Canadian competition policy has been driven by the economic and political exigencies of the moment and the weaknesses inherent in previous legislation. It was definitely not the result of a planned, coherent process reflecting thoughtful analysis and a broad construction of the public interest. No wonder Bismarck is said to have stated that there were two activities that should be shielded from the public's eyes lest they become disillusioned: the making of sausages, and the making of legislation.

7.5 Fluctuations in Intensity of Enforcement

This study indicates that the enforcement of the *Combines Investigation Act* and the *Criminal Code* sections relevant to competition policy between

---

135. Ball (1934, p. 37) states that by 1910, "the country under the protection of a consistently high tariff policy had witnessed a constantly rising price level for several years.... The large number of industrial mergers, trade association activities and wide publicity given to monopoly evils in both Canadian and American press during these years was a stimulus for reform."

136. The Board of Commerce had exclusive authority to authorize prosecutions under the *Code* or the *Combines and Fair Prices Act* (which replaced the *Combines Investigation Act* of 1910). After November 11, 1921, the Board ceased to function as its enabling legislation had been declared unconstitutional by the Privy Council (1922) 1 A.C. 191-201.

1889 and 1952 fluctuated with respect to two very important sets of political factors. First, there were factors which transcended political parties and were outside the control of the Canadian state. In the first six decades of competition policy legislation, the most obvious examples were the two World Wars and the Great Depression. During wartime, direct price controls and the allocation of critical materials by central government in co-operation with firms, meant that competition policy was a virtual dead letter. In the Great Depression the prevailing ideology changed. The "ruinous" effects of "cutthroat competition" led to an aversion to competition policy which was reflected in non-enforcement of the *Combines Investigation Act* by the political authority and the attempt, in 1935, to allow industry self-regulation.[137] This was struck down by the courts in 1937 (Appendix A). In other words enforcement of the *Combines Investigation Act* was suspended or the whole basis of competition was changed in response to specific political and economic crisis.[138] Such a response also occurred, at least in part, in other Western democracies. During periods of high unemployment and slow growth, a possible policy response by the political authorities might be to decrease the role of competition policy. On the other hand competition policy may be seen to be the solution in which case its significance will increase. Either way, a severe recession may result in policy moves which effect competition policy significantly

The second set of political factors which influence the level of enforcement is the ideological commitment of the two major political parties to competition policy in Canada. The evidence suggests that both political parties support varied from indifference to outright hostility. Eric Kierans has commented as follows, "Despite the lip service paid to laissez-faire capitalism, competition and the virtues of the individual enterprise and initiative no Canadian government has ever believed in, to the extent of practising these principles" (in Rea and McLeod, 1976, p. 204). In the late 1940s, when the Registrar (McGregor) became "too active," he was forced to resign. Indeed, in a memorandum attached to his letter of resignation the Registrar was clearly apprehensive that the government of the day would introduce an amendment to the *Combines Investigation Act* with the "result of limiting the effectiveness of the Registrar" at a time when there was "a greater need for

---

137. See McConnell (1971) and Finkel (1979).

138. A similar pattern occurred in the U.S. in the 1920s, the average number of antitrust prosecutions was about 11 p.a. (Weaver, 1977, p. 28). However, with the advent of Roosevelt's *National Industrial Recovery Act* under which sanctioned industry-wide cooperation, prosecutions fell to a level of only six per year. This was sharply reversed when the *NRA* was declared unconstitutional and Thurman Arnold became assistant attorney general for antitrust. He got the budget increased, hired some economists and increased the number of lawyers from 59 to 144 in one year (Weaver, 1977, p. 28). Prosecutions rose to over 50 p.a. before Arnold left the post in 1943.

strong action than there has been at any time in the past twenty-five years" (as quoted in Rosenbluth and Thorburn, 1963, pp. 11-12). Such lack of support for the enforcement of competition policy by the cabinet is consistent with the left-wing view of the world (see Young, 1974). If true, it implies real limits on the extent to which competition policy can be expected to go.

Few would deny that a democratically elected government has the right to determine an appropriate policy response in times of national crisis (i.e., the Great Depression, World Wars). This may even require radical changes to competition policy. In more normal times perhaps the official in charge of the enforcement of competition policy should be given more independence. At all times, the decision to prosecute has been a political decision (see Weaver, 1977). Presumably if Parliament has passed a law it wants it to be enforced and not subject to the whim of a particularly strong pressure group. One way in which Parliament could, perhaps, have ensured more compliance with its wishes would have been to let the Registrar have the power to decide whether a case should be prosecuted. This would require that the federal Department of Justice give up its monopoly over the decision to prosecute. However, even here one must tread carefully. Under the *Competition Act* of 1986 today's equivalent of the Registrar was given considerable discretion in bringing certain civil categories of cases before an expert tribunal (Competition Tribunal) - see Stanbury (1986). However, the way that power has been used has been severely criticized (Davidson, 1989). Even the Tribunal in the Texaco/Imperial case noted in its November 10, 1989 comments that some of the Director's actions were considered by at least one Tribunal member "highly presumsptious, if not arrogant. The message that might be taken by some people from that conduct is that the Director has determined to approve the merger regardless of what the Tribunal decides."[139] Even in the area of routine or bare cartels, administration and enforcement has consisted of negotiated settlements rather than prosecutions in some important cases (Stanbury, 1991). Thus if one believes in vigorous prosecution of bare cartels and in clarifying the law, an optimal enforcement strategy giving today's Registrar (Director) greater independence, as the reforms in 1986 have done, is only a necessary not a sufficient condition for implementation of such a strategy.

7.6 Competition Policy Reflects Basic Values

If a nation's laws and administrative practices quite closely reflect its character, our review of the administration and enforcement of competition over the period 1889-1952 reveals the following about Canadians and their federal government. First, Canadians have been extremely reluctant to do more than rhetorically condemn a wide variety of restraints of trade. They

---

139. Competition Tribunal, "Comments Delivered on November 10, 1989" re DIR and Imperial Oil Limited, CT-89/3, p. 21.

were unwilling to create machinery that would in <u>practical</u> terms investigate and take tough-minded action that would go to the root of such restraints. As described above, the government was very slow (at least in the period 1889-1923) to learn how to create even a minimally effective regime to enforce the laws in restraint of trade. It was also very slow to create new substantive legislation to deal with monopoly, and resale price maintenance/refusal to supply. Although mergers that lessened competition to the public detriment were condemned in 1910 (at the height of a huge merger boom), the first two prosecutions (both unsuccessful) occurred in 1935 and 1949 respectively. (The next two merger cases were decided in 1960; again the Crown was unsuccessful in both cases - see Rosenbluth and Thorburn, 1963.)

Second, the design flaws in the legislation of 1889, 1910, and 1919 with respect to the offence provisions and procedural matters were so serious, judged by comparison to the U.S., that it is difficult to avoid the conclusion that the legislation was never intended to be effective. It could fairly be construed as a series of symbolic gestures to "solve" short term political crises while - by design - not actually having any or much impact on restraints of trade. Recall also that under the *Combines Investigation Act* of 1910, the firms or individuals whose conduct had been impugned and against whom a judge had found a *prima facie* case (advanced by a private individual, not the Crown) was given the power to recommend to the Minister the name of a person to serve on the three-person *ad hoc* Board of Investigation. In other words, King set up the process like an arbitration panel dealing with an interest dispute. However, while there are good reasons why employee and employer representatives should participate in a labour board, it is diifficult to see why that model applies to restraint of trade cases.

While his rhetoric was concerned about the public interest and protecting consumers from high prices established by cartels, King was totally unable "to screw up his courage to the sticking point" in specifying enforcement procedures to treat price fixing as a crime analogous to conspiracy to engage in robbery. Note further that King sought - with a quite predictable lack of success - to rely primarily on the therapeutic powers of publicity to stamp out existing and deter future combines. Under his Act a fine could be imposed - and quite a modest one of $1000/day given the potential stakes for the accused - only if the combine continued in operation for <u>more</u> than 10 days <u>after</u> the Board's report found them guilty of unduly lessening competition or unreasonably enhancing the price of an article. In other words, operating a combine was not illegal under the 1910 Act.[140]

---

140. Note, however, that the *Criminal Code* provisions remained in force (until 1960) so that an individual could lay an Information in an effort to persuade the provincial or federal Attorney General to undertake a prosecution. Such a prosecution would, of course, be aided by an unfavorable report by a Board of Investigation. "It was believed that when an odious combine had been revealed there would be no alternative for the administrators but to pursue a vigorous prosecution" (Ball, 1934, p. 40).

Having seen the utter failure of the 1910 Act, King continued to embrace the rhetoric of publicity in introducing the 1923 Act, but now he provided for prosecution as the logical outcome of the investigation, appraisal and report functions. King, however, in sharp contrast to the U.S. approach, created a process which had a number of "filters" in which by inaction or deliberate political decision a combine might be spared the slight embarrassment of prosecution. These included

- the reliance on the use of *ad hoc* Special Commissioners to conduct formal inquiries,
- Ministerial discretion over the publication of a report by the Registrar (but not by a Special Commissioner, and
- giving the Minister of Justice discretion over whether an unfavorable report will be referred to a provincial attorney-general for prosecution.

Should a prosecution be brought and be successful, the traditional penalty or remedy was a fine with a modest maximum: $10,000 for corporations charged under the *Criminal Code* and $25,000 under the *Combines Investigation Act* (see Stanbury, 1976). Since the vast majority of conspiracy cases (there were very few monopoly or merger cases) were brought under the *Code*,[141] the lower ceiling on fines prevailed.

The history of competition policy from 1889 to 1952 makes it clear that only some of the more egregious restraints of trade were addressed by federal legislation. The critical point is that in the highest council of government (i.e., the cabinet) it seems that there has never been any intention to do otherwise. This was not a case of the reach exceeding the grasp. The law and machinery were an accurate reflection of the men that put them in place. If the intent had been to have an antitrust policy at least as effective as that in the U.S., it is inconceivable that the architects could have designed the building so badly several times. Even a modest amount of *a priori* analysis would have made the serious defects apparent. Even 20/60 foresight would have been sufficient. The point is that there was no political will, and that failure of will was not simply due to conflicting political pressures.

The architects did not believe in the efficacy of freely competitive processes and that the state should be active in striking down private restraints on trade. There was (and is even today) a remarkable naivete about the putative benefits of "combinations."[142] Recall King's plaintive desire in passing the 1910 Act to "conserve to the public some of the benefits which arise from large organizations of capital for the purpose of business and commerce." The

---

141. It should be noted that of the first 13 prosecutions (those prior to W.W. II), eight were brought under both the *Code* and the *Act* (Stanbury, 1991). Thereafter, the Code was used almost exclusively (except in merger or monopoly cases).

142. This point is developed in more detail in Stanbury (1991).

blunt fact is that legislators at least up to the mid-1930s were confused about the nature of the problem they said they wished to address. While the Act of 1889 was clearly focused on agreements to fix prices or limit output, the first *Combines Investigation Act* defined a combine so as to include price-fixing/market sharing conspiracies and "what is known as a trust, monopoly or merger." While a merger was defined, neither a trust nor monopoly were. Yet King evidently knew what a monopoly was and what its effects were. In an article in 1911, he defined a "modern trust" as "a monopoly in its purpose, its plans and its culmination. It is a combination that strikes down all competitors. The parties combine to control the market and to control it without competition" (King, 1911, p. 104). He was referring to a series of mergers which led to a monopoly. The objective of such arrangements, King (1911, p. 105) made clear, is to fix the prices at which they purchase raw materials and to fix their selling prices. The point is that King never did distinguish between bare cartels and other "combinations" which might or might not be, on balance, against the public interest.

In summary, competition legislation and its enforcement in Canada between 1889 and 1952 was an accurate reflection of the set of values that dominated the nation's economy and public policy. Only some of the most severe forms of anti-competitive behaviour were addressed, the tools were faulty, and the remedies very largely ineffective.

REFERENCES

Alward, Silas (1900) "Contracts in Restraint of Trade," *Canada Law Journal*, Vol. 36(21), November, pp. 612-619.

Andrews, E.B. (1889) "Trusts According to Official Investigations," *Quarterly Journal of Economics*, Vol. 3, January, pp. 117-132.

Ashley, C.A. (1940) "Investigation into an Alleged Combine of Wholesalers and Shippers of Fruit and Vegetables in Western Canada," *Canadian Journal of Economics and Political Science*, Vol. 6(2), May, pp. 288-292.

Ashley, W.J. (1890) "The Canadian Sugar Combine," *University Quarterly Review* (Toronto) Vol. 1, February, pp. 24-39. Reprinted in his *Surveys, Historic and Economic* (London, New York, etc.: Longmans, Green), pp. 361-377.

Baggaley, Carman D. (1991) "Tariffs, Combines and Politics: The Beginning of Canadian Competition Policy, 1888-1900" in R.S. Khemani and W.T. Stanbury (eds.) *Historical Perspectives on Canadian Competition Policy* (Halifax: The Institute for Research on Public Policy).

Ball, J.A. (1934) *Canadian Antitrust Legislation* (Baltimore: William and Wilkins).

Bladen, V.W. (1932) "A Note on the Reports of Public Investigations Into Combines in Canada, 1889-1932" in *Contributions to Canadian Economics* (Toronto: University of Toronto Press), pp. 61-76.

Bladen, V.W. (1938) "The Role of Trade Associations in the Determination of Prices," *Canadian Journal of Economics and Political Science*, Vol. 4, May, pp. 223-230.

Bladen, V.W. (1940) "Note on Paperboard Shipping Containers Report," *Canadian Journal of Economics and Political Science*, Vol. 6, May, pp. 293-296.

Bladen, V.W. (1945) "Canada and Cartels," *Behind the Headlines*, Vol. 6(1), October, pp. 1-24.

Bladen, V.W. (1956) "Combines & Public Policy" in *An Introduction to Political Economy* Third Edition (Toronto: University of Toronto Press), Chapter VIII, pp. 209-266.

Bliss, Michael (1973) "Another Anti-Trust Tradition: Canadian Anti-Combines Policy, 1889-1910," *Business History Review*, Vol. 47(2), Summer, pp. 177-188.

Bliss, Michael (1974) *A Living Profit* (Toronto: McClelland & Stewart).

Bliss, Michael (1987) *Northern Enterprise: Five Centuries of Canadian Business* (Toronto: McClelland and Stewart).

Boyle, James E. (1911) "How Canada Controls Her Trusts," *Twentieth Century Magazine*, August.

Boyle, James E. (1913) "Canada's Combines Investigation Act, A Lesson for the United States," *Quarterly Journal of the University of North Dakota*, Vol. III(2), January, pp. 164-170.

Brecher, Irving (1960) "Combines and Competition: A Re-appraisal of Canadian Public Policy," *Canadian Bar Review*, Vol. 38(4), December, pp. 523-593.

Brown, R.C. and R. Cook (1974) *Canada 1896-1932, A Nation Transformed* (Toronto: McClelland and Stewart).

Canada (1952) Parliament. House of Commons Committee to Study Combines Legislation. *Report and Interim Report on Resale Price Maintenance* (Ottawa: Queen's Printer) [the MacQuarrie Committee report].

Canada (1973) Consumer and Corporate Affairs, *Proposals for a New Competition Policy for Canada, First Stage*, Second Edition, (Ottawa: Information Canada).

Canada (1888) House of Commons, Select Committee to Investigate and Report Upon Alleged Combinations in Manufactures, Trade and Insurance in Canada, *Report*, Appendix (No. 3) to *Journal of the House of Commons of Canada*, Vol. 22 (Ottawa: Queen's Printer).

Canada (1935) Royal Commission on Price Spreads, *Report of the Royal Commission on Price Spreads* (Ottawa: King's Printer).

Cheffins, Brian R. (1989) "The Development of Competition Legislation, 1890-1940: A Re-Evaluation of a Canadian and American Tradition," *Osgoode Hall Law Journal*, Vol. 27, pp. 449-490.

Cheffins, Brian R. (1991) "One Step Forward, Two Steps Back, One Step Forward: Canadian Competition Law Reform, 1919 and 1935" in R.S. Khemani and W.T. Stanbury (eds.) *Historical Perspectives on Canadian Competition Policy* (Halifax: The Institute for Research on Public Policy).

Chipman, Warwick (1923) "Combinations in Restraint of Trade," *Canadian Bar Review*, Vol. 1(3), March, pp. 236-242.

Chrysler, A.C. (1963) "What Does the Common Law Say About Restraint of Trade?" *Canadian Business*, September, pp. 110-118.

Cohen, Maxwell (1938) "The Canadian Anti-Trust Laws - Doctrinal and Legislative Beginnings," *Canadian Bar Review*, Vol. 16,pp. 439-465.

Combines Investigation Board (1912) "Report of the Board of Investigation Constituted Under the Combines Investigation Act to Enquire Into the United Shoe Machinery Company of Canada," *Labour Gazette*, Vol. XIII, Nov., pp. 464-476.

Corry, J.A. (1938) "The Law on Resale Price Maintenance in Canada" in Canada, Department of Labour, Combines Investigation Commission, *Report of an Investigation into an Alleged Combine in the Province of Alberta and Elsewhere in Canada* Annex 3, Appendix 1 (Ottawa: King's Printer), pp. 89-97.

Curtis, L.A. (1938) "Resale Price Maintenance," *Canadian Journal of Economics and Political Science*, Vol. 4(3), pp. 350-361.

Davidson, Roy M. (1991) "Independence Without Accountability Won't Last" in R.S. Khemani and W.T. Stanbury (eds.) *Competition Law and Policy at the Centenary* (Halifax: The Institute for Research on Public Policy).

Dunlop, Bruce (1979) "Price Discrimination, Predatory Pricing and Systematic Delivered Pricing" in J.R.S. Prichard et al. (eds.) *Canadian Competition Policy* (Toronto: Butterworths), pp. 405-420.

Dunlop, Bruce, David McQueen & Michael Trebilcock (1987) *Canadian Competition Policy: A Legal and Economic Analysis* (Toronto: Canada Law Book).

Edgar, W.W. (1906) "Trade Combinations in Canada," *Journal of Political Economy*, Vol. 14, July, pp. 427-434.

Edwards, Corwin D. (1943) "Thurman Arnold and the Antitrust Laws," *Politican Science Quarterly*, Vol. 58(3), September, pp. 338-355.

Epp, A.E. (1973) *Cooperation Among Capitalists: The Canadian Merger Movement 1909-1913* (Baltimore: John Hopkins University, unpublished Ph.D. thesis).

Ferns, H.S. and B. Ostry (1955) *The Age of Mackenzie King* (London: William Heinemann Ltd.).

Finkel, Alvin (1979) *Business and Social Reform in the Thirties* (Toronto: James Lorimer).

Forster, Donald F. (1962) "The Politics of Combines Policy: Liberals and the Stevens Commission," *Canadian Journal of Economics and Political Science*, Vol. 28(4), pp. 511-526.

Forster, Donald F. and Colin Read (1979) "The Politics of Opportunism: The New Deal Broadcasts," *Canadian Historical Review*, Vol. 60, September, pp. 324-349.

Gillis, Peter (1980) "Big Business and the Origins of the Conservative Reform Movement in Ottawa, 1890-1912," *Journal of Canadian Studies*, Vol. 15(1), Spring, pp. 93-109.

Goodwin, C.D.W. (1961) "Industrial Combinations" in *Canadian Economic Thought: The Political Economy of a Developing Nation, 1814-1914* (Durham, N.C.: Duke University Press), pp. 138-141.

Gordon, Sanford D. (1963a) "Attitudes Towards Trusts Prior to the Sherman Act," *Southern Economic Journal*, Vol. 30, October, pp. 156-167.

Gordon, Sanford D. (1963b) "Attitudes of Economists Toward Industrial Combinations in the Decade Preceding Passage of the Sherman Act," *Western Economic Journal*, Vol. 2, Fall, pp. 24-37.

Gorecki, Paul K. (1981) *The Administration and Enforcement of Competition Policy in Canada, 1960 to 1975*, Research Monograph No. 6, Bureau of Competition Policy (Ottawa: Minister of Supply and Services Canada).

Gorecki, Paul K. and W.T. Stanbury (1979) "Canada's *Combines Investigation Act*: The Record of Public Law Enforcement" in J.R.S. Prichard, W.T. Stanbury and T.A. Wilson (eds.) *Canadian Competition Policy: Essays in Law and Economics* (Toronto: Butterworths).

Gorecki, Paul K. and W.T. Stanbury (1981a) "History of Attempts to Amend Canada's Original Competition Legislation, 1890-1900" (Vancouver: University of British Columbia, Faculty of Commerce and Business Administration).

Gorecki, Paul K. and W.T. Stanbury (1981b) "Declaring the Common Law: The Genesis of Canadian Competition Policy" (Vancouver: University of British Columbia, Faculty of Commerce and Business Administration).

Gorecki, Paul K. & W.T. Stanbury (1984) *The Objectives of Canadian Competition Policy, 1888-1983* (Montreal: The Institute for Research on Public Policy).

Gosse, R.F. (1962) *The Law on Competition in Canada* (Toronto: Carswell).

Hamilton, Walton and Irene Till (1940) *Antitrust in Action*, Monograph No. 16, U.S. Temporary national Economic Commission: Investigation of Concentration of Economic Power (Washington, D.C.: USGPO).

Hawley, Ellis (1966) *The New Deal and the Problem of Monopoly* (Princeton: Princeton University Press).

Hodges, Edward P. (1940) "Complaints of Antitrust Violations and Their Investigation: The Work of the Complaints Section of the Antitrust Division," *Law and Contemporary Problems*, Vol. 7(1), Winter, pp. 90-95.

Hodgins, Frank E. (1901) "Restraint of Trade by Societies Which are Not Trade Unions," *Canadian Law Times*, Vol. 21(1), January, pp. 1-15.

Hunter, Tamara (1991) "History of Resale Price Maintenance Legislaton" in R.S. Khemani and W.T. Stanbury (eds.) *Historical Perspectives on Canadian Competition Policy* (Halifax: The Institute for Research on Public Policy).

King, W.L.M. (1911) "How to Curb Trusts," *Lawyer and Banker and Bench and Bar Review*, Vol. 4, pp. 102-109.

King, W.L.M. (1912) "The Canadian Combines Investigation Act" in *Industrial Competition and Combination* (Philadelphia: American Academy of Political and Social Science), pp. 149-155.

Lindsey, J.D. (1987) "Reconstructing Capitalism: Business-Government Relations During the Keynesian Revolution, 1939-1950" (Ph.D. Thesis, York University, Toronto).

MacCrimmon, M.T. and W.T. Stanbury (1978) "The Reform of Canada's Merger Law and the Provisions of Bill C-13" in J.W. Rowley and W.T. Stanbury (eds.) *Competition Policy in Canada: Stage II, Bill C13* (Montreal: The Institute for Research on Public Policy), pp. 65-107.

MacDonald, T.D. (1955) "Canadian Anti-Combines Legislation," *University of Toronto School of Law Review*, Vol. 13, Spring, pp. 4-16.

MacLeod, F.N. (197?) "Combines Investigation Act: 'Detriment'" (Ottawa: Department of Justice, unpublished paper, mimeo, no date).

Magwood, J.M. (1981) *Competition Law of Canada* (Toronto: Carwell).

McConnell, W.H. (1971) "Some Comparisons of the Roosevelt and Bennett 'New Deals'," *Osgoode Hall Law Journal*, Vol. 9, November, pp. 221-260.

McFall, R.J. (1922) "Regulation of Business in Canada," *Political Science Quarterly*, Vol. 37(2), June, pp. 177-210.

McGregor, F.A. (1932) "Canadian Combines Legislation," Speech to the International Alumni Association of Toronto, April 1, mimeo.

McGregor, F.A. (1944) "Speech to the Conference of Business Newspaper Editors," Ottawa, September (Ottawa: Historical Collection, Department of Consumer and Corporate Affairs).

McGregor, F.A. (1945a) "Control of Prices in Peace and War - Some Contrasts," *Commerce Journal* (New Series), No. 5, May, pp. 1-12.

McGregor, F.A. (1945b) "Speech to the Standard-Imperial Oil Conference," Toronto, 25 October (Ottawa: Historical Collection, Department of Consumer and Corporate Affairs).

McGregor, F.A. (1946a) "Speech to the Business Newspapers Association," Toronto, 22 February (Ottawa: Historical Collection, Department of Consumer and Corporate Affairs).

McGregor, F.A. (1946b) "Speech to the Ottawa Women's Forum," Ottawa, 5 March (Ottawa: Historical Collection, Department of Consumer and Corporate Affairs).

McGregor, F.A. (1946c) "Speech to the Canadian Advertiser's Association," Toronto, 17 September (Ottawa: Historical Collection, Department of Consumer and Corporate Affairs).

McGregor, F.A. (1954) "Preventing Monopoly - Canadian Techniques" in E.H. Chamberlain (ed.) *Monopoly, Competition and Their Regulation* (London: International Economics Association), pp. 359-384.

McGregor, F.A. (1962) *The Fall and Rise of Mackenzie King: 1911-1919* (Toronto: Macmillan).

Porritt, E. (1911) *The Revolt in Canada Against the New Feudalism* (London: Cassel and Co.).

Posner, Richard (1976) *The Robinson-Patman Act: Federal Regulation of Price Differences* (Washington, D.C.: American Enterprise Institute).

Quinlan, J.J. (1966a) "Notes on Jurisprudence Relating to Canadian Anti-Combines Legislation" in L.A. Skeoch, *Restrictive Trade Practices in Canada* (Toronto: McClelland and Stewart), pp. 46-66.

Quinlan, J.J. (1966b) "Canadian Anti-Combines Legislation: 'Unduly' and 'Public Detriment'" in L.A. Skeoch, *Restrictive Trade Practices in Canada* (Toronto: McClelland and Stewart), pp. 67-75.

Restrictive Trade Practices Commission (1959) *Report Concerning the Manufacture, Distribution and Sale of Ammunition in Canada* (Ottawa: Queen's Printer).

Reynolds, L.G. (1940) *The Control of Competition in Canada* (Cambridge, Mass.: Harvard University).

Rea, K.J. and McLeod, eds. (1976) *Business and Government in Canada* (Toronto: Methuen), 2nd edition.

Robinette, J.J. (1955) *Competition and Combines in Canada* (Toronto: Gilbert Jackson and Assoc.).

Rosenbluth, G. and H.G. Thorburn (1963) *Canadian Anti-Combines Administration, 1952-1960* (Toronto: University of Toronto Press).

Safarian, A.E. (1959) *The Canadian Economy in the Great Depression* (Toronto: University of Toronto Press).

Sanderson, Margaret and W.T. Stanbury (1989) *Competition Policy in Canada: The First Hundred Years* (Ottawa: Department of Consumer & Corporate Affairs).

Seligman, E.R.A. and R.A. Love (1932) *Price Cutting and Price Maintenance* (New York: Harper and Bros.).

Shorthill, Cynthia and J.C.H. Jones (1990) "Ends, Means and Utility Functions: The Efficiency Criterion and Enforcement Activity in Canadian Antitrust, 1970-1981," *Osgoode Hall Law Journal*, Vol. 28(2), pp. 449-483.

Skeoch, L.A. (1957) "The Combines Investigation Act: Its Intent and Application," *Canadian Journal of Economics and Political Science*, Vol. 22(1), pp. 17-37.

Skeoch, L.A. (1964) "The Abolition of Resale Price Maintenance: Some Notes on the Canadian Experience," *Economica*, Vol. 31(123), August, pp. 260-269. Reprinted in Dkeoch (1966b, pp. 156-157).

Skeoch, L.A. (1966a) "Canada" in B.S. Yamey (ed.) *Resale Price Maintenance* (London: Weidenfeld and Nicolson), pp. 25-64.

Skeoch, L.A., ed. (1966b) *Restrictive Trade Practices in Canada* (Toronto: McClelland and Stewart).

Sommerfeld, S.F. (1948) "Free Competition and the Public Interest," *University of Toronto Law Journal*, Vol. 7(2), pp. 413-446.

Stanbury, W.T. (1976) "Penalties and Remedies Under the Combines Investigation Act," *Osgoode Law Journal*, Vol. XIV(3), December, pp. 571-631.

Stanbury, W.T. (1978) "Monopoly, Monopolization and Joint Monopolization: Policy Development and Bill C-13" in J.W. Rowley and W.T. Stanbury (eds.) *Competition Policy in Canada: Stage II, Bill C-13* (Montreal: The Institute for Research on Public Policy), pp. 133-175.

Stanbury, W.T. (1979) "Services and Competition Policy in Canada: A Legislative History, 1888-1976" (Unpublished paper, The Institute for Research on Public Policy, Ottawa).

Stanbury, W.T. (1981) "The Legislative Development of Canadian Competition Policy, 1888-1981," *Canadian Competition Policy Record*, vol. 2(2), pp. 1-18.

Stanbury, W.T. (1986) "The New Competition Act and Competition Tribunal Act: 'Not With a Bang, But a Whimper'," *Canadian Business Law Journal*, Vol. 12(1), pp. 2-42.

Stanbury, W.T. (1991) "Legislation to Control Agreements in Restraint of Trade in Canada: Review of the Historical Record and Proposals for Reform" in R.S. Khemani and W.T. Stanbury (eds.) *Canadian Competition Law and Policy at the Centenary* (Halifax: The Institute for Research on Public Policy).

Stanley, George J. (1912) *Report of Anti-Trust Legislation in the British Self-Governing Dominions* (London: HMSO, Cd. 6439) pp. 5-12 contain a copy of the 1910 Combines Investigation Act.

Stapells, H.G. (1922) *Recent Consolidation Movement in Canadian Industry* (Toronto: University of Toronto, unpublished Masters thesis).

Stewart, D.M. (1898) "What Constitutes Unwise Competition Between Banks?" *Journal of the Canadian Bankers Association*, January.

Strekaf, Jo'Anne (1991) "Private Enforcement of Canadian Competition law" in R.S. Khemani and W.T. Stanbury (eds.) *Competition Law and Policy at the Centenary* (Halifax: The Institute for Research on Public Policy).

Strickland, Philip (1936) "A Comparative Study of the Anti-Trust Laws of the British Dominions and of Their Administration," *Journal of Comparative Legislation and International Law*, Vol. 18, November, pp. 240-256.

Swanson, W.W. (1910) "Curbing the Combines by Boards of Investigation," *Queen's Quarterly*, Vol. 17(4), April/May/June, pp. 351-356.

Terrel, Charles L. (1940) "Processes in the Investigation of Complaints," *Law and Contemporary Problems*, Vol. 7(1), Winter, pp. 99-103.

Traves, T.D. (1974a) "Some Problems with Peacetime Price Controls: The Case of the Board of Commerce of Canada, 1919-20," *Canadian Public Administration*, Vol. 17(1), Spring, pp. 85-95.

Traves, T.D. (1974b) "The Board of Commerce and the Canadian Sugar Refining Industry: A Speculation on the Role of the State," *Canadian Historical Review*, Vol. 54(2), June.

Traves, T.D. (1979) *The State and Enterprise: Canadian Manufacturers and the Federal Government, 1917-1931* (Toronto: University of Toronto Press).

Trebilcock, Michael J. (1986) *The Common Law Restraint of Trade: A Legal and Economic Analysis* (Toronto: Carswell).

Underhill, F.A. (1944) "The Close of an Era: Twenty-Five Years of Mr. Mackenzie King," *Canadian Forum*, Sept. All page references refer to F.A. Underhill (1960) *In Search of Canadian Liberalism* (Toronto: Macmillan Co. of Canada), pp. 114-119.

Waite, P.B. (1971) *Canada 1874-1896, Arduous Destiny* (Toronto: McClelland and Stewart).

Walker, Francis (1912) "Policies of Germany, England, Canada and the United States Towards Combinations" in American Academy of Political and Social Science, Philadelphia, *Industrial Competition and Combination*, pp. 183-201.

Waverman, Leonard (1985) "The Abuse of Dominant Position and Eddy Match Revisited" (University of Torontno, Law and Economics Programme, Faculty of Law, January 23, mimeo).

Weaver, Suzanne (1977) *Decision to Prosecute: Organization and Public Policy in the Antitrust Division* (Cambridge, Mass.: MIT Press).

Weldon, J.C. (1966) "Consolidations in Canadian Industry, 1900-1948" in L.A. Skeoch (ed.) *Restrictive Trade Practices in Canada* (Toronto: McClelland and Stewart), pp. 228-279.

Winnipeg Free Press (1949) *The McGregor Controversy and The Combines Act*, Winnipeg Free Press Pamphlet, No. 29 (Winnipeg: Winnipeg Free Press).

Wolfe, J.N. (1957) "Some Empirical Issues in Canadian Combines Policy," *Canadian Journal of Economics and Political Science*, Vol. 23(1), pp. 113-121.

Wollman, Henry (1902) "Trusts and How They Refuse to be Exterminated," *Canadian Law Review*, Vol. 1(10-11), July-August, pp. 499-501.

Young, B. (1974) "Corporate Interests and the State," *Our Generation*, Vol. 10(1), Winter/Spring, pp. 70-83.

Table 1

ANTI-COMBINES PROSECUTIONS IN CANADA: 1889 to 1922/23[1]

Case Title, R. v.	Source of Case	Calendar or Fiscal[2] Year of Trial Decision	Final Court Level	Final Result	Penalty (Total Fine)	Offence
1. American Tobacco Company of Canada	A Private Citizen Laid the Information[3]	1897	Trial	Acquitted	--	Conspiracy
2. Elliott[8] (Pres. of Ont. Coal Assoc.)	No Data	1903/04	Appeal	Conviction	$4,000	Conspiracy
3. Master Plumbers and Steam Fitters Co-operative Association Ltd. et al.	Private Individual[4]	1904/05	Appeal	Conviction	$10,000	Conspiracy
4. Armstrong[10] et al.	No data	1904/05	Trial	Conviction	na	Conspiracy
5. McKittrick[10] et al.	No data	1904/05	Trial	Conviction	na	Conspiracy
6. McGuire et al.[8]	Arose Out of Master Plumbers[4]	1906	Trial	Conviction	$10,000	Conspiracy
7. McMichael[8]	Arose Out of Master Plumbers[7]	1907/08	Trial	Convicted	$250 + costs	Conspiracy
8. Gage et al. (members of Winnipeg Grain Exchange)	No Data	1907/08	Appeal	Acquitted	-	Conspiracy
9. Clarke[8] (Pres. of Alta. Retail Lumber Dealers Assoc.)	A Parliamentary Committee[6]	1907/08	Appeal	Convicted	$500	Conspiracy
10. Beckett et al. (Dominion Wholesale Grocers Guild)	Statement Before the Tariff Commission[5]	1909/10	Trial	Acquitted	-	Conspiracy
11. Canadian Wholesale Grocers Association et al.	No Data	1922/23	Appeal	Acquitted[9]	-	Conspiracy

1. All prosecutions were under the Criminal Code, S. 520 which was renumbered as S.498 in 1906.
2. Ending March 31. In some cases the fiscal year could not be ascertained.
3. Gosse (1962, p. 75, footnote 26).
4. Edgar (1906, pp. 429-430).
5. Edgar (1906, p. 430). Also a parliamentary inquiry in 1888. (See Ball, 1934, p. 32 for details.)
6. Bladen (1932, pp. 61, 70).
7. Ball (1934, p. 29).
8. Only individuals were charged; one in every case except McGuire et al. in which 38 individuals or unincorporated enterprises were charged.
9. Held that Attorney General of Ontario had no *locus standi* to bring a civil action.
10. Unreported cases tried at same assizes as Master Plumber. Defendants included members of the Assoc. and the Assoc. itself (per F.N. MacLeod, BCP Legal Branch).

Source: Ball (1934), Bladen (1932), Edgar (1906), Stanbury (1976) and the court judgments.

Table 2

CLASSIFICATION OF CASE FILES OPENED UNDER THE
COMBINES INVESTIGATION ACT, 1923/24 TO 1951/52

Fiscal Year	Requests for Advice as to Legality	Six-Citizen Formal Applications	Other Complaints	Initiated by Registrar/ Commissioner	Total	
1923/24	1	-	17	1	19	
1924/25	1	3	20	1	25	
1925/26	-	6	16	1	23	(24)[2]
1926/27	3	6	18	-	27	
1927/28	2	1	23	6	32	
1928/29	-	2	15	7	24	(23)
1929/30	4	4	18	4	30	
1930/31	6	4	24	1	35	(27)
1931/32	7	2	32	-	41	(47)
1932/33	4	4	37	2	47[1]	(46)
1933/34	6	6	34	-	46	(45)
1934/35	6	3	35	-	44	(46)
1935/36	3	2	24	-	29	
1936/37	2	1	30	-	33	
1937/38	7	3	24	-	34	
1938/39	7	6	17	-	30	
1939/40	4	2	16	-	22	
1940/41	3	2	23	-	28	
1941/42	-	-	8	-	8	
1942/43	-	-	2	-	2	
1943/44	-	-	1	-	1	(2)
1944/45	2	-	4	-	6	(3)
1945/46	4	-	15	1	20	(23)
1946/47	7	-	23	11	41	
1947/48	11	-	50	15 (16)[2]	76	(80)
1948/49	na	na	(6)[2]	na	na	(65)
1949/50	na	na	(2)[2]	na	na	(66)
1950/51	na	na	(13)[2]	na	na	(89)
1951/52	na	na	(17)[2]	na	na	(180)

na = not available
1. Includes one file opened at the request of the Minister.
2. Figures in brackets are from data collected by Gorecki from Bureau of Competition Policy records.

Sources of Formal Applications, 1923-1947/48

Consumers	10
Competitors	12
Other Dealers	24
Primary Producers (farmers)	11
Total	57

Source:　Bureau of Competition Policy Records.

Table 3

SOURCES OF PRELIMINARY INQUIRIES UNDER THE COMBINES INVESTIGATION ACT, 1923/24 TO 1951/52

Source of Preliminary Inquiry	Period						1923-46 1950/51 1951/52	
	1923-1946		1950/51		1951/52			
	Number	%	Number	%	Number	%	Number	%
Informal Complaints	507	86.7	70	60.3	122	88.4	699	83.3
Formal Applications by Six Citizens	57	9.7	0	0.0	0	0.0	57	6.8
Registrar/Commissioner[1]	21	3.6	46	39.6	16	11.6	83	9.9
TOTAL	585[4]	100	116[2]	100	138[3]	100	839	100

1. Registrar from 1923/24 to 1935/36; Commissioner from 1937/38 to 1952/53. Between 1937 and 1946 the Commissioner could not start inquiry on his own initiative.
2. Compare to 89 files opened in Table 2.
3. Compare to 180 files opened in Table 2.
2. Compare to 604 files opened 1923/24 to 1945/46 in Table 2.

Percentages may not add to 100 due to rounding.

Sources: House of Commons *Debates*, July 2, 1946, pp. 3076-3077; Registrar's *Annual Report 1950/51* (p. 3), *Annual Report 1951/52* (p. 27).

Table 4

THE INITIATION OF FORMAL INVESTIGATIONS[1]
UNDER THE COMBINES INVESTIGATION ACT,
1923/24 to 1951/52

Period[2]	Source of Initiation			
	Six Citizen Application	Minister	Registrar/ Commissioner[3]	Not Known
1923/24 to 1928/29	7	0	0	1
1929/30 to 1933/34	5	2	3	1
1934/35 to 1936/37	0	0	0	0
1937/38 to 1939/40	6	1	0[5]	1
1940/41 to 1944/45	0	0	0[5]	0
1945/46 to 1948/49	0	1	9	1
1949/50 to 1952/53[4]	1	0	2	0
	Summary by Period			
1923/24 to 1933/34				
Number	12	2	3	2
Percentage	63%	11%	16%	11%
1934/35 to 1939/40				
Number	16	1	0	1
Percentage	89%	6%	0%	6%
1945/46 to 1952/53[4]				
Number	1	1	11	1
Percentage	7%	7%	79%	7%
1923/24 to 1952/53[4]				
Number	19	4	14	4
Percentage	46%	10%	34%	10%

1. Formal investigations are defined here as those which led to a report which was transmitted to the Minister. The list of such reports is found in Skeoch (1966b, pp. 97-116). See also Table 5.

2. For fiscal year ending March 31. The 1923/24 fiscal year started in August 1923, the date of the Registrar's appointment. The date in the table refers to when the formal investigation began. As can be seen by reference to Table A-1 the receipt of the complaint and the start of the formal inquiry was virtually always in the same financial year. However, the dates with respect to when the formal inquiry started are much more reliable and hence are used here.

3. Registrar, 1923/24 - 1935/36; Commissioner, 1937/38 - 1952/53.

4. Carried out under authority of the 1923 Act prior to 1952 amendments to the *Combines Investigation Act*.

5. The Commissioner had no authority to initiate an investigation during this period.

Sources: *Annual Reports* of Registrar, Commissioner, Dominion Trade & Industry Commission; Reports of the Registrar, Commissioner & Special Commissioner; Rosenbluth & Thorburn (1963, Table II, p. 42); Skeoch (1966b, pp. 97-116).

Table 5

REPORTS BY REGISTRAR, SPECIAL COMMISSIONER OR COMMISSIONER,
UNDER THE COMBINES INVESTIGATION ACT, 1923 TO 1952

Skeoch No.	Name	Date	Report Published	Spec. Comm (SC) Registrar (R) Commissioner (C)	Resulting Case	Alleged Offence
1.	Fruits and Veg., W. Canada	Feb. 18, 1925	Yes	SC	R. v. Simington et al. (1926)	price fixing
2.	Coal, Western Canada	Feb. 28, 1925	Yes	SC	none (Report not adverse)	price fixing
3.	Potatoes, New Brunswick	June 9, 1925	Yes	R	none (Report submitted to N.B. Attorney-General)	price fixing
4.	Bread, Montreal	Mar. 25, 1926	Yes	R	none (Report not adverse)	price fixing
5.	Fruits and Vegetables, Ont.	July 31, 1926	Yes	SC	none (Report submitted to Ontario Attorney-General)	price fixing
6a.	Druggists, P.A.T.A.	Sept. 6, 1926	Yes	R	none, Min. of Labour appointed S.C. (6b)	RPM
6b.	Druggists, P.A.T.A.	Oct. 24, 1927	Yes	SC	Constitutional challenge, Privy Council upheld Can. law Jan. 29, 1931	RPM
7.	Milk Distribution, Montreal	Mar. 15, 1929	No	R	none (no combine said Report)	price fixing
8.	Matches, Canada, See 35.	Mar. 25, 1929	No	R	none - at this time	monopoly
9.	Plumbing and Heating Contractors (Amalgamated Builders' Council)	Oct. 31, 1929 (Interim) Dec. 18, 1929 (Final)	Yes	R & SC	R. v. Singer et al. (1931); Belyea v. R. (1931); Weinraub v. R. (1931); R. v. White et al. (1932)	price fixing
10.	Electrical Contractors, Toronto	Oct. 4, 1930	Yes	SC	R. v. Alexander (1932)	price fixing
11.	Breadbaking Industry, See 31.	Feb. 5, 1931	Yes[1]	R	Report not adverse	price fixing
12.	Motion Picture Industry	Apr. 30, 1931	Yes	SC	R. vs. Famous Players (1932)	price fixing
13.	Flour Milling Industry, See 32.	Dec. 30, 1931	No	Spec. Asst. to Reg.	Report adverse, but no prosecution	price fixing
14.	Radio Tubes and Sets	July 10, 1931 Oct. 24, 1931 June 7, 1932	No	R + Prof. Taylor	Report adverse, prosecution announced by Ontario A-G, not carried out	price fixing
15.	Canadian Fruit Basket Pool	Mar. 18, 1932	No	R	R. v. Chapman et al. (1933)	price fixing
16.	Tobacco Mfg., Ontario	Mar. 4, 1933	Yes	R by D. Sutherland	Report not adverse	price fixing
17.	British anthracite coal	April 21, 1933	Yes	R (later Royal Commission)	R. v. Hartt & Adair Coal Co. (1935); R. v. Canadian Import (1933, 1935)	price fixing and merger
18.	Rubber footwear, Canada	Mar. 29, 1934	No	R	Report adverse, but tentative, no prosecution	price fixing
19.	Gasoline refiners and dist., Ontario	May 29, 1934	No	R & Prof. Taylor	Report adverse, but tentative, no prosecution	price fixing
20.	Vitrified clay products, Ontario	Nov. 30, 1937	No	C	Report not adverse	monopoly
21.	Fruits and vegetables, B.C.	May 3, 1938	No	C	Report not adverse	price fixing

Table 5 - continued

Skeoch No.	Name	Date	Report Published	Spec. Comm (SC) Registrar (R) Commissioner (C)	Resulting Case	Alleged Offence
22.	Tobacco products	Aug. 31, 1938	Yes	C	R. v. Imperial Tobacco et al. (1941)	price fixing
23.	Paperboard shipping containers	Mar. 14, 1939	Yes	C	R. v. Container Materials (1942); H.J. Badden (1942)	price fixing
24.	Gasoline industry, Manitoba	May 23, 1939	No	C	Report not adverse	price discrim.
25.	Fruits and vegetables, Western Canada	Oct. 31, 1939	Yes	C	R. v. Staples et al (1940)	price fixing and merger
26.	Wood preservation industry	Dec. 30, 1939	No	C	Report not adverse	price fixing
27.	Optical goods (patents) See 30.	Feb. 18, 1941	Yes	C	Action to impeach patents after after W.W.II	patents
28.	Ammunition (C.I.L. Ltd.) See 66	Sept. 3, 1946	No	C	None, C.I.L. changed policy	refusal to supply
29.	Dental supplies	July 28, 1947	Yes	C	R. v. Ash-Temple Co. et al. (1948), led to amendments in 1949	price fixing
30.	Optical goods (patents) See 27	April 24, 1948	Yes	C	Action brought in Exchequer Court	patents
31.	Breadbaking, Western Canada	Nov. 3, 1948	Yes	SC	R. v. McGavin Bakeries et al. (1948)	price fixing
32.	Flour Milling	Dec. 29, 1948	Yes (delayed)	C	None (resignation of Commissioner F.A. McGregor)	price fixing
33.	Gasoline retailers, Montreal	July 8, 1949	No	C	Report not adverse	price fixing
34.	Flat glass	Dec. 13, 1949	Yes	C	R. v. Hobbs Glass et al. (1950), later tariffs reduced	price fixing
35.	Wooden matches	Dec. 27, 1949	Yes	C	R. v. Eddy Match (1951, 1953)	merger & monopoly
36.	Rubber products (6 branches)	May 21, 1952	Yes	C	R. v. Goodyear (1953), R. v. Dominion Rubber (1953), R. v. Firestone (1953)	price fixing
37.	Bread, Winnipeg	July 7, 1952	Yes	C	None, union action deemed not to been deliberate	price fixing (union)
38.	Fine Papers	Oct. 23, 1952	Yes	C	R. v. Howard Smith (1954, 1955, 1957)	price fixing
39.	Coarse Papers	Jan. 22, 1953	Yes	C	R. v. Crown Zellerbach (1955, 1957)	price fixing
40.	Maple Products, Quebec	Mar. 20, 1953	Yes	C	Report not adverse	price fixing
41.	Electrical wire and cable	Nov. 13, 1953	Yes	SC	R. v. Northern Electric et al.	price fixing

1.   Skeoch (1966b) says it was not published whereas in fact it was.

Sources: Skeoch (1966b, pp. 97-115). See also Ball (1934, Ch. 9) for a discussion of the first 17 reports.

Table 6

AUTHOR OF REPORTS UNDER THE COMBINES INVESTIGATION ACT,[1]
1923/24 TO 1951/52

Period[2]	Author of Report	
	Registrar/ Commissioner[5]	Special Commissioner
1923/24 to 1928/29	5[3]	4[3]
1929/30 to 1933/34	6	5
1934/35 to 1936/37	0	0
1937/38 to 1939/40	8	0
1940/41 to 1944/45	0	0
1945/46 to 1948/49	10	1
1949/50 to 1952/53[4]	2	1
1923/24 to 1952/53	31	11

1. Reports which were transmitted to the Minister responsible for the administration of the Combines Investigation Act. The list of such reports is found in Skeoch (1966b, pp. 97-116) and Table 5.

2. For fiscal year ending March 31. The 1923/24 fiscal year started in August 1923, the date of the Registrar's appointment. Reports are dated by when formal investigation started.

3. In one instance (#6), a report was written by both the Registrar and the Special Commissioner. Hence totals add to 42, whereas there were only 41 separate investigations.

4. Carried out under the authority of the 1923 Act prior to the 1952 amendments of the Combines Investigation Act.

5. Registrar, 1923/24 to 1935/36; Commissioner, 1937/38 to 1952/53.

Sources: Annual Reports of the Registrar, Commissioner, Dominion Trade & Industry Commission; Reports of the Registrar, Commissioner & Special Commissioner; Rosenbluth & Thorburn (1963, Table 11, p. 42); Skeoch (1966b, pp. 97-116).

Table 7

THE PUBLICATION OF REPORTS BY THE REGISTRAR OR COMMISSIONER UNDER THE COMBINES INVESTIGATION ACT, 1923/24 TO 1953/54[1]

Period[2]	Number of Reports Transmitted to the Minister by the Registrar or Commissioner[5]	Number of the Reports Published by the Minister
1923/24 to 1926/27	3	3
1927/28	0	0
1928/29 to 1934/35	10[3]	3[4]
1935/36 to 1936/37	0	0
1938/39 to 1940/41	8	3
1941/42 to 1945/46	0	0
1946/47 to 1948/49	4	3
1949/50 to 1953/54	8	7
Total	33	19

1. Reports which were transmitted to the Minister responsible for the administration of the Combines Investigation Act. The list of such reports is found in Skeoch (1966b, pp. 97-116).

2. For fiscal year ending March 31. The 1923/24 fiscal year started in August 1923, the date of the Registrar's appointment. Reports are dated by when transmitted to the Minister. In those instances where the data lists several reports (i.e., interim, final) the date in the table refers to the final report.

3. In Table 5 Reports #13, 16 were treated as though they were written by a Special Commissioner because the evidence suggested that the reports were written on behalf of the Registrar, although not by a special commissioner as such. However, for the purposes of this table they are treated as though they were written by the Registrar because legally they were.

4. Skeoch (1966b, p. 103) incorrectly specifies that Report #11 was not published whereas in fact it was published.

5. Registrar, 1923/24 to 1935/36; Commissioner, 1937/38 to 1952/53.

Sources: Reports of the Registrar, Commissioner, Special Commissioner; Skeoch (1966b, pp. 97-116).

Table 8

THE FINDINGS OF REPORTS BY THE REGISTRAR OR COMMISSIONER
UNDER THE COMBINES INVESTIGATION ACT, 1923/24 TO 1953/54[1]

Period[2]	Published Reports		Unpublished Reports	
	Found a Contravention of Act	Found no Contravention of Act	Found a Contravention of Act	Found no Contravention of Act
1923/24 to 1926/27	2	1	0	0
1927/28	0	0	0	0
1928/29 to 1934/35[3,5]	1	2	5	2
1935/36 to 1936/37	0	0	0	0
1938/39 to 1940/41	3	0	1	4
1941/42 to 1945/46	0	0	0	0
1946/47 to 1948/49	3	0	1[4]	0
1949/50 to 1953/54	6	1	0	1
Total	15	4	7	7

1. Reports which were transmitted to the Minister responsible for the administration of the <u>Combines Investigation Act</u>. The list of such reports is found in Skeoch (1966b, pp. 97-116) and Table 4. Registrar, 1923/24 to 2935/36; Commissioner, 1937/38 to 1952/53.

2. For fiscal year ending March 31. The 1923/24 fiscal year started in August 1923, the date of the Registrar's appointment. Reports are dated by when transmitted to the Minister. In those instances where the data lists several reports (i.e., interim, final) the date in the table refers to the final report.

3. In Table 6 Reports #13 and #16 were treated as though they were written by a Special Commissioner because the evidence suggested that the reports were written on behalf of the Registrar, although not by a special commissioner as such. However, for the purposes of this table they are treated as though they were written by the Registrar because legally they were.

4. From available information not clear if a contravention was found. (See Skeoch, 1966b, pp. 109-110, Report #28.)

5. Skeoch (1966b, p. 103) incorrectly specifies that #11 was not published whereas in fact it was published.

Sources: <u>Reports</u> of the Registrar, Commissioner, Special Commissioner; Skeoch (1966b, pp. 97-116).

Table 9

RESPONSIBILITY BETWEEN FEDERAL AND PROVINCIAL AUTHORITIES
IN UNDERTAKING ANTI-COMBINES PROSECUTIONS IN CANADA,[1]
1923/24 TO 1953/54[2]

Fiscal Year of Report Leading to Prosecution[3]	Case Title	Prosecuting Authority	Area of Canada Which was Subject of Report
1924/25	Symington et al.	Federal	Western Canada
No Report	Stinson-Reeb et al.	Quebec	Not applicable
1929/30*	Amalgamated Builders Council	Fed/Ontario[4]	Ontario
1929/30*	Singer et al.	Fed/Ontario[4]	Ontario
1929/30*	White et al.	Fed/Ontario[4]	Ontario
1930/31	Alexander Ltd. et al.	Ontario	Toronto
1931/32	Famous Players et al.	Ontario[6]	Canada
1931/32	Chapman et al.	Ontario	Ontario
1933/34*	Hartt and Adair Coal Co. Ltd. et al.	Quebec	Eastern Canada
1933/34*	Canadian Import Co. et al.	Quebec	Eastern Canada
1938/39	Imperial Tobacco Co. of Canada Ltd. et al.	Alberta	Alberta and Elsewhere in Canada
1938/39*	Container Materials Ltd. et al.	Federal	Canada
1938/39*	Bathurst Power & Paper (& H.J. Badden)	Federal	Canada
1939/40	Staples et al.	British Columbia	Western Canada
1947/48	Ash-Temple Co. Ltd. et al.	Federal	Canada
1948/49	McGavin Bakeries et al.	Alberta/Fed[5]	Western Canada
1949/50	Hobbs Glass Limited et al.	Federal	Ontario & Quebec
1949/50	Eddy Match Co. Ltd. et al.	Federal	Canada
1952/53*	Goodyear Tire & Rubber Co. of Canada Ltd. et al.	Federal	Canada
1952/53*	Firestone Tire & Rubber Co. of Canada Ltd. et al.	Federal	Canada
1952/53*	Dominion Rubber Co. Ltd. et al.	Federal	Canada
1952/53	Howard Smith Paper Mills Ltd. et al.	Federal	Canada
1952/53	Crown Zellerbach Canada Ltd. et al.	Federal	British Columbia
1953/54	Northern Electric Co. Ltd. et al.	Federal	Canada

1. Prosecutions under the Combines Investigation Act and/or the Criminal Code of Canada. Excluded is one case involving patents taken to the Exchequer Court. (See Skeoch, 1966b, pp. 110-111.) In other words the table refers only to regular criminal proceedings through the courts. All except Eddy Match and Staples were conspiracy cases. Canadian Import involved both merger and conspiracy charges.

2. Carried out under authority of the Act prior to the 1952 amendments to the Combines Investigation Act.

3. Reports are dated by when transmitted to the Minister. In those instances where the data source lists several reports (i.e.. interim, final) the date in the table refers to the final report. Fiscal year ends March 31.

4. Prosecution started by federal government, but concluded by Province of Ontario.

5. Although started by Alberta not clear if federal government involved in later stages or not. Annual Report of Commissioner (1948/49, p. 5) indicates federal involvement.

6. House of Commons Debates (April 1, 1932, p. 2625) states that prosecution was by Ontario and the federal government.

* denote instances where more than one prosecution arose from the same report.

Sources: Annual Reports of Registrar or Commissioner; Reports of the Registrar, Commissioner, Special Commissioner; Skeoch (1966b, pp. 97-116); judgments of the individual cases.

Table 10

REPORTS WHICH FOUND A COMBINE BUT
IN WHICH NO PROSECUTION WAS INSTITUTED,
1923/24 TO 1952/53[1]

Report[2]	Date Report Transmitted to Minister[3]	Comment
#3, Potatoes, New Brunswick	June 9, 1925	Transmitted to Attorney-General of New Brunswick. No action taken. Reynold's (1940, p. 160) remarks this may have been due to "political considerations."
#6, Druggists, PATA	October 24, 1927	Skeoch (1966b, p. 99) states that "There was no direct prosecution. Rather, the Government was requested by the persons involved in the case to refer the question of the constitutional validity of the Combines Investigation Act and of section 498 of the Criminal Code to the Supreme Court of Canada. In an unanimous judgment the Supreme Court held that both the Act and section 498 were _intra vires_ the Parliament of Canada. An appeal from this judgment was taken to the Judicial Committee of the Privy Council. Judgment was delivered on Jan. 29, 1931, upholding the decision of the Supreme Court."
#13, Flour Milling	December 30, 1931	Not clear if case was even referred to Provincial Attorney-General.
#14, Radio Tubes and Sets	June 7, 1932	Referred to Attorney General of Ontario. Skeoch (1966b, p. 104) states that "The intention to prosecute was announced and counsel appointed. It was later decided on the advice of counsel, not to prosecute."
#18, Rubber Footwear	March 29, 1934	Skeoch (1966b, p. 106) states that the finding was "tentative." No indication of whether it was referred to a Provincial Attorney-General.
#19, Gasoline refining and distribution	May 29, 1934	Again Skeoch (1966b, p. 106) comments that the "Report made a tentative finding of a combine..." No indication of whether the case was referred to a Provincial Attorney-General.
#32, Flour Milling	Dec. 29, 1948	The Federal Government refused to prosecute despite strong evidence of a conspiracy. (This was the _Flour-Milling Report_ which led to the Commissioner's resignation in 1949.)
#37, Bread, Winnipeg	July 7, 1952	Skeoch (1966b, p. 114) states that "The Minister of Justice announced that the evidence did not indicate a deliberate intention on the part of the local labour union to contravene the Combines Investigation Act, and that, in view of the publicity which the matter had received, the same considerations against prosecution would not apply in a future like case."

1. Carried out under authority of the Combines Investigation Act of 1923 prior to the 1952 amendments.

2. By Registrar, Commissioner or Special Commissioner.

3. Reports are dated by when transmitted to the Minister. In those instances where the data source lists several reports (i.e., interim, final) the date in the table refers to final report. Fiscal year ends March 31. In report #28 (as Table 8) it is not clear if a contravention was found in this case. Skeoch (1966b, pp. 109-110) comments that the cause of the complaint was removed by the company.

Sources: Annual Reports of the Registrar or Commissioner; Skeoch (1966b, pp. 97-116).

Table 11

RESULTS OF ANTI-COMBINES PROSECUTIONS[1]
IN CANADA, 1923/24 TO 1955/56

Case Title (R. vs. ...)	Fiscal Year of Trial Decision[2]	Final Court Level	Final Results	Total Fines	Offence	Charged Under Combines Invest. Act or Criminal Code
1. Symington et al.	1925/26	Trial	Charges Dropped[3]	-	Conspiracy	Both
2. Stinson-Reeb et al.	1925/26	Supreme Court	Conviction	$6000	Conspiracy	Code
3. Amalgamated Builders Council	1930/31	Trial (g)	Conviction	$26,500	Conspiracy	Code
4. Singer et al.	1930/31	Supreme Court[4]	Conviction	$17,600	Conspiracy	Both
5. White et al.	1932/33	Trial	Conviction	$1,100	Conspiracy	Both
6. Alexander Ltd. et al.	1931/32	Trial	Conviction	$20,000	Conspiracy	Both
7. Famous Players et al.	1931/32	Trial	Acquitted	-	Conspiracy	Both
8. Chapman et al.	1932/33	Trial (g)	Conviction	$1500	Conspiracy	Code
9. Hartt and Adair Coal Co. Ltd. et al.	1934/35	Appeal	Conviction	$13,500	Conspiracy	Code
10. Canadian Import Co. et al.	1933/34	Appeal (d)	Conviction[8]	$30,000	Merger and Conspiracy	Both
11. Imperial Tobacco Co. of Canada et al.	1941/42	Appeal (d)	Conviction[9]	$15,000	Conspiracy	Act
12. Container Materials Ltd. et al. (incl. H.J. Badden)	1940/41	Supreme Court	Conviction	$159,000	Conspiracy	Code
13. Bathurst Power & Paper (& H.J. Badden)	1941/42	Trial (g)	Conviction	$17,000	Conspiracy	Code
14. Staples et al.	1940/41	Trial	Acquitted	-	Merger	Act
15. Ash-Temple Co. Ltd. et al.	1947/48	Appeal	Acquitted	-	Conspiracy	Both
16. McGavin Bakeries et al.	1951/52	Trial	Conviction	$30,000 + $19,402 costs	Conspiracy	Code
17. Hobbs Glass Limited et al.	1950/51	Trial (g)	Conviction	$44,000	Conspiracy	Code
18. Eddy Match Co. Ltd. et al.	1951/52	Appeal (d)	Conviction	$85,000	Monopoly	Act
19. Goodyear Tire & Rubber Co. of Canada Ltd. et al.	1953/54	Trial[5] (g)	Conviction	$50,000[7]	Conspiracy	Code
20. Firestone Tire & Rubber Co. of Canada Ltd. et al.	1953/54	Trial (g)	Conviction	$90,000[7]	Conspiracy	Code

Table 11 - continued

Case Title (R. vs. ...)	Fiscal Year of Trial Decision[2]	Final Court Level	Final Results	Total Fines	Offence	Charged Under Combines Invest. Act or Criminal Code
21. Dominion Rubber Co. Ltd. et al.	1953/54	Trial (g)	Conviction	$80,000[7]	Conspiracy	Code
22. Howard Smith Paper Mills Ltd. et al.	1954/55	Supreme Court	Conviction	$242,000[7]	Conspiracy	Code
23. Crown Zellerbach Canada Ltd. et al.	1955/56	Appeal[6]	Conviction	$58,000[7] + costs	Conspiracy	Code
24. Northern Electric Co. Ltd. et al.	1954/55	Trial	Conviction	$82,000[7] + costs	Conspiracy	Code

1. Under the <u>Combines Investigation Act</u> and/or the <u>Criminal Code</u> of Canada where the investigation began prior to the 1952 amendments.
2. Year ending March 31.
3. The accused were convicted, however, of fraud and offences under the <u>Secret Commissions Act</u>.
4. Belyea and Weinraub only.
5. Appealed unsuccessfully to Supreme Court of Canada on the constitutionality of prohibition orders.
6. All the accused but Crown Zellerbach and Bartram pleaded guilty. Their appeal from conviction was dismissed.
7. In addition, a Prohibition Order was made.
8. Found not guilty on merger count.
9. Only one firm (W.C. Macdonald Inc.) which did not appeal was convicted of both conspiracy and one count of monopoly according to Bureau of Competition Policy records.

(d) = Leave to appeal to Supreme Court of Canada was denied.
(g) = pleaded guilty

Sources: Derived by the authors from reported judgments; Stanbury (1976).

Table 12

AVERAGE TIME INTERVALS FOR REPORTS[1]
AND PROSECUTIONS MADE UNDER THE
COMBINES INVESTIGATION ACT,[2]
1923/24 TO 1951/52

	Period	All Reports	Reports Completed Between 1923/24 and 1939/40	Reports Completed Between 1945/46 and 1953/54	Reports Completed Between 1945/46 and 1953/54 Revised[5]
		(Months)			
T1	File opened to report transmitted to Minister	20.4 (N = 40)	13.2 (N = 26)	33.8 (N = 14)	23.3 (N = 12)
T1 (T5)	File opened to report transmitted to Minister where no prosecution	16.3 (N = 23)	12.6 (N = 17)	26.8 (N = 6)	15.4 (N = 5)
T1	File opened to report transmitted to Minister where prosecution[3]	25.9 (N = 17)	14.3 (N = 9)	39.0 (N = 8)	35.9 (N = 7)
T2	Report transmitted to Minister to institution of court proceedings[3]	7.2 (N = 22)	4.3 (N = 12)	10.7 (N = 10)	
T3	Institution of court proceedings to trial decision	10.9 (N = 22)	13.2 (N = 12)	8.2 (N = 10)	
T4	Institution of court proceedings to final disposition of case	17.9 (N = 22)	17.1 (N = 12)	18.8 (N = 10)	
T5	File opened to final disposition where prosecution	50.9 (N = 23)[4]	33.9 (N = 13)[4]	73.0 (N = 10)	

1. Reports which were transmitted to the Minister responsible for the administration of the Combines Investigation Act. This list of such reports is found in Skeoch (1966b, pp. 97-116) and Table 5. The table excludes consideration of Report #27, which involved a lengthy court case concerning patents. The time taken to complete the report to the Minister was 17 months.

2. Or the Criminal Code of Canada. Most prosecutions were under the Criminal Code. See Table 11.

3. Since one report could lead to a number of prosecutions, the sample sizes across these two rows differ.

4. Sample size is N = 23, and N = 13, whereas for T2 to T2 N = 22, N = 12 respectively. The difference reflects unavailability of data for institution of legal proceedings for the case arising out of Report #15. If T5 is recalculated for N = 22, N = 12, then the respective averages are 51.8 and 34.2.

5. To eliminate two reports on which no work was done during World War II.

Source: See Table 15.

Table 13

EXPENDITURES ON THE ADMINISTRATION AND ENFORCEMENT
OF THE COMBINES INVESTIGATION ACT, 1923-1952

Year	Nominal Dollars	1949 Dollars[1]
1923/24 and 1924/25	$ 40,535	
1925/26	90,000	
1926/27	56,616	
1927/28	28,704	
1928/29	50,000	
1929/30	95,000	
1930/31	21,925	
1935/36	3,400	$ 5,700
1936/37	--	--
1937/38	14,600	23,200
1938/39	52,500	82,400
1939/40	45,300	71,600
1940/41	61,800	94,000
1941/42	57,500	82,600
1942/43	23,400	32,100
1943/44	25,200	34,000
1944/45	24,900	33,400
1945/46	34,600	46,100
1946/47	77,600	100,100
1947/48	124,800	147,200
1948/49	169,400	174,600
1949/50	168,800	168,800
1950/51	221,100	214,900
1951/52	205,800	181,000
1952/53	267,000	229,100

1.   Based on Consumer Price Index for calendar year preceding the fiscal year.

Sources: Ball (1934, p. 100); Rosenbluth and Thorburn (1963, p. 46).

Table 14

ROSENBLUTH AND THORBURN'S ANALYSIS OF
CERTAIN COMBINES CASES, 1948-1953

Industry	Date of Report	Relative Size of the Market ($ per $1000 of GNP)	Court Result	Classification
Rubber (19-21)[1]	1952	11.90	$220,000[2] + P.O.	A
Electrical wire and cable (24)	1953	6.17	$82,000 + P.O.	A
Coarse papers, B.C. (23)	1953	0.29	$58,000 + P.O.	B
Optical goods (na)	1948	1.54	Not prosecuted	B
Bread, Western Canada (16)	1948	2.33	$30,000	B
Flat glass (17)	1949	1.52	$44,000	B
Dental supplies (15)	1947	0.41	Acquitted	C
Matches (18)	1949	0.27	$85,000	C
Flour milling (not prosec.)	1952	7.37	Not prosecuted	C
Fine papers (22)	1952	2.27	$242,000	C

A = monopolistic situation effectively handled by combines machinery; court issued a restraining order

B = monopolistic situation in which conviction has been secured without a restraining order

C = monopolistic situations not effectively handled; cases mentioned in reports, but no effective action taken

1. Case number in Table 11.

2. There were three cases (mechanical rubber goods, rubber footwear, and rubber tires). The fines were $50,000, $80,000, and $90,000 respectively.

Source: Rosenbluth and Thorburn (1963, pp. 60-63); Stanbury (1976).

Table 15

IMPORTANT DATES IN REPORTS AND PROSECUTIONS UNDER
THE COMBINES INVESTIGATION ACT: 1922/23 to 1951/52[1]

Report[2]	Date File Opened[3]	Date Report Transmitted to Minister[4]	Date of Instituting Legal Proceedings[5]	Date of Trial Decision[6]	Date of Appeal Court Decision[6]	Date of Supreme Court Decision[6]
1	02:24	02:25	09:25	03:26	--	--
2	10:24	02:25	--	--	--	--
3	01:24	06:25	--	--	--	--
4	09:24	03:26	--	--	--	--
5	02:25	07:26	--	--	--	--
6	10:25	10:27	--	--	--	--
7	10:28	03:29	--	--	--	--
8	01:28	03:29	--	--	--	--
9(a)	05:28	12:29	02:30	05/06:30	--	--
9(b)	05:28	12:29	09:30	03:31	06:31	02:32
9(c)	05:28	12:29	02:30	04:32	--	--
10	09:29	10:30	09:31	01:32	--	--
11	04:30	02:31	--	--	--	--
12	06:29	04:31	10:31	03:32	--	--
13	03:30	12:31	--	--	--	--
14	06:30	05:32	--	--	--	--
15	06:30	03:32	N/A	01:33	--	--
16	11:32	03:33	--	--	--	--
17(a)	10:32	04:33	07:33	12:33	10:34	--
17(b)	10:32	04:33	07:33	10:35	06:35	--
18	04:33	03:34	--	--	--	--
19	09:33	05:34	--	--	--	--
20	03:37	11:37	--	--	--	--
21	01:38	05:38	--	--	--	--
22	01:38	08:38	11:38	07:41	02:42	--
23(a)	01:38	03:39	09:39	09:40	05:41	--
23(b)	01:38	03:39	09:39	03:42	--	--
24	06:38	05:39	--	--	--	--
25	07:38	10:39	12:39	05:40	--	--
26	10:38	12:39	--	--	--	--
27	09:39	02:41	The Patent Case		--	--
28	11:45	09:46	--	--	--	--
29	03:46	07:47	01:48	03:48	02:49	--
30	02:41	04:48	--	--	--	--
31	08:47	11:48	01:50	10:51	--	--
32	09:47	12:48	--	--	--	--
33	03:49	07:49	--	--	--	--
34	04:47	12:49	04:50	10:50	--	--
35	06:46	12:49	10:50	10:51	10:52	--
36(a)	04:47	05:52	01:53	09:53	04:54	02:56
36(b)	04:47	05:52	09:53	11:53	--	--
36(c)	04:47	05:52	09:53	11:53	--	--
37	06:51	07:52	--	--	--	--
38	09:48	10:52	09:53	06:54	06:55	05:57
39	03:48	01:53	02:54	04:55	11:56	--
40	06:50	03:53	--	--	--	--
41	08:50	11:53	09:54	03:55	--	--

1. Table refers to prosecutions undertaken as a result of reports carried out under the authority of the Combines Investigation Act or the Criminal Code prior to the 1952 amendments.
2. Report # follow Skeoch (1966b, pp. 97-116). Letters in brackets denote cases. See Table 5 for cross-reference.
3. Taken from a list which detailed all files opened by the Registrar between 1922/23 and 1951/52. The list was kindly supplied by the Records Office of the Bureau of Competition Policy. Note in report #30 the file open is dated from the conclusion of report #27. This seemed more appropriate than dating them both from 09:39. See Skeoch (1966b) for details.
4. Taken from Skeoch (1966b, pp. 97-116).
5. Taken from various issues of the Annual Reports of the Registrar, Commissioner and Dominion Trade and Industry Commission. Note for report #15 it was not possible to date the beginning of the legal proceedings.
6. Judgments and same sources as in footnote 5. In report #9 case (a) it was not clear if the judgment was on the 5th or 6th month. All calculations in Table 12 assumed it was the 5th.

Note: Dates recorded by month, year.
Source: Annual Reports of the Registrar, Commissioner, Dominion Trade and Industry Commission; Skeoch (1966b, pp. 97-116); judgments; data supplied by Records Office, Bureau of Competition Policy.

Figure 1

COMPARISONS OF THE CHARACTERISTICS OF THE ADMINISTRATION AND ENFORCEMENT
OF COMPETITION POLICY IN CANADA IN THREE PERIODS BETWEEN 1889 AND 1952

	1889-1910	1910-1919	1923-1935, 1937-1952
Offences	- Conspiracies or agreements in restraint of trade	- Conspiracies or agreements in restraint of trade (in both the *Act* and the *Criminal Code*); and mergers	- Conspiracies or agreements in restraint of trade; and mergers
Federal official responsible for enforcement	- None; left to provincial Attorneys General	- None; enforcement under the *Criminal Code* by provincial Attorney-General	- Registrar, 1923-1935; Dominion Trade and Industry Commission, 1935-37; Commissioner 1937-52
Initiation of an inquiry	- Individuals could complain to a provincial Attorney-General - Attorney General of a province	- Under the Act, a formal 6-citizen application to a judge (required to make a *prima facie* case) who could recommend that an *ad hoc* Board of Investigation be appointed by the Minister	- Formal 6-citizen application to the Registrar - Registrar on his own volition - Direction from Minister
Appraisal and report	- None; to be done internally by provincial Attorney-General	- Board of Investigation (1 person appointed by complainants, 1 by persons under investigation, neutral chairman)	- Report by Registrar or *ad hoc* Special Commissioner. The latter's report had to be made public.
Formal powers of investigation	- Same as for any other criminal case handled by the police	- Board held hearings in public and had full power of a court of record in civil cases. It could compel witnesses to attend and testify under oath and compel the production of documents.	- Registrar or Special Commissioner had full power to summon and examine witnesses under oath, examine records and to require the production of documents.
Prosecution	- At the discretion of provincial Attorney-General	- Provincial Attorney-General could prosecute under *Criminal Code*	- Cases referred first to provincial Attorneys-General; then the federal Attorney General could prosecute under *Code* or *Act*. However, an individual had to lay an Information and the federal Cabinet had to approve prosecution
Penalties and remedies	- Fine of $200 to $4000 or up to two years imprisonment for individuals - Fine of $1000 to $10,000 for corporations - Reduce or remove tariffs (from 1897) if a judge found a combine	- Under 1910 Act, fines of $1000/day could only be imposed if the combine did not cease its offence within 10 days of the publication of the Report - Same fines as in 1889 for offences under the *Criminal Code* - Reduction or removal of tariffs at the Cabinet's discretion if a combine was found - Could apply to the Exchequer Court to revoke a patent	- Fine of up to $25,000 for corporations and up to $10,000 or two years imprisonment for individuals for offences under the Act. - Fines of up to $10,000 for corporations convicted under the *Criminal Code*. - Reduction or removal of tariffs at the Cabinet's discretion if a combine was found. - Could apply to Exchequer Court to revoke a patent.
Civil law enforcement	- No provision	- No provision	- No provision

Appendix A

CHRONOLOGY OF MAJOR CHANGES IN COMPETITION POLICY LEGISLATION IN CANADA, 1889 - 1952

1889: Parliament enacts *An Act for the Prevention and Suppression of Combinations Formed in Restraint of Trade* (52 Victoria, c. 41). It made it an offence to conspire or agree "unlawfully"' to lessen competition "unduly" by limiting facilities, restricting output or unreasonably enhancing the price of an article or commodity. Enforcement was left up to the Attorneys General of the provinces.

1892: The Act of 1889 was incorporated in Canada's first *Criminal Code* as sections 516, 517 and 520 (55-56 Victoria, c. 29).

1897: The *Customs Tariff Act* was amended (S. 18) such that when the Cabinet believed that a combine had unreasonably enhanced the price of article or unduly promoted the advantage of the manufacturer at the expense of the consumer, it might order an investigation by a judge. If the report found a combine and if the disadvantage to consumers was facilitated by the tariff, the Cabinet could reduce or remove the duty (60-61 Victoria, c. 16). The provision was used only once, in 1902, in respect to newsprint. The tariff was reduced from 25 percent to 15 percent (Ball, 1934, pp. 14-16).

1899: The words "unduly" and "unreasonably" were deleted from S.520 (*Criminal Code Amendment Act*, 1899, 62-63 Victoria, c. 46).

1900: Both "unduly" and "unreasonably" were restored to S.520, but "unlawfully" was deleted (*Criminal Code Amendment Act*, 1900, 63-64 Victoria, c. 46).

1906: Sections 516, 517, 520 of the *Criminal Code* were renumbered as S. 496, 497, 498 (63-64 Victoria, c. 35, s.3).

1907: The *Customs Tariff Act* was amended by repealing S.18 and inserting a new S.12. It was similar to the 1897 provision, but it also gave the Cabinet the power to reduce or remove tariffs if a court found a combine existed. A similar provision was put into the *Combines Investigation Acts* of 1910 and 1923. In addition, the Cabinet could appoint a judge to inquire into combine or conspiracy alleged to exist "among manufacturers or dealers in any article of commerce to unduly promote the advantage of the manufacturers or dealers in such article at the expense of the consumers..." The judge was to make his report to the Cabinet which could reduce the tariffs on such articles "to give the public the benefit of reasonable competition in the article..." The judge was given the power to "compel the attendance of witnesses and examine them under oath and require the production of books and papers." The Cabinet could also give him other "necessary powers."

1910: The first *Combines Investigation Act* was enacted effective May 4. It made combines illegal. A combine was defined in S.2(c) as

> any contract, agreement, arrangement or combination which has or is designed to have, the effect of increasing or fixing the price or rental of any article of trade or commerce or the cost of the storage or transportation thereof, or of the restricting competition in or of controlling the production, manufacture, transportation, storage, sale or supply thereof, to the detriment of consumers or producers of such article of trade or commerce and includes the acquisition, leasing or otherwise taking over, or obtaining by any person to the end aforesaid, of any control over or interest in the business, or any portion of the business, of any person, and also includes what is known as a trust monopoly or merger...

The Act provided for citizens to apply to a judge to order an independent investigation of alleged combines. If a *prima facie* case was established, the judge could order that a three-person Board of Investigation be convened. If it found that a combine existed, the accused had to cease their impugned activities within 10 days or face a fine of up to $1000 per day and costs.

1916: Under the *War Measures Act* of 1914, the Cabinet passed an Order-in-Council (P.C. 2777) S.2 part 3 of which repealed S.498 of the *Criminal Code* only insofar as necessaries of life were concerned (staples and ordinary food, clothing, fuel...). Section 498 was reasserted with the important elimination of the words "unduly" and "unreasonably." Section 3 of the Order-in-Council provided that no person should accumulate necessaries of life beyond the reasonable amount required for home or business (Ball, 1934, p. 51). The Minister of Labour was empowered to make full investigations. Prosecutions could only be conducted with the consent of relevant provincial Attorney-General. Subsequent orders amended and changed the original Order (Ball, 1934, p. 52).

1919: The *Combines Investigation Act* of 1910 was repealed and replaced by the *Board of Commerce Act* and the *Combines and Fair Practices Act* (effective July 7) (see Cheffins, 1991). The new Acts were ruled *ultra vires* of the federal government by the Privy Council on November 11, 1921 [(1922) 1 A.C. 191].

1923: The second *Combines Investigation Act* was passed effective June 13. S. 32 provided that

> Every one is guilty of an indictable offence and liable to a penalty not exceeding ten thousand dollars or to two years imprisonment, or if a corporation to a penalty not exceeding twenty five thousand dollars, who is a party or privy to or knowingly assists in the formation or operation of a combine within the meaning of this Act.
> A combine was defined in S.2 as follows

> In this Act, unless the context otherwise requires,
> (1)   combines which have operated or are likely to operate to the detriment or against the interest of the public, whether consumers, producers or others, and which
>   (a)   are mergers, trusts or monopolies, so called; or
>   (b)   result from the purchase, lease, or other acquisition by any person of any control over or interest in the whole or part of the business of any other person; or
>   (c)   result from any actual or tacit contract, agreement, arrangement, or combination which has or is designed to have the effect of
>   (i)   limiting facilities for transporting, producing, manufacturing, supplying, storing or dealing, or
>   (ii)   preventing, limiting or lessening manufacture or production, or
>   (iii)   fixing a common price or resale price, or a common rental, or a common cost of storage or transportation, or
>   (iv)   enhancing the price, rental or cost of article, rental, storage or transportation, or
>   (v)   preventing or lessening competition in, or substantially controlling within any particular area or district or generally, production, manufacture, purchase, barter, sale, storage, transportation, insurance or supply, or
>   (vi)   otherwise restraining or injuring trade or commerce, are described by the word "combine."

The new Act provided for the appointment of a permanent official, the Registrar, to receive complaints and applications for investigations of combines from six citizens and to investigate alleged combines. He could also initiate investigations on his own volition and he was required to undertake investigations at the request of the Minister. The Act provided for formal investigatory powers: search for documents; compulsory written returns of information requested by the Registrar or Special Commissioner appointed to conduct a formal inquiry.

1935: The *Dominion Trade and Industry Commission Act* was passed effective July 5. The Commission was to administer the *Combines Investigation Act* rather than the Registrar and to authorize prosecutions under S.498 of the *Criminal Code* (i.e., the conspiracy provision). The Act was also aimed at unfair trade practices. It included a more comprehensive definition of a "combine" to include mergers and monopolies (see Skeoch, 1966b). Services, however, were exempted.

Effective July 5 the *Criminal Code* was amended (S. 498A) to prohibit discriminatory discounts, rebates and allowances, regional price discrimination, and predatory pricing.

> Every person engaged in trade or commerce or industry is guilty of an indictable offence and liable to a penalty not exceeding one thousand dollars or to one month's imprisonment, or, if a corporation, to a penalty not exceeding five thousand dollars, who
> (a)   is a party or privy to, or assists in, any transaction of sale which discriminates, to his knowledge, against competitors of the purchaser in that any discount, rebate or allowance is granted to the purchaser over and above any discount, rebate or allowance available at the time of such transaction to the aforesaid competitors in respect of a sale of goods of like quality and quantity;
> The provisions of this paragraph shall not, however, prevent a co-operative society returning to producers or consumers, or a co-operative wholesale society returning to its constituent retail members, the whole or any part of the net surplus made in its trading operations in proportion to purchases made from or sales to the society;
> (b)   engages in a policy of selling goods in any area of Canada at prices lower than those exacted by such seller elsewhere in Canada, for the purpose of destroying competition or eliminating a competitor in such part of Canada;
> (c)   engages in a policy of selling goods at prices unreasonably low for the purpose of destroying competition or eliminating a competitor (S.C. 1935, c. 45, s. 9).

1937: Part of the *Dominion Trade and Industry Commission Act* (passed in 1935) was held to be *ultra vires* of the federal government's power, i.e., S.14 which permitted industrial agreements to prevent "wasteful" or "demoralizing" competition as authorized by the Commission. Again, the Supreme Court, [(1935) S.C.R. 379] and the Privy Council, [(1937) A.C. 405; 1 D.L.R. 702], were largely in agreement. Note - the Privy Council upheld the *DTIC Act*, but S.14 was excluded from the reference. On the day of the Supreme Court's ruling, Senator Arthur Meighen exclaimed, "We struggled so much to legitimize combines that we exceeded the Constitution" (Senate, *Debates*, June 17, 1936, p. 525).

> The *Combines Investigation Act* was amended effective April 10, 1937 to put the administration of the Act in the hands of a permanent Commissioner (title changed from Registrar), and provision was made for the appointment of *ad hoc* Commissioners to investigate and report to the Minister of Labour (then responsible for the administration of the Act). The Commissioner's ability to initiate investigations on his own volition was deleted. This change was pushed by R.B. Bennett (House of Commons, *Debates*, April 1, 1937, pp. 2436-2439). The Act was changed to permit the Attorney-General of Canada to bring cases on his own under the *Act* or *Criminal Code*.

1941: The *Wartime Prices and Trade Board*'s Maximum Prices Regulations came into effect December 1, 1941. The Board was established in September 1939. Commissioner McGregor (Registrar between 1925 and 1935 and Commissioner since 1937) was appointed as an Enforcement Administrator. The enforcement of the combines legislation in the *Act* and the *Criminal Code* was effectively suspended, but not with Parliament's consent (see House of

Commons, *Debates*, November 23, 1949, p. 2142). The price ceiling on a wide range of commodities was suspended until January 1947.

1946: Amendments were made to the *Combines Investigation Act* effective August 31. They provided for the appointment of up to three deputy-commissioners. The Commissioner was authorized to make studies of cartels or other monopolistic conditions and report to the Minister. (Regulations in this respect were passed by Order-in-Council No. 1291, April 3, 1947.)

> The Commissioner was now permitted to investigate complaints in respect to S.498 and 498A of the *Criminal Code* which were removed from the jurisdiction of the Dominion Trade and Industry Commission. From 1935 it had responsibility to make inquiries into breaches of S. 498 and 498A. This was done with the approval of the Commission and the Minister of Trade and Commerce. The Commissioner was permitted, on his own, to initiate preliminary inquiries, a power which had been in the 1923 Act, but was deleted in the 1937 amendments (see above).
>
> The principal substantive change, said Mr. St. Laurent (Minister of Justice), was S.9 which authorized the Exchequer (now the Federal) Court to issue an order revising or cancelling a patent licence or pooling agreements or trade mark agreements where such agreements have been used to the detriment of the public.
>
> At the insistence of Mr. Diefenbaker (then a Conservative MP), the Liberals accepted an amendment permitting individuals to lay an Information, a power they had always had under the *Criminal Code*. Such prosecutions would then be taken over by the Attorney-General.

1949: Amendments to the *Combines Investigation Act* were made effective December 10. One major amendment made it clear that documents found in the possession of individuals are admissible in evidence against them and extended it to apply to companies and to unincorporated businesses which act through employees (result of the *Ash-Temple* case [(1949) 93 C.C.C. 267].

> The *Combines Investigation Act* was also amended to provide that the Attorney-General of Canada may institute and conduct proceedings under the *Combines Investigation Act* or S. 498 or 498A of the *Criminal Code*. Because they no longer had to wait three months after a case had been referred to a provincial Attorney-General, federal officials were finally given equal status to the provincial Attorneys-General in prosecuting combines cases.

1951: The *Combines Investigation Act* was amended (S. 37A) effective December 29 to prohibit resale price maintenance and refusals to supply. See Hunter (1991).

1952: The *Combines Investigation Act* was amended effective November 1 to
- split the functions of the Commissioner by creating the position of Director of Investigation and Research (investigation, enforcement, research) and the Restrictive Trade Practices Commission (appraisal, report and permission for DIR to use formal powers)
- permit the use of a Prohibition Order as the sole remedy
- have all prosecutions conducted by the federal Department of Justice
- provide for general inquiries into restraints of trade
- allow for dissolution of a merger, trust or monopoly (first structural remedy)
- remove the ceiling on fines in conspiracy cases under S.32 of the Act of S.498 of the Criminal Code.

Source: adapted from Stanbury (1981).

Appendix B

PRIVATE ACTIONS INVOLVING
COMPETITION LEGISLATION, 1889 TO 1923

1.   *Consumer's Cordage Company v. Connolly* (1901) 31 S.C.R. 244; (1903) 89 L.T.R. 347 **(Privy Council)**: The plaintiff was the sole producer of binder twine in Canada shortly after 1890. The Ontario government started a binder twine plant in a prison. Prices fell. The private firm had two nominees bid secretly on its behalf. One of them won and took over the prison plant where production was kept down to keep prices up. The SCC found there was an illegal conspiracy, but did not refer to the combines section at all or any cases (Gosse, 1962, pp. 90-93).

2.   *Hatley v. Elliott* (1905) 9 O.L.R. 185: Successfully relied on S. 520(d). Association of coal dealers in Brantford fixed prices and had a tendering scheme. Dispute over a particular tender.

3.   *Wampole et al. v. John T. Lyons* (1904) Q.B. 390; (1905) Q.B. 53: [get information]

4.   *Gibbins v. Metcalfe* (1905) **Man. L.R. 583**: Unsuccessfully relied on S. 520(c) and (d). The members of the Winnipeg Grain exchange refused to deal with the plaintiff as he was not abiding by its rules for a fixed commission for dealers - see *R. v. Gage*.

5.   *Wampole and Co. v. Karn Co.* (1906) 11 O.L.R. 619: Successfully relied on S. 520(c) and (d). Action on an RPM agreement adopted by national retail and wholesale associations whose object was to prevent price cutting. Prices apparently not fixed by the associations nor any collective enforcement. The judge found the RPM scheme was so effective as to "destroy competition."

6.   *Lefebvre v. Knott* (1907) 13 C.C.C. 223: Unsuccessfully relied on S. 498(d). Agreement by members of Master Plasters Association in Montreal in anticipation of a strike. Agreement to lock out strikers was valid.

7.   *United Shoe Machinery Co. v. Brunet* (1905) Que. S.C., 200-217; (1909) A.C. 330 **(Privy Council)**: United Shoe sought an injunction and damages to prevent certain shoe manufacturers from violating the lease they had made with United Shoe. The lease contained tying clauses requiring that the machines be used only on products which had been processed by machines of the same company.
     The defendants pleaded that they had been induced to take the machines under false representation and that the leases were unjust and oppressive because of the monopoly of United Shoe, hence were in restraint of trade and therefore void. While the Quebec courts sustained the shoe manufacturers, they were overruled by the Privy Council. The case led to an application for a Board of Investigation under the new *Combines Investigation Act* (see Ball, 1934, p. 32).

8.   *Weidman v. Shragge* (1910) 20 M.R. 178 (trial); (1910 20 M.R. 188 (appeal); (1912) 46 S.C.R. 1 **(SCC)**: Successfully relied on S. 498(d) at trial, but reversed upon appeal. Contract between two largest junk dealers in the prairie provinces with the object of controlling the trade - they had over 90% of the market. They had agreed on prices they were to pay for junk and to split profits. The agreement was ultimately found to have been an undue lessening of competition.

9.   *Stearns v. Avery* (1915) 33 O.L.R. 251: Successfully relied on S. 498(c). Apparently this was an RPM contract between a manufacturer and a customer.

10.   *Dominion Supply Co. v. Robertson Manufacturing Co.* (1917) 39 O.L.R. 495: Successfully relied on S. 498(b) and (d). Association of nail makers fixed prices and divided markets with penalties for violation. Customer was said to have failed to resell at the Association's prices.

11.   *MacEwan v. Toronto General Trusts Co.* (1917) 35 D.L.R. 435; (1917) 54 S.C.R. 381: Unsuccessfully relied on S. 498(d). The owner of a salt works leased them for five years. The owner retained the right to make salt, at prices fixed by the lessee, to the local retail trade. The lessee turned out to be acting for the Dominion Salt Agency, which controlled 90% of the salt produced in Canada.

12.   *Stewart v. Thorp* (1917) 27 C.C.C. 409 (Trial); (1917) 36 D.L.R. 752 (Alta C.A.); (1918) 49 D.L.R. 694 (SCC): Successfully relied on S. 498(d) at trial, but reversed on appeal. Two related coal-mining companies agreed to buy out a third in the same district where there were no other competitors. The object of the purchase was to close the third down. The selling firm gave no covenant not to restart.

13.   *Peloquin v. La Traverse* (1919) 33 C.C.C. 165; (1920) 54 D.L.R. 181: Successfully relied on S. 498(c) and (d). Price of installation of electrical lighting system in a house not agreed on in advance. The plaintiff billed on the basis of current prices agreed upon by local contractors in Montreal.

Chapter 3

ONE STEP FORWARD, TWO STEPS BACK, ONE STEP FORWARD: CANADIAN COMPETITION LAW REFORM, 1919 AND 1935

Brian R. Cheffins[*]
Faculty of Law
University of British Columbia

1.0 INTRODUCTION

Parliament greatly modified Canadian competition law in 1919 and 1935.[1] Recent events cast a favourable light on these reforms. In contrast to the federal government's hesitant approach to competition law revision between 1960 and 1986, Parliament acted quickly in 1919 and 1935.[2] Furthermore, both times the legislation seemed to be a step forward for Canadian competition policy. This paper will show, however, that the 1919 and 1935 reforms really involved two steps backward and that the government was taking a step forward when it dismantled the legislation.

---

[*]. The author would like to thank Brad Daisley and Professor W.A. Neilson, University of Victoria Law Faculty, for their advice and assistance in the preparation of this article.

1. *Board of Commerce Act*, S.C. 1919, c. 37; *Combines and Fair Prices Act*, S.C. 1919, c. 45; *Combines Investigation Act Amendment Act*, 1935, S.C. 1935, c. 54; *Dominion Trade and Commerce Act*, S.C. 1935, c. 59; and *Criminal Code Amendment Act*, 1935, S.C. 1035, c. 56, s.9.

2. The 1960-1986 period is briefly discussed by W.T. Stanbury, "The New Competition Act and Competition Tribunal Act: 'Not With a Bang, but a Whimper'," *Canadian Business Law Journal*, Vol. 12, 1986/87, pp. 4-8.

2.0 THE 1919 REFORMS

Prior to the 1919 reforms, two pieces of legislation formed the basis of Canada's competition policy. One was a *Criminal Code* provision which prohibited agreements that lessened competition unduly.[3] The other was the 1910 *Combines Investigation Act*.[4] The 1910 *Act* reflected the philosophy of W.L. Mackenzie King, who was the Minister responsible for drafting the legislation and steering it through Parliament. In carrying out his task, King espoused the advantages of big business and suggested that only "bad" trusts needed to be regulated. The 1910 legislation reflected these considerations, as it only prohibited mergers, monopolies and combines which operated to the detriment of the public.

Despite the existence of this legislation, Canadian competition policy was largely ineffective. Prosecutions were sporadic under the *Criminal Code* and the investigation procedure under the 1910 *Act* was used only once.[5] On the positive side, there was very little federal legislation restricting market forces. Some industries, such as banking, insurance and railways, were regulated and high tariffs did constrain competition, but prior to World War 1 the federal government generally refrained from intervening in the market's operation.[6]

The political, social and economic dynamics, however, were favourable to government regulation when World War 1 ended. During the War the federal government gained unprecedented experience in regulating the economy by creating the Wheat Board, the Imperial Munitions Board, the Food Controller, the Fuel Controller and the Cost of Living Commissioner.[7] These agencies were dismantled immediately after the armistice, but volatile economic and social conditions soon forced Robert Borden's Unionist government to consider reentering the regulatory field. The volatility arose from a rapid price rise in 1919, which, in turn exacerbated simmering labour

---

3. On the history of this provision see W.T. Stanbury, "Legislation to Control Agreements in Restraint of Trade: Review of the Historical Record and Proposals for Reform" in R.S. Khemani and W.T. Stanbury (eds.) *Canadian Competition Law and Policy at the Centenary* (Halifax: The Institute for Research on Public Policy). The modern equivalent is s.32 of the *Competition Act*, R.S.C. 1985, c. C-34.

4. S.C. 1910, c. 9. The origins of the legislation are discussed in Brian R. Cheffins, "The Development of Competition Policy, 1890-1940: A Re-Evaluation of a Canadian and American Tradition," *Osgoode Hall Law Journal*, Vol. 27, 1989, pp. 461-62.

5. Paul K. Gorecki and W.T. Stanbury, "The Administration and Enforcement of Competition Policy in Canada, 1889-1952," Chapter 2 in this volume.

6. See Carman D. Baggaley, *The Emergence of the Regulatory State in Canada, 1867-1939* (Ottawa: Economic Council of Canada, Technical Report No. 15, 1981) pp. 264-267.

7. *Ibid.*, p. 50; Bernard J. Hibbits, "A Bridle for Leviathan: the Supreme Court of Canada and the Board of Commerce," *Ottawa Law Review* Vol. 21, 1989, p. 67, and R.J. McFall, "Regulation of Business in Canada" *Political Science Quarterly*, Vol. 37, 1922, pp. 182-198.

tensions, the ultimate product of which was the Winnipeg General Strike. Consequently, M.P.s, the financial press and others expressed concern about strikes and class tension.[8] The government's immediate response was to establish a select committee of the House of Commons to inquire into the reasons for the high cost of living.

The outcome of the select committee's hearings was a bit surprising.[9] The Committee found that the rise in prices was due primarily to War demand and said that business could not be criticized for its pricing policies, since profit margins were reasonably close to actual cost and profiteering was no more common than in peace-time. Given this, one might have expected that the Committee would have suggested no legislative changes. Instead, it recommended the creation of a federal regulatory agency to deal with the high cost of living, perhaps because Robert Borden's Unionist government had already decided to pass such legislation.

The Committee suggested that the agency be authorized to impose price and profit controls and that it have the power to investigate and regulate combines, trusts and mergers. From a modern perspective, this is an odd combination, given that anti-combines legislation seeks to promote market competition while price and production controls operate in the opposite direction. The likely explanation is that at the time anti-combines legislation was thought to be an anti-inflation measure as much as a device for preserving competitive forces.[10]

Acting on the select committee's recommendations, Parliament created a Board of Commerce and vested it with regulatory power over prices and combines. The most important element of the Board's authority over prices was the power to investigate and prohibit the making or taking of unfair profits in relation to "necessaries of life," which were defined to include food, clothing and fuel.[11] Regarding combines, Parliament authorized the Board to

---

8. See Thomas Traves, *The State and Enterprise: Canadian Manufacturers and the Federal Government, 1917-1931* (Toronto: University of Toronto Press, 1979), pp. 7, 29; Thomas Traves, "Some Problems with Peacetime Price Controls: The Case of the Board of Commerce of Canada, 1919-20," *Canadian Public Administration*, Vol. 16, 1973, pp. 86-87; House of Commons, *Debates*, 1919, pp. 394, 4499, 4505 and *Monetary Times*, June 20, 1919, pp. 6, 10.

9. On the committee and its report, see Hibbits, *supra*, note 7, pp. 71-72; Lloyd Reynolds, *The Control of Competition in Canada* (Cambridge, Mass.: Harvard University Press, 1940), p. 141; Thomas Traves, "The Board of Commerce and the Canadian Sugar Refining Industry: A Speculation on the Role of the State in Canada," *Canadian Historical Review*, Vol. 55, 1974, pp. 159-60 and J. Castell Hopkins, *Canadian Annual Review, 1919* (Toronto: The Canadian Annual Review Ltd., 1920), pp. 333-34, 426-27.

10. See Paul K. Gorecki and W.T. Stanbury, *Objectives of Canadian Competition Policy, 1888-1983* (Montreal: The Institute for Research on Public Policy, 1984), pp. 116-18.

11. *Combines and Fair Prices Act*, *supra*, note 1, ss. 16, 18. These provisions may have been modelled after England's *Profiteering Act*, 9 & 10 Geo. 5, c. 66, which empowered the Board of Trade to investigate and fix maximum prices and profits.

investigate and restrain mergers, trusts, monopolies and agreements which had the effect of preventing or lessening competition and which operated to the detriment of the public. Furthermore, Parliament made the authority absolute by stipulating that the anti-combines provisions in the *Criminal Code* could not be utilized without Board approval. Finally, the 1919 legislation gave the Board the power to issue cease and desist orders to enforce its decisions. This is striking. This was the first time Parliament authorized the use of civil remedies to enforce competition legislation. Also, this was the only time prior to the 1970s that Canadian competition legislation contained such sanctions, which is rather surprising given the prominent role of regulatory, non-criminal remedies in the present *Competition Act*.[12]

Parliament created the Board of Commerce very abruptly, as the relevant legislation was passed only nine days after the Committee's report was published.[13] This stands in contrast to the time consuming creation of the U.S. Federal Trade Commission, with which the Board was often compared.[14]

The 1919 legislation was also a distinct shift in government policy. In 1910 King said it was unnecessary and undesirable to create a trade commission to regulate the 1910 *Combines Investigation Act*. Also, the Unionist Cabinet had shown no prior interest in the matter despite having had possession of draft trade commission legislation since 1917.[15] The upshot was that the Board was the first Canadian agency to have general regulatory authority over commercial and business practices.

---

12. *Combines and Fair Prices Act, supra*, note 1, ss. 2, 4 and 11(2),(4) and (5). The leading civil remedies provisions in the *Competition Act, supra*, note 3 are ss. 51(1),(2) and 64(1) and 70. On the introduction of civil remedies in the 1970s, see G. Kaiser, "The Stage I Amendments: An Overview" in J.R.S. Prichard, W.T. Stanbury and T.A. Wilson, eds. *Canadian Competition Policy: Essays in Law and Economics* (Toronto: Butterworths, 1979), pp. 33-41.

There are, not surprisingly, important differences between the civil remedies provisions in the 1919 legislation and the present legislation. For example, under the *Combines and Fair Prices Act*, the Board of Commerce was both investigator and adjudicator. Under the *Competition Act*, the Competition Tribunal, which issues the regulatory sanctions, only has an adjudicative function. Furthermore, while the *Competition Act* largely segregates civil remedies from criminal reinforcement, the Board of Commerce's regulatory powers were strongly buttressed by potential criminal sanctions. Primarily, the *Combines and Fair Prices Act* stipulated that failing to comply with a cease and desist order was a criminal offence and authorised the Board to recommend to provincial Attorneys-General that breaches of the *Act* be prosecuted.

13. The select committee issued its report on June 26th, the government introduced the legislation to Parliament on June 28th and the Governor-General gave Royal assent on July 7th.

14. The Federal Trade Commission's origins are discussed by Martin Sklar, *The Corporate Reconstruction of American Capitalism, 1890-1916: The Market, the Law and Politics* (Cambridge: Cambridge University Press, 1988), pp. 203-332. On comparisons between the F.T.C. and the Board of Commerce, see Canada, House of Commons, *Debates*, 1919, pp. 4519, 4526; W.T. Jackman, "Should the Board of Commerce be Retained," *Monetary Times*, June 4, 1920, p. 5; Canada, House of Commons, *Debates*, 1923, pp. 2594-95 and Reynolds, *supra*, note 9, p. 141.

15. See Canada, House of Commons, *Debates*, 1910, pp. 6859 and 1919, 4506-07.

The dramatic change in policy arose primarily from the desire to provide a signal to the public that the government was responding to the high cost of living and the resulting social strife.[16] G.B. Nicholson, who was a member of the special committee which recommended the 1919 legislation, said:

> In that connection it is well to ask ourselves, if the Bill is important why is it important? It is important chiefly for the reason that from one end of this country to the other there is a feeling that something must be done before this Parliament prorogues to grapple with the question of the high cost of living, and the undue profiteering which so many of our people believe is enhancing that cost.[17]

There was some skepticism in Parliament whether the legislation would have much impact on inflation.[18] Nevertheless, for M.P.s such as Horatio Hacken, a publisher from Toronto, the legislation was still worth supporting because "the appointment of a tribunal such as this...will remove ninety-five per cent of the dissatisfaction or the grouching that is going on."[19]

Still, the legislation's rapid passage is striking because the business community traditionally opposes competition legislation and has successfully blocked competition policy reform at other points in Canadian history.[20] Lack of influence was certainly not the reason for the absence of a similar phenomenon in 1919. Indeed, commercial and industrial interests had substantial connections with governments of the time.[21] The explanation instead is that most of the business community was cautiously supportive of or at least neutral toward the 1919 legislation.[22] While certain business people were critical of how quickly the legislation was passed, most understood why the government took rapid action and sympathised with the government's desire to reduce inflation and social strife.[23] Also, some business groups

---

16.   Traves, *supra*, note 9, pp. 159-60.

17.   Canada, House of Commons, *Debates*, 1919, p. 4499.

18.   *Ibid.*, pp. 4498-99, 4504, 4507-08.

19.   *Ibid.*, p. 4505.

20.   See, for example, W.T. Stanbury, *Business Interests and the Reform of Canadian Competition Policy, 1971-1975* (Toronto: Carswell/Methuen, 1977), especially pp. 45-46, 175-98, 208-14. See also Stanbury, *supra*, note 2 and Ian Clark, Chapter 6 in this volume.

21.   The relationship between business and government prior to World War II is discussed by Baggaley, *supra*, note 6, pp. 17-24, 276-83; Reynolds, *supra*, note 9, pp. 271-073; and Alan Finkel, *Business and Social Reform in the Thirties* (Toronto: James Lorimer & Co., 1979), pp. 4-20.

22.   Hibbits, *supra*, note 7, p. 74. The sugar refining industry in fact was involved with the creation of the legislation. See Traves, *State, supra*, note 8, p. 60 and Traves, *supra*, note 9, p. 161.

23.   See "Inflated Conditions Must be Removed," *Monetary Times*, May 30, 1919, 7 and July 2nd, 1919 letter from Montreal Board of Trade quoted in Canada, House of Commons, *Debates*, 1919,

thought Board investigations of commercial matters would be beneficial because the Canadian people would see that business in the country was being conducted properly.[24]

For most members of the business community, however, any support for the Board of Commerce was conditional on how the Board operated. Arthur Meighen, the Minister responsible for guiding the legislation through the House of Commons, was cognizant of such concerns and did his best to alleviate them by saying that the Board would not "be continually digging at the roots of our industrial life."[25] Still, there was some skepticism. The Canadian Manufacturers' Association said of the new provisions:

> If they are administered sanely there can be no great objection to such legislation, especially if it will have any real effect on the high cost of living. If the personnel of the Board of Commerce is made up of men who have had no business experience, or who are visionaries and theorists, the harm they can do is almost incalculable.[26]

The business press echoed these sentiments.[27]

Any concerns the business community had about the Board's use of its anti-combines powers should have been alleviated by its initial composition. The chairman, H.A. Robson, a Manitoba judge, had no enthusiasm for the Board's jurisdiction over combines and was sceptical of government intervention in the economy.[28] W.F. O'Connor who was assistant chairman and had close connections to major sugar refiners, said "the key note of this Act is that a combine is not necessarily an evil thing."[29] The remaining initial member was James Murdock, who, when he was Minister of Labour in the early 1920s, carefully denied that he had ever been any type of trust-buster.[30]

---

p. 4553.

24. Canada, House of Commons, *Debates*, 1919, p. 4505; "Economics, Prices and the War," *Monetary Times*, August 1, 1919, pp. 7-8; and "Duty of the Court of Commerce," *Financial Post*, July 12, 1919, p. 10.

25. Canada, House of Commons, *Debates*, 1919, p. 4557.

26. Quoted in Traves, *supra*, note 9, p. 160.

27. *Financial Post*, "A Square Deal for Business," July 5, 1919, p. 1.

28. Hibbits, *supra*, note 7, n. 149 and Traves, "Some," *supra*, note 8, p. 91. Even James Murdock, a fellow commissioner, alleged that Robson was "the 'safe and sane' representative of the 'big interests'" - J. Castell Hopkins, *Canadian Annual Review*, 1920 (Toronto: The Canadian Review Ltd., 1921).

29. Quoted in Jackman, *supra*, note 14, p. 5. O'Connor frequently acted as counsel for St. Lawrence Sugar Co. and other refiners. See generally Traves, *supra*, note 9, pp. 161, 168-70.

30. Canada, House of Commons, *Debates*, 1923, p. 2568.

These attitudes were manifested in the Board's anti-combines policy. During its tenure, the Board only took affirmative action against one combine, this being when it ordered some French Canadian bakers to dissolve their trade combination.[31] Also, the Board was reluctant to investigate alleged anti-competitive arrangements. For example, it declined to investigate alleged restaurant, shoe and clothing combines even after being presented with "a trunkload of evidence" by the the health officer of the City of Toronto.[32]

Even when the Board investigated anti-competitive activity its lack of enthusiasm was evident. In March 1920, upon the request of the Attorney-General of Ontario, it held an enquiry into a wholesale grocers' trade combination in Hamilton. The Board dismissed all charges on the basis that it was not contrary to the public interest for the members of the combine to establish a selling policy and to refuse to deal with those that would not comply with it. In the course of the proceedings O'Connor identified the Crown's informant and reproved the unlucky individual for his actions. The informant, an employee of one of the combine's members, was summarily fired from his position.[33]

Potentially the most significant action the Board took against combines was to require all parties to existing or proposed mergers, price-fixing arrangements and other trade combinations to identify themselves and to establish that they were not operating against the public interest.[34] Because the Board suspended operations within six months of issuing the order, it is not clear whether the filed information would have been used to develop a more aggressive competition policy. There is reason to doubt, however, that this would have occurred. Given its history, the Board probably would have been more inclined to sanction trade combinations than attack them.[35] Furthermore, even if it had intended to use the filed information to attack anti-competitive activity, resource problems may have proved intractable. For example, the Board suspended its investigation of a combine in the canning industry on the grounds that it could not secure the services of a qualified

31. Traves, "Some," *supra*, note 8, p. 90.

32. Canada, House of Commons, *Debates*, 1923, p. 2596. The Board did instruct the health officer to contact the Attorney-General.

33. Canada, House of Commons, *Debates*, 1920, p. 568; Hibbits, *supra*, note 7, pp. 69-70; McFall, *supra*, note 7, pp. 207-8 and *Canadian Annual Review*, 1920, *supra*, note 28, pp. 44-45.

34. Traves, *supra*, "Some," note 8, pp. 91-92.

35. The U.S. experience lends credence to this suggestion. The short-lived Industrial Board of the Department of Commerce, which bore some resemblance to the Board of Commerce, was created primarily to stabilize price structures in U.S. industries. See Robert Himmelberg, "Business, Antitrust Policy, and the Industrial Board of the Department of Commerce, 1919," *Business History Review*, Vol. 42, 1968, pp. 1-?.

accountant.[36] Clearly, then, the government would have to have supplied the Board with additional staff and funding if any rigorous attack on anti-competitive activity was going to be mounted.

Despite its alleged resource problems, the Board used its jurisdiction over unfair prices often enough to place itself in serious political trouble.[37] Retailers and farmers were particularly vocal opponents of the Board since they were the primary targets of its attack on unfair profits. Also, by early 1920 the cautious support of the Canadian Manufacturers' Association had turned into opposition, primarily because of the Board's attack on prices charged in the textile industry. The opposition took its toll, and in February 1920 Robson resigned as Chairman, saying that price-fixing and profit restrictions should not be a part of the permanent statute law. Furthermore, by April, M.P.s were criticizing the Board in the House of Commons.

At the same time, problems arose in the courts. In April 1920, in an application to strike down an order on newsprint prices, the Supreme Court of Canada interpreted "necessaries of life" narrowly, which case doubt on the scope of the Board's jurisdiction over unfair profits.[38] Two months later, in a reference on the constitutionality of the 1919 legislation, the Supreme Court split evenly on whether Parliament had the authority to legislation in relation to unfair price and profits.[39]

O'Connor, who had acted as counsel for the federal government in the constitutional reference, was frustrated by these setbacks. Consequently, he suggested to Prime Minister Borden that legislative amendments should be made to clarify the Board's authority. When Borden proved unreceptive, O'Connor resigned in June 1920. Murdock resigned soon after, saying that the Cabinet was out of sympathy with the Board of Commerce legislation.[40]

Three new members were appointed in July 1920, but the Board's fortunes did not improve. In October, after appeals by sugar refining companies for relief from rapidly falling prices, the Board fixed the retail price

---

36.   Traves, "Some," *supra*, note 8, p. 92 and "Board of Commerce Activities Suspended," *Monetary Times*, October 29, 1920, p. 7. The Board's refusal to follow up on the Toronto city health office's allegations was also attributed to resource considerations - Traves, *ibid.*, p. 91.

37.   Hibbits, *supra*, note 7, pp. 75-78, 110-11; *Canadian Annual Review*, 1919, *supra*, note 9, p. 336, and *Canadian Annual Review, 1920, supra*, note 28, pp. 484-90.

38.   Re *Price Brothers and Co. and the Board of Commerce* (1920) 60 S.C.R. 265. See Hibbits, *supra*, note 7, pp. 80-87, 97-102.

39.   Re *The Board of Commerce Act and the Combines and Fair Prices Act of 1919* (1920) 60 S.C.R. 456. The Board itself had referred the case to the Supreme Court. It had the authority to do so under the *Board of Commerce Act, supra*, note 1, s. 32. The case is discussed in detail by Hibbits, *supra*, note 7, pp. 79-80, 87-102.

40.   Hibbits, *supra*, note 7, pp. 108-9, 112; Traves, *supra*, note 9, p. 166 and *Canadian Annual Review, supra*, note 28, pp. 489-90.

of sugar at a level higher than the market price. This caused a storm of protest, which led the government to suspend the operations of the Board pending the appeal of the Supreme Court of Canada's constitutional reference decision to the Judicial Committee of the Privy Council.[41] Ultimately, the Privy Council held that the unfair profits and prices powers were invalid on the grounds that regulation of the accumulation and pricing of commodities was within the provinces' jurisdiction over property and civil rights.[42] Even though the anti-combines provisions survived without adverse comment, the federal government responded to the decision by immediately disbanding the Board of Commerce.

Because the Board had exclusive jurisdiction over the area, its dissolution left Canada without any enforceable competition legislation. W.L. Mackenzie King, who became Prime Minister in 1921, responded by orchestrating the enactment of the *Combines Investigation Act* in 1923.[43] King's views on competition law changed little since 1910 and the new legislation reflected this. For example, the 1923 *Act* reintroduced the provision which prohibited only those combines which were not in the public interest. Furthermore, because King still did not feel that it was necessary to have a permanent commission regulating competition law, the new legislation contained no direct equivalent to the Board of Commerce. The 1923 *Act* made an important improvement over the 1910 legislation, however, as responsibility for initiating investigations was placed in the hands of a government official, the Registrar.

3.0 THE 1935 REFORMS

The 1923 *Act* functioned more satisfactorily than its predecessors, as for the first time investigations and prosecutions were commenced with some regularity. The change came about primarily because the Registrar's office operated on an ongoing basis and was efficiently run. Overall, however, Canada's anti-combines policy remained poorly funded and unambitious.[44] Because of this, one might have thought that strengthening competition law

---

41. *Ibid.*, p. 492; Traves, *supra*, note 8, p. 93 and Traves, *supra*, note 9, pp. 166-70.

42. Re the *Board of Commerce Act, 1919* and *The Combines and Fair Prices Act, 1919* [1922] 1 A.C. 191. See Hibbits, *supra*, note 7, pp. 113-14.

43. S.C. 1923, c. 9. The 1910 *Act* was repealed in 1919 - *Combines and Fair Prices Act, supra*, note 1, s. 15. On King's views and the enactment of the 1923 legislation, see *supra*, note 4, pp. 468-69; Reynolds, *supra*, note 9, pp. 145-46 and Canada, House of Commons, *Debates*, 1923, pp. 2520-36, 2569-76, 2594-2609.

44. See *supra*, note 5, pp. 53-70; Reynolds, *supra*, note 9, pp. 146, 152, 166-71, 264-81; "To Tighten Combines Act," *Financial Times*, February 9, 1934, p. 1; "New Powers for Tariff Board," *Financial Post*, June 8, 1935, p. 2; Canada, *Report of the Royal Commission on Price Spreads* (Ottawa: King's Printer, 1937), pp. 251, 305, 476; and Gorecki and Stanbury, Chapter 2 in this volume.

was the primary objective of the 1935 anti-combines reforms. This is incorrect. Most people who advocated competition law revision in the mid-1930s wanted anti-combines enforcement to be weakened and wanted the Canadian government to increase its involvement in the regulation of market forces. These impulses in turn helped to shape the 1935 legislation.

The pressure for reform arose primarily because of economic distress. In good times and bad, Canadian business people have attempted to control competition within their trades and industries.[45]   During the Depression, however, it was more difficult to do so successfully.[46]   Furthermore, the consequences of failure were dramatic, because prices fell much more quickly in trades and industries where price competition could not be regulated.[47] Not surprisingly, then, competition was unpopular and was often referred to as being "cutthroat" and "destructive".[48]

Some business people also complained that the *Combines Investigation Act* made it more difficult to escape the effects of market forces.[49] Given the unambitious enforcement of the *Act*, their comments have to be treated with some skepticism. As the *Financial Post* said in 1934:

> The pat answer is that the *Combines Investigation Act* keeps the businessmen apart. The answer is inadequate and not entirely accurate. Because competition has gone to extremes, we cannot wisely jump to the conclusion that the [anti-]combines legislation is entirely or even largely to blame.[50]

Still, the complaints made were not entirely groundless. This was because of the pattern of enforcement and the Depression's influence on price control methods.   Limited resources forced the Registrar to rely almost entirely on informal reports to find out about prospective violations.   Most

---

45. See Traves, *State, supra*, note 8, pp. 9-10, 81-86; Reynolds, *supra*, note 9, pp. 53-54; and *supra*, note 20, p. 45.

46. See generally Reynolds, *supra*, note 9, pp. 97-102. The pattern was also evident in particular industries, such as baking. See *Price Spreads Report, ibid.*, p. 100 and *Special Committee on Price Spreads and Mass Buying: Proceedings and Evidence* (Ottawa: King's Printer, 1934), p. 300.

47. This is borne out by Reynolds' study of wholesale prices between 1926-1938. He examined nearly 40 industries which together encompassed four-fifths of the new product of Canadian manufacturing. He found that while price levels fell uniformly prior to 1929, between 1929 and 1933 prices fell 36% in competitive industries, 18% in industries where there were price agreements and 10% in monopoly industries. See *supra*, note 9, pp. 7-8, 71-78. His observations are borne out by the experiences of individual industries, such as furniture and rubber footwear. See *Price Spreads Report, supra*, note 44, pp. 73-75, 102-03.

48. See *Price Spreads Report, ibid.*, pp. 5-10 and Reynolds, *supra*, note 9, pp. 85, 94-96, 106.

49. See, for example, *R. v. Alexander* [1932] 2 D.L.R. 109, pp. 115-23; *Price Spreads Report, supra*, note 44, p. 95 and *infra*, notes 63-65.

50. See April 7, 1934, "Codes for Canada: 1. Why Do We Want Them?" p. 8.

complaints were made by business persons who had been disciplined for non-compliance with anti-competitive agreements or associational structures in their industry. The Registrar in turn was inclined to investigate such arrangements because evidence was easy to collect in comparison to other anti-competitive activities.

Consequently, between the Wars enforcement focused almost entirely on formal price fixing arrangements.[51] This pattern of enforcement probably was more distressing to business people than would have been the case in better economic times. This is because numerous sectors of the business community were having to rely increasingly on formal methods of price control, such as trade associations or holding companies, to regulate the intensive competition brought by the Depression.[52]

Independent retailers were the business sector most adversely affected by the Depression and the operation of anti-combines enforcement.[53] Prior to the Depression, chain stores had steadily grown at independents' expense. This occurred because the chains obtained their supplies more cheaply from manufacturers and used efficient distribution procedures. The Depression made matters worse for independent retailers as consumers became more conscious of the price advantages of chain stores and unemployed workers attempted to enter the retail trade despite declining demand. Furthermore, in terms of anti-combines policy, retailers were one of the sectors of the economy which had a legitimate reason to feel threatened. This was illustrated by the fate of the Proprietary Articles Trade Association. In order to help counteract the competitive advantages of chain stores, in the mid-

51. On the pattern of anti-combines enforcement between the Wars and the dynamics involved, see *supra*, note 5, pp. 29-40, 48-53, 86-87; Stanbury, *supra* note 3; Reynolds, *supra*, note 9, pp. 151-60; the summaries of formal investigations by the Registrar in L.A. Skeoch, *Restrictive Trade Practices in Canada* (Toronto: McClelland and Stewart, 1966), pp. 97-116 and R.A. Posner, *Antitrust Law: An Economic Perspective* (Chicago: University of Chicago Press, 1976).

52. On the differences between formal and informal control arrangements, see Reynolds, *supra*, note 9, p. 12. Examples of industries where a successful shift was made from tacit agreements to more formal methods of price control were rubber footwear and paper products. See Traves, *State*, *supra*, note 8, p. 71; Reynolds, *ibid.*, pp. 18-21 and *Price Spreads Report, ibid.*, p. 73. The device used in the paper products industry was Container Materials Ltd., which was prosecuted and convicted under the conspiracy provisions of the *Criminal Code - R. v. Container Materials Ltd.* [1942] S.C.R. 147. On trade associations in the 1930s, see Reynolds, *ibid.*, pp. 17-19 and V.W. Bladen, "The Role of Trade Associations in the Determination of Prices" *Canadian Journal of Economics and Political Science*, Vol. 4, 1938, pp. 223-. Unsuccessful formal price control arrangements are discussed by Reynolds, *ibid.*, pp. 21-30.

53. The retail trade and chain stores are discussed by Reynolds, *supra*, note 9, pp. 109-30 and the *Price Spreads Report, supra*, note 44, pp. 200-33. For contemporary accounts, see "Codes for Canada: 2. Competition As It Is Today," *Financial Post*, April 14, 1934, p. 9 and "Codes for Canada: 4. Role of Big Business," *Financial Post*, April 28, 1934, p. 8. Similar factors were at work in the U.S. See Ellis Hawley, *The New Deal and the Problem of Monopoly: A Study in Economic Ambivalence* (Princeton: Princeton University Press, 1966), pp. 247-50.

1920s the Association operated a nationwide retail price maintenance scheme for the drug trade. The Association, however, disbanded after an investigation under the *Combines Investigation Act.*[54]

H.H. Stevens, the Minister of Trade and Commerce in the Conservative Government led by R.B. Bennett, was receptive to the independent retailers' complaints. Stevens took their cause up in a speech to the Retail Shoe Merchants' Association in January 1934 in which he denounced chain stores and lauded local independent businessmen. His speech was favourably received in many quarters and generated considerable political momentum. This led the Conservatives to establish a select committee of the House, with Stevens as chairman, to investigate mass buying and price spreads.[55]

The committee hearings gave those who were dissatisfied with the competitive conditions in their industry the opportunity to express their concerns. E.J. Young, who wrote a dissent in the final report of the Price Spreads Commission, aptly summarized the tenor of the evidence given when he said:

> Witnesses appearing before the Price Spreads Commission were of all sorts and classes. They came to us with their grievances; we listened to them and then asked remedies they had to suggest. In nearly every case the suggested remedy was the same. They all said "eliminate our competition and we'll be alright."[56]

More specifically, those involved in the agricultural and livestock industries expressed concerns about unstable price and supply conditions.[57] Smaller retail merchants, on the other hand, complained primarily about

54. See *Investigation into the Proprietary Articles Trade Association, Interim Report of the Registrar* (Ottawa: F.A. Acland, 1926); *supra*, note 5, pp. 69-70, quoting *Annual Report of the Registrar, 1929/30*, and *Price Spreads: Evidence*, *supra*, note 46, pp. 471-72, 2579, 2582-83, 2608-10, 2618.

55. See Richard Wilbur, *H.H. Stevens: 1878-1973* (Toronto: University of Toronto Press, 1977), pp. 105-15 and Ernest Watkins, *R.B. Bennett: A Biography* (Toronto: Kingswood House, 1963), pp. 198-204.

56. Canada, House of Commons, *Debates*, 1935, p. 3539.

57. *Price Spreads...Evidence*, *supra*, note 46, pp. 247-29, 285-86 (per J.S. McLean, President Canada Packers Ltd.); pp. 304-5, 319-20 (per Warren Cook, Canadian Association of Garment Manufacturers), pp. 607-09, 619 (per Roderick MacLeay, rancher, Alberta), pp. 735-39 (per Jack Byers, Western Stock Growers Association), pp. 831-32 (per H.P. Kennedy, president Edmonton Stockyard Ltd.), pp. 998-1000 (per D.G. McKenzie, Minister of Agriculture, Manitoba), pp. 1194-95 (per J.F. McKay, president Ontario Tobacco Plantations ltd.), pp. 1254-58 (per George Hoadley, Alberta Minister of Agriculture), pp. 1429-30 (per Mark Bredin, president Canadian Bakers Association), pp. 1879-82 (per A.G. Munich, president Benson & Hedges of Canada), pp. 2579-81 (per Arthur Wilkinson, chairman Canadian Pharmaceutical Association) and pp. 3922-23 (Report of Enquiry into Fishing Industry).

competition from chain stores.[58] Despite the differing complaints, witnesses from all of these groups suggested their problems would be alleviated if the government actively regulated competition through industrial and commercial codes or marketing boards.[59] Many retail merchants also suggested that the federal government should control volume discounts, price discrimination and other allegedly unfair activities carried out by chains.[60] They argued that the government could do this by establishing of a federal commission which would have authority over trade practices.[61]

In terms of the *Combines Investigation Act*, the Retail Merchants' Association, the Canadian Plumbing and Heating Institute and the Canadian Pharmaceutical Association recommended that administration of the *Act* be shifted to a government department which would treat business groups more

---

58. *Price Spreads...Evidence, ibid.*, pp. 291-92, 296-97, 300, 304-6 (per Warren Cook, Canadian Association of Garment Manufacturers), pp. 324-26, 335-37, 339-48, 352 (per George Hougham, Retail Merchants' Association, Ontario), pp. 361-62 (per A.E. Grassby, Retail Merchants' Association, Manitoba), pp. 375-80, 384-84 (per C.C. Falconer, Retail Merchants' of Manitoba), pp. 395-402 (per W.L. McQuarrie, Retail Merchants' Association, Saskatchewan), pp. 433-45 (per Alexander MacKay, Retail Merchants' Association, Alberta), pp. 1346-48 (per J. Jette, president Caron Ltd., Montreal bakers), pp. 1359-65 (per Cecil Morrison, Morrison-Lamothe Ltd., Ottawa baker), pp. 1974-79 (per M.M. Robinson, chairman Ontario Growers' Markets Council), pp. 2169-70 (per E.S. Sargeant, vice-president, Canadian Goodrich Ltd.), pp. 2595-96, 2601-02, 2606-07 (per R.J. Sparks, counsel, Canadian Pharmaceutical Association) and pp. 3923-24 (Report of Enquiry into Fishing Industry).

59. *Price Spreads...Evidence, ibid.*, pp. 292-94 (per Warren Cook, Canadian Association of Garment Manufacturers), pp. 353-56 (per George Hougham, Retail Merchants' Association, Ontario), pp. 365-68 (per A.E. Grassby, Retail Merchants' Association, Manitoba), pp. 610, 623-24 (per Roderick MacLeay, rancher, Alberta), pp. 648-56 (per R.H.M. Bailey, president, Alberta Milk and Cream Producers Association), pp. 702-07, 712-15 (per Ingimar Ingaldson, manager Canadian Live Stock Co-operative - Western, Ltd.), p. 795 (per Rosario Messier, Retail Merchants Association, Quebec), pp. 835-36, 905-10 (per H.P. Kennedy, president Edmonton Stockyard Ltd.), p. 931 (letter from Saskatchewan Livestock Board), pp. 1103-05 (per Robert Wright, president Western Canada Live Stock Union), pp. 1165-66 (per E.C. Scythes, president Victoria Tobacco Plantations), pp. 1242-43 (per Archibald Leitch, tobacco grower), pp. 1264-66, 1279-87, 1291 (per George Hoadley, Alberta Minister of Agriculture), p. 1434 (per Mark Bredin, president Canadian Bakers Association), pp. 1613-14, 1638 (per Gray Miller, president Imperial Tobacco Co.), pp. 2175, 2177-79, 2183-87 (per C.H. Carlisle, president of Goodyear Rubber Co. of Canada), pp. 3843-44 (per R.J. Sparks, Canadian Pharmaceutical Association) and p. 3924 (Report of Enquiry into Fishing Industry).

60. *Price Spreads...Evidence, ibid.*, p. 369 (per A.E. Grassby, Retail Merchants' Association, Manitoba), pp. 381, 392 (per C.C. Falconer, Retail Merchants of Manitoba), pp. 400-01 (per W.L. McQuarrie, Retail Merchants' Association, Saskatchewan), pp. 467-68 (per J.C. Doyle, Retail Merchants' Association, Nova Scotia), p. 795 (per Rosario Messier, Retail Merchants' Association, Quebec), p. 1347 (per J. Jette, president Caron Ltd., Montreal bakers).

61. *Price Spreads...Evidence, ibid.*, p. 353 (per George Hougham, Retail Merchants' Association, Ontario), pp. 457-58 (per Alexander MacKay, Retail Merchants' Association, Alberta), p. 795 (per Rosario Messier, Retail Merchants' Association, Quebec), p. 2188 (per C.H. Carlisle, president of Goodyear Rubber Co. of Canada) and pp. 2618, 3842 (per R.J. Sparks, counsel Canadian Pharmaceutical Association).

favourably.[62] Some also suggested that Parliament amend the *Act* to legalize arrangements like the Proprietary Articles Trade Association.[63] Others even recommended that the *Act* be repealed.[64]

Stevens, who dominated the proceedings of the Committee in its early stages, was very sympathetic to the complaints made and the corresponding proposals for legislative change. This in turn increased his political popularity, especially among independent retailers, wholesalers and smaller agricultural interests.[65] Consequently, there was reason to think in mid-1934 that the Committee's recommendations would reflect Stevens' views and that legislation along similar lines would result.[66]

After the initial euphoria, however, the momentum behind the Stevens program slowed. The business community probably played a role in this process.[67] If there had been unanimous business support for the proposals made, the prospects for legislative reform would have been good, especially given the influence of industrial and commercial interests over government.[68] There was, however, no such consensus. To start, important sectors of the business community had little reason to support the proposals made before the Committee. This was because in industries where competition could be controlled without formal arrangements there was little need to ask for relief from the *Combines Investigation Act* or for assistance in controlling competition. Hence, it is not surprising that participants in such industries

---

62.   *Price Spreads Report, supra*, note 44, p. 477.

63.   *Price Spreads...Evidence, supra*, note 46, pp. 352-53 (per George Hougham, Retail Merchants' Association, Ontario) and pp. 2603-04, 2607, 2611, 2615-18 (per R.J. Sparks, counsel Canadian Pharmaceutical Association). Some others proposed that their own industry should be exempt - see pp. 1391-93 (per James Dempster, Toronto baker).

64.   *Price Spreads...Evidence, ibid.*, pp. 2174, 2177-78, 2184 (C.H. Carlisle, president Goodyear Tire and Rubber Company of Canada) and *Price Spreads Report, supra*, note 44, p. 474.

65.   *Wilbur, supra*, note 55, pp. 125, 130-31, 144, 162-63.

66.   "Codes for Canada: 5. Who is to Control?" *Financial Post*, May 5, 1934, p.9, and "Stevens' Methods, Not His Objectives, Are Bad," *Financial Post*, September 1, 1934, p. 6.

67.   Robert Himmelberg's work influence the interpretation of the business community's role given here. He has argued in another context that the competitive conditions of industries divided the business community and put a brake on antitrust reform. He has argued that the movement for antitrust revision in the U.S. in the 1920s because those in profitable industries were indifferent to or opposed complete dismantling of the Sherman Act. See his *The Origins of the National Recovery Administration: Business, Government and the Trade Association Issue* (New York: Fordham University Press, 1976). Traves' analysis of the 1917-31 period is also consistent with this line of analysis. See, for example, *State, supra*, note 8, pp. 8-9, 155-67.

68.   As Traves has said about the years between the Wars, "when the business community united behind a specific policy its influence was often decisive" - *State, supra*, note 8, p. 9.

generally did not use the Price Spreads investigation as a platform for legislative reform.[69]

Beyond being indifferent, however, significant elements of the business community likely opposed at least some of the proposed legislative changes. In some cases, such as with chain stores, business had self-interested reasons for disagreeing with the changes being proposed before the Price Spreads Committee. There was opposition, however, among sectors of the business community which were not directly implicated in the proceedings.[70] Price and production controls were probably the least popular proposal. This was primarily because of the history of the National Recovery Administration (NRA), which was created as part of Franklin Roosevelt's New Deal in 1933. Under the NRA, industries were authorized to create codes of fair competition which the NRA was to enforce. Some codes prohibited sales below cost and allowed liberal exchanges of statistical information while others established direct price controls. By 1934, however, the NRA had run into difficulties because it had become a bureaucratic nightmare and had not met the expectations of the U.S. business community. Citing these problems, the financial press argued that the Canadian government should not experiment with price and production controls.[71] The evidence suggests that significant elements in the business community shared these views.[72]

The absence of consensus in the business community probably allowed other factors to play a more prominent role in determining the fate of the Price Spreads Committee and its recommendations. One of these factors was a growing political rift between Stevens and Bennett. The conflict led Stevens to resign from the Cabinet just before the Committee was to recommence hearings in December 1934, this time as a Royal Commission. Stevens' resignation, which was prompted by his refusal to apologize for comments

---

69. Among the industries which Reynolds classified as monopoly or informal agreement, the Price Spreads commission only investigated the agricultural implements industry.

70. For instance, the financial press was skeptical about the charges being made against chain stores and there was criticism of the proposal that the *Combines Investigation Act* be repealed. See "Large Scale Merchandising Goes on Trial," *Financial Post*, February 17, 1934, p. 6; and "A Clear Field for Big Trusts?" *Financial Post*, June 30, 1934, p. 2.

71. "Probe Can Learn From US Codes," *Financial Post*, March 17, 1934, p. 1; "Mere Action is Not Progress," *Financial Post*, April 21, 1934, p. 6; "Regulation or Regimentation," *Financial Post*, June 2, 1934, p. 1; "The Blue Eagle - A Sick Bird," *Financial Times*, October 5, 1934, p. 8; "Competition in Favour Again," *Financial Post*, October 15, 1934, p. 2 and "Policeman of Business," *Financial Post*, October 15, 1934, p. 6. The NRA was dismantled in 1935 after its powers were successfully challenged in *Schechter* v. *U.S.* 295 U.S. 495. On the history of the NRA, see Hawley, *supra*, note 53, pp. 56-61, 66-72, 114-17, 122-26 and 130.

72. On business opposition to the NRA and the other Stevens proposals, see Finkel, *supra*, note 21, pp. 33, 38 and "Ottawa Reforms Still Further Modified," *Financial Times*, June 7, 1935, p. 6. On other evidence of opposition, see Wilbur, *supra*, note 55, pp. 145-46 and Canada, House of Commons, *Debates*, 1934, p. 203.

made about the directors of Simpson's department store, meant that he was not made chairman of the Royal Commission. While Stevens' reduced duties allowed him to make speeches across the country, he spent less time at the hearings, which probably had a moderating influence on the proceedings.[73]

Another factor which may have had a moderating influence on the proceedings was the prospect that the Royal Commission's recommendations would be transformed into legislation. The chances of this occurring grew as a result of a series of speeches which Bennett gave in early 1935. Bennett, who was attempting to recreate the spirit of Roosevelt's New Deal, said in one of his speeches that he would invite Parliament to take action in accordance with the Commission's recommendations.[74]

Whatever the reasons, the Royal Commission's recommendations did not fully accord with the wishes of either Stevens or the many witnesses who wanted legislative reform.[75] Instead, it drew on the NRA experience and opposed comprehensive government involvement in price and production control. In addition, the Royal Commission noted that chain stores operated efficiently and declined to recommend government regulation of them.

The Royal Commission, however, did support a number of the suggested changes. To start, its final report recommended the creation of regulatory boards to assist livestock producers and fishermen. The Royal Commission also said that Parliament should establish a government trade commission and suggested that the trade commission be given regulatory authority over some of the conduct which concerned the witnesses who had appeared before it. For example, the final report recommended that the trade commission have the power to supervise price and production agreements in industries where competition had gone to extremes.[76] Furthermore, the Royal Commission said the new agency should have the authority to hold fair trade conferences and

---

73. Wilbur, *ibid.*, pp. 134, 141-45, 156-61 and John H. Thompson and Allen Seager, *Canada 1922-39: Decades of Discord* (Toronto: McClelland and Stewart, 1985), pp. 260-61.

74. Speech of January 7, 1935, set out in J.R.H. Wilbur, *The Bennett New Deal: Fraud or Portent* (Toronto: Copp Clark Publishing, 1968), p. 86. The speeches are discussed by Thompson and Seager, *ibid.*, pp. 261-64. Bennett's and Roosevelt's legislative initiatives are analysed in detail by W.H. McConnell, "Some Comparisons of the Roosevelt and Bennett 'New Deals'," *Osgoode Hall Law Journal*, Vol. 9, 1971, pp. 221-60.

75. For contemporary accounts of Stevens' objectives and the drafting of the *Report*, see "Price Spreads Final Report's Progress Slow," *Financial Post*, March 2, 1935, 1; "More Commissions to Rule Business," *Financial Post*, April 27, 1935, p. 1 and "The Bitter Bit," *Financial Post*, June 8, 1935, p. 6. The recommendations are set out in *Price Spreads Report, supra*, note 44, pp. xviii-xxv, 232-33, 256-58, 260-75.

76. The holding of fair trade conferences by the U.S. Federal Trade Commission in the 1920s was probably the source of the Royal Commission's trade conference recommendation. The Federal Trade Commission conferences drafted codes of conduct for particular industries which in turn served as blueprints for co-operation among industry members. See Himmelberg, *supra*, note 67, pp. 62-65.

should be given regulatory authority over unfair trade practices. The final report also suggested that the legislative definition of unfair trade practice should be left open, with territorial price discrimination, discriminatory discounts and predatory conduct being included as examples.

In addition, the final report proposed that the trade commission should be able to declare specific industries to be monopolies. Such industries would then be regulated by the trade commission but would be exempt from prosecution under combines legislation. Finally, the Royal Commission recommended that administration of the *Combines Investigation Act* be shifted to the new agency.

The legislative package which the Bennett Government introduced, and which Parliament enacted, was based largely on the Price Spreads Commission's recommendations. The package, however, was significantly less ambitious. For example, the Government refrained from establishing independent regulatory boards for live stock producers and fishermen.[77] Also, no independent trade commission was created, because the body Parliament established, the Dominion Trade and Industry Commission, was to be made up of the members of the Tariff Board.[78] The Government argued on this point that the Tariff Board could adequately perform the Commission's duties and that money would be saved by not setting up an independent board.[79] Opposition M.P.s, however, were skeptical of the Government's motives, and pointed out that since the Tariff Board was already very busy, the Commission's functions would probably be neglected.[80] Concern about the issue was understandable, as the Price Spreads final report had specifically recognized that the success or failure of the trade commission depended almost entirely on its members.[81]

Another government modification of the Price Spreads recommendations was its refusal to give the Trade and Industry Commission regulatory jurisdiction over monopolies. The government relied on a legal opinion based on the Privy Council's judgment in the *Board of Commerce* constitutional reference as grounds for its decision. For similar reasons, it also declined to give the Trade Commission the power to regulate unfair trade practices by way of regulatory, non-criminal sanctions. The government instead made criminal some conduct which the Price Spreads Commission had classified as unfair trade practices, namely certain types of price discrimination and

---

77. Canada, House of Commons, *Debates*, 1935, p. 3486.

78. *Dominion Trade and Industry Commission Act, supra*, note 1, s. 3(2).

79. Canada, House of Commons, *Debates*, 1935, pp. 3444, 3511-12.

80. See Canada, House of Commons, *Debates*, 1935, pp. 3445. 3519, 3525 and 3535. On the tariff board, see also "New" *supra*, note 44 and Reynolds, *supra*, note 9, p. 148.

81. *Supra*, note 44, p. 265.

predatory pricing. The Trade Commission's authority in this area was limited to investigating and recommending the prosecution of violations of the new criminal legislation and other federal laws which prohibited unfair trade practices.[82]

The government's legislative package did, however, match the Royal Commission's recommendations in some respects. For example, the Trade and Industry Commission replaced the Registrar as the administrator of the *Combines Investigation Act.* In addition, Parliament authorized the Trade Commission to conduct fair trade conferences. Furthermore, the Commission was given the power to approve price and production agreements in industries where "wasteful" or "demoralizing" competition was occurring. If the Governor in Council agreed with the Commission's decision, the agreement was then immune from prosecution.[83]

The financial press and some elements in the business community praised the legislative package on the basis that it would be cheaper and would interfere less with business than legislation which faithfully followed the Royal Commission's recommendations.[84] Many M.P.s, however, were critical of the package. Some were frustrated by the government's reliance on constitutional arguments as a justification for not enacting more ambitious legislation.[85] Others argued that the price discrimination and predatory pricing provisions would be unenforceable and did not go far enough to meet the concerns of small business. Some M.P.s asserted, on the other hand, that price competition would be hindered if these provisions were in fact enforced.[86] Concerns about the reduction of competition also led to criticism of the Trade Commission's power to approve price and production agreements. As J.E. Isley, a Liberal M.P., said:

> We believe it is thoroughly illogical to confer upon the commission, as its primary function, the prevention of combines and then, further down the list, to confer on it the power to sanction combines. That is thoroughly illogical and contradictory.

---

82. Canada, House of Commons, *Debates,* 1935, pp. 3476-78 and 3508-10; *Dominion Trade and Industry Commission Act, supra,* note 1, ss, 2(h), 20 and *Criminal Code Amendment Act, supra,* note 1. On the constitutional validity of price discrimination provisions, see Canada, House of Commons, *Debates,* 1935, pp. 3482-83, 3488, 3490.

83. *Dominion Trade and Industry Commission Act, supra,* note 1, ss. 14, 23 and Canada, House of Commons, *Debates,* 1935, pp. 3533, 3537.

84. "Ottawa," *supra,* note 72. The *Financial Post* and a number of daily newspapers had criticized the Price Spreads Report for recommending the creation of numerous bureaucratic commissions. See Canada, House of Commons, *Debates,* 1935, p. 3484.

85. Canada, House of Commons, *Debates,* 1935, pp. 3513, 3519-20 and 3534.

86. Canada, House of Commons, *Debates,* 1935, pp. 3476-79, 3488-98. The conflicting themes underlying the criticism of the legislation are described by Gorecki and Stanbury, *supra,* note 10, pp. 122-25. The concern about unenforceability has been borne out, see *infra* note 95.

> I admit that in times of distress and depression you will find highly competitive industries where there seems to be cutthroat competition, waste and chaos. But our contention is that competition is the best protection the public has....We believe in the *Combines Investigation Act* and do not believe in its nullification by conferring on the trade and industry commission or on the government, on the advice of the commission, the power to sanction combines....[87]

The Liberals were soon to have the opportunity to restore the *Combines Investigation Act* to its pre-1935 form. Despite passing the *Dominion Trade and Industry Commission Act*, amending the *Combines Investigation Act* and the *Criminal Code* and enacting a number of other important legislative changes, the Conservatives' attempt to capture the spirit of the New Deal failed. Also, Stevens, unhappy with the manner in which his legislative proposals had been treated, left the Conservatives and formed the Reconstructionist Party. His party, which not surprisingly was supported by retail merchants and small manufacturers, cut into Conservative support, which in turn contributed to a landslide victory for Mackenzie King's Liberals.[88]

King, who was not enthusiastic about government regulation of the economy, ultimately referred the entire Bennett New Deal to the courts.[89] In relation to the competition law reforms, the provisions giving the Trade and Industry Commission the power to sanction price and production agreements were struck down. The courts, however, upheld the price discrimination and predatory pricing provisions and much of the *Dominion Trade and Industry Commission Act*.[90]

Even though some elements of the 1935 reforms survived judicial scrutiny, the Liberals enacted new anti-combines legislation in 1937.[91] In so doing, they essentially restored the 1923 legislation. Consequently, the 1937 *Combines Investigation Act* prohibited the same conduct as its 1923

---

87. House of Commons, *Debates*, 1935, p. 3528. See also pp. 3522, 3539 and 3541.

88. Wilbur, *supra*, note 55, pp. 177-200 and Thompson and Seager, *supra*, note 73, pp. 272-76.

89. H. Blair Neatby, *William Lyon Mackenzie King: The Prism of Unity* (Toronto: University of Toronto Press, 1976), p. 38 and McConnell, *supra*, note 74 at pp. 252-56.

90. *A.G. Ont.* v. *A.G. Can.* (Reference re *Dominion Trade and Industry Commission Act, 1935*) [1936] S.C.R. 379 (S.C.C.), varied [1937] A.C. 405 (J.C.P.C.) and *A.G. B.C.* v. *A.G. Can.* (Reference re s. 498A of the *Criminal Code*) [1936] S.C.R. 363 (S.C.C.), affd. [1937] 368 (J.C.P.C.). The federal government did not appeal the Supreme Court of Canada's decision that the price and production agreement provisions were *ultra vires*.

91. The powers created by the *Dominion Trade and Industry Commission Act* remained vested in the Tariff Board, but were rarely used before they were repealed in 1946.

counterpart and the administrative structure and the investigative procedure were almost the same.[92]

The Liberals also retained the criminal prohibitions of price discrimination and predatory pricing.[93] Indeed, these provisions remain on the statute books today.[94] They have, however, rarely been enforced.[95] This is probably fortunate. Given that Parliament enacted the provisions in response to complaints about the effects of competition, logically, strict enforcement would have dulled the operation of market forces.[96]

U.S. experience bears this out. In 1936 Congress responded to retail merchants' complaints about chain stores by enacting price discrimination prohibitions in the *Robinson-Patman Act*.[97] In the 1960s and early 1970s, the U.S. government enforced the provisions quite rigorously.[98] The experience was not a happy one. By the 1980s, academics and government officials agreed that *Robinson-Patman* enforcement probably limited competition rather than promoting it.[99] Consequently, the U.S. government now rarely attacks price discrimination.[100]

---

92.   S.C. 1937, c. 23. See Reynolds, *supra*, note 9, pp. 150-52 and Canada, House of Commons, *Debates*, 1937, pp. 1346-53. One difference was that the official in the charge was referred to as the Commissioner.

93.   These provisions were in the *Criminal Code* until 1960 when Parliament moved them to the *Combines Investigation Act* - S.C. 1960, c. 45, s. 13.

94.   *Competition Act*, *supra*, note ss. 34(1)(a) - (c).

95.   Gorecki and Stanbury, *supra*, note 10, Appendix B, Table 2-B and D.G. McFetridge and S. Wong, "Predatory Pricing in Canada: The Law and Economics," *Canadian Bar Review*, Vol. 63, 1985, p. 688.

96.   Contemporary examinations of the economic underpinnings of Canadian price discrimination and predatory pricing legislation include McFetridge and Wong, *ibid.*, pp. 703-33 and B. Dunlop, D. McQueen and M. Trebilcock, *Canadian Competition Policy: A Legal and Economic Analysis* (Toronto: Canada Law Book Inc., 1987), pp. 208-31.

97.   15 U.S.C., s. 13, amending the *Clayton Act*, 15 U.S.C. 21. See Hawley, *supra*, note 53, pp. 247-54.

98.   The legislation can be enforced by the Federal Trade Commission, by the Department of Justice or by private plaintiffs. The Federal Trade Commission was responsible for most of the U.S. government enforcement. See R. Posner, *The Robinson-Patman Act: Federal Regulation of Price Differences* (Washington, D.C.: American Enterprise Institute for Public Policy Research, 1976), pp. 29-31 and A. Stone, *Economic Regulation and the Public Interests: The Federal Trade Commission in Theory and Practice* (Ithaca, N.Y.: Cornell University Press, 1977), pp. 98-101, 118-19.

99.   Stone, *ibid.*, pp. 101-19 and H. Hansen, "Robinson-Patman Law: A Review and Analysis," *Fordham Law Review*, Vol. 51, 1983, pp. 1114-19, 1188-96.

100.   Hansen, *ibid.*, pp. 1174-86. Private plaintiffs, however, still bring actions with some regularity.

4.0 CONCLUSION

For those who followed the attempts to reform Canadian competition legislation between 1960 and 1986, the speed with which legislative changes were made in 1919 and 1935 might have been cause for amazement and envy. A closer look at the 1919 and 1935 reforms, however, reveals a different picture. The rapid changes were not the result of a long-term shift in attitudes toward competition. Instead, the competition law reforms were components in larger legislative packages which were enacted quickly in order to alleviate political pressure arising from distressed economic conditions. The urgency involved in turn led the federal government to test the limits of its constitutional jurisdiction and likely contributed to the hasty dismantling of the reforms when political and economic circumstances changed.

The collapse of the 1919 and 1935 legislative packages was not a setback for Canadian competition policy. As products of poor economic times, the 1919 and 1935 reforms focused more on controlling competitive forces than enhancing the operation of the market. Consequently, while the reforms were in some way a step forward, in others they were two steps back. Taken as a whole, it likely was a step forward for the long-term interests of Canadian competition policy when the 1919 and 1935 reforms were dismantled and replaced, even if ultimately competition law ended up in much the same position in 1937 as it was in 1923.

Chapter 4

HISTORY OF PRICE MAINTENANCE LEGISLATION IN CANADA

Tamara Hunter
Davis & Company
Vancouver

The purpose of this paper is to trace the origins and development of the legislation in respect to price maintenance in Canada. Section 1 covers the period prior to 1950 in which there was no specific legislation dealing with price maintenance and its companion offence, refusal to supply. Section 2 describes the work of the MacQuarrie Committee in 1950 which led to the first legislation in 1951. The new legislation and changes made in 1952 are outlined in Section 3. Section 4 describes the loss-leader defence and other amendments made in 1960. Section 5 traces the efforts to amend the 1951 legislation in the decade ending with the amendments of 1976. Finally, in Section 6, the 1986 amendments are described very briefly.

1.0 1889 TO 1950

Until 1951, Canadian competition law did not contain a specific prohibition of resale price maintenance.[1] However, the practice was recognized as problematic for the maintenance of competitive markets long before it was addressed by legislation.[2] At first, the law of price maintenance

---

*. Ms. Hunter was a Third Year Law student at the University of British Columbia, when this paper was written. She was a Clerk to the Honourable Mr. Justice Antonio Lamer, Supreme Court of Canada in 1990-91.

1. See the discussion in Gorecki and Stanbury, Chapter 2 in this volume.

2. See, for example, *Investigation into the Proprietary Articles Trade Association*, Report of Commissioner - Combines Investigation Act (Ottawa: October 24, 1927).

in Canada closely followed the English Common Law.[3] By the nineteenth century, the English case law had established that agreements to maintain resale prices were agreements in restraint of trade. However, agreements in restraint of trade would be lawful and enforceable if the restraint was "reasonable" (taking into account the interests of the parties concerned and the interests of the public).[4] The case law established a general rule which presumed restraints of trade to be unreasonable until proven otherwise by the party relying on them, but many cases indicated that the parties themselves were the best judges of reasonableness. In 1889, the Canadian Parliament passed an Act[5] which made it an offence to conspire, combine, agree or arrange unlawfully to (inter alia): "unduly prevent, limit, or lessen the manufacture or production of any such article or commodity, or to unreasonably enhance the price thereof." On the basis of this legislation, certain agreements of the type used to maintain prices would be criminal offences, not merely unenforceable agreements as was the case under the English common law. Under the Combines Investigation Act of 1923,[6] any combination resulting from an agreement or arrangement to limit facilities, to prevent or lessen production, or competition, to enhance price or to fix a common price or resale price was a criminal offence if the combination had operated or was likely to operate to the detriment or against the interest of the public.

The Canadian case law interpreting these provisions of the Criminal Code and the Combines Investigation Act indicated that a scheme of resale price maintenance could "probably" come within the prohibition where there was an agreement to limit, supply and regulate price, made between two or more persons who dominate the trade in a particular product through their control of the greater portion of the available supply.[7] No Canadian decision found the provisions to be violated where a single person or corporation had a dominant position in a trade and endeavoured to maintain resale prices.[8] Thus, prior to the 1951 legislation, resale price maintenance could only constitute an offence where it formed part of an illegal combination.

---

3. See: J.A. Corry, "The Law of Resale Price Maintenance in Canada" forming Appendix I of Investigation into An Alleged Combine in the Distribution of Tobacco Products, Report of the Commissioner (Ottawa: King's Printer: August 31, 1938).

4. See M.J. Trebilcock, The Common Law Restraint of Trade: A Legal and Economic Analysis (Toronto: Carswell, 1986).

5. 63-64 V., c. 46, s. 3 (the parent of s. 498 of the Criminal Code, R.S.C. 1927, Ch. 36).

6. Combines Investigation Act, S.C. 1923, c. 9, ss. 2 & 26.

7. J.A. Corry, supra, note 3.

8. Ibid. See also L.A. Skeoch, "Canada" in B.S. Yamey (ed.) Resale Price Maintenance, London, Weidenfeld & Nicholson, 1966, p. 29.

According to the Economic Council of Canada,[9] it was a controversy involving publicity and the suspension of anticombines activity during the Second World War, when production, the allocation of resources, and the setting of prices were subject to direct control, which led to the establishment of the MacQuarrie Committee and ultimately to the establishment of the first legislation on price maintenance in 1951.   In 1949 the Combines Commissioner, Mr. F.A. McGregor, resigned after his report to the Minister of Justice regarding price fixing agreements in the flour-milling industry was largely ignored.[10]   The flour-milling inquiry had uncovered that price fixing agreements had been maintained in the industry since at least 1936, that these agreements remained in force during the war, and that the firms had colluded in bidding for government contracts.   Mr. McGregor called for a stronger statute with a clear statement of government policy with respect to enforcement, and raised the issue of an industry being condemned for carrying out policies sanctioned by the War-time Prices and Trade board during the war and tacitly allowed by the government in the subsequent period of decontrol.   This incident resulted in a great deal of criticism being levelled at the government.

2.0   MACQUARRIE COMMITTEE

In 1950, the federal government appointed the MacQuarrie Committee to study both the purposes and methods of the *Combines Investigation Act* and related Canadian statutes, and the legislation and procedures of other countries.   The Committee (named after its chairman) was asked to recommend "...what amendments, if any, should be made to our Canadian legislation in order to make it a more effective instrument for the encouraging and safeguarding of our free economy."[11]

The MacQuarrie Committee examined resale price maintenance in the light of two standards of judgment:[12] does resale price maintenance favour a free economy? and does it promote economic efficiency? After hearing representations from interested parties and conducting studies of its own, the Committee concluded that the direct and immediate effect of resale price maintenance was the elimination of price competition among retailers in price-maintained goods. Although price maintenance might shift competition from

---

9. Economic Council of Canada, *Interim Report on Competition Policy* (Ottawa, Information Canada: July 1969), pp. 56-57.

10. See the discussion in Gorecki and Stanbury, Chapter 2 in this volume.

11. See Statement of the Minister of Justice, House of Commons, June 27th 1950, cited in *Report to the Minister of Justice*, Committee to Study Combines Legislation (Ottawa: Queen's Printer) March 8, 1952, p. 55.

12. *Ibid.*, p. 57.

price to service, resale price maintenance prevented the trader from providing the alternative of less service and lower prices to consumers. Furthermore, resale price maintenance was found to facilitate and make more effective horizontal agreements among manufacturers, thus producing an effect similar to that which would result from direct collusion. Where measures of enforcement were involved in a scheme of price maintenance, it established "a private system of law allowing no appeal to the courts of justice."[13] In summary, the Committee found that the practice of resale price maintenance was detrimental to a free economy.

In relation to the standard of economic efficiency, the Committee found that while there was some evidence that resale price maintenance contributed to price stability, it led to a higher level of prices than would exist under more competitive, unstable conditions. The Committee found that resale price maintenance prevented two possible forms of monopolistic practices which tend to produce unreasonable retail prices, namely, the use of monopoly power at the retail level and the "loss-leader" device. Retail monopoly power was thought to be prevented by the fact that maintained prices constituted both a minimum and a maximum. However, the Committee indicated that the practice of resale price maintenance was an overly broad mechanism for enforcing maximum prices. Similarly, while resale price maintenance afforded protection against loss-leading, more direct and desirable weapons could be found to curb these practices. While resale price maintenance could act to protect the small business outlets (by maintaining margins), the Committee felt that this benefit was exaggerated. Finally, while resale price maintenance did help to protect the reputation of branded goods and facilitated advertising, the Committee noted that advertising was a powerful force and indicated that the slight disadvantage which might arise from the prohibition of resale price maintenance was not significant. In summary, the Commission found that resale price maintenance was not desirable on the grounds of economic efficiency.

The findings of the MacQuarrie Committee thus indicated that resale price maintenance was not justified by either of the stated standards. Therefore, the Committee recommended that:

"It should be made an offence for a manufacturer or other supplier:
1. To recommend or prescribe minimum resale prices for his products.
2. To refuse to sell, to withdraw a franchise or to take any other form of action as a means of enforcing minimum resale prices."[14]

The Committee further recommended that suppliers should be free to suggest and enforce maximum resale prices and that issuing list prices should not in

---

13. *Ibid.*, p. 68.

14. *Ibid.*, p. 71.

itself be prohibited as long as it was made clear that the price mentioned was not recommended or prescribed by the manufacturer as a minimum.

3.0 NEW LEGISLATION, 1951 AND 1952

The conclusions and recommendations of the MacQuarrie Committee regarding resale price maintenance were considered by Parliament in December 1951, and an amendment to the *Combines Investigation Act* was passed. A Joint Committee of the Senate and the House of Commons on Combines Legislation was formed to review the Report of the MacQuarrie Committee and to recommend proposed implementing legislation to the House of Commons. The Joint Committee was provided with a draft bill, prepared by the Combines Branch, which was virtually identical to the provisions which were eventually enacted.[15] The Joint Committee heard submissions from various parties and generally discussed the merits of enacting an offence of resale price maintenance, but did not conduct a clause by clause analysis of the proposed bill. A great deal of concern was expressed over the problem of loss-leader selling by various members of the Committee, but the Joint Committee recommended in its final report that this problem be addressed by vigorous enforcement of the "predatory pricing" offence contained in s. 498A of the *Criminal Code* (which had been enacted in 1935). The offence of price maintenance was introduced into Canadian law as s. 37A of the *Combines Investigation Act*.[16]

In 1952, this offence was renumbered as section 34,[17] and subsections 4, 5 and 6 were repealed and a new provision was substituted.[18] There were five substantive changes introduced by the 1952 amendment. First, the distinction in penalty as between a person and a corporation was removed. Second, the fine was changed from a fixed sum to a fine in the discretion of the court. Third, the penalty was changed from a fixed fine or two years imprisonment, to a fine or a prison term not exceeding two years, or both. Thus the penalty could now include both a fine and a prison term and the latter could be less than two years.   Fourth, the provision authorizing the Commissioner to institute and conduct an inquiry in regard to the offence of price maintenance

---

15.   The only difference was that s. 37A(2)(e), s. 37A(3)(a)(v), and s. 37A(3)(b)(iii) - all dealing with maximum discounts - were not part of the draft bill. See Joint Committee of the Senate and The House of Commons on Combines Legislation, *Minutes of Proceedings and Evidence*, Final Report #15, December 7, 1951.

16.   R.S.C. 1927, c. 26 by *An Act to Amend the Combines Investigation Act* S.C. 1951 [2nd sess.] c. 30, s. 1. The text of S.37A is contained in Appendix A.

17.   *An Act to Amend the Combines Investigation Act and the Criminal Code* S.C. 1952, c. 39, s. 4.

18.   See Appendix A.

was repealed.   A more general provision authorizing inquiries by the Commissioner was added as s. 8 of the *Act*. Finally, the provision dealing with a report of an inquiry respecting this offence was repealed.

4.0   LOSS LEADER DEFENCE, 1960

At the time of the MacQuarrie Report, those opposed to the abolition of resale price maintenance had argued that the practice of loss-leader selling would be disastrous for small distributors.[19] The MacQuarrie Report itself stated that the "loss-leader device" was a monopolistic practice which was not compatible with the public interest. However, the MacQuarrie Committee indicated that loss-leader selling was not an immediate danger and that better methods than resale price maintenance could be derived through careful study to control the practice.

In 1954-55, the Restrictive Trade Practices Commission (RTPC) conducted an extensive inquiry into the practice of selling articles at prices below net purchase cost was not prevalent and had no significant effect on the industries studied. Where the practice did exist, it was found to occur for short durations and was restricted to a very limited range of articles. Therefore, the RTPC made no recommendation for legislative action in the area of loss-leader selling.[20] It concluded that the abolition of resale price maintenance had not led to a situation where loss-leader selling was operating as a monopolistic device detrimental to the public interest.

Despite the conclusions of the RTPC, the advocates of price maintenance mounted another attack on loss-leader selling after the defeat of the Liberal Government (which had brought in the original offence in 1951) in 1957 by the Conservatives under John Diefenbaker.

In 1960, E.D. Fulton, Minister of Justice, put Bill C-58 before the House of Commons. In moving for Second Reading of the Bill, Mr. Fulton indicated that the purpose of the proposed amendment was to improve the current legislation by maximizing the reconciliation between the interests of small businessmen and the interests of consumers. The Minister indicated that the Government had received many complaints and representations regarding the problem of loss-leader selling. He stated that the previous legislation left small businesses "completely defenceless" against the operation of their more powerful competitors and the large retail chains, and that the provisions were designed to prevent the monopolization of certain trades by particular merchants through unfair and undesirable business practices.[21]

---

19.   See L.A. Skeoch, *supra*, note 8 at pp. 35-36.

20.   RTPC, *Loss Leader Selling* (Ottawa: Queen's Printer, 1955).

21.   *Debates*, House of Commons, Vol. IV 1960, May 30, 1960, pp. 4339-4356.

The Bill was referred to the Standing Committee on Banking and Commerce and was reported out of Committee with only one minor proposed amendment.[22] Thus, in 1960, the offence of price maintenance was amended.[23] Subsection 5 was added. It delineated the several defences: loss-leadering, "bait and switch," misleading advertising, and inadequate level of servicing.[24]

In 1966, the Supreme Court of Canada upheld the constitutionality of the price maintenance provisions in *Regina* v. *Campbell*.[25]

In the 1970 revision of the Statutes of Canada,[26] the offence was renumbered as section 38.

5.0 1976 AMENDMENTS

The process of change leading up to the 1976 amendments took place over a ten year period. In 1966, the federal government asked the Economic Council of Canada to prepare a report on competition policy. The Council issued its report in July of 1969.[27] With respect to price maintenance, the Council recommended that it should continue to be subject to *per se* prohibition under criminal law. The Council suggested that a manufacturer who printed a retail price on a package should be required to indicate clearly that it was a suggested price only. The Council's major recommendation was that the defences set out in s. 34(5) be eliminated (loss leadering was to be considered in more detail before deciding whether it should be eliminated). The Council stated that if the practices referred to in the subsection were undesirable, they should be more directly and generally prohibited. The Council stated: "To discourage an undesirable practice by weakening the prohibition of another is not a sound principle."[28]

Following the submission of the Council's Report, the government introduced Bill-256, the *Competition Act*, in the House of Commons. This Bill was unpopular with business, and was scrapped after the October 1972

---

22. The original Bill contained five defences. Section 34(5)(e) would have read: "that the other person was unfairly disparaging the value of articles supplied by the person charged, in relation to their price or otherwise." The Committee felt that this wording was too vague and the subsection was unnecessary. See Standing Committee on Banking and Commerce, *Minutes of Proceedings and Evidence*, No. 8, July 19, 1960.

23. *An Act to Amend the Combines Investigation Act and the Criminal Code* S.C. 1960, c. 45, s. 14.

24. The text can be found in Appendix A.

25. (1964), 46 D.L.R. (2d) 83 (Ont. C.A.); affirmed (1966), 58 D.L.R. (2d) 673 (S.C.C.).

26. *Combines Investigation Act* R.S.C. 1970, c. C-23.

27. *Interim Report on Competition Policy, supra*, note 9.

28. *Interim Report on Competition Policy, supra*, note 9 at p. 105.

general election in which the Liberals became a minority government.[29]   In July of 1973, the government began implementing its competition policy in two stages. The first stage was introduced as Bill C-227, an act to amend the *Combines Investigation Act.* The government indicated that the amendments to the price maintenance provisions were designed to correct weaknesses in the existing provisions.[30]

Because price maintenance could be accomplished without a requirement to sell at a specific price, minimum mark-up or maximum discount, the existing provisions were reworded (changed to "attempt to influence upward, or to discourage the reduction of" a price) to cover the situation where the supplier simply directed the other party to "get your price up" until the supplier was satisfied with the price level. Under the previous provisions, this situation was thought to fall outside of the words of the offence.   The government also stated that experience had shown that the initiative in price maintenance could come not only from the supplier, but also from other customers who put pressure on the supplier to control the pricing policies of their competitors.[31] Therefore, the new provisions referred not to the supplier who supplies a product for resale, but to "any person engaged in the business of producing or supplying a product."

The government did not state a specific rationale for extending the section to a person who had intellectual property rights with respect to a product.

The government indicated that the "saving provision" contained in s. 38(2) was necessary to prevent the section applying to communications between members of a firm or between affiliated companies. The government stated: "Such communications should be regarded as internal to one economic entity and not within the ban against resale price maintenance."[32]   Bill C-227 also adopted the Economic Council of Canada's recommendation that the defences in s. 38(5) be discontinued.

The government did not give any explanation for the changes embodied in ss. 38(3) and 38(4), but with respect to the pre-ticketing exemption, the following explanation was offered:

---

29.   See W.T. Stanbury, *Business Interests and the Reform of Canadian Competition Policy, 1971-1975* (Toronto, Carswell/Methuen, 1977).

30.   *Proposals for a New Competition Policy,* First Stage, Bill C-227, November 1973, Ottawa, Department of Consumer and Corporate Affairs, pp. 81-83.

31.   *Ibid.,* p. 81.

32.   *Ibid.,* p. 81.

> One reason for this qualification is that it avoids many small merchants the time-consuming and costly necessity of pricing individually the many articles on their shelves. It also places Canadian manufacturers and middlemen on an equal footing with those who affix or apply a resale price outside Canada to an article that is to be exported into Canada, and who are beyond the reach of Canadian law.[33]

The effect of s. 38(6) was said to be that it would make it an offence for a large retailer to tell a manufacturer that he will not buy his product unless he withholds it from another retailer whose competition the first supplier fears because of the low pricing policy of the second merchant.

After the Christmas recess of Parliament, Bill C-227 was reintroduced unchanged as Bill C-7. After six days of debate, the Bill was referred to the House Standing Committee on Finance, Trade and Economic Affairs. While Bill C-7 was in the Committee stage, the minority Liberal government was defeated on a non-confidence motion.[34] When Parliament reconvened, M. Andre Ouellet, the new Minister of Consumer and Corporate Affairs, introduced Bill C-2 (identical to Bill C-7 and Bill C-227). Bill C-2 was referred to the House Standing Committee on Finance, Trade and Economic Affairs after Second Reading. The Minister proposed thirty amendments to Bill C-2 in Committee, five of which dealt with the offence of price maintenance. All of these amendments were made and remain in the current offence of price maintenance.

M. Ouellet proposed that ss. 38(1)(b) and 38(6) have added to them the words "because of the low pricing policy of that person," so that it would be explicit that the provisions were aimed at a refusal to sell on account of a low pricing policy and not on some other basis. The Minister indicated that while the possibility of some other interpretation being put on the sections was "remote," concern had been expressed on this point.[35]

The Minister also proposed that s. 38(2)(b) have added to it the words "or where the person attempting to influence the conduct of another person and that other person are principal and agent." Some concern had been expressed that the provision might prevent a principal from instructing his agent as to the prices at which the latter was to sell the former's products. While the Minister believed such concern to be unwarranted, he noted that it would be allayed by the amendment proposed.[36]

M. Ouellet proposed an amendment to s. 38(3), whereby the word "evidence" was changed to the word "proof" - the amended provision would

---

33. *Ibid.*, p. 82.

34. May 8, 1974 - see W.T. Stanbury, *supra*, note 29, p. 220.

35. Standing Committee on Finance, Trade and Economic Affairs, *Minutes of Proceeding and Evidence*, #15, December 3, 1974, Appendix J.

36. *Ibid.*

require proof that the person making a suggestion of a retail price also made it clear that the suggested retail price was not obligatory. This amendment was proposed "for the purpose of meeting the possible argument that any scintilla of evidence, no matter how unsatisfactory, would upset the burden of proof."[37]

Finally, the Minister proposed that s. 38(7.1) be added to the proposed legislation on the basis that a definition of "control" was required, as the term was used in s. 38(7).

The extension of the prohibition contained in s. 38(1) to "one who extends credit by way of credit cards" was moved in Committee by Mr. Cafik, the Minister's parliamentary secretary.[38] M. Ouellet in supporting the amendment stated: "Therefore, by putting the credit card apparatus there, we allow the retailers who honour credit cards the possibility of giving a cash discount to a customer if he so desires to do this." The restoration of the defences now contained in s. 38(9) was also suggested by Mr. Cafik and the provisions were contained in the proposed legislation in the final report of the Standing Committee to the House.[39] M. Ouellet stated in Committee that "we thought it might perhaps be better not to interfere with the act for the time being."[40] This change may also have been due to the extensive lobbying carried out by business interests during the period of legislative change.[41]

The penalties now set out in s. 38(8) were increased from a fine in the discretion of the court and/or two years imprisonment to a fine and/or five years imprisonment via an amendment made by Mr. Rodriguez (NDP). M. Ouellet did not oppose the amendment.[42]

Bill C-2 received Third Reading, passed through the Senate without further amendment to the provisions regarding price maintenance and came into force on January 1, 1976.[43]

In 1976, the offence was considerably broadened and altered.[44] The entire section 38 was repealed and replaced. Here is a summary of the

---

37. *Ibid.*

38. Standing Committee on Finance, Trade and Economic Affairs, *Minutes of Proceeding and Evidence*, #55, June 3, 1975.

39. Standing Committee on Banking, Trade and Commerce, *Minutes of Proceedings and Evidence*, Final Report, June 5, 1975.

40. *Ibid., Minutes of Proceedings and Evidence*, June 3, 1975, p. 61.

41. See W.T. Stanbury, *supra*, note 29.

42. Standing Committee on Finance, Trade and Economic Affairs, *Minutes of Proceeding and Evidence*, #55, June 3, 1975.

43. W.T. Stanbury, *supra*, note 29, p. 221.

44. *An Act to Amend the Combines Investigation Act* S.C. 1974-75-76, c. 76, s. 18(1).

substantive changes introduced in 1976. The former definition of "dealer" was removed from the section. A new category of persons who could be liable for the offence of price maintenance was established, and included persons who produce a product, those who extend credit and those who have exclusive rights and privileges conferred by a patent, trade mark, copyright or registered industrial design. The phrase "person engaged in <u>manufacturing</u>" was deleted from the category, and was presumably replaced by the term <u>producing</u>. The phrase "person engaged in ... selling" was also deleted from the category. The prohibition against price maintenance where accomplished through the exercise of patents, trade marks, copyrights or registered industrial designs was now clearly delineated.   This point was in some doubt prior to the amendment.[45]

The phrase "article or commodity" was replaced by the word "product" which includes an article and a service.[46]

The phrase "any other means whatever," which refers to modes of influencing a purchaser of products, was changed to read "any <u>like</u> means."

The offence of price maintenance was no longer tied to a situation of resale. This change had two effects: it expanded the practices which constitute price maintenance and it expanded the range of liability.   Modes of interference now include the supply, offer to supply, or advertisement of a product.

The offence was now limited to any other person engaged in business <u>in Canada</u> who supplies, offers or advertises a product <u>within Canada</u>.   The limitation "within Canada" is new and applies to paragraphs 38(1)(a) and (b).

Prior to this amendment, it was an essential ingredient of the offence that there be an inducement to sell at a <u>specified</u> price, discount or markup. The amendments broaden the prohibition considerably by providing that no producer or supplier may attempt to influence the price upwards or discourage the reduction of any price.[47] A specific price, discount or markup is no longer an essential ingredient of this offence.

The amendment compiled into one the prohibition of influencing price upward or discouraging the reduction of a price, the various methods of price maintenance previously delineated in the former ss. 38(2)(a) to 38(2)(e).

The prohibition of refusal to sell or supply was amplified to include refusal to supply a product or to otherwise discriminate against another person. In order to avoid confusion, it is important to note that in the prior legislation, the subject heading "refusal to sell" referred to refusal of a dealer

45.   Gordon Kaiser, "The Stage I Amendments: An Overview" in J.R.S. Prichard, W.T. Stanbury and T.A. Wilson (eds.) *Canadian Competition Policy: Essays in Law and Economics* (Toronto: Butterworths, 1979), pp. 41-42.

46.   See Interpretation section (s. 2).

47.   Kaiser, *supra*, note 45.

to sell to a reseller. In the amended provisions, the subject heading "refusal to supply" refers to the inducement of a supplier, by a third person, not to sell to another.

The various specific prohibitions of refusal to sell or supply goods set out in the former s. 38(3), were compiled into one broad prohibition declaring it an offence to refuse to supply, or to otherwise discriminate against a person "because of the low pricing policy of that other person."

The amended provisions exclude affiliated companies and other affiliated parties from the scope of the offence of price maintenance.

Suggested retail prices and publications by a supplier (other than a retailer) of resale prices are *prima facie* attempts to influence upward the selling price.

The amendments clearly delineate what appears to be a new offence (s. 38(6)). This provision states that <u>no person</u> shall induce a <u>supplier</u> (as a condition of his doing business with the supplier) to refuse to supply a product to another because of the low pricing policy of that other person. This provision makes it an offence to <u>induce</u> a supplier to refuse to supply products. It is possible that this was formerly prohibited within the parameters of the old s. 38.

The defences relating to refusal or counselling of refusal to sell or supply products arise only "in a prosecution under paragraphs (1)(b)." The defences section previously read "in a prosecution under this section." The phrase "refusal to supply a product" is used rather than the previous phrase "refusal to sell or supply." However, "supply" includes the word "sell" (s. 1(6)).

Pre-ticketing is specifically exempted from the provisions which deem suggested retail prices or advertisements an "attempt to influence the price upward."[48]

The amendments increased the penalty of imprisonment from a term not exceeding two years, to imprisonment for five years.

6.0 1986 AMENDMENTS

In 1986,[49] subsections 38(7) and 38(8.1), which defined "affiliated companies" for the purpose of subsection (2), were repealed. A more expanded definition of "affiliated companies" was added to s.2, the definitions section.

The wording of the offence of price maintenance remains the same today, however, in the 1985 revision of the Statutes of Canada, the offence was

---

48.   *Ibid.*

49.   *An Act to establish the Competition Tribunal and to amend the Combines Investigation Act and the Bank Act and other Acts in consequence thereof*, S.C. 1986, c. 26, s. 38. It was by this legislation that the name of the Act was changed to the *Competition Act* (ss. 18 & 19).

renumbered as section 61.[50] Accordingly, subsections 61(7) and 61(8) have been repealed.[51]

50. *Competition Act*, R.S.C. 1985, c. C-34.

51. *An Act to establish the Competition Tribunal and to Amend the Combines Investigation Act and the Bank Act and other Acts in consequence thereof*, R.S.C. 1985, c. 19 (2nd. Supp) s.36. Sections 61(7) and 61(8) of R.S.C. 1985 correspond to sections 38(7) and 38(7.1) of R.S.C. 1970.

Appendix A

TEXT OF LEGISLATION AND AMENDMENTS THERETO

1.   *An Act to Amend the Combines Investigation Act*, S.C. 1951 [2nd sess.], c. 30, s. 1 amending *Combines Investigation Act*, R.S.C. 1927, c. 26.

37A. (1) In this section "dealer" means a person engaged in the business of manufacturing or supplying or selling any article or commodity.

(2) No dealer shall directly or indirectly by agreement, threat, promise or any means whatsoever, require or induce or attempt to require or induce any other person to resell an article or commodity

(a) at a price specified by the dealer or established by agreement,
(b) at a price not less than a minimum price specified by the dealer or established by agreement,
(c) at a markup or discount specified by the dealer or established by agreement,
(d) at a markup not less than a minimum markup specified by the dealer or established by agreement, or
(e) at a discount not greater than a maximum discount specified by the dealer or established by agreement, whether such markup or discount or minimum markup or maximum discount is expressed as a percentage or otherwise.

(3) No dealer shall refuse to sell or supply an article or commodity to any other person for the reason that such other person

(a) has refused to resell or to offer for resale the article or commodity
       (i) at a price specified by the dealer or established by agreement;
       (ii) at a price not less than a minimum price specified by the dealer or established by agreement,
       (iii) at a markup or discount specified by the dealer or established by agreement,
       (iv) at a markup not less than a minimum markup specified by the dealer or established by agreement, or
       (v) at a discount not greater than a maximum discount specified by the dealer or established by agreement, or
(b) has resold or offered to resell the article or commodity
       (i) at a price less than a price or minimum price specified by the dealer or established by agreement,
       (ii) at a markup less than a markup or minimum markup specified by the dealer or established by agreement, or
       (iii) at a discount greater than a discount or maximum discount specified by the dealer or established by agreement.

(4) Every person who violates subsection two or three is guilty of an indictable offence and is liable on conviction to a penalty not exceeding ten thousand dollars or to two years' imprisonment, or if a corporation to a penalty not exceeding twenty-five thousand dollars.

(5) The Commissioner has authority to institute and conduct an inquiry into all such matters as he considers necessary to inquire into with a view of determining whether this section has been or is being violated and to make a report thereon in writing to the Minister, and for such purposes the Commissioner has all the powers,

authority, jurisdiction and duties that are conferred upon him by this Act, including sections sixteen and seventeen, with respect to an inquiry as to whether a combine exists or is being formed.

(6) A report of an inquiry under this section shall be dealt with in the same manner as a report of an inquiry or investigation under this Act as to whether a combine exists or is being formed.

2.   *An Act to Amend the Combines Investigation Act and the Criminal Code*, S.C. 1952, c. 39, s. 4.

The amendment renumbered the provision as section 34 and repealed and substituted subsections 4, 5 and 6 with a new subsection 4:

(4) Every person who violates subsection two or three is guilty of an indictable offence and is liable on conviction to a fine in the discretion of the court or to imprisonment for a term not exceeding two years or to both.

3.   *An Act to Amend the Combines Investigation Act and the Criminal Code*, S.C. 1960, c. 34, s. 14.

(5) Where, in a prosecution under this section, it is proved that the person charged refused or counselled the refusal to sell or supply an article to any other person, no inference unfavourable to the person charged shall be drawn from such evidence if he satisfies the court that he and any one upon whose report he depended had reasonable cause to believe and did believe

(a) that the other person was making a practice of using articles supplied by the person charged as loss-leaders, that is to say, not for the purpose of making a profit thereon but for the purposes of advertising;
(b) that the other person was making a practice of using articles supplied by the person charged not for the purpose of selling such articles at a profit but for the purpose of attracting customers to his store in the hope of selling them other articles;
(c) that the other person was making a practice of engaging in misleading advertising in respect of articles supplied by the person charged; or
(d) that the other person made a practice of not providing the level of servicing that purchasers of such articles might reasonable expect from such other person.

4.   *Combines Investigation Act*, R.S.C. 1970, c. C-23

The section was renumbered as section 38 as part of the 1970 revision of the Statutes of Canada.

5.   *An Act to Amend the Combines Investigation Act*, S.C. 1974-75-76, c. 76, s. 18(1)

The amendment repealed the entire section and replaced it with the following:

38. (1) No person who is engaged in the business of producing or supplying a product, or who extends credit by way of credit cards or is otherwise engaged in a business that relates to credit cards, or who has the exclusive rights and privileges conferred by a patent, trade mark, copyright or registered industrial design shall, directly or indirectly,

(a) by agreement, threat, promise or any like means, attempt to influence upward, or to discourage the reduction of, the price at which any other person engaged in business in Canada supplies or offers to supply or advertises a product within Canada; or

(b) refuse to supply a product to or otherwise discriminate against any other person engaged in business in Canada because of the low pricing policy of that other person.

(2) Subsection (1) does not apply where the person attempting to influence the conduct of another person and that other person are affiliated companies or directors, agents, officers or employees of

(a) the same company, partnership or sole proprietorship, or
(b) companies, partnerships or sole proprietorships that are affiliated,

or where the person attempting to influence the conduct of another person and that other person are principal and agent.

(3) For the purposes of this section, a suggestion by a producer or supplier of a product of a resale price or minimum resale price in respect thereof, however arrived at, is, in the absence of proof that the person making the suggestion, in so doing, also made it clear to the person to whom the suggestion was made that he was under no obligation to accept the suggestion and would in no way suffer in his business relations with the person making the suggestion or with any other person if he failed to accept the suggestion, proof of an attempt to influence the person to whom the suggestion is made in accordance with the suggestion.

(4) For the purpose of this section, the publication by a supplier of a product other than a retailer, of an advertisement that mentions a resale price for the product is an attempt to influence upward the selling price of any person into whose hands the product comes for resale unless the price is so expressed as to make it clear to any person to whose attention the advertisement comes that the product may be sold at a lower price.

(5) Subsections (3) and (4) do not apply to a price that is affixed or applied to a product or its package or container.

(6) No person shall, by threat, promise or any like means, attempt to induce a supplier, whether within or without Canada, as a condition of his doing business with the supplier, to refuse to supply a product to a particular person or class of persons because of the low pricing policy of that person or class of persons.

(7) For the purposes of subsection (2),

(a) a company is affiliated with another company if
    (i) one is a subsidiary of the other
    (ii) both are subsidiaries of the same company
    (iii) both are controlled by the same person, or
    (iv) each is affiliated with the same company; and
(b) a partnership or sole proprietorship is affiliated with another partnership, sole proprietorship or a company if both are controlled by the same person.

(7.1) For the purposes of this section, a company is deemed to be controlled by a person if shares of the company carrying voting rights sufficient to elect a majority of the directors of the company are held, other than by way of security only, by or on behalf of that person.

(8) Every person who violates subsection (1) or (6) is guilty of an indictable offence and is liable on conviction to a fine in the discretion of the court or to imprisonment for five years or to both.

(9) Where, in a prosecution under paragraphs (1)(b), it is proved that the person charged refused or counselled the refusal to supply a product to any other person, no inference unfavourable to the person charged shall be drawn from such evidence if he satisfies the court that he and any one upon whose report he depended had reasonable cause to believe and did believe

(a) that the other person was making a practice of using products supplied by the person charged as loss-leaders, that is to say, not for the purpose of making a profit thereon but for purposes of advertising;
(b) that the other person was making a practice of using products supplied by the person charged not for the purpose of selling such products at profit but for the purpose of attracting customers to his store in the hope of selling them other products;
(c) that the other person was making a practice of engaging in misleading advertising in respect of products supplied by the person charged; or
(d) that the other person made a practice of not providing the level of servicing that purchasers of such products might reasonably expect from such other person.

6.   *An Act to establish the Competition Tribunal and to amend the Combines Investigation Act and the Bank Act and other Acts in consequence thereof,* S.C. 1986, c. 26, s. 38.

The amendment repealed subsections 38(7) and (7.1) and a more expansive definition of affiliated companies was put in S.2.

7.   *An Act to establish the Competition Tribunal and to amend the Combines Investigation Act and the Bank Act and other Acts in consequence thereof,* R.S.C. 1985, c. 19 (2nd Supp), s. 36.

This is the 1985 revision to the Statutes of Canada. Section 38 became S. 61 effective December 12, 1988.

Chapter 5

MISLEADING ADVERTISING AND DECEPTIVE MARKETING PRACTICES: THE EVOLUTION OF LEGISLATION, ADJUDICATION AND ADMINISTRATION

W. Chris Martin
Marketing Practices Branch
Bureau of Competition Policy
Department of Consumer & Corporate Affairs

Firmness-Audacity   French Scientific Bureau   Success-Happiness
P.O. Box 169, Hochelaga, Montreal, Canada
Audaces fortuna juvat.   Montreal, Canada

       Madam, -- In going over our books we find that nine only out of the hundreds of people who had written to us, have deferred ordering our marvellous home treatment against self-consciousness, bashfulness and self-diffidence.

       You are one of them, and as we have as yet no one in your locality or in that neighbourhood who has been in a position to experience the happy results ensured by our treatment, the Bureau has decided to let you have the benefit of our treatment at a loss, for the sole purpose of advertising it. We shall send you our twelve lessons in 'Auto-Suggestion' with fifty three of our tablets 'Anti-Geno', the full treatment for one dollar ($1), under the express understanding that you will refrain from imparting this information to any one.

       Now then, if you are a sufferer from the thousand inconveniences inflicted by shyness, if you find that you are beaten in the race by your neighbour, though she may not be more clever than yourself, if in love, as well as in business matters you do not attain that measure of success which your sterling qualities would seem to warrant, you alone will be to blame for it. As for us, we have done all that it was in the power of human beings to do.

                       Please accept our best compliments,
                       Bureau Scientifique Francais.
                       (1914 circular)[1]

---

1.   Taken from House of Commons Debates, May 8, 1914, v. IV, at 3467-8.

1.0 LEGISLATIVE ORIGINS

1.1 1914-1960 - The Criminal Code

While the 100th anniversary of anti-combines legislation was recognized in 1989,[2] another anniversary of sorts also occurred. It was 75 years since the first enactment of a law dealing with false advertising. On June 12, 1914, *An Act to amend the Criminal Code*[3] received Royal Assent, thereby adding the following provision to the criminal law of Canada:

> 406A. Every person who knowingly publishes or causes to be published any advertisement for either directly or indirectly promoting the sale or disposal of any real or personal movable or immovable property, or any interest therein, containing any false statement or false representation which is of a character likely to or is intended to enhance the price or value of such property or any interest therein or to promote the sale or disposal thereof shall be liable upon summary conviction to a fine not exceeding two hundred dollars or to six months' imprisonment or to both fine and imprisonment.

While one might expect the police authorities to be eager to test the breadth of this new provision in the courts, that is exactly what didn't happen. In fact, there appears to be only one reported case dealing with the provision and its successors over the next 44 years.[4] Thus, in the absence of any reported court decisions on what the legislation meant, it is necessary to look at what the legislators said as reported in Hansard.

Upon motion for First reading in the House of Commons, the Minister of Justice, C.J. Doherty, indicated that the Bill was being introduced in response to:

> very wide-spread abuses in connection with the advertising of properties for sale, more particularly with regard to the advertising for sale of real property. The Act, of course, does not purport to go further than to make it an offence for a person knowingly to make a statement representing something to be a fact which is not a fact.[5]

He elaborated on Second reading:

---

2. *An Act for the Prevention and Suppression of Combinations formed in restraint of Trade*, S.C. 1889, c. 41.

3. S.C. 1914, c. 24.

4. It should be emphasized, however, that the absence of reported cases does not mean that the provision was not being enforced or, in any event, having the desired deterrent effect. Reference is made during the Parliamentary debates to prosecutions being carried out. Moreover, the offence was but a summary conviction matter (until the 1954 amendments), prosecuted before magistrates. Thus, in the scheme of the criminal process, it was not likely to have a high profile.

5. *Supra*, note 1, at 3397-8 (May 7, 1914).

Of course, every one understands that persons advertising will make the very best of the things they have to sell, and we do not propose to restrict a man's good opinion of his own goods or his right to express it. But the Act proposes to make it a criminal offence for a man knowingly to make a false statement of a nature to deceive people as regards the value of the thing that he has to offer. I have had representations from all parts of the country, and I think more especially from the western provinces, that there was really a system of deception carried on in the advertising of properties for sale, such as townsites... The purpose here is to make it a criminal offence to publish as actually existing facts things that do not exist.[6]

Upon Second reading in the Senate, Senator Lougheed proffered a further raison d'être for the Bill:

This legislation is largely due to the reckless advertising which has taken place, not only throughout the westerly part of Canada, although more particularly there, but throughout the whole Dominion of Canada as to townsites, as to mining properties, and as to the various classes of speculative investment. A very great deal of misrepresentation has been indulged in, and very serious losses have taken place on the part of those who were least able to sustain such losses. The object of the amendment is to do away with that class of advertising. I think I may say it has been initiated by the advertising clubs of Calgary and Edmonton, because probably that class of advertising ran as wildly in that province as in any other.[7]

In the House of Commons at Second reading, an exchange provides insight into the legislators' intent:

Mr. Knowles: Under this a man is liable before he has had any results from his false advertisement. I think this is very dangerous legislation, and for the reason that there are a great many such clauses in the Criminal Code which are used by speculators and by people who rue their bargains. In my own practice I have defended quite a number of people who have been accused when the purchaser has rued his bargain and is not ready to stand by his speculation...

Mr. Doherty: What we are doing here is merely making it an offence for a man[8] to publicly and deliberately lie, and scatter his lies broadcast in an endeavour to inveigle people into investing in worthless things, whether he succeeds or does not succeed: *The evil that is sought to be stopped is an evil which in its effects reaches a large number of small investors, none of whom will be sufficiently interested, even if he has the means, to bring criminal prosecution, if you leave the law in a condition where the transaction must have been actually carried out before there is any criminal responsibility. What we want to try to do, if it can be done, is to suppress the lying advertisement without regard to whether the liar succeeds in getting something or not.*[9]

...

---

6. *Ibid.*, at 3466.

7. Debates of the Senate, 1914, at 464 (May 26, 1914).

8. It was indicated during the debate that it was not expected that corporations would be subject to the provision.

9. *Supra*, note 1, at 3470, emphasis added.

> Mr. Doherty: What I said in comparing the two offences was that, I thought, as we had now a very well defined doctrine as to what was a false pretense in the case of obtaining goods under false pretenses, that doctrine would find its natural application in the determination of what is a false statement or representation under this Bill. The difference between the two things, it seems to me, is this, that the obtaining of goods by false pretenses deals with an offence that is consummated and carried to its ultimate conclusion, and whereby somebody is actually fradulently [sic] deprived of goods or money, whereas, here we are limiting ourselves to the attempt to do that.[10]

The provision was renumbered in the next statutory revision as subsection 406(2).[11] It was first amended in 1931 in a Bill amending numerous provisions of the *Criminal Code* which, *inter alia*, sought to prohibit nude parades, chicken stealing and the use of living bacilli as rat poison:[12]

> (2) Every person who publishes, or causes to be published, any advertisement for either directly or indirectly promoting the sale or disposal of any real or personal, movable or immovable property, or any interest therein, *which contains any statement purporting to be one of fact which is untrue, deceptive or misleading, shall be liable upon summary conviction to a fine not exceeding two hundred dollars or to six months imprisonment, or to both fine and imprisonment: Provided that any newspaper publishing any such advertisement accepted in good faith in the ordinary course of its business shall not be subject to the provisions of this subsection. Provided further, that in any prosecution under this subsection the case may be dismissed if it be established to the satisfaction of the Court upon proper evidence that the accused acted in good faith* (amendment emphasized)[13]

Upon introduction for first reading, it was indicated that this amendment was asked for by retail merchants' associations and better business associations.

At Second reading, the then Minister of Justice explained what he saw as the reason for, and the effect of, the amendment:

> Mr. Guthrie: Formerly the penalty was provided for one who "knowingly" publishes, and the real change that is made here is to strike out the word "knowingly." The question has been raised by some very prominent business people in Canada as to the propriety of striking out that word, and of putting a saving clause at the end of the section. They represent that many bona fide advertisers are mistaken in some of the statements they make, through not fault of their own in many cases, and that it is hard to penalize them for statements innocently made. The difficulty with the word "knowingly" in the clause as it now stands is that it imposes upon the

---

10. *Ibid.*, at 3471.

11. *Criminal Code*, R.S.C. 1927, c. 36.

12. *An Act to Amend the Criminal Code*, S.C. 1930-31, c. 28, s. 5.

13. This further proviso was added to the Bill during Second reading. It is arguable that the addition rendered the first one respecting newspapers superfluous.

prosecution the burden of proving that a certain thing was stated knowing it to be false or untrue, and very often the prosecution is not able to prove that knowledge on the part of the accused, and consequently the prosecution fails. If the word "knowingly" is struck out the section becomes much broader...

[The "good faith" proviso places the onus on] the accused to show that he acted in good faith, and if he had so acted and convinced the court of that fact the court might forgive him of his offence. In the present section the word "knowingly" appears and the result is that prosecutions have failed because the crown has not been able to establish the fact a man has knowingly inserted a false advertisement, knowing it to be false.[14]

The Senate passed the amendment without comment.

The next legislative adjustment occurred in 1935.[15] The two provisos contained in subsection (2) were repealed and the following was substituted in their place:

Provided that any person publishing any such advertisement accepted in good faith in the ordinary course of his business shall not be subject to the provisions of this subsection.

As well, a new subsection was added:

(3)(a) Every person who publishes, or causes to be published, any advertisement containing any statement or guarantee of the performance, efficacy or length of life of any product for the purpose of either directly or indirectly promoting the sale or disposal of such product and which statement or guarantee is not based upon an adequate and proper test, shall be guilty of an offence and liable upon summary conviction to a fine not exceeding two hundred dollars or to six months imprisonment, or to both fine and imprisonment: Provided that any person publishing any such advertisement accepted in good faith in the ordinary course of his business shall not be subject to the provisions of this subsection;

(b) Without excluding any other adequate and proper test, a test by the Honorary Advisory Council for Scientific and Industrial Research or any other public department shall be considered an adequate and proper test for the purposes of this subsection, but no reference shall be made in any such advertisement to the fact that a test has been made by such Council or other public department;

(c) On any prosecution under this subsection, the burden of proof that an adequate and proper test has been made shall lie on the defendant.

These considerable changes evoked no substantive debate in the House of Commons. The Senate record indicates that the amendments arose out of

14. House of Commons Debates, 1931, v. IV, at 4137 (July 24, 1931).

15. *An Act to Amend the Criminal Code*, S.C. 1935, c. 56, s. 6.

the Royal Commission on Price Spreads and that advertisements over the radio were thought not to come within the prohibitions.[16]
    Once again, in 1939, subsection (2) was amended:[17]

> (2) Every person who publishes, or causes to be published, any advertisement for promoting either directly or indirectly the sale or disposal of any real or personal, movable or immovable property, or any interest therein, *or promoting any business or commercial interests*... shall be liable (amendment emphasized).

The Parliamentary record gives no assistance as to why this amendment was made.
    In 1944, another branch was added to subsection (2) requiring intent:[18]

> (2) Every person who publishes, or causes to be published, any advertisement for promoting either directly or indirectly the sale or disposal of any real or personal, movable or immovable property, or any interest therein, or promoting any business or commercial interests, which contains any statement purporting to be one of fact which is untrue, deceptive or misleading, *or which advertisement is intentionally so worded or arranged as to be deceptive or misleading*, shall be liable... (amendment emphasized)

Louis St. Laurent, the then Minister of Justice, explained the reason for the change:

> This was asked for by the Better Business Bureau [of Toronto], and we were told that there were signs being published with the word "no", in small type, and the words "fire sale here" in larger type. Such a sign would have in large type the words "fire sale here", but if one looked at it closely he would see that it read "no fire sale here."[19]

Later, the record discloses a discussion on the necessity for *mens rea*:

> Mr. Graham: Would the section not be improved by leaving out the word "intentionally"? *Mens rea* must be an ingredient, anyway...
>
> Mr. St. Laurent: I should be afraid it might be held that if in fact it happened to be worded or arranged in a manner that did not convey the correct information, the very fact that it was so worded or arranged, without *mens rea*, might be held to constitute an offence. I think the hon. member will agree that there should not be a conviction unless there is *mens rea*...[20]

---

16. But see the discussion in House of Commons Debates, 1953-54, v. III, at 2492-3, where the then Minister of Justice, the Honourable S. Garson, expressed the opposite view.

17. *An Act to Amend the Criminal Code*, S.C. 1939, c. 30, s. 7.

18. *An Act to Amend the Criminal Code*, S.C. 1943-44, c. 23, s. 11.

19. House of Commons Debates, 1943, v. V, at 5010 (July 17, 1943).

20. *Ibid.*, at 5011.

The Senate record provides no further insight into the meaning of the amendment.

Finally, during its tenure in the *Criminal Code*, the misleading advertising provision was restructured by the extensive amendments to the Code in 1954.[21] It was otherwise substantively unaltered but for the addition of heavier penalties:

> 306 (1) Every one who publishes or causes to be published an advertisement containing a statement that purports to be a statement of fact but that is untrue, deceptive or misleading or is intentionally so worded or arranged that it is deceptive or misleading, is guilty of an indictable offence and is liable to imprisonment for five years, if the advertisement is published
>> (a) to promote, directly or indirectly, the sale or disposal of property or any interest therein, or
>> (b) to promote a business or commercial interest.
>
> (2) Every one who publishes or causes to be published in an advertisement a statement or guarantee of the performance, efficacy or length of life of anything that is not based upon an adequate and proper test of that thing, the proof of which lies upon the accused, is, if the advertisement is published to promote, directly or indirectly, the sale or disposal of that thing, guilty of an...
>
> (3) Subsections (1) and (2) do not apply to a person who publishes an advertisement that he accepts in good faith for publication in the ordinary course of his business.
>
> (4) For the purposes of subsection (2), a test that is made by the National Research Council of Canada or by any other public department is an adequate and proper test, but no reference shall be made in an advertisement to indicate that a test has been made by the National Research Council or other public department unless the advertisement has, before publication, been approved and permission to publish it has been given in writing by the president of the National Research Council or by the deputy head of the public department, as the case may be.
>
> (5) Nothing in subsection (4) shall be deemed to exclude, for the purposes of this section, any other adequate or proper test.

1.2 1960-Present: The Combines Investigation Act and the Competition Act

In 1960, misrepresentations about prices were, for the first time, made an offence under the *Combines Investigation Act*.[22]

> 33C. (1) Every one who, for the purpose of promoting the sale or use of an article, makes any materially misleading representation to the public, by any means whatever, concerning the price at which such or like articles have been, are, or will be, ordinarily sold, is guilty of an offence.
>
> (2) Subsection (1) does not apply to a person who publishes an advertisement that he accepts in good faith for publication in the ordinary course of his business.

---

21. *Criminal Code*, S.C. 1953-54, c. 51, s. 306.

22. *An Act to amend the Combines Investigation Act and the Criminal Code*, S.C. 1960, c. 45, s. 13.

The Justice Minister at the time, E.D. Fulton, explained the change in emphasis the new provision embodied:

> It was our intention here to go a little further than the Criminal Code goes but in one particular field only, the field of misrepresentation by misleading advertising with respect to pricing. We wanted to cover that as a special and separate field, as one of those provisions which we are now introducing to improve the situation of the independent merchant because this is one of the respects in which he is particularly vulnerable to unscrupulous practices especially by those who use the power of the purse as one of the main devices against their weaker competitors...
>
> It will be appreciated, I think, that this is a special type of misleading advertising; it is misleading advertising related to price alone; and so we have felt it was proper to have a provision in the combines legislation dealing with the matter, because of its relation to other subjects with which this legislation now deals, namely the provision designed to protect and improve the position of the independent merchant.
>
> Another reason for having it in here in this form is that we do not police the Criminal Code; that is the ordinary provisions of the Criminal Code are not normally the responsibility of the combines branch to supervise or to enforce, and I think that it would be the subject of criticism if we took the ordinary provisions of the Criminal Code and put our officers in charge of supervision and enforcement.[23] There would be a change in the normal division of responsibility for enforcement of the ordinary Criminal Code provisions. That is why we put it especially in here.[24]

In 1969, section 306 of the *Criminal Code* was transferred into the Combines Investigation Act, becoming section 33D, pursuant to the *Criminal Law Amendment Act*, 1968-89.[25] The move was explained by the Justice Minister, John N. Turner, during motion for second reading of the Bill:

> [The amendment] gives the federal Attorney General jurisdiction over... prosecution. I cannot resist saying that the consumer has a fundamental right to correct information and that truth in advertising is essential to any charter for the consumer. I hope these amendments will more effectively protect the consumer's right to correct information in future. The Minister of Consumer and Corporate Affairs (Mr. Basford) and I intend that *there shall be vigorous enforcement of these provisions on a national basis.*[26]

23.　In retrospect this turned out to be an ironic statement, for this is exactly what happened, in part as a result of the growing consumer movement during the latter part of the 1960s.

24.　House of Commons Debates, 1960, v. VII, at 6984 (July 26, 1960).

25.　S.C. 1968-69, c. 38, s. 116, in force July 31, 1969. Sections 33C and 33D were renumbered sections 36 and 37 by virtue of R.S.C. 1970, c. C-23, in force July 15, 1971.

26.　House of Commons, 1969, at 4723-4 (January 23, 1969), emphasis added. For a discussion on the effect of this amendment, see Part 3, *infra*.

Prior to this, the Government initiated a process which was to culminate in the most fundamental legislative changes to date. On July 22, 1966, it asked the Economic Council of Canada to undertake a study respecting certain aspects of the impending responsibilities of the newly created ministry of the Registrar General of Canada.[27] The terms of reference were as follows:

> [I]n the light of the Government's long-term economic objectives, to study and advise regarding:
> (a) the interests of the consumer particularly as they relate to the functions of the Department of the Registrar General;
> (b) combines, mergers, monopolies and restraint of trade;
> (c) patents, trade marks, copyrights and registered industrial designs.

On August 7, 1969, the Council issued its *Interim Report on Competition Policy*.[28] It made a number of fundamental proposals for new legislation directed towards attaining maximum economic efficiency in the interests of the general consumer. The Minister of Consumer and Corporate Affairs,[29] Ron Basford, then revealed that a complete revision of the *Combines Investigation Act* would take place, after extensive consultation with interested individuals, organizations and companies.

While appearing before the House of Commons Committee on Health, Welfare and Social Affairs on March 3, 1970, the Minister indicated the high priority he gave to the Economic Council's recommendations:

> The revision of this legislation to make it more effective to accomplish the objectives of competition policy is our most important single project in this field. Since the council's report was received last August, my officials and I have been studying the recommendations intensively and developing the scheme of the new act. I have the benefit of advice not only from officials of my department, but also from officials of other departments directly concerned and of experts outside the government service. In addition, I have asked for and received representations from people in the private sector, all of which are...
>
> I am happy to report that very considerable progress has been made in preparing a revision of the Act in so far as we are now in a position to be discussing it interdepartmentally within government. It is our object to produce first-class legislation to correct some of the inadequacies of the existing law which my officials have had to work under for many years.[30]

---

27. See Ministerial/Departmental Responsibility, *infra*.

28. This was something of a misnomer as a "final" report was never issued.

29. The successor ministry to the Department of the Registrar General of Canada.

30. Annual Report of the Director of Investigation and Research for the year ended March 31, 1970, at 10. [Hereafter referred to as Annual Report, 1969/70.]

When the Minister appeared before the same Committee on March 11, 1971, the legislation was still in the preparatory stage. On that occasion, he indicated that the Bill would reflect a broad policy towards restrictive trade practices and competition policy in general. He anticipated that the Bill would be fully examined by a parliamentary committee which would hear representations from interested parties, thus ensuring that its final version would be "broadly accepted and able to withstand the test of time."[31]

On June 29, 1971, Bill C-256[32] was presented for first reading in the House of Commons.

> [T]he then Minister, the Honourable Ron Basford, made it clear that he did not intend to carry it through the legislative process during the current session but wished to cause a debate to take place for the purpose of perfecting the legislation. He invited all sections of the public to make representations. The representations duly came in, and there were over 300 detailed briefs and hundreds of additional letters. These briefs and press comments disclosed that some of the provisions were strongly opposed by the business sector, in some leading instances for valid reasons. Careful attention was then given to the detail of the criticisms and to changes that would be necessary to meet what was considered to be well-founded.[33]

On March 17, 1972, the new Minister, Robert K. Andras, indicated his intention to introduce a revised bill with substantial changes. After consultations with members of the public and the provincial governments, he would decide upon the final form of the proposed legislation to be submitted to Cabinet.

In the interim, on April 2, 1973, the First Report of the Special Committee of the House of Commons on Trends in Food Prices recommended that provisions relating to "consumer protection"[34] be enacted in separate legislation. The then Minister, Herb Gray, on November 5, 1973, introduced for first reading in the House of Commons Bill C-227.[35] That Bill died on the order paper, proceeding no further than firsts reading. However, it was reintroduced as Bill C-7 on March 11, 1974. After having been given second reading and receiving approval in principle, it was sent for clause-by-clause examination to the House of Commons Committee on Finance, Trade and Economic Affairs. That Committee's deliberations were cut short when, on May 8, 1974, Parliament was dissolved.

---

31. *Annual Report*, 1970/71, at 10.

32. *Bill C-256, The Competition Act* (Ottawa: Queen's Printer, 1971).

33. *Annual Report*, 1971/72, at 10.

34. Which came to be known as the Stage I amendments.

35. See *Proposals for a New Competition Policy for Canada -- First Stage* (Ottawa: Information Canada, 1973).

On October 2, 1974, the new Minister, André Ouellet, reintroduced Bill C-7 as Bill C-2. That Bill was enacted in 1975.[36] Sections 36 and 37, *inter alia*, were repealed and new sections 36 to 36.4 and 37 to 37.3 were substituted in their place.[37]

The amended Act covered services for the first time. It contained new or strengthened prohibitions regarding certain specified practices. The general misleading advertising provision was extended to cover representations made in any manner whatsoever.[38] Other provisions related to sales above advertised prices and the deceptive use of warranties and guarantees, tests and testimonials and promotional contests.

In 1985, a fourth defence was enacted regarding the offence of selling above the advertised price.[39] Paragraph (d) was added to subsection 58(3) making that section inapplicable to a "sale of a product by or on behalf of a person who is not engaged in the business of dealing in that product."

The Stage II[40] amendments[41] did not affect the substantive misleading advertising provisions. Yet, substantial changes were effected by the new Competition Act in other respects which impacted upon the administration of those provisions. Section 2.1 removed Crown immunity for agent Crown corporations engaged in commercial activities in actual or potential competition with other firms.

The Director's[42] powers respecting search and seizure, ordering hearings before a presiding officer, the production of documents and returns of information under oath were also completely revised. In line with the Canadian *Charter of Rights and Freedoms*, his exercise of these powers were made subject to scrutiny by the judiciary; the authority to issue warrants and subpoenas now resided with judges.[43]

---

36. *An Act to amend the Combines Investigation Act*, S.C. 1974-75-76, c. 76, s. 18, in force January 1, 1976.

37. Sections 36 to 37.3 were renumbered sections 52 to 60 by virtue of R.S.C. 1985, c. C-34.

38. Although it should be noted that some of the other provisions were restricted solely to representations in the form of published advertisements.

39. *Criminal Law Amendment Act*, 1985, R.S.C. 1985, c. 27 (1st Supp.), s. 189, in force December 4, 1985.

40. See W.T. Stanbury, "The New Competition Act and Competition Tribunal Act: Not With a Bang, But a Whimper," *Canadian Business Law Journal*, Vol. 12(1), 1986, pp. 2-42.

41. *Competition Act*, S.C. 1986, c. 26, s. 19, in force June 19, 1986 (except ss. 80-95).

42. The role of the Director of Investigation and Research is discussed, *infra*.

43. The newly-created Competition Tribunal was given a purely adjudicative function.

2.0   SELECTED JURISPRUDENCE[44]

2.1   Constitution Act, 1867

Historically, anti-combines legislation has been upheld as validly enacted federal legislation by virtue of subsection 91(27) of the Constitution Act, 1867, the Criminal Law Power.[45] More recently, however, the Supreme Court of Canada has upheld the constitutionality of the Competition Act by virtue of subsection 91(2), the Trade and Commerce Power.[46]

Québec Ready Mix Inc. v. *Rocois Constr. Inc.*,[47] and *General Motors of Canada Ltd.* v. *City National Leasing*,[48] held subsections 36(1)(a)[49] and 36(3)[50]

---

44.   It is beyond the scope of this paper to include an extensive consideration of the judicial decisions relating to the various misleading advertising and deceptive marketing practices provisions. Accordingly, only some of the highlights will be covered here; only some of the more important cases from the Supreme Court of Canada and provincial Courts of Appeal will be mentioned. For a more detailed consideration of the current state of the law, see George Addy, "Deceptive Marketing Practices" in R.S. Khemani and W.T. Stanbury (eds.) *Canadian Competition Law and Policy at the Centenary* (Halifax: The Institute for Research on Public Policy, 1991).

45.   "Peace, order and good government" has also been mentioned: *R.* v. *Hoffman-La Roche Ltd.* (Nos. 1 and 2) (1981), 58 C.P.R. (2d) 1 (Ont. C.A.); Bruce C. McDonald, "Constitutional Aspects of Canadian Anti-Combines Law Enforcement," 47 *Can. B. Rev.* 161 (1969); Peter W. Hogg and Warren Grover, "The Constitutionality of the Competition Bill," 1 *Can. Bus. L.J.* 197 (1976). See also the paper by Rutherford and Tyhurst, Chapter 8 in this volume.

46.   The Court in *Hoffman-La Roche* also held that the predatory pricing provision in the Combines Investigation Act [s. 50(1)(b)] was validly enacted federal legislation not only by reason of the Criminal Law Power but also because of the Trade and Commerce Power.

47.   (1985), 25 D.L.R. (4th) 373, 64 N.R. 209 (F.C.A.), affd [1989] 1 S.C.R. 695.

48.   (1986), 28 D.L.R. (4th) 158 (Ont. C.A.), affd [1989] 1 S.C.R. 641. While these two cases dealt with price discrimination, they, nevertheless, had a significant impact on misleading advertising.

49.   That section states:
>   36(1) Any person who has suffered loss or damage as a result of
>   (a) conduct that is contrary to any provision of Part VI,or
>   (b) the failure of any person to comply with an order of the Tribunal or other court under this Act,
>   may, in any court of competent jurisdiction, sue for and recover from the person who engaged in the conduct or failed to comply with the order an amount equal to the loss or damage proved to have been suffered by him, together with any additional amount that the court may allow not exceeding the full cost to him of any investigation in connection with the matter and of proceedings under this section.

For convenience, the current provisions will be referred to by the most recent (R.S.C. 1985) section numbers. Concordance is as follows: Old (1976)/New (1985): 36/52, 36.1/53, 36.2/54, 36.3/55, 36.4/56, 37/57, 37.1/58, 37.2/59, 37.3/60.

50.   That subsection states: "For the purposes of any action under subsection (1), the Federal Court of Canada is a competent jurisdiction."

to be constitutionally valid federal legislation under the trade and commerce power and, in particular, its "second branch" over "general" trade and commerce.

In the *General Motors* case, the practice of price discrimination contrary to section 50(1)(a) was alleged to have caused loss to City National Leasing. The Supreme Court held that the following questions should be answered in the affirmative:

> (1) whether the *Combines Investigation Act*, either in whole or in part, was *intra vires* Parliament under s. 91(2) of the Constitution Act, 1867, and
>
> (2) whether [s. 36] was within the legislative competence of Parliament.[51]

The Criminal Law Power nevertheless continues to remain important. In *R. v. Shaklee Canada Inc.*,[52] where the impugned provision was section 55, it was held to be criminal legislation and not a colourable invasion of the provinces' legislative jurisdiction over property and civil rights.

2.2 Substantive Developments

Under both sections 33C and 33D [old sections 36 and 37], as well as their successors, *mens rea* has been held not to be an element.[53] Moreover,

---

51.   From page 4 of the headnote: "The Court has advanced several hallmarks of validity for legislation under the second branch of the trade and commerce power: (1) the impugned legislation must be part of a general regulatory scheme; (2) the scheme must be monitored by the continuing oversight of a regulatory agency; (3) the legislation must be concerned with trade as a whole rather than with a particular industry; (4) the legislation should be of a nature that the provinces jointly or severally would be constitutionally incapable of enacting; and (5) the failure to include one or more provinces or localities in a legislative scheme would jeopardize the successful operation of the scheme in other parts of the country. These indicia do not represent an exhaustive list of traits that will tend to characterize general trade and commerce legislation and the presence or absence of any of them is not necessarily determinative. On any occasion where the general trade and commerce power is advanced as a ground of constitutional validity, a careful case by case analysis remains appropriate" [1989] 1 S.C.R. 695.

52.   [1985] 1 F.C. 593, 4 C.P.R. (3d) 433 (C.A.), afd [1988] 1 S.C.R. 622, 84 N.R. 385.

53.   There is a plethora of cases on this point: *R. v. Allied Towers Merchants Ltd.*, [1965] 2 O.R. 628, 46 C.P.R. 239 (H.C.J.); *R. V. Imperial Tobacco Products Ltd.* (1971), 3 C.P.R. (2d) 178, 22 D.L.R. (3d) 51 (Alta. S.C. App. Div.); *R. v. J. Clark & Son Ltd.* (1972), 9 C.P.R. (2d) 192, 32 D.L.R. (3d) 479 (N.B.S.C. App. Div.); *Paramount Industries Inc. v. The Queen* (1973), 10 C.P.R. (2d) 216 (Que. C.A.); *R. v. Leaman Group Ltd.* (1976), 13 N.B.R. (2d) 336, 28 C.P.R. (2d) 152 (S.C. App. Div.); *R. v. Birchcliff Lincoln Mercury Sales Ltd.* (1987), 17 C.P.R. (3d) 99, 43 D.L.R. (4th) 417 (Ont. C.A.). However, where guilt is predicated upon the accused being an aider and abettor, pursuant to section 21 of the Criminal Code, *mens rea* is required in that the accused must be shown to have had knowledge of the circumstances constituting the alleged offence although he need not have known that they amounted to an offence: *R. v. F.W. Woolworth Co. Ltd.* (1974), 18 C.C.C. (2d) 23 (Ont. C.A.); *R. v. Fell* (1981), 59 C.P.R. (2d) 34, 131 D.L.R. (3d) 105 (Ont. C.A.).

the statutory defence provided in section 57(3) precludes the common law defence of due diligence.[54]

The Court must consider the advertisement in its entirety. Thus, it is an error of law to construe a word in an advertisement without reference to its context. Whether an advertisement is misleading is solely a question of law.[55]

Although the law has been found to be directed towards the general public including the ignorant, the unthinking and the credulous,[56] that standard has been diminished by subsequent standards.[57] The focus is on the ultimate impression made on the minds of readers of the statement, having regard to what is actually said and, as well, what can reasonably be implied.[58]

The words in sections 33C ["have been, are or will be ordinarily sold"][59] and 33D ["untrue, deceptive or misleading"][60] each created not three but one offence which could be committed in three different ways.

---

54. R. v. International Vacations Ltd. (1980), 56 C.P.R. (2d) 251, 124 D.L.R. (3d) 319 (Ont. C.A.); R. v. Consumers Distributing Co. (1980), 54 C.P.R. (2d) 50, 57 C.C.C. (2d) 317 (Ont. C.A.). But see R. v. Westfair Foods Ltd. (1986), 41 Man. R. (2d) 205, 11 C.P.R. (3d) 345 (Q.B.), discussed infra.

It is interesting to note that the statutory defence was enacted for the opposite reason. It was included because, in the pre R. v. Sault Ste. Marie period, the government was of the opinion that no due diligence defence would otherwise be available. During the Standing Committee on Finance, Trade and Economic Affairs' consideration of Bill C-2, the sponsoring Minister, the Honourable André Ouellet, stated: "As you know, Mr. Chairman, many of the briefs that have been submitted to this Committee and to the department request that [the] defence of honest error, due diligence in preventing errors and the like, be provided under proposed [sections 52 and 53] which relate to misleading representation and testimonial. The fact is that the kind of offence created by these sections are the offence of strict liability; that is, they permit no defence of error or precaution. We reviewed the section and the act and we came to the conclusion that the argument presented to us in the Department and also presented to the members of this Committee has great merit. This is why I am suggesting to the members of this Committee to accept that this amendment will allow due diligence as a defence" [Minutes of Proceedings and Evidence of the Standing Committee on Finance, Trade and Economic Affairs, Chairman: Robert Kaplan, No. 55, at 52 (June 3, 1975).]

55. R. v. Imperial Tobacco Products Ltd., supra; Alberta Giftwares Ltd. v. The Queen, [1974] S.C.R. 584, 3 D.L.R. (3d) 321.

56. R. v. Imperial Tobacco Products Ltd., supra.

57. See, e.g., R. v. T. Eaton Co. Ltd. (1975), 26 C.P.R. (2d) 118 (Alta. S.C.), where the readers of an advertisement were assumed to have had some common sense, and R. v. International Vacations Ltd., supra, where those considering an advertisement for European air flights were assumed to be literate, intelligent and careful readers.

58. R. v. Viceroy Construction Co. Ltd. (1975), 11 O.R. (2d) 485, 23 C.P.R. (2d) 281 (C.A.).

59. R. v. Morse Jewellers (Sudbury) Ltd., [1964] 1 O.R. 103, 42 C.P.R. 130 (S.C.), affd [1964] 1 O.R. 466, [1964] 1 C.C.C. 293 (C.A.).

60. R. v. Firestone Stores Ltd., [1972] 2 O.R. 327, 5 C.P.R. (2d) 193 (C.A.); R. v. T. Eaton Co. Ltd. (1974), 15 C.P.R. (2d) 25, 47 D.L.R. (3d) 746 (Man. C.A.).

It is not a defence that the breach of the statute was inadvertent or against company policy.[61] So, statements made on an in-store display sign, which were similar to, and based on, the manufacturer's statements which appeared on the product's cartons, were held to come within the ambit of section 52(2)(c).[62] Where an advertisement is prepared by a licensee of the accused and screened by the accused's employees, criminal liability will flow.[63] The Crown need not show that anyone was misled by the statement.[64]

Section 52(1)(b) placed the burden on the accused to lead evidence in support of the alleged tests after which the Crown could lead rebuttal evidence to show that the tests were not "adequate and proper."[65]

The failure of an airline to supply in reasonable quantities the flights it advertised, contrary to section 57(2), was not saved by a disclaimer ("some flights may be sold out") as that section imposes a positive duty not to advertise unless reasonable quantities are available.[66]

2.3 The Canadian Charter of Rights and Freedoms

The first Charter case to be decided by the Supreme Court of Canada struck down the search and seizure provision, then section 10, of the *Combines Investigation Act*.[67]

Whether the reverse onus provision contained in section 52(1)(b) is reasonable under the Charter is yet to be considered by a provincial Court of Appeal. There are contradictory lower court decisions. However, it has been held that section 60(2) is contrary to section 7. It was found effectively to render section 52(1) an absolute liability offence where the accused meets the

---

61. *R. v. G. Tamblyn Ltd.* (1972), 6 C.P.R. (2d) 97, 26 D.L.R. (3d) 436 (Ont. C.A.); *R. v. Steinberg's Ltd.* (1976), 26 C.P.R. (2d) 109, 70 D.L.R. (3d) 624 (Ont. C.A.).

62. *R. v. Consumers Distributing Co., supra.*

63. *R. v. Hudson's Bay Co.* (1977), 33 C.P.R. (2d) 131, 35 C.C.C. (2d) 61 (Ont. C.A.).

64. *R. v. Imperial Tobacco Products Ltd., supra; R. v. Alexanian & Sons Ltd.* (1974), 22 C.P.R. (2d) 37, 23 C.C.C. (2d) 249 (Ont. C.A.), affd [1976] 2 S.C.R. v; *R. v. MacKay* (1979), 36 N.S.R. (2d) 553 (S.C. App. Div.).

65. *R. v. Bristol-Myers of Canada Ltd.* (1979), 45 C.P.R. (2d) 228, 48 C.C.C. (2d) 384 (Ont. Co. Ct.), affd January 29, 1981 (C.A.), unreported.

66. *R. v. Air Canada* (1987), 17 C.P.R. (3d) 397 (Ont. Dist. Ct.).

67. *Southam v. Hunter,* [1984] 2 S.C.R. 145, 11 D.L.R. (4th) 641. As a result of this decision, section 443 Criminal Code search warrants were relied on from the time of the decision in the court below until the 1986 amendments - a five year period.

common law test for due diligence but fails to satisfy the requirements of paragraphs 60(2)(c) and (d).[68]

It has been held that subsections 55(2) and (3), which prohibit pyramid selling schemes where they are otherwise not regulated by the provinces, do not violate section 15 of the Charter. While only some of the provinces had undertaken such regulation, nevertheless, the federal prohibition applied uniformly across Canada. Section 15, it was said, guarantees the uniform application of the law, not uniformity of the law.[69]

2.4 Penalties/Remedies[70]

The Courts have traditionally been reluctant to impose substantial fines. Indeed, the seriousness of the public deception is only slowly being recognized.[71] In one case, for example, where a substantial corporation had a record of eight prior convictions over the previous ten years and past fines were treated by it as licence fees, a total fine of $1 million was imposed.[72] On another occasion, the accused was sentenced to two years incarceration, later reduced to one year on appeal.[73] Nevertheless, the deterrent effect of such penalties remains uncertain.[74]

---

68. *R.* v. *Westfair Foods Ltd.* (1985), 5 C.P.R. (3d) 373, 16 D.L.R. (4th) 668 (Sask. Q.B.). The accused was faced with a Hobson's choice. To avail itself of the section 60(2) defence, it had to comply, *inter alia*, with the notice requirements in paragraphs (c) and (d). But this would force it to admit committing the *actus reus* even if it honestly believed it hadn't. See also *R.* v. *Westfair Foods Ltd.*, (Man.), *supra*, which held not only that section 60(2) violated section 7 of the Charter [not "in accordance with the principles of fundamental justice"] but also section 11(b) [reverse onus]. But see *R.* v. *Independent Order of Foresters* (1986), 13 C.P.R. (3d) 563 (Ont. Dist. Ct.), where it was held that the combined effect of sections 52(1) and 60(2) was constitutional.

69. *R.* v. *CLP Canmarket Lifestyle Products Corp.*, [1988] 2 W.W.R. 170 (Man. C.A.), per Twaddle and Monnin JJ.A., O'Sullivan J.A. concurring for other reasons.

70. See Table 1 which sets out the penalties currently provided under the *Competition Act*.

71. For selected statistics on fines imposed see Tables 2 and 3.

72. *R.* v. *Simpson-Sears Ltd.*, [1985] C.C.L. 11437 (Ont. Co. Ct.). During sentencing, the Court applied a number of sentencing factors: protection of the public interest in free competition, the nature of the offence, deterrence to the corporation and to others, the factor that the fine must not be considered as constituting a licence fee, the nature of the market and the number of competitors, dealers and sellers of the product marketed, fines imposed in the past, whether the company was aware it was breaking the law, the net profit, the income and ability to pay of a convicted company, the presence or absence of moral turpitude, whether persons were misled as a result of the unlawful advertising scheme and the character of the convicted company.

73. *R.* v. *O'Brien* (1975), 11 N.S.R. (2d) 629, 25 C.P.R. (2d) 143 (S.C. App. Div.).

74. Prohibition orders are being sought with increasing frequency, especially subsection 34(2) orders.

3.0 ADMINISTRATION

3.1 Ministerial/Departmental Responsibility

Until December 22, 1965, the Department of Justice had responsibility for administering the *Combines Investigation Act*.[75] On that date, interim responsibility in respect of those powers, duties and functions of the Minister of Justice, except those vested in his guise as Attorney General of Canada (and those under section 13), was transferred to the President of the Privy Council.[76]

This interim measure was taken pending a planned reorganization of departmental responsibilities. On June 16, 1966 the Government Organization Act, 1966[77] was enacted. Among other things, it established the new Department of the Registrar General. The duties, powers and functions of the Registrar General of Canada included all matters over which the Parliament of Canada had jurisdiction not by law assigned to any other department, branch or agency of the Government of Canada relating to (a) combines, mergers, monopolies and restraint of trade; (b) patents, copyrights and trade marks; (c) bankruptcy and insolvency; and (d) corporate affairs.

The Act was proclaimed in force on October 1, 1966 and Guy Favreau was appointed Registrar General.[78] On April 4, 1967 John N. Turner assumed the office.

The Department of the Registrar General of Canada was subsumed in the new Department of Consumer and Corporate Affairs, whose Minister had a broader mandate, including "consumer affairs."[79] Soon after its creation, the Department established a mailing address (The Consumer, Box 99, Ottawa) to receive consumer complaints and enquiries. By the end of May 1968, over 1,000 complaints or enquiries had been received; by the end of December

75. Justice Ministers from 1960 to this date were E. Davie Fulton, Donald M. Fleming, Lionel Chevrier, Guy Favreau and Lucien Cardin.

76. Order in Council, P.C., 1954-2281, effective January 1, 1966, pursuant to the *Public Service Rearrangement and Transfer of Duties Act*, R.S.C. 1952, c. 227, s. 2.

77. S.C. 1966-67, c. 25.

78. He had previously been responsible for these matters in his capacity as President of the Privy Council.

79. Department of Consumer and Corporate Affairs Act, S.C. 1967, c. 16, in force December 21, 1967. The intention was to place under one department all the federal agencies whose mandates dealt with regulation of the marketplace. From 1968 to 1991 there were 17 Ministers of Consumer and Corporate Affairs.

1971, they numbered 61,000. Deceptive trade practices such as misleading advertising accounted for 64 percent of the complaints.[80]

3.2 The Director of Investigation and Research[81]

At the time the first misleading advertising provision was incorporated into the *Combines Investigation Act*, the Director of Investigation and Research's duty was to further the philosophy behind the anti-combines legislation. He considered that to be:

> to assist in maintaining fee and open competition as a prime stimulus to the achievement of maximum production, distribution and employment in a system of free enterprise. To this end, the legislation seeks to eliminate certain practices in restraint of trade which serve to prevent the nation's economic resources from being most effectively used for the advantage of all citizens.[82]

That philosophy is now embodied in the "purpose" section of the *Competition Act*:[83]

> 1.1 The purpose of this Act is to maintain and encourage competition in Canada in order to promote the efficiency and adaptability of the Canadian economy, in order to expand opportunities for Canadian participation in world markets while at the same time recognizing the role of foreign competition in Canada, in order to ensure that small and medium-sized enterprises have an equitable opportunity to participate in the Canadian economy and in order to provide consumers with competitive prices and product choices.

The importance of preventing misleading advertising in relation to this philosophy has been highlighted:

> [The] misleading advertising provisions played a significant role within the overall framework of competition policy in ensuring that the market mechanism operated effectively and the consumers were protected from deceptive practices which might otherwise have occurred in the marketplace. It was with this purpose in mind that the original misleading advertising provisions were included in the *Combines Investigation Act*. Moreover, it can be shown that where there is a lack of complete information or where distorted information in relation to a product is fed into the

---

80. Department of Consumer and Corporate Affairs, Consumer Services Branch, *Consumer Communiqué*, No. 1 (July 1968). This early publication was intended to educate its readers about consumer legislation, government activities in consumer affairs, trade practices and "actual shopping methods."

81. The Director is the person designated by the *Combines Investigation Act* to enforce its provisions. Between 1960 and 1991 there were seven Directors of Investigation and Research.

82. *Annual Report*, 1960/61, at 7.

83. R.S.C. 1985, c. C-34, s. 1.1.

marketplace, its functioning will be adversely affected and the distortion will be injurious to honest competitors.[84]

The Director's role was, and continues to be, to investigate matters relating to the prohibitions contained in the *Combines Investigation Act*. Such an investigation was usually commenced on the Director's initiative when he had "reason to believe" that a contravention had taken, or was about to take, place.[85]

Where there were reasonable grounds to believe that an offence had occurred or was incipient, the Director could obtain from the Restrictive Trade Practices Commission (a body consisting of not more than three members) authorization to examine witnesses under oath, enter premises and examine and remove files and records and require sworn returns of information.

When the Director had gathered sufficient information which he believed proved the existence of prohibited practices, he would submit a statement of the evidence to the Commission and to the parties believed to be responsible. The Commission would convene a hearing into the matter, giving the parties the opportunity to be heard and, thereafter, submit a report to the Minister which appraised the effect on the public interest of the practices disclosed.[86] The Minister would then take appropriate action.

Section 33C was a summary conviction offence where proceedings had to be commenced within six months of the time when the offence took place.[87] The practice developed, due to the time constraint and the nature of the offence, whereby evidence received as a result of inquiries, which warranted consideration as to possible prosecution, was referred directly to the Attorney General of Canada, bypassing the Restrictive Trade Practices Commission.[88]

---

84. *Annual Report*, 1976/77, at 40.

85. This "reason to believe" was usually supplied by informal complaints received from the public. An investigation could also be instigated by the formal, written application of six Canadian citizens or by direction of the Minister.

86. With the Stage I amendments, the Commission was given the added responsibility, as a court of record, to receive applications from the Director to review various situations restrictive of competition and make remedial orders binding upon the persons to whom they were addressed. The Commission was abolished by the 1986 amendments which created in its place the Competition Tribunal. That Tribunal is responsible for the adjudication of the non-criminal matters in the *Competition Act* including mergers and abuse of dominant position.

87. *Criminal Code*, S.C. 1953-54, c. 51, subsection 693(2). The limitation period is now two years by virtue of section 67(6) of the *Competition Act*.

88. This practice was authorized by section 15 of the *Combines Investigation Act*. The final decision as to whether or not to proceed with a prosecution rested with the Attorney General of Canada.

From the beginning, complainants held misconceptions about the Director's role. His function was to enforce the Act in the interests of the public in general and not to act on any individual complainant's behalf. Since inquiries usually took months or years to complete, complaints did not and could not bring complainants quick relief.

> Further, it should be understood that the *Combines Investigation Act* does not provide the Director with any authority to regulate business practices. The Director may not, therefore, require those complained against to discontinue or alter the course of action which has given rise to the complaint. If a breach of the Act is disclosed, however, enforcement proceedings may ordinarily be expected to follow.[89]

As the *Combines Investigation Act*'s ambit was widened over the years, so too were the Director's duties and responsibilities. While the number of cases dealing with misleading advertising remained proportionally small during the 1960s, those numbers began to increase dramatically after the 1969 amendment and with the growing tide of consumerism.[90]

The enactment of section 33D in 1969,[91] while not presaging a change in the philosophy behind the Director's role vis-a-vis the *Combines Investigation Act*, nevertheless had a significant effect on the Bureau of Competition Policy's efforts.[92] The need to adopt a more specialized approach to investigation and enforcement was recognized. Accordingly, a small staff of officers whose professional training was in investigation, rather than in law or economics, was recruited.

In the ensuing years, increasing resources were directed towards enforcing the misleading advertising provisions as well as assessing the provisions' ability to provide protection for the public interest in an accurate market information system.[93] Towards this end, in 1970, investigators were

---

89.   *Annual Report*, 1962/63, at 9-10.

90.   The numbers of completed prosecutions under old sections 36 and 37 for the years ending March 31, 1962 to 1973 can be found in the *Annual Report*, 1973, at 57. It indicates that from 1962 to 1968 the number did not exceed 10 p.a. By 1971 the number had increased to 58 and then it rose over 80 in 1972 and 1973. Table 4 sets out the statistics respecting Inquiries, investigations and prosecutions for the years 1972/73 to 1989/90.

91.   It was a natural addition, removing the duty to enforce the previous provision (s. 306 of the *Criminal Code*) from the seemingly disinterested provincial authorities (local police, etc.) and giving the newly recruited Bureau officers the opportunity to bring to bear their ever-increasing expertise, as well as the more flexible investigative powers provided in the *Combines Investigation Act*. The Bureau of Competition Policy appears to have been so named during fiscal year 1973-74.

92.   See *Annual Report*, 1969/70 at 60 and Table 3.

93.   The Trade Practices Section initially had operational responsibility for the provisions. Later becoming the Misleading Advertising Division in the Trade Practices Branch, in 1977 it was established as the Marketing Practices Branch.

stationed in each of the five regional offices of the Department (Halifax, Montreal, Toronto, Winnipeg and Vancouver) "as a further step in the campaign against false and misleading advertising."[94]

With the Stage I amendments came record numbers of inquiries and, consequently, prosecutions.   By 1979, the Marketing Practices Branch's priorities in dealing with the ever-increasing numbers of complaints it received were well established. Limited staff resources had to be concentrated on the cases most likely to produce an overall improvement in the quality of market information directed to the public, thus furthering the objectives of the legislation.

> The principles followed in assessing the priority of complaints are the degree of coverage of the representation, its impact on the public and the deterrent effect of a successful prosecution. A high priority is also given to cases that will afford a court the opportunity of establishing new principles or of clarifying the law.[95]

Administrative authorities, however, feel that the enforcement process being relied on could be improved.

3.3   Enforcement and the Compliance-Oriented Approach

The efforts of the Marketing Practices Branch are directed towards enforcement and compliance. In fiscal year 1989/90 some 14,610 complaints in respect of the misleading advertising and deceptive marketing practices provisions were received, up from 10,668 in 1985/86.[96]

Compliance with the Act is currently encouraged through the Program of Advisory Opinions (formerly the Program of Compliance) which provides, when requested, oral or written non-binding advice on potential infringements of the law by proposed advertising. It is also facilitated by increased general awareness on the part of business and consumers as to what the law requires of advertisers. The Bureau's Speech Program, whereby the Director and senior officials attend numerous speaking engagements each year, aids in achieving this goal.

The practice of holding informal discussions with interested persons regarding the interpretation of the anti-combines legislation had been longstanding by the time the misleading advertising provisions were introduced into the *Combines Investigation Act* in 1960. This practice, which came to be known as the Program of Compliance, provided an alternative to the criminal process, the sole statutory mechanism to encourage compliance with the Act.

---

94. *Annual Report*, 1969/70 at 10. At present, in addition to the head office in Hull, Quebec, there are branch field offices in Vancouver, Edmonton, Calgary, Winnipeg, London, Toronto, Hamilton, Montreal, Quebec City, Dartmouth and St. John's.

95. *Annual Report*, 1978/79, at 76.

96. *Annual Report*, 1989/90 at 30.

By 1979, advisory opinions were provided to 158 firms which had requested a review of proposed promotional material. The majority of compliance opinions then, and now, related to promotional contests. Throughout the 1980s, these numbers continued to rise.[97] In 1986, the Marketing Practices Branch commenced efforts to inform small businesses of the availability of the Program.

During 1988, the Compliance and Coordination Branch was created, responsible for the further development of the compliance-oriented approach and the public information program.[98] The Program of Advisory Opinions has been given renewed priority.

> Historically, enforcement of the *Competition Act* has focussed on investigating violations of the Act, with a view to prosecution and the imposition of criminal penalties. However, *it has become clear that in many instances the goals of maintaining and encouraging competition can be pursued with greater effectiveness and certainty, and with less time and expense, through an approach to enforcement which stresses the promotion of continuing voluntary compliance with the Act and relies on a broader range of responses to non-compliant behaviour* (emphasis added).

> For this reason, the Director is placing more emphasis than in the past on communication and public education as a means of promoting a better understanding of the Act and its application.[99] As well, the Director is encouraging business persons to make more use of the Program of Advisory Opinions, and to discuss proposed conduct or transactions with his office at the earliest possible stage. Finally, the Director is relying to a greater extent on alternative case resolution instruments in appropriate circumstances as a means of achieving early and effective remedies for non-compliant behaviour.[100]

While it would seem that the Program's success has reduced reliance on the criminal process, it has been made clear that that avenue of redress continues to be relied on.

> While we are making greater use of alternatives to litigation where this approach is appropriate, we nonetheless have a considerable number of cases before the courts. When resort to contested proceedings is the appropriate course of action, I [the Director] will not hesitate to refer potential offences to the Attorney General

---

97. In 1980 and 1981, 156 and 182 firms respectively received such opinions. By 1988/89 the number had risen to 377 (*Annual Report*, 1988/89, at 36). In 1989/90, the number was 323 (*Misleading Advertising Bulletin*, Vol. 4, 1990, p. 7).

98. The Bureau's enforcement Branches continue to have responsibility for day-to-day compliance efforts.

99. In June 1989, a comprehensive Information Bulletin (No. 3) was produced setting out the various features of the Program which applied to all aspects of the Bureau's mandate.

100. *Annual Report*, 1987/88 at p. 4.

of Canada or to make an application to the Competition Tribunal for a remedial order.[101]

One mechanism to disseminate information on both current case law and the Director's position in relation to those matters which, amongst other things, may not yet have been adjudicated upon, is the *Misleading Advertising Bulletin*.

Although lists of prosecutions under the misleading advertising provisions were issued quarterly as far back as 1971, they were only available upon written request.[102] This practice became systematized through dialogue with the public, resulting, in December 1974, in the publication of the first quarterly issue of the *Misleading Advertising Bulletin*. With wide distribution to the news media, the advertising industry and other interested parties, it reported on the activities of the then Misleading Advertising Division of the Bureau of Competition Policy.

In the ensuing years, the *Misleading Advertising Bulletin* provided the Director with a means to express his positions on a variety of topics:

- 1976: double ticketing, fuel economy advertising, promotional contests, adequate and fair disclosure, comparative advertising;
- 1977: testimonials and endorsements, ordinary price claims, energy conservation and advertising, liability of advertising agencies, the non-availability of advertised specials;
- 1978: simulations of product characteristics in advertising, "silver dollar" premium offers, strict or absolute liability in relation to sections 52 to 59, sale above advertised price, the general impression test;
- 1979: pyramid selling provisions;
- 1980: retailers' use of manufacturers' suggested list prices for comparison purposes in advertising, deeming provisions related to offences under section 52;
- 1981: section 52(1)(b): adequate and proper test, image advertising;
- 1982: the use of the Director's formal powers in Marketing Practices cases, the Program of Compliance;
- 1983: misleading advertising in relation to the housing industry, false reasons for distress sales, adequate and fair contest disclosures at point of sale;

---

101. *Annual Report*, 1987/88 at p. viii.

102. The only other source which provided relatively up-to-date information on prosecutions was the Director's *Annual Report* - a document not likely to be found in the average advertiser's library.

- 1984:   section 57(2) "raincheck" defences, test markets, section 55 pyramid sales scheme exemption, representations, employment-related advertising;[103]
- 1985:   advertising guidelines for the automobile industry, pyramid sales, "made in Canada";
- 1986:   use of disclaimers, advertising by Crown corporations, continuous sales, interest-free financing, schemes that take advantage of businesses, grey marketing, counterfeit goods;
- 1987:   comparative price advertising;
- 1988:   practices of the window-blind industry;
- 1989:   weight loss schemes.

While the Bulletin's circulation varies significantly from year to year, the last edition was sent to over 15,000 recipients.

3.4 Report of the Standing Committee on Consumer and Corporate Affairs[104]

There have been continuing calls for reform since the mid 1970s. Following this trend, in 1988, the Standing Committee on Consumer and Corporate Affairs considered the subject of misleading advertising and produced a report. Numerous groups and individuals appeared before the Committee to make submissions. Some witnesses stated that the Bureau's efforts to educate have failed to impart a sufficient degree of consumer awareness. Consumers are felt to be unfamiliar with the function of the Department of Consumer and Corporate Affairs and its mandate to prevent misleading advertising.[105]

The Consumers' Association of Canada expressed its concern over what it perceived as a widening gap between the level of sophistication of consumers and the business community. The lack of available information has forced consumers to rely increasingly on information supplied by the product manufacturers themselves. It is the CAC's view that the government should address this concern through consumer education programs.

The Committee, which commended the Marketing Practices Branch for its work in enforcing its mandate, recognized that its financial and human

---

103. Summaries of compliance opinions which had been provided to members of the business community were also included in the Bulletin commencing in 1984.

104. In June 1988 the Standing Committee, chaired by Mary Collins, M.P. produced its *Report... on the Subject of Misleading Advertising* [hereafter referred to as the Committee and the Report].

105. Report, at 7.

resources were limited.[106] Nevertheless, it concluded that increased resources should be devoted to the task of education.

It recommended that the Director adopt a more pro-active role in seeking to educate consumers and the business community, with additional financial and human resources to be allocated by the Department. The Director should consider a multi-media informational approach, possibly using film, television and radio. As well, the Committee recommended that, where appropriate, the Director should undertake such education programs as joint ventures with the business community, consumer groups and other organizations.[107]

It has long been recognized that use of the criminal process to combat deceptive marketing practices is not appropriate in all circumstances. In fact, it is often wholly inappropriate. This opinion was reiterated before the Committee:

> Several witnesses felt that there were significant problems with the current approach. The criminal process was viewed as cumbersome, costly and slow, ill-suited to matters of this nature. One witness described it as a ridiculous misuse of society's resources, another said it was too blunt an instrument, while yet another questioned its deterrent effect.[108]

Taking its cue from the remedies employed by the U.S. Federal Trade Commission, the Committee recommended that the Act be amended to permit courts to require the disclosure of essential facts previously omitted from a representation. This would have the twofold effect of countering past deception through future advertising and providing a greater deterrent than fines.

Courts should also be given the power to order corrective advertising. This requires advertisers to acknowledge that certain claims in previous advertisements were false. Such orders can specify the method to be used in carrying out such advertising, as well as its content, form, frequency and duration. This remedy would also be available as a term in consent agreements.

The Director should be empowered to enter into binding consent agreements or assurances of voluntary compliance [AVCs] with advertisers

---

106. The number of person years allocated to the Marketing Practices Branch since 1976/77 has ranged from 61 in 1980/81 to 80 in 1985/86. In 1989/90 the number was 71, but it was reduced to 69 in 1990/91 and 68 in 1991/92.

107. Report, at 51. Recognizing the importance of the provinces' role in education and enforcement, the Committee also recommended that the Minister of Consumer and Corporate Affairs coordinate with his provincial counterparts.

108. Report, at 17.

who thereby agree to cease and desist from misleading advertising or deceptive marketing practices.[109]

Finally, the Committee considered the desirability of rules and regulations which would define or specify acts or marketing practices which are misleading or deceptive.

The Committee concluded that, although the Director has endeavoured to make known his position regarding certain industry practices, such efforts lack the weight of statutory authority. As the *Competition Act* is not a regulatory statute, thus making it inappropriate that the Director should have the rule-making power, it was recommended that the power should reside with the Governor-in-Council.[110]

3.5 The Response of the Federal Government

The Committee's report contained numerous invaluable recommendations which represented not only a blueprint for reform but a status report on the effectiveness of the current laws and practices. While the government could not respond to the Report before Parliament was dissolved for the 1988 general election, the Marketing Practices Branch felt it useful to examine some of the reform issues raised. The Branch undertook several internal studies and was encouraged to continue the process of consultation.

Beginning in June 1989, a consultation letter was sent out by the Bureau to business associations, consumer interest groups and academics, as well as to provincial authorities, indicating that the desirability of the amendments to the misleading advertising provisions of the *Competition Act* was being examined. Recipients were invited to review and critique what was called a "framework for reform," developed in part as a response to the Report. The

---

109.   Such authority would simplify and facilitate current practice: "Although the *Competition Act* does not specifically provide for a consent procedure, officials of the Department of Consumer and Corporate Affairs informed the Committee that, on occasion, the Director has negotiated a prohibition order with an advertised and has had the order approved by a court under [subsection 34(2)] of the Act. In this way, the Director can avoid initiating a criminal prosecution." [Report, at 25.] To avoid what it perceived as the potential for abuse of the AVC mechanism, the Committee also recommended that the Director develop and publish guidelines for the use of such consent procedures. It also recommended that they be part of the public record, to ensure "some form of public oversight of the use of the procedure" [at 25].

110.   The Committee also recognized that some feel that there may be constitutional constraints on reform, the concern being that as one moves away from the criminal sphere, legislative authority must increasingly depend on the trade and commerce power. The Committee agreed with the conclusions of one of its witnesses who noted: "that a major hurdle for federal parliamentarians and regulators is the "constitutional mindset" which stresses that the control of misleading advertising must be based on the criminal law power. In his opinion, the immediate need is to rediscover and resuscitate the trade and commerce power and to create a national trade practices policy beginning with the broadening of the techniques available to the federal government to deal with misleading advertising" [Report, at 19]. The recent decisions by the Supreme Court of Canada, *Rocois* and *General Motors*, discussed *infra*, lend credence to this viewpoint.

framework did not propose to widen the scope of the misleading advertising provisions but was, rather, "confined to allowing improved and more equitable options for dealing with matters that are currently within the ambit of the Act, but are adjudicated by the criminal courts."

The letter addressed four concerns raised in the Report. It gave some indication of the Bureau's "preliminary positions" regarding a non-criminal case adjudication process, remedial orders, interpretative rule-making and assurances of voluntary compliance. Preliminary positions, which were "not [to] be seen as carrying the endorsement of the Department of the Minister," were set out, intended to "stimulate and focus comment from interested parties." Responses received were numerous and detailed and were being studied at the end of 1989. The process of reform is ongoing. But that must remain the subject of another paper.[111]

Order Form[112]

Bureau Scientifique Français, P.O. Box 169,
Hochelaga, Montreal, Canada

Gentlemen, -- You will find herewith $1 for your full home treatment against self-consciousness, bashfulness and self-diffidence (including twelve lessons in 'Auto-Suggestion' and fifty three tablet(s) 'Anti-Gêno' as described in your pamphlet entitled 'The Road to Success'. I agree, moreover, to spread as much as I can acknowledge of your treatment among my friends and acquaintances, when cured.

Name . . . .
Address . . . .

---

111.   See William A.W. Neilson, "Reforming Federal Misleading Advertising Law: Review and Prognosis" in R.S. Khemani and W.T. Stanbury (eds.) *Canadian Competition Law and Policy at the Centenary* (Halifax: The Institute for Research on Public Policy, 1991).

112.   *Supra*, note 1.

Table 1

MAXIMUM PENALTIES FOR MISLEADING ADVRTISING AND DECEPTIVE MARKETING PRACTICES

1. **Summary Conviction**

    Maximum Fine

    * $25,000: ss. 52, 53, 55, 56, 57, 58 and 59.

    * $10,000: s. 54

    Maximum Imprisonment

    *   1 year for all offences.

2. **Indictment**

    Maximum Fine

    *   In the discretion of the Court for all offences where indictment is available (i.e., not ss. 54, 57 and 58).

    Maximum Imprisonment

    *   5 years for all offences where indictment is available (i.e., not ss. 54, 57 and 58).

Source: *Competition Act*, R.S.C. 1985, c. C-34.

Table 2

CONVICTIONS AND FINES
IN MISLEADING ADVERTISING CASES,
1976/77 TO 1979/80

	1976/77	1977/78	1978/79	1979/80
Number of individuals/ corporations convicted:				
S.36(1)(a)	22	57	77	61
S.36(1)(b)	0	0	0	3
S.36(1)(d)	6	6	13	8
S.36.2	2	3	1	1
S.37(2)	0	2	0	3
S.37.1	1	6	11	30
S.37.2	0	1	7	2
Total	98	96	123	110
Average fine per case:				
S.36(1)(a)	$ 597	$1,030	$1,558	$1,970
S.36(1)(b)	-	-	-	387
S.36(1)(d)	660	483	1,427	944
S.36.2	500	800	2,000	500
S.37(2)	-	750	-	1,833
S.37.1	1,000	3,108	448	7,943
S.37.2	-	750	479	1,500
All sections	$1,242	$1,481	$1,810	$3,710

Source: Director of Investigation and Research, *Annual Report*, 1976/77.

Table 3

**CONVICTIONS AND FINES IN MISLEADING ADVERTISING CASES,
1980/81 TO 1989/90**

	1980/81	1981/82	1982/83	1983/84	1984/85	1985/86	1986/87	1987/88	1988/89	1989/90
Number of Individuals/ Corporations Convicted										
S.52(1)(a)	85	58	87	84	84	87	80	78	73	37
S.52(1)(b)	8	14	11	16	14	10	12	6	9	7
S.52(1)(c)	0	0	0	1	0	1	2	0	2	0
S.52(1)(d)	7	17	10	16	23	18	20	8	9	8
S.53	0	1	0	0	3	0	0	0	0	0
S.54	1	2	0	2	1	0	0	1	0	0
S.55	0	0	0	3	2	3	3	2	1	0
S.57	0	4	1	3	3	4	5	24	3	2
S.58	15	4	25	33	17	4	4	2	1	2
S.59	1	3	3	7	5	1	5	4	1	3
Total	123	103	136	156	130	128	131	125	99	59
Average Fine per Case:										
S.52(1)(a)	$2,043	$3,188	$ 5,296	$19,832	$ 4,811	$ 6,561	$ 7,608	$ 8,232	$10,538	$10,854
S.52(1)(b)	5,385	1,904	10,893	1,918	3,454	2,028	5,919	3,030	3,569	29,786
S.52(1)(c)	-	-	-	300	-	-	20,000	-	6,500	-
S.52(1)(d)	2,366	1,200	1,430	1,431	2,587	3,705	4,809	6,925	4,978	20,781
S.53	-	-	-	-	800	-	-	-	-	-
S.54	200	125	-	7,040	22,500	-	-	2,000	-	-
S.55	-	-	-	-	12,000	30,500	20,000	4,250	8,000	-
S.57	-	1,250	2,500	1,333	4,400	18,750	2,400	52,660	4,500	8,500
S.58	8,516	1,239	4,073	3,824	10,042	5,875	3,562	1,875	4,500	19,000
S.59	8,000	1,333	2,875	2,967	19,660	700	2,740	5,625	9,000	1,667
All sections	$3,457	$2,395	$ 5,047	$11,679	$ 5,679	$ 6,384	$ 7,120	$10,430	$ 9,033	$14,175

Source: Bureau of Competition Policy, *Misleading Advertising Bulletin*, various issues.

Table 4

MISLEADING ADVERTISING INVESTIGATIONS
AND PROSECUTIONS, 1972/73 TO 1989/90

	72/73	73/74	74/75	75/76	76/77	77/78	78/79	79/80	80/81	81/82	82/83	83/84	84/85	85/86	86/87	87/88	88/89	89/90
• Number of complete investigations[1]	609	911	1047	1373	1895	2113	2135	2234	2147	2319	2457	2068	2145	2151	2188	2187	1937	1803
• Total number of cases referred to the Attorney General	84	125	127	120	117	139	174	129	167	142	199	181	136	175	151	83	75	56
• Informations laid during the year (proceedings commenced)																		
• former section 36	23	21	29	9	3													
• former section 37	43	89	84	95	35													
• new provisions																		
section 36(1)(a)				3	56	86	94	89	78	95	93	97	78	108	81	[detail not available]		
section 36(1)(b)				1	1	2	5	4	13	14	22	21	13	8	10			
section 36(1)(c)					0	1	0	1	1	1	1	1	0	2	0			
section 36(1)(d)					9	14	17	8	11	25	25	21	40	21	26			
section 36.1					0	0	2	0	1	0	2	1	4	0	0			
section 36.2					3	2	2	1	3	0	0	1	0	0	0			
section 36.3					0	0	1	0	1	0	0	5	4	0	4			
section 36.4					1	1	1	1	0	0	0	0	0	0	0			
section 37					1	3	5	1	3	8	1	2	5	7	9			
section 37.1					4	11	18	29	24	31	33	5	1	6	7			
section 37.2					0	4	4	3	2	3	1	9	3	6	6			
Total Informations laid	66	110	113	108	113	123	149	137	136	176	178	163	148	158	143	131	110	84

1. In the 1989/90 Annual Report, this category was broken down into "completed examinations/inquiries" and "information contacts." From 1985/86 to 1989/90, the number of "completed examinations and inquiries" was 1042, 882, 670, 612 and 493 respectively.

Source: Director of Investigation and Research, Annual Reports, various years (Ottawa: Minister of Supply and Services Canada).

Chapter 6

LEGISLATIVE REFORM AND THE POLICY PROCESS: THE CASE OF THE COMPETITION ACT

Ian D. Clark
Deputy Minister
Department of Consumer and Corporate Affairs

1.0 INTRODUCTION

As the title indicates, I intend to focus on the recent reform process that culminated in passage of the *Competition Act* in 1986.[1] It may be useful by way of introduction to relay a rather telling remark on the enthusiasm with which economists addressed early antitrust legislation. Professor George Stigler (1982, p. 1) has remarked that:

> For much too long a time, students of the history of the American antitrust policy have been at least mildly perplexed by the coolness with which American economists greeted the Sherman Act. Was not the nineteenth century the period in which the benevolent effects of competition were most widely extolled? Should not a profession praise a Congress which seeks to legislate its textbook assumptions into universal practice? And with even modest foresight, should not the economists have seen the Sherman Act would put more into economists' purses than perhaps any other law ever passed?

Since that time certain economists have come to embrace competition legislation. For others, indifference, and even antagonism, has grown.

In the case of Canada, competition policy represents one of the most studied, debated and revised pieces of legislation in Canadian history. Debate

---

1. The earlier history is reviewed in Sanderson and Stanbury (1989), Gorecki and Stanbury (1984), and Baggaley, Chapter 1 in this volume.

over proposed reforms has always been lively and sometimes acrimonious.[2] Indeed, some observers have suggested that these debates have led to a higher than average turnover of ministers in this portfolio. Between 1967, when it was created, and the fall of 1989, the Department of Consumer and Corporate Affairs has had no fewer than 14 ministers. No wonder senior officials in our department find the subject of the reform of competition legislation in Canada intriguing.

I have been in the public service during most of the period in which the government proposals to reform competition law were being discussed. Although I have never been directly involved in the attempts to amend competition law, I have watched its evolution -- and signed numerous briefing notes on the subject -- during my 18 years in Ottawa. In this paper I provide some of my personal observations on this long process of legislative revision.

2.0   REFORM PROCESS, 1966-1978

When I took my first summer job in Ottawa in the Planning Branch of the Treasury Board in 1971, reform of competition legislation was one of the top Government planning initiatives.   As you will recall, the Pearson government had asked the newly-formed Economic Council of Canada to undertake a study of combines, mergers, monopolies and restraint of trade, among other matters, in 1966. The Council released its *Interim Report on Competition Policy* in July of 1969 -- just months after the election of the Trudeau government. In its report, the Council called for a fundamental change in Canadian competition legislation-- namely, the adoption of an approach based on a mixture of criminal and civil law, employing the single, clear objective of furthering the interest of Canadian consumers through an efficiently functioning economy (McDonald, 1970).

Legislation incorporating many of the Council's proposals was given first reading in the House of Commons in the summer of 1971 (Canada, 1971). In the eyes of some, the proposals found in Bill C-256 went far beyond the Council's recommendations in the extent of its advocacy for consumer interests (see Stanbury, 1977a; Skeoch, 1972).   When introducing the legislation, the then Minister of Consumer and Corporate Affairs, the Honourable Ron Basford, stated that the Bill sought to develop a clear and precise statute which was also economically sound. In Mr. Basford's words:

---

2.   See, for example, Block (1982), Brecher (1982), Business Council on National Issues (1981a), (1981b), Green (1981), Lecraw (1981), MacCrimmon and Stanbury (1977), McDonald (1970), McQueen (1976), Moore (1970), Reschenthaler and Stanbury (1981), Rochwerg (1977), Skeoch, ed. (1972), Skeoch (1979), Stanbury (1977a), (1977b), (1978), (1981), (1985), (1988), Stanbury and Reschenthaler (1981).

> ... we face many challenges in devising a new competition policy. It is more than a
> challenge, however. It is an opportunity to help create an economy that is efficient,
> growing and equitable for all Canadians. With those objectives who can disagree?

Needless to say, a few Canadians were found to disagree.

The critique of Bill C-256 from the business community was vigorous from the beginning. Generally, the Bill was perceived as being "solely concerned with consumer benefits and not at all with the survival of domestic industry." The legislation was described in Orwellian terms as "centralizing ... decision-making power in the hands of a group of technocrats bound only by the vaguest rules." In the words of one editorial, "if enacted in [its] present form, [Bill C-256] could well spell the death knell of private enterprise as it is known in this country." In 1972, I was made personally aware of the fallout of this controversy when I took an assignment as Mr. Basford's Executive Assistant in his new responsibilities as Minister of State for Urban Affairs.

Perusal of ministerial speeches reveals the optimism with which Mr. Basford and successive ministers of Consumer and Corporate Affairs approached the reform process in the face of such strongly held views. Each recognized the large task ahead, yet believed legislation could be enacted in a relatively short time. Reaction to Bill C-256 provided an indication of exactly how difficult the amendment process would be.

In an effort to respond to the recognized complexities of Bill C-256 and the Bill's application to different sectors of the economy, Mr. Basford had sought to provide opportunity for consultation with interested parties. In all, some 300 briefs and submissions were reportedly received. A series of seminars with interested parties and meetings with the provinces were also embarked upon. Nonetheless, criticism remained fierce (see Stanbury, 1977a).

Five months after the Bill's introduction, the *Financial Post* claimed: "Not since the early days of the great tax debate has a single government proposal aroused the ire of the business community to the extent that the Competition Act has." One of the principal criticisms of Bill C-256 was that it was too theoretical -- the Bill was perceived to have been "drafted in isolation." Business leaders professed to have little faith in the economic models upon which the Bill was thought to be based. Business spokesmen also complained that, in addition to being excessively concerned with price competition and low prices for consumers, the proposed reforms granted far too much power to the proposed Competitive Practices Tribunal. Moreover, the cost of compliance with the proposed Act was estimated by business spokesmen to be enormous.

Critics felt government already had too much control over business. By closely following Government initiatives in the areas of energy and tax, competition legislation was regarded as yet another attempt by the federal government to gain greater control over business behaviour. Thus, Bill C-256 acted to deepen the business community's sense of alienation from Ottawa in the mid-1970s. Attempting reform in such an atmosphere of distrust would prove to be a major feat.

To expedite the process of putting competition legislation before Parliament, the minority Liberal Government announced in 1973 that it would split the Bill into two stages, noting at that time that "the scope of the policy areas to be covered were ... wide and the administrative effort and Cabinet time required were ... extensive." Dividing legislative reform into stages proved to be a relatively successful approach. It has since been adopted in other areas of this portfolio, such as the *Copyright Act* and the *Patent Act*.

The least contentious proposed revisions to the *Combines Investigation Act*, were introduced as Stage I Amendments in November of 1973 (Canada, 1973). The Trudeau government returned with a majority in 1974 and these amendments were passed within a year, after incorporating numerous House of Commons and Senate Committee revisions. They came into effect in January 1, 1976, one decade after the Pearson government's reference to the Economic Council (see Kaiser, 1979).

However, the Stage II Amendments, relating to adjudication, mergers, monopolies and other disputed issues, were not completed for another decade. Several bills were introduced and reintroduced throughout the late 1970s in the face of continuing business criticism.[3] Recall that in October 1975 the Government imposed temporary wage and price controls to deal with historically high levels of inflation. They stayed in place for three years.

The Government's policy approach in respect of the post-control period was outlined in the discussion paper "The Way Ahead" in 1976. In this 1976 document, the Government expressed its commitment to both increased reliance on and effectiveness of the market system:

> The role of government policy should not be to direct and manage the economy in detail. The interplay of dynamic forces that results from the market system and has led to continuing economic growth must be encouraged.

To assist the Government in developing a coordinated policy response to the post-control period, the Prime Minister established an *ad hoc* committee of ten deputy ministers, known as the DM 10 Committee. Representation on the Committee came from all the major social and economic departments of Government, including Consumer and Corporate Affairs.

At this time, I joined the staff of the newly created Board of Economic Development, headed by Mr. Robert Andras, the man who had replaced Mr. Basford at Consumer and Corporate Affairs six years earlier. Competition policy was once again near the top of the Government's policy agenda. Indeed, because it is so obviously a key part of any country's policy

---

3. See Canada (1977), MacCrimmon and Stanbury (1977), Rochwerg (1977), Rowley and Stanbury, eds. (1978).

framework, competition legislation generally moved to the top of Ottawa's economic policy agenda whenever a major planning exercise was being embarked upon. This occurred in the late 1970s in response to inflation. It also occurred later in the early 1980s in response to the imperatives of economic renewal and deficit control.

Let me briefly summarize the legislative initiatives during this period. Mr. Anthony Abbott introduced the first attempt at Stage II reform to the House of Commons in March of 1977 (Canada, 1977). The legislation, Bill C-42, was subsequently reintroduced to the House after referral to, and significant revision by, the House of Commons Standing Committee on Finance, Trade and Economic Affairs, commonly referred to as the Cafik Committee after its chairman Mr. Norman Cafik (see MacCrimmon and Stanbury, 1977). Bill C-42 did not, however, move beyond second reading. Mr. Warren Allmand replaced Mr. Abbott as Minister of Consumer and Corporate Affairs in September of 1977. Bill C-13 followed in 1978, but died on the Order Paper (see Rowley and Stanbury, eds., 1978).

3.0 REFORM PROCESS, 1979-1986

Following the election of the Clark government in 1979, Mr. Allan Lawrence was appointed Minister of Consumer and Corporate Affairs. With a crowded policy agenda and a relatively short time in office, no legislative action was taken on competition legislation during the Clark government.

Mr. André Ouellet was appointed Minister in 1980 following the Trudeau Government's return to office. In 1981, Mr. Ouellet released a discussion paper on competition legislative reform (Canada, 1981). But once again, most of the spokesmen for Canada's business community were critical (Business Council on National Issues, 1981a, 1981b). Feelings against the Minister's proposals were so deep that the Canadian Chamber of Commerce released a film to its members depicting the sands of time running out for the average businessman. In the film version of reform, businessmen pursuing "legitimate" growth would likely be thrown behind bars. Members were urged to write the Government in order to protest the proposed reforms.[4]

In recognition of the indisputable role business interests had played throughout the reform process, extensive consultation with business was embarked upon following the effective withdrawal of Mr. Ouellet's 1981 proposals. Initially, general concepts and theoretical propositions were discussed between a team of senior officials and what became known as the "Gang of Three" -- the Canadian Manufacturers Association, Canadian Chamber of Commerce, and the Business Council on National Issues which pushed the idea of a less confrontational approach. This group was later

---

4. For different critiques, see Lecraw (1981), Stanbury and Reschenthaler (1981), the papers in Block ed. (1982), and Green (1981).

extended to include the Grocery Products Manufacturers of Canada and the Canadian Bar Association. The Consumers Association of Canada and interested academics were also regularly consulted (Stanbury, 1985, 1986).

Business and government officials approached each other with considerable caution in the early stages of consultation. This should not be surprising in view of the fact that most of the legislation governing competition was of a criminal nature. Naturally, the traditional lines of prosecutor and defendant were felt to exist. However, as weekly meetings continued, guards were gradually dropped.

The goal of the government representatives, by then reporting to a new Minister, Mrs. Judy Erola, was to develop a consensus with business on the ultimate objectives of competition legislation. By working towards increased business understanding of the Government's objectives, officials sought to create a business protagonist for competition policy reform. Pursuing a consultative approach to reform proved to considerably reduce the distance between policy formulation and the view of concerned parties. Policy-making was by no means proceeding in a vacuum; a frequent criticism of earlier attempts at reform. The Business Council on National Issues has since described this process, before the MacDonald Commission, as an exemplary model for policy development. While Bill C-29 was introduced in 1984 it was not enacted before the next general election was called.[5]

After the election of the Mulroney government in September, 1984, the consultative process was continued under Mr. Michel Côté. I had observed the last four years of the process with the emotional detachment that one acquires in the Privy Council Office, where I was concerned with such arcane machinery of government matters as the implications of subjecting agents of Her Majesty, in this case Crown corporations, to the non-criminal provisions of the proposed legislation. Eventually, the various positions were reconciled and Bill C-91 was introduced in December 1985,[6] and in June 1986 passed into law as the *Competition Act*. I must say that at the time I had no idea that I would soon have the responsibility, as Deputy Minister of Consumer and Corporate Affairs, to help the new Director of Investigation and Research put the appropriate people, systems and financial resources in place to implement the new law.

4.0 LESSONS

In looking back at this rather strenuous process of legislative reform, I believe several lessons may be learned. We will temporarily set aside

---

5. See Canada (1984a), (1984b) and Stanbury (1985).

6. See Canada (1985a), (1985b) and Stanbury (1986).

Bismarck's warning that: "there are two things in this world one does not wish to know how are made -- sausages and legislation."

First, it should not be surprising that revising competition policy generated so large and extended a debate, given the fundamental role played by competition within our society. Competition affects <u>all</u> members of society, giving each participant a vested interest in how competition policy is administered. Clearly, divergent views will arise. Consumers have different interests from those of small business which have different interests from those of larger enterprises. When a policy affects numerous diverse groups, extensive consultations will need to take place. I believe Professor W.T. Stanbury (1977a, p. 36) described the situation well, when he stated that:

> [Policy-makers] learned, perhaps painfully, that the <u>technical quality</u> of a policy solution is only one part of the problem. Policy solutions must be <u>acceptable</u> to the dominant participants in the policy environment. Acceptability and technical quality may be independent or even opposed to each other.

While the individuals attempting to reform Canadian competition policy were always aware of the need for a consultative process, they initially failed to recognize the extent that the process required. Few if any attempts were made to prepare the public for competition legislation reform between release of the Economic Council's recommendations in 1969 and introduction of Bill C-256 in 1971.

Furthermore, despite Mr. Basford's stated objective to use Bill C-256 as an "exposure draft" rather than a regular bill, business perceived the bill as stated Government policy having been composed without an adequate attempt to obtain business views. In fact, reform of the *Combines Investigation Act* was one of the Government's first attempts at release of a "draft bill published solely for consultation purposes." Such a strategy had not previously been common. Later attempts at consultation were also regarded with considerable suspicion. For example, the *Financial Times* referred to Mr. Basford's press seminars as part of a "road show," asking "where does explanation end and propaganda begin?"

The second point I wish to make is that competition policy represents an extremely important piece of legislation. It is advanced in pursuit of numerous objectives. To paraphrase the work of Gorecki and Stanbury (1984), Canadian competition policy has been historically associated with three major objectives: maintaining free competition; preventing abuses of market power; and achieving economic efficiency. In addition, a number of supplementary objectives for Canadian competition policy have been identified. These include codifying the common law doctrine of restraint of trade; fighting inflation; protecting small business; preserving the free enterprise system; and ensuring fairness and honesty in the marketplace. In many ways competition legislation provides a link between political and economic objectives. As a single piece of legislation, it has a big impact.

In Canada, most attention has been focused on the economic implications of competition law. But in many countries, the focus of competition policy has also been closely linked to the objective of developing and maintaining democratic institutions.

In Japan, for example, prior to World War II, great importance was placed on a policy of rapidly fostering modern industries by means of government leadership, aid and assistance. Large combines developed. Furthermore, cartels were promoted and reinforced by legislation. After the war this policy was fundamentally altered. In 1947, the *Act concerning Prohibition of Private Monopoly and Maintenance of Fair Trade* was enacted under the strong influence of the Allied Forces, the objectives of which included the decentralization of economic and political influence of large firms in the economy.

Likewise, competition policy was significantly strengthened in Germany following the war. Although legislation attempting to control cartels had previously existed in Germany, cartels were legitimized in the late 1930s. After the war, the Allies instituted a program of decartelization and deconcentration. Laws against restrictive business practices were introduced by the western allied military governments in 1946 and 1947. In 1957, Germany established comprehensive competition legislation. It is noteworthy that the body presently governing antitrust legislation in Germany is known as the Federal Cartel Office.

More generally, most economists agree that the promotion of the efficient use of resources through adherence to competition policy lessens the need for what they regard as alternative, more interventionist and expensive, forms of control such as regulation and public ownership. Whereas in the past there was a view in favour of government intervention to correct perceived market failures, there has gradually developed a consensus in respect of the limitations of direct intervention in the marketplace.

This phenomenon is one which has been experienced world-wide. For instance, in the Economic Declaration from the 1988 Toronto Summit, the leaders of the "G7" countries and the European Community recognized the need for a "shift from short-term considerations to a medium-term framework for the development and implementation of economic policies, and a commitment to improve efficiency and adaptability through greater reliance on competitive forces and structural reform."

A somewhat similar position is now being promoted throughout the Eastern block countries as reforms in Hungary and the Soviet Union attest to. Moreover, the importance of a "market-oriented, growth-led strategy" to deal with the problems of Third World indebtedness in an expeditious and cost-effective manner have also been advanced.

In the case of Canada, competition policy was considered to be an increasingly important tool after anti-inflation controls were phased out in the late 1970s. In its 1976 White Paper, *Attack on Inflation*, the Government expressed its commitment to encouraging market forces as a method of steering the Canadian economy out of the controls period: "Over the longer term, we must make our economic system more innovative, dynamic and efficient by reducing existing rigidities and intensifying competition." The White Paper went on to explicitly recognize the major role which competition policy was to play in ensuring a smooth transition from the controls period.

Finally, I believe it is important not to lose sight of the "revolutionary" approach proposed by the Economic Council in 1969. The introduction of civil law standards for mergers, monopolies and certain practices in restraint of trade represented a definitive break from the past (McDonald, 1970). New rules of evidence and burden of proof would be adopted. In addition, the proposed Competitive Practices Tribunal was in many ways unique. Adjudication by an independent group of economic, legal and business experts with the powers of a superior court was, at that time, unheard of in Canada. In fact, the controversy surrounding the last 20 years of attempted reform may be distilled down to two issues: adjudication and the proposed test for mergers.

Progressive proposals will always require increased efforts on the part of government officials to properly inform affected parties of possible outcomes. One should keep in mind that part of the Government's reference to the Economic Council was "preparedness": preparing competition legislation to meet the prospective needs of the Canadian economy. In this respect, the resulting legislation is an excellent example of long-term planning.

Governments are often criticized for not looking beyond the next election, yet here is a policy thrust supported by successive Governments over two decades which anticipated the Canadian economy would become increasingly integrated with a global economic system. New pressures and opportunities would flow from new technologies and organizational methods. Industry adjustment processes would need to accelerate in reaction. Competition policy was regarded by its advocates as having an important contribution to make to both the responsiveness and accountability of Canadian business.

This continues to be the case today. The 1986 *Competition Act* attempts to prevent domestic abuses of market position without hindering Canadian firms' ability to competitively respond to international rivals. Further reform is never foreclosed -- although both my Minister and I are relieved that, so far at least, there have not been any compelling reasons to reopen the Act during our watch. But the Government is well aware that, to remain effective, all legislation must evolve in response to the changing environment. I trust that the experience of the last two decades will be put to use in developing whatever future amendments are required.

REFERENCES

Block, Walker (1982) *Response to the Framework Document for Amending the Combines Investigation Act*, Technical Report 82-10 (Vancouver: The Fraser Institute).

Brecher, Irving (1982) *Canada's Competition Policy Revisited: Some New Thoughts on an Old Story* (Montreal: The Institute for Research on Public Policy).

Business Council on National Issues (1981a) *A Consideration of Possible Amendments to the Combines Investigation Act* (Ottawa: BCNI).

Business Council on National Issues (1981b) "Supplementary Response from BCNI to the Hon. André Ouellet Concerning Conspiracy Law Amendments Raised in Proposals for Amending the Combines Investigation Act - A Framework for Discussion, April 1981" (Ottawa: BCNI, September).

Canada (1971) *Bill C-256, The Competition Act*, First Reading, 29 June 1971 (Ottawa: Queen's Printer).

Canada (1973) Department of Consumer and Corporate Affairs, *Proposals for a New Competition Policy for Canada, First Stage* (Ottawa: Information Canada).

Canada (1977) Department of Consumer and Corporate Affairs, *Proposals for a New Competition Policy for Canada, Second Stage* (Ottawa: Minister of Supply and Services Canada).

Canada (1981) Minister of Consumer and Corporate Affairs, "Proposals for Amending the Combines Investigation Act: A Framework for Discussion" (Ottawa: Bureau of Competition Policy).

Canada (1984a) Department of Consumer and Corporate Affairs, *Amendments to the Combines Investigation Act: A Schematic Presentation of the Act and the Bill* (Ottawa: Consumer and Corporate Affairs Canada).

Canada (1984b) Department of Consumer and Corporate Affairs, *Combines Investigation Act Amendments 1984: Clause-By-Clause Analysis* (Ottawa: Consumer and Corporate Affairs Canada).

Canada (1985a) Department of Consumer and Corporate Affairs, *Reform of Competition Policy in Canada: A Consultation Paper* (Ottawa: Consumer and Corporate Affairs Canada).

Canada (1985b) House of Commons, *Bill C-91: An Act to Establish the Competition Tribunal and to amend the Combines Investigation Act and the Bank Act and other Acts in consequence thereof: First Reading, December 17, 1985* (Ottawa: Supply and Services Canada).

Economic Council of Canada (1969) *Interim Report on Competition Policy* (Ottawa: Queen's Printer).

Gorecki, P.K. and W.T. Stanbury (1984) *The Objectives of Canadian Competition Policy, 1888-1983* (Montreal: The Institute for Research on Public Policy).

Green, Christopher (1981) "Canadian Competition Policy at a Crossroads," *Canadian Public Policy*, Vol. 7 (Summer), pp. 418-32.

Kaiser, Gordon E. (1979) "The Stage I Amendments: An Overview" in J.R.S. Prichard, W.T. Stanbury and T.A. Wilson (eds.) *Canadian Competition Policy: Essays in Law and Economics* (Toronto: Butterworth), pp. 25-54.

Lecraw, Donald J. (1981) "Proposals for Amending the Combines Investigation Act - A Business Economist's Views," *Canadian Business Law Journal*, Vol. 5, pp. 438-69.

MacCrimmon, M.T. and W.T. Stanbury (1977) "Policy Death by Administrative Restriction: The House Committee's Report on Bill C-42, The Competition Act of 1977," *Osgoode Hall Law Journal*, Vol. 15, pp. 485-500.

McDonald, ,Bruce C. (1970) "Canadian Competition Policy: Interim Report of the Economic Council of Canada," *Antitrust Bulletin*, Vol. 15, pp. 521-545.

McQueen, David (1976) "Competition Policy in Stages: Recent Developments in Canada," *Antitrust Bulletin*, Vol. 20(Winter), pp. 751-768.

Moore, Milton (1970) *How Much Price Competition? The Prerequisites of an Effective Canadian Competition Policy* (Montreal: McGill-Queen's University Press).

Reschenthaler, G.B. and W.T. Stanbury (1981) "Recent Conspiracy Decisions in Canada: New Legislation Needed," *Antitrust Bulletin*, Vol. 26 (Winter), pp. 839-69.

Rochwerg, Martin J. (1977) "Proposed Stage II Amendments to Canadian Combines Legislation - Bill C-42," *Osgoode Hall Law Journal*, Vol. 15, pp. 51-69.

Rowley, J.W. and W.T. Stanbury, eds. (1978) *Competition Policy in Canada: Stage II, Bill C-13* (Montreal: The Institute for Research on Public Policy).

Sanderson, Margaret and W.T. Stanbury (1989) *Competition Policy in Canada: The First Hundred Years* (Ottawa: Bureau of Competition Policy, Consumer and Corporate Affairs Canada).

Skeoch, L.A., ed. (1972) *Canadian Competition Policy: Proceedings of a Conference held at Queen's University, 20-21 January, 1972* (Kingston: Queen's University Industrial Relations Centre).

Skeoch, L.A. (1979) "The Dynamic Change Report and the Proposed Competition Act" in J.R.S. Prichard, W.T. Stanbury and T.A. Wilson (eds.) *Canadian Competition Policy: Essays in Law and Economics* (Toronto: Butterworth), pp. 79-94.

Stanbury, W.T. (1977a) *Business Interests and the Reform of Canadian Competition Policy, 1971-1975* (Toronto: Carswell/Methuen).

Stanbury, W.T. (1977b) "Dynamic Change and Accountability in a Canadian Market Economy: Summary and Critique," *Osgoode Hall Law Journal*, Vol. 15, pp. 1-50.

Stanbury, W.T. (1978) "The Background of Bill C-13: The Stage II Amendments in Historical Perspective" in J.W. Rowley and W.T. Stanbury (eds.) *Competition Policy in Canada: Stage II, Bill C-13* (Montreal: The Institute for Research on Public Policy), pp. 133-75.

Stanbury, W.T. (1981) "The BCNI Study on Competition Policy: A Review," *Canadian Competition Policy Record*, Vol. 2 (September), pp. 15-28.

Stanbury, W.T. (1985) "Half a Loaf: Bill C-29, Proposed Amendments to the Combines Investigation Act," *Canadian Business Law Journal*, Vol. 10(1), pp. 1-34.

Stanbury, W.T. (1986) "The New Competition Act and Competition Tribunal Act: Not With a Bang, But a Whimper," *Canadian Business Law Journal*, Vol. 12(1), pp. 2-42.

Stanbury, W.T. (1988) "The Politics of Canadian Competition Policy, 1977-1986" (Vancouver: University of British Columbia, Faculty of Commerce and Business Administration).

Stanbury, W.T. and G.B. Reschenthaler (1981) "Reforming Canadian Competition Policy: One More Unto the Breach," *Canadian Business Law Journal*, Vol. 5, pp. 381-437.

Stigler, George J. (1982) "The Economists and the Problem of Monopoly," *American Economic Review*, Vol. 72(2), May, pp. 1-11.

Chapter 7

THE YOLK OF THE TRUSTS: A COMPARISON OF CANADA'S COMPETITIVE ENVIRONMENT IN 1889 AND 1989

Michael Bliss
Department of History
University of Toronto

1.0 INTRODUCTION

This paper is a comparison of the competitive environment Canada faced in 1989 with that of 1889, the year in which the young Dominion became the first country in the modern world to pass legislation aimed at protecting competition in the national marketplace. The 1889 *Act for the Prevention and Suppression of Combinations formed in restraint of Trade* (S.C. 1889, 52 Vic., c.41) anticipated the American *Sherman Act* by one year, and began the one hundred year tradition of competition law and policy examined in this volume. In this paper I am not so foolish as to attempt elaborate statistically-based comparisons between the highly-developed, immensely complex post-industrial economy we have in Canada today, and the comparatively tiny and undeveloped, still largely agricultural society in which our great-grandfathers lived. What I do is wander around a bit in the fog known as the climate of opinion in the two ages (some of the opinions being my own), pointing out some of the concerns underlying competition policy in both periods. My conclusions will circle around the ambivalence which drove policy in those days, and has haunted competition policy in Canada ever since.

2.0   ORIGINS OF THE 1889 LEGISLATION

It all began[1] with the Toronto mayoralty election in 1887, when a local Conservative Member of Parliament, Mr. N. Clarke Wallace, intervened in the campaign to charge that the "purity and good government" candidate, Mr. Elias Rogers, was actually a leading member of a coal ring that was fixing prices and gouging Torontonians. Wallace got something of a reputation as a foe of combines, and in 1888 was appointed chairman of a House of Commons Select Committee with a mandate to investigate the extent and operations of combinations in the Canadian marketplace.   Wallace's committee conducted lengthy hearings and promptly reported that while "the evils produced by combinations... have not by any means been fully developed as yet in this country, ...sufficient evidence of their injurious tendencies and effects is given to justify legislative action for suppressing the evils arising from these and similar combinations and monopolies" (Canada, 1888, p. 10). Wallace introduced a bill, which in 1889 was passed in greatly revised form, to suppress the evils uncovered (see Gorecki and Stanbury, 1984, pp. 108-112). Before considering this bill and its impact, it is necessary to take a long look at the dimensions of the problem as it seemed to have developed in 1888-1889 and compare that situation with that of 1989.

In 1887 the Montreal *Journal of Commerce* remarked "there are few branches of trade in this or any country which are not represented by associations which seek to prevent unprofitable competition."[2] The House of Commons Select Committee investigated many of these associations - of distributors or producers of groceries, watch-cases, binder-twine, coal, oatmeal, stoves, agricultural implements, and undertakers' supplies. Most of these, including the Coal Section of the Toronto Board of Trade, were attempting to fix prices, divide markets, and/or limit production and entry in their line of business.   As Clarke Wallace put it, Canadians were being burdened by combines "from the cradle to the grave... from Nestle's food in infancy to the coffin in which they were carried to the grave."[3] Noticing that egg buyers in Ontario had combined to set a common purchase price from farmers, the *Journal of Commerce* noted that even eggs had fallen under the "yolk" of the trusts.[4]

---

1. For the origins of Canadians combines policy see Bliss (1973) and (1974). Some of my interpretations have been challenged, unsuccessfully I believe, in Carman D. Baggaley, Chapter 1 in this volume. For the later history, stressing its changing goals, see Gorecki and Stanbury (1984).

2. *Journal of Commerce*, July 15, 1887, pp. 66-7.

3. *Canadian Grocer*, November 7, 1890.

4. *Journal of Commerce*, March 30, 1888, p. 607.

In fact that word "trust" was not properly applicable to the Canadian situation in 1889. (With the exception of banks and the great railway companies, notably the CPR, most firms were still small and unincorporated. Trade associations were voluntarist organizations, with no way of enforcing their agreements other than boycott.) It was in the United States, where lawyers were developing the organizational form of the trust as a way of solidifying and enforcing combination agreements that the term became synonymous with anti-competitive behaviour and with the ensuing antitrust legislation. In Canada we did not yet have trusts; we had combines. We were of course conscious of American developments (it was a country plagued by "Alps upon Alps of combines," a Member of Parliament said in 1889[5]) and we legislated partly on the assumption that Canada had to be alert to stave off industrial trends bound to replicate themselves north of the border. Late 19th century Canada wanted to replicate the United States in all the good facets of industrial growth. Partly in the hope of doing this we had in 1879 and after made it our "National Policy" to erect high tariff walls, very similar to American trade barriers. Most Canadian free-traders, like American ones, saw these government-created barriers to competition as the legislative parent making possible so much anti-competitive activity domestically. The tariff, they never tired of saying, was the mother of the trusts.

Generally, Canadian commentators in the late 1880s were struck by the ways in which collective organization leading to the concentration of power seemed to be a new and salient feature of modern industrial life. Combines and rings and corporations seemed to be sprouting everywhere - not only in business, but among professionals - as organizations of lawyers and doctors were exercising extensive powers of self-government and restricting competition among their members - and even among workingmen themselves, whose trade unions seemed to have much the same price-fixing intent as businessmen's trade associations. "This is emphatically an age of combinations," the *Journal of Commerce* suggested.

> Nothing is more marked among the tendencies of modern times than this increasing effort to merge a comparatively feeble individuality into a powerful combination and thus exert a collective force that will command respect...
>
> No matter in what quarter of the commercial horizon we may look the same tendency is apparent. The wholesome individuality of our fathers is a thing of the past and on every hand we notice the growing habit of centralization, of the desire to collect in masses, and to deliver over one's freedom of action to the guidance of two or three master minds capable of swaying the bulk of their followers. Modern man, whether merchant or artisan, finds a certain relief in surrendering his individuality to the leaders of a 'trust' or 'union', content that if he loses his personal freedom in all save the name, at least he may count upon the increased gain that membership in such an association must secure him.... As, in the long run, a well

---

5. House of Commons, *Debates*, April 22, 1889, p. 1441.

conducted despotism must naturally triumph over individual efforts, we may expect to see these aggregations of capital gradually increase until they reach a culminating point...[6]

3.0   PERSPECTIVE OF 1969

Just 20 years ago Canadian analysts might have argued that little had changed in eighty years, except that collectivism and industrial organization had moved ever closer to the culminating point. From the 1880s through the 1960s there was a very influential, possibly a dominant (certainly dominant in popular discourse) view of economic evolution to the effect that the visible hands of management were steadily replacing the invisible, unorganized forces of the marketplace, and thereby creating a capitalist order increasingly dominated by a small number of very large corporations. In the late 1960s, with the popularity of books like John Kenneth Galbraith's (1967) *New Industrial State* or Jean-Jacques Servan-Schreiber's *La Defi Americaine* it was fashionable to suggest that the competitive future belonged to giant multi-divisional, multi-national firms.[7] A small number of these, some thought, already dominated the global economy. In the future their size would probably grow and their numbers shrink. The immense power of these collectivities could only be checked by other power blocs - large international trade unions on the one hand, the organized power of political collectivities, notably the nation state, on the other. Many would have argued in 1969 that the fundamental rationale for Canadian competition policy[8] had not changed in 80 years: a national competition policy was vital to suppress the evils arising from collectivities trying to dominate the marketplace.

4.0   PERSPECTIVE OF 1989

In 1989 the picture was not so clear. Globally, in the past twenty years we have seen a remarkable demonstration of the capacity of the invisible hands of the marketplace to challenge the collectivist order put in place by big business, big labour, and, above all, big government.

This is not a small topic. If I tried seriously to touch on its broadest and most important manifestation, the collapse of Marxist economics and politics,

---

6.   *Journal of Commerce*, November 25, 1887, p. 100. See also Bliss (1972).

7.   The writings of A.D. Chandler (1977), the dominant business historian in the United States, powerfully influenced the notion that the rise of these firms was the central theme in the evolution of modern business. For a consideration of these trends in the 1960s and changes through the mid-1980s in Canadian business see the latter chapters of Bliss (1987a).

8.   Recall that the process of trying to reform Canadian competition policy began in 1969. See Economic Council of Canada (1969).

I would never get back within Canadian borders. If I limited myself to the resurgence of competition in our domestic economy and tried to address the issues swirling around concentration and its measurement in Canada,[9] it would be easy to become lost in a thicket of statistics. So I will try to hold to an impressionistic middle ground, offering a few more or less connected observations on what might be called the crisis of the visible hand in our time. It is also the crisis of the large organization, and it can be summed up in the single image of the big organization as dinosaur.

Empirically, we have seen example after example in the past twenty years of those huge corporations whose planning mechanisms Galbraith (1967) had told us were next to infallible, in fact stumble and fail. The list is too long to enumerate - perhaps one Canadian corporation, Massey Ferguson, can stand as a symbol, or the enterprises of one Canadian plutocrat, the symbol of corporate concentration in the 1950s, who died virtually forgotten in 1989 - E.P. Taylor (see Cook, 1981). Or we could re-read Peter C. Newman's 1970s books about the wonderfully powerful Canadian establishment,[10] and ask ourselves, where are they now.[11]

5.0   1889 REVISITED

Or we might consider recent news about two Canadian corporations that were actually around in 1889. In that year the Canadian Pacific Railroad Company was by far the largest and most powerful corporation in Canada, arguably as powerful in the country as the government of Canada itself - and was viewed by many farmers as a gouging, grinding monopoly. (Sir John A. Macdonald suggested to the president of the CPR during one of its struggles, that it simply buy control of the legislature of Manitoba.) We know that for most of its history, the CPR continued to grow and expand, becoming a great transportation conglomerate and diversifying into heavy manufacturing and a host of other enterprises (Goldenberg, 1983). We also know that in 1989, the Canadian Pacific empire, already shrinking as a result of the sale of some of its less profitable subsidiaries,[12] has been thought a prime takeover candidate - not because of its muscle, size and power - but because of the prospect that it can be profitably dismantled. What was once a great Imperial institution seems destined for the same fate as the British Empire itself.

---

9.   See Khemani (1988) and Khemani (1986).

10.   See Newman (1975), (1978), (1981), (1982).

11.   Ed. Note: They have been supplanted to some extent by new aggregations of corporate wealth. See, for example, Goldenberg (1984), Foster (1986) and Shortell and Best (1988).

12.   For example, in December 1986 CP Air was sold to PWA Corp. for $300 million.

In 1889 there was one Canadian pork-packing plant exporting sides of bacon to Great Britain, the William Davies Company of Toronto. It soon grew into the largest pork-packing firm in the British Empire, came to dominate the Canadian market, and was the principal target in the agitation against the "food trust" that was primarily responsible for the first major revision of our combines law, the advent of the *Combines Investigation Act* in 1910. Then, when transformed into the Canada Packers "combine" in the 1920s and afterwards, the meat-packing firm became the target for periodic outbursts of populist anti-combines sentiment. In the fall of 1989 Canada Packers was put up for sale;[13] it is a barely profitable company in a brutally competitive industry, which under new owners was apt to be dismembered and its parts sold off. In other words Canada Packers, like Canadian Pacific, and other failed conglomerates, relics of an earlier age, seemed headed for the ruthless abattoir of the modern marketplace.

6.0 GROWING COMPETITIVE PRESSURES

Twenty years ago entrepreneurship was almost a forgotten word in the lexicon of management. Small business was seen as a kind of slum, a shrinking fringe on the "real" world of the large corporation. In the 1980s we have seen a renaissance of small business, a resurgence of entrepreneurship and the entrepreneurial spirit almost completely unforseen a generation earlier. The thrashing around of the corporate dinosaurs has been paralleled by a population explosion of scurrying little furry corporate creatures, who may well inherit the earth. On the day in October 1989, for example, that the effective death of Wardair as a distinct airline was formally announced,[14] causing shivers among the friends of competition in Canada's skies, a small regional airline, Inter-Canadien, announced its intention of becoming a national carrier.[15] Earlier the demise of Wardair as an independent airline had immediately induced the appearance of new firms in the charter

---

13. In April 1989 Canada Packers was acquired by Hillsdown Holdings PLC which will merge its Maple Leaf Mills Ltd. with Canada Packers. Hillsdown will end up with 56% of the new entity. See *Financial Post*, April 23, 1990, p. 1; *Globe and Mail*, April 21, 1990, pp. B1, B6; Toronto *Star*, April 21, 1990, p. C1. Hillsdown said it would likely sell off Canada Packers beef slaughtering assets (*Financial Post*, April 24, 1990, p. 7).

14. The takeover of Wardair by PWA Corp., owner of Canadian Airlines International, was announced in January 1989. Although the takeover resulted in a duopoly in the airline industry, it was not challenged by the Bureau of Competition Policy as Wardair was deemed to be a failing firm.

15. For more details on Intair (formerly Inter-Canadian), see *Financial Post*, March 1, 1990, p. 30. Intair was aiming at 15% of the eastern Canadian market.

business.[16] The tremendous vigour of the small business sector was a sign of the fundamental health of competitive forces in the Canadian economy in 1989. Individualism is alive and well here, as it is everywhere in a world where collectivist ideas and practices are in stunning retreat.

The dinosaurs have no place to hide. In our time changes in capital markets have wiped out most of the protection that size gave to firms. Today even the most widely-held public company is a potential takeover target.[17] In industries where economies of scale or the benefits of monopoly still appear to protect firms, they are nonetheless vulnerable to challenges from competitors that first grew large and efficient in the Japanese or Korean or some other new market, and are now large enough to do battle in North America. It is a cliché of our time to say that the marketplace has become global, that international competition in most industries is more intense than at any time in history, and that it shows few signs of diminishing. It appears that competition, from abroad and from within, even affects law firms today - and when lawyers have to compete the old order has indeed crumbled.

At the risk of treading into economists' territory, it might be worth considering that the problem of big business in our time is a function of the challenges caused by the increasing depth and efficiency of markets in a widening range of industries. A firm whose in-house transaction costs exceeded open-market transaction costs is in dinosaur country. Is the tendency of most industries in that direction? See Bliss (1987a, pp. 569-70).

7.0   GOVERNMENT RESTRAINTS ON COMPETITION

If modern corporate management is about down-sizing, dis-integration, fostering intrapreneurship and other ways of rejuvenating the competitive spirit, similarly modern governments have begun to move, ponderously to be sure, to try to correct their own obsolescence. Deregulation and privatization in North America and Europe,[18] *perestroika* in the Eastern bloc, are sides of the same coin, as governments reverse the tendency of the last century of Western history and reduce their interference with freely-operating markets. We have our Canadian examples of these movements, of course. Above all, we have trade liberalization - both as a result of the half-century of the GATT, and, since the beginning of 1989 in the free-trade agreement with our

---

16. However, one of the largest entrants, Odyssey International, ceased service when its parent Soundair Corp. went into receivership in April 1990. It was the fourth charter carrier to cease operations in 1990. See *Globe and Mail*, April 28, 1990, pp. B1, B18. Some 3000 travellers were stranded (*Globe and Mail*, April 28, 1990, pp. A1-A2).

17. The case of KKR's acquisition of RJR Nabisco for almost U.S. $26 billion in 1989 makes this point.

18. See, for example, Walker (1988).

dominant trading partner, the United States. In 1989 it was no longer Canada's National Policy to use tariffs to keep foreigners from competing in our markets. This is a striking, radical change from the protectionism of 1889. We can now look forward to the time when in most industries it will no longer be said that the tariff is mother to the trusts.

This is not to say that our governments have not found other ways to give birth to or nurture anti-competitive practices. Those naive trade associationists of 1889, with their simple little price-fixing conspiracies,[19] would marvel, at the ingenuity with which certain producers and distributors have been able to use a friendly and often ignorant political system for their ends. In 1889, for example, the egg combine got nowhere. At that time the device of the marketing board had not yet been invented. Now in 1989 in Canada eggs were firmly under the yolk of one of the strongest, most unassailable of all the "trusts," a gouging monopoly created and enforced by the state.[20] If there is still a rationale for competition policy in Canada in an age when competitive forces are in the ascendancy practically everywhere else in our economy, it is surely in areas like this where government itself is the main villain. These areas are substantial, extending to "strategic" or "key" industries where foreign competition is restricted and to many regulated industries, such as broadcasting and telecommunications. Perhaps supply management schemes are the most pernicious of the new state-created conspiracies against the marketplace. It might be said that in the 1990s the Bureau of Competition Policy will not be fully engaged in the struggle against the evils of monopoly until it is prepared to get egg on its face.[21]

But of course the Bureau has no mandate to attack the marketing boards because Parliament believes that they exercise restraints on cutthroat competition which are in fact in the public interest. To use a phrase from the 1880s, these are surely "righteous combinations," and it is our policy to leave them alone (unless, as some fear and others hope, the free trade agreement and/or GATT does them in).[22] Our official attitudes towards marketing boards are one example of the ambivalence we feel towards competitive forces in the Canadian environment as we face the 1990s.

---

19. The record of price-fixing prosecutions over the past century is traced by Stanbury (1991b).

20. Generally see Economic Council of Canada (1981). On the ability of farmers to extract various kinds of help from government see "Embarassing cost of protecting jobs on Canadian farms," *Globe and Mail*, April 2, 1990, p. B2 reporting on an OECD (1990) study. See also Jeffrey Simpson, "Cowed politicians, contented farmers," *Globe and Mail*, April 5, 1990, p. A6.

21. Janigan (1990) describes the power and cost of the chicken marketing scheme.

22. In April 1990 Canada actually proposed to GATT that it be easier for countries to impose import quotas in support of supply management marketing boards. See "Canada teased for its farm trade proposal," *Globe and Mail*, April 14, 1990, p. B1.

In some ways it is the same ambivalence that characterized policy-making a century ago. At that time there were fierce arguments about the restraints of trade apparently exercised by combines. Were all of their activities necessarily evil? Could there be reasonable combines exercising reasonable or due restraints of trade? Surely trade unions, for example, in their struggle to get a "living wage" for their members, were not fit subjects for prosecution under anti-combines laws. They certainly did not think so. Nor did Parliament, which explicitly exempted them from the 1889 legislation and has not seriously considered applying anti-combines laws to unions ever since.

But if it was legitimate to combine to get a living wage, people asked in those days, what was wrong with working together in the hope of making a "living profit"? In 1889 there was a strong body of opinion, in business and in government, that it was perfectly reasonable for trade associations to fix prices, or work out schemes of retail price maintenance in collusion with manufacturers,[23] in the hope of getting for their members that "living profit," or to stop the "cutthroat competition," "demoralization," "waste," "vulgarization of business" (a phrase used by Canada's leading economist of the time) and other disorderly and unprofitable accompaniments of free markets.[24] And that was just the tip of the iceberg, for there was a vast range of restrictionist practices - from supply management and controlling entry through early closing and anti-Christmas present agreements - about the goods or evils of which reasonable people could disagree. Finally, of course, there was that overwhelming question of the National Policy itself, the protective tariff. In the eyes of the Conservative government of Canada in 1889, the tariff was a perfectly reasonable, indeed a marvelously beneficial interference with the marketplace, that had nothing at all to do with combines or trusts or the limitation of righteously Canadian competition.

As Canadians began to think about competition and combination in the late 1880s, they quickly backed away from a doctrinaire commitment to intervening to force businesses to compete in all things. Led by the person who started it all, N. Clarke Wallace, MP, Parliament watered-down various drafts of its anti-combines legislation until the final product, "An Act to Declare the Common Law" had clauses so qualified by the words "unlawfully," "unduly" and "unreasonably," that it was almost universally considered a farce, meaningless political posturing, possibly useful to the government as a sop to free trade ideas that might otherwise focus on the National Policy. In a way, we honored in 1989 the centenary of a non-event, at best the centenary of a symbol, certainly not the commencement of serious anti-combines legislation in North America. For that we should join the Americans in the celebration of the 100th birthday of their *Sherman Act* in 1990. That legislation did

---

23. See Gorecki and Stanbury (1991).

24. For discussion of that opinion see Bliss (1974).

contain unqualified language that struck at the heart of anti-competitive activities.[25]

In 1889, then, Canadian competition law was born in ambivalence (and no little ridicule from the Opposition) about the collectivist activities that seemed to be increasingly characterizing the Canadian marketplace. Ambivalence has continued to steer or confuse our considerations of our competition law since. It was not long after 1889, for example, that new kinds of combinations, in the form of corporate mergers or giant business organizations like department stores, began to dominate certain markets to the detriment of competition. But if bigness led to efficiency, surely a certain amount of market domination was not unreasonable, a consideration still at the heart of today's legislation.[26] And then we saw the development of doctrines of "natural" monopoly, state regulation, and a host of other rationales for accepting anti-competitive behaviour in both the public and private sector (see Baggaley, 1981).

In 1989 the pendulum of economic thought and public policy seems to have swung considerably in the other direction. Not just Canada but the whole world believes in the efficiency of free markets and the desirability of extending market-like competitive practices into more and more of the areas traditionally closed off. We believe it is good that stock brokers and real estate agents and lawyers are not allowed to engage in their traditional collusive practices (see Goldman, 1991). In the 1990s we will surely see major new inroads made by competitive practices - perhaps into telephone service,[27] perhaps in broadcasting, possibly even in the removal of eggs from the yoke of marketing boards. We will still have serious concerns about concentrated economic power. Perhaps we will shift our focus from abuses of market power to problems of concentrated ownership.[28] Perhaps we will continue to worry about the nationality of those who provide our goods and services, and will insist on using the power of the state to maintain Canadian presences in certain markets. Still, it is surely fair to predict that in the business environment that we have seen evolve in our time and will face in the future, competition will be healthier and more widespread than ever before.

---

25. Indeed, the substantive parts of Sections 1 and 2 of the *Sherman Act* have remained unchanged for a century. This is in contrast to the situation in Canada. With respect to the evolution of the law in respect of price fixing and similar agreements, see Stanbury (1991b).

26. See the discussion in Stanbury (1986).

27. For example, Unitel Communications Inc. applied for the second time to the CRTC in May 1990 to offer competition in the public voice long distance market which is now a monopoly. The case for competition in this market is made by Stanbury (1991a).

28. Aside from the papers in this volume, the best introduction to shifting concepts of concentration in the 1980s, is to be found in Khemani, Shapiro and Stanbury eds. (1988).

There is an argument, though, that competition has always been healthier and more widespread than observers have tended to assume. The combinations that Parliament worried about and legislated against back in 1888-1889 were not much of a threat to anyone. Most collapsed under competitive pressure within months of their formation. Throughout the next century most combinations in the private sector, including mergers aimed at market domination, failed to maintain their position in the face of the competition that their realization of monopoly profits inevitably induced. Usually the market took care of itself, without the help of Canada's enfeebled, ambivalent trustbusters.[29] Thus the points made earlier in this paper about the health of the marketplace in Canada. Thus our ability to ask ourselves whatever happened to Canadian Breweries and Argus Corp. and Power Corp. and Massey-Ferguson and the CPR and Canada Packers, even General Motors and IBM, and those other symbols of efficiency and/or oligopoly. Because of the marketplace, not because of the visible hands of the state, they do not oppress us with their power.

Finally, it may even become thinkable that in our considerations of competition law and policy we may in the 1990s debate the need for any state surveillance of industries in sectors where markets and informed consumers have the capacity to be such fine natural watchdogs and regulators. Perhaps in the second century of Canadian competition policy, our trustbusting institutions will gradually wither away. Or they may assume their most logical functions, as watchdogs against the proclivities of government and politicians to limit competition, equality of opportunity, efficiency, and economic growth.

---

29. This is a central theme of and has been elaborated upon in Bliss (1987b).

REFERENCES

Baggaley, Carman (1981) *The Emergence of the Regulatory State in Canada, 1890-1939* (Ottawa: Economic Council of Canada, Regulation Reference Technical Report No. 15, August).

Bliss, Michael (1972) "The Protective Impulse: An Approach to the Social History of Oliver Mowat's Ontario," in D. Swainson, ed., *Oliver Mowat's Ontario* (Toronto: MacMillan), pp. 174-88.

Bliss, Michael (1973) "Another Anti-Trust Tradition: Canadian Anti-Combines Policy, 1889-1910," *Business History Review*, Vol. XLVII(2), pp. 177-88.

Bliss, Michael (1974) *A Living Profit: Studies in the Social History of Canadian Business, 1883-1911* (Toronto: McClelland & Stewart).

Bliss, Michael (1987a) *Northern Enterprise: Five Centuries of Canadian Business* (Toronto: McClelland and Stewart).

Bliss, Michael (1987b) "Enterprise in a Cold Climate: Reflections on the History of Canadian Business" (Ottawa: University of Ottawa, J.J. Carson Lecture).

Canada (1888) *Report of the Select Committee to Investigate and Report Upon Alleged Combinations in Manufactures, Trade and Insurance in Canada*, House of Commons, *Journals*, 1888, Appendix 3.

Chandler, A.D. (1977) *The Visible Hand: The Managerial Revolution in American Business* (Cambridge, Mass.: Harvard University Press).

Cook, Peter (1981) *Massey at the Brink* (Toronto: Collins Publishers).

Economic Council of Canada (1969) *Interim Report on Competition Policy* (Ottawa: Queen's Printer).

Economic Council of Canada (1981) *Reforming Regulation* (Ottawa: Minister of Supply and Services), Ch. 6.

Foster, Peter (1986) *The Master Builders* (Toronto: Key Porter Books).

Francis, Diane (1986) *Controlling Interest: Who Owns Canada?* (Toronto: Macmillan).

Galbraith, J.K. (1967) *The New Industrial State* (Boston: Houghton-Mifflin).

Goldenberg, Susan (1983) *Canadian Pacific: A Portrait of Power* (Toronto: Methuen).

Goldenberg, Susan (1984) *The Thomson Empire* (Toronto: Seal Books).

Goldman, Calvin S. (1991) "The Impact of the Competition Act of 1986" in R.S. Khemani and W.T. Stanbury (eds.) *Canadian Competition Law and Policy at the Centenary* (Halifax: The Institute for Research on Public Policy).

Gorecki, Paul K. and W.T. Stanbury (1984) *The Objectives of Canadian Competition Policy, 1888-1983* (Montreal: The Institute for Research on Public Policy).

Janigan, Mary (1990) "Why Chickens Don't Come Cheap," *Report on Business Magazine*, October, pp. 87-98.

Khemani, R.S. (1986) "The Extent and Evolution of Competition in the Canadian Economy" in D.G. McFetridge (ed.) *Canadian Industry in Transition* (Toronto: University of Toronto), pp. 135-176.

Khemani, R.S. (1988) "The Dimensions of Corporate Concentration in Canada" in R.S. Khemani, D.M. Shapiro and W.T. Stanbury (eds.) *Mergers, Corporate Concentration and Power in Canada* (Halifax: Institute for Research on Public Policy), pp. 17-38.

Khemani, R.S., D.M. Shapiro and W.T. Stanbury eds. (1988) *Mergers, Corporate Concentration and Power in Canada* (Halifax: Institute for Research on Public Policy).

Khemani, R.S. and W.T. Stanbury, eds. (1991) *Canadian Competition Law and Policy at the Centenary* (Halifax: Institute for Research on Public Policy).

Newman, Peter C. (1975) *The Canadian Establishment* (Toronto: McClelland and Stewart).

Newman, Peter C. (1978) *The Bronfman Dynasty: The Rothschilds of the New World* (Toronto: McClelland and Stewart).

Newman, Peter C. (1981) *The Canadian Establishment, Vol. II, The Acquisitors* (Toronto: McClelland and Stewart).

Newman, Peter C. (1982) *The Establishment Man: A Portrait of Power* (Toronto: McClelland and Stewart).

OECD (1990) *Economy-Wide Effects of Agricultural Policies in OECD Countries* (Paris: OECD, Economic Studies No. 13).

Servan-Shreiber, Jean Jacques (1969) *The American Challenge [La Defi Americaine* translated from the French by Ronald Steel] (New York: Avon).

Shortell, Ann and Patricia Best (1988) *The Brass Ring* (Toronto: Random House).

Stanbury, W.T. (1986) "The New Competition Act and Competition Tribunal Act: Not With a Bang But a Whimper," *Canadian Business Law Journal*, Vol. 12(1), pp. 2-42.

Stanbury, W.T. (1991a) "The Case for Competition in Public Long Distance Telephone Service in Canada" in Jan Fedorowicz (ed.) *From Monopoly to Competition: Telecommunications In Transition* (Mississauga: Informatics Publishing), pp. 147-198.

Stanbury, W.T. (1991b) "Legislation to Control Agreements in Restraint of Trade in Canada: Review of the Historical Record and Proposals for Reform" in R.S. Khemani and W.T. Stanbury (eds.) *Canadian Competition Law and Policy at the Centenary* (Halifax: Institute for Research on Public Policy).

Walker, Michael A., ed. (1988) *Privatization: Tactics and Techniques* (Vancouver: The Fraser Institute).

Chapter 8

COMPETITION LAW AND THE CONSTITUTION: 1889-1989 AND INTO THE TWENTY-FIRST CENTURY*

Douglas Rutherford, Q.C.
Associate Deputy Minister
Department of Justice, Canada
and
J.S. Tyhurst
Counsel
Department of Justice, Canada

1.0 INTRODUCTION

In April, 1989 the Supreme Court of Canada gave judgment in the *City National Leasing*[1] and *Rocois Construction*[2] cases. For the first time in the 100 years that Canada has had competition legislation, the highest court has confirmed that such legislation as a whole is a valid exercise of a head of legislative authority other than the criminal law, namely, the trade and commerce power. The court also sustained the legislative private civil damage action as being connected to a valid scheme of regulating competition in the *Combines Investigation Act* (now the *Competition Act*).[3]

The decisions pave the way for more effective public and private enforcement of the legislation. For several decades proposals for competition

---

*. The views and opinions expressed in this paper are those of the authors and do not necessarily reflect those of the Department of Justice or of the Government of Canada.

1. *General Motors of Canada Limited v. City National Leasing et al.*, (1989), 58 D.L.R. (4th) 255 (S.C.C.).

2. *Quebec Ready Mix Inc. et al. v. Rocois Construction Inc.*, (1989), 60 D.L.R. (4th) 124 (S.C.C.).

3. R.S. 1985 c.C-34; as amended by c.19 (2nd Supp.).

law reform, and, since 1976, legislation employing civil remedies have been clouded with doubt as to their constitutional validity. The move to civil remedies was motivated in large part by a growing concern that the criminal law was no longer appropriate for the type of detailed economic analysis and flexible remedial action that modern competition policy requires. At last, it appears that competition law has a constitutional foundation that is broad and flexible enough to carry it into the 21st century.

This paper will examine the Supreme Court's recent decisions from a historical perspective. Over the past century three potential constitutional heads of power have been advanced for competition legislation as a whole: criminal law, the residual power or "peace order and good government" (POGG) and trade and commerce. The focus of this paper will be on the criminal and trade and commerce heads, which have played the most prominent role in the constitutional history of competition legislation. The criminal law power has been the central basis for such legislation since its inception 100 years ago. The trade and commerce power, on the other hand, has until recently been given little prominence or scope by the courts. The review of the case law that follows suggests that breathing life into the trade and commerce power in *City National Leasing* and *Rocois Construction* is another step by the Supreme Court of Canada in the process of rationalizing the constitutional balance between federal and provincial authority in the light of current economic circumstances.

2.0 EARLY CONSTITUTIONAL HISTORY: THE CRIMINAL LAW BASIS

The first competition legislation of 1889 consisted of one substantive section directed at "every person who conspires, combines, agrees or arranges with any other person ... unlawfully" to do certain anti-competitive acts.[4] This conduct was made a misdemeanour.[5] In the general codification of the criminal law in 1892, the Act of 1889 became a section of the *Criminal Code* and the offense was made an indictable one.[6] The reliance on the criminal law was in keeping with the feeling that what was at issue was morally

---

4. S.C. 1889, c.41, s.1.

5. *Competition Act*, R.S. 1985, c.C-34, as amended, s.45 is the current revision of that section. Its evolution is described in W.T. Stanbury, "Legislation to Control Agreements in Restraint of Trade in Canada: Review of the Historical Record and Proposals for Reform"in R.S. Khemani and W.T. Stanbury (eds.) *Canadian Competition Law and Policy at the Centenary* (Halifax: The Institute for Research on Public Policy, 1991).

6. S.C. 1892, c.29, s.520. For a description of the early legislative changes, see *Report to the Minister of Justice, Committee to Study Combines Legislation* (MacQuarrie Report) (Ottawa: King's Printer, 1952), pp.9-11.

reprehensible and abusive behaviour.[7] Over time, reliance on the criminal law became a practical necessity as attempts to go beyond the traditional confines of the criminal law were struck down on constitutional grounds by the Judicial Committee of the Privy Council in England.

The first such attempt was the establishment of the Board of Commerce in 1919 in response to the rapid rise in the cost of living in the aftermath of the First World War. The Board was given the administration of the *Combines and Fair Prices Act* under which it had two main functions. The first was to investigate and restrain combinations, monopolies, trusts and mergers constituting a "combine." The second was to inquire into and enforce prohibitions against hoarding and profiteering. The profiteering provisions led to a constitutional challenge. The Board made an order prohibiting certain clothing manufacturers in Ottawa from charging higher than specified profit margins. The constitutionality of the legislation as a whole was tested in the Supreme Court of Canada by way of reference case.

The Supreme Court split evenly on the constitutionality of the legislation,[8] but on appeal it was unanimously struck down as *ultra vires* by the Privy Council.[9] Viscount Haldane rejected peace order and good government, trade and commerce and criminal law as basis for the legislation. In relation to criminal law, he suggested that to qualify under this head of power, the subject matter would have to fall within a fixed "domain of criminal jurisprudence".[10]

Despite Viscount Haldane's limiting statements, in 1931 the Privy Council in *Proprietary Articles Trade Association v. A.G. Canada*[11] finally confirmed a criminal law constitutional foundation for both the administrative structure and substantive aspects of competition law. In 1923 Parliament had enacted the *Combines Investigation Act*,[12] which repealed the Board of Commerce legislation and established a new scheme of competition laws. The legislation provided the origin of the structure of the law currently in place. A "registrar" was established to inquire into and report on "combines", defined as "mergers,

---

7.   M. Cohen "The Canadian Anti-Trust Laws - Doctrinal and Legislative beginnings" (1938), 26 C.B.R. 439 at pp.449-454. B.C. McDonald "Criminality and the Canadian Anti-Combines Laws" (1965), 4 *Alberta Law Review* 67; *Report of the Select Committee appointed February 29, 1888, to Investigate and Report upon alleged Combinations in Manufacturing, Trade and Insurance in Canada* 51-52 Vict. Sess. Papers (2d. Sess.) May 16, 1988. See also W.T. Stanbury and Paul K. Gorecki, *Objectives of Canadian Competition Policy 1888-1983* (Montreal: The Institute for Research on Public Policy, 1984), at pp.14-17; 177.

8.   *Re Board of Commerce Act* (1920), 60 S.C.R. 456.

9.   *Re Board of Commerce Act* [1922] 1 A.C. 191 (P.C.).

10.   *Ibid.*, p.199. The "domain of criminal jurisprudence" contemplated that no new crimes could be created beyond those existing in 1867.

11.   [1931] A.C. 310 (P.C.).

12.   S.C. 1923, c.9.

trusts or monopolies so-called ... which have operated or are likely to operate to the detriment or against the interests of the public..." It was made a criminal offense to be "a party or privy to or knowingly assist in the formation or operation of a combine."

This legislation was challenged along with section 498 of the *Criminal Code*, the successor to the original 1889 prohibition. The Supreme Court of Canada upheld both the prohibitions and scheme of inquiry and report as being valid exercises of the criminal law power.[13] This decision was sustained by the Privy Council.[14] In doing so, Atkin L.J. repudiated Viscount Haldane's restrictive "domain of criminal jurisprudence" test. He held:

> The substance of the Act is by s.2 to define, and by s.32 to make criminal, combines which the legislature in the public interest intends to prohibit. The definition is wide, and may cover activities which have not hitherto been considered to be criminal ... [I]f Parliament genuinely determines that commercial activities which can be so described are to be suppressed in the public interest, their Lordships see no reason why Parliament should not make them crimes. "Criminal law" means "the criminal law in its widest sense": *Attorney-General for Ontario v. Hamilton Street Ry. Co.* It certainly is not confined to what was criminal by the law of England or of any Province in 1867. The power must extend to legislation to make new crimes...[15]

This statement became a fundamental expression of the scope of the federal criminal law power, and confirmed its potential application to business and commercial activities.[16] The *P.A.T.A.* decision also sustained, under the taxation (91(3)) and patent (91(22)) powers, respectively, remedies in the *Combines Investigation Act* for reducing customs tariffs and revoking patents in response to anti-competitive conditions. These heads of power could support only these isolated provisions, however, and the basic framework of the Act depended for its validity on the criminal law power.

From the *P.A.T.A.* case until the passage of the 1976 "Stage I" amendments to the *Combines Investigation Act*, the reliance on this basic criminal law structure continued. Several decisions over this period confirmed that criminal law was a "safe harbour" for competition legislation from a constitutional standpoint. Two of these decisions arose from legislation enacted in 1935. The first concerned the *Dominion Trade and Industry Commission Act*.[17] The Commission was given the administration of the combines laws as well as additional powers including the ability to grant exemptions to certain types of agreements found to be in the public interest.

---

13. [1929] 2 D.L.R. 802 (S.C.C.).

14. [1931] A.C. 310 (P.C.).

15. *Ibid.*, pp.323-324.

16. Peter Hogg, *Constitutional Law of Canada*, 2d.ed. (Agincourt, Ont.: Carsell, 1985), p. 407.

17. S.C. 1935, c.59.

On a reference on the constitutionality of this scheme, the Supreme Court of Canada upheld the general investigative powers of the Commission on criminal law grounds, but struck down the power to approve agreements.[18] The latter issue was not appealed to the Privy Council, although the Supreme Court's support for the investigative powers of the Commission was sustained.[19]

The other case involved an amendment to the *Criminal Code* to prohibit price discrimination and predatory pricing.[20] The Supreme Court upheld this provision under the criminal law power.[21] This decision was sustained by the Privy Council.[22] Lord Atkin, who had written the *P.A.T.A.* decision, continued to take a broad view of the criminal law power. He held that:

> The only limitation on the plenary power of the Dominion to determine what shall or shall not be criminal is the condition that Parliament shall not in the guise of enacting criminal legislation in truth and in substance encroach on any of the classes of subjects enumerated in s.92. It is no objection that it does in fact affect them.[23]

After the abolition of appeals to the Privy Council, the Supreme Court of Canada continued to support competition provisions on criminal law grounds. In the 1956 decision of *Goodyear Tire & Rubber Co. v. The Queen*[24] the Court upheld a section providing for the making of prohibition orders which had been added to the legislation in 1952. Such an order could "prohibit the continuation or repetition" of an offence under the Act as well as "the doing of any act or thing ... directed toward the continuation or repetition of the offence."[25] The Court reasoned per Locke J.:

> The power to legislate in relation to criminal law is not restricted, in my opinion, to defining offences and providing penalties for their commission. The power of Parliament extends to legislation designed for the prevention of crime as well as to punishing crime. It was, apparently, considered that to prohibit the continuation or repetition of the offence by order ... would tend to restrain its repetition.[26]

---

18. *Ref Re Dominion Trade and Industrial Commission Act* [1936] 3 D.L.R. 607, [1936] S.C.R. 379.

19. *A.G. Ont. v. A.G. Can.* [1937] 1 D.L.R. 703, [1937] A.C. 405 (P.C.).

20. S.C. 1935, c.56, s.9.

21. *Re Section 498A of the Criminal Code* [1936] 3 D.L.R. 593 (S.C.C.).

22. *A.G. B.C. v. A.G. Can.* [1937] 1 D.L.R. 688, [1937] A.C. 368 (P.C.).

23. *Ibid.*, p.375 (A.C.).

24. [1956] 2 D.L.R. (2d) 11 (S.C.C.).

25. S.31(1), *Combines Investigation Act*, R.S.C. 1927, c.26, as amended by 1952, c.39, s.3.

26. [1956] 1 D.L.R. (2d) 11 (S.C.C.) at p.19.

In 1966, in *R. v. Campbell*[27] the Supreme Court sustained a decision of the Ontario Court of Appeal[28] upholding the constitutionality of the resale price maintenance prohibition in the *Combines Investigation Act* which had been added in 1960. In two more recent decisions, *Canadian National Transportation*[29] and *Shaklee Canada*,[30] the Supreme Court upheld as valid criminal law, the *Combines Investigation Act* conspiracy prohibition and pyramid selling provision, respectively.

Although the criminal law had provided a safe constitutional haven for nearly three quarters of a century, concerns began to be expressed in the 1960's that competition legislation founded on such a basis might not be effective. Bruce McDonald wrote in 1965:

> The demands of 1889 are not the demands of the 1960's, and the combines cases illustrate the contortions through which the courts have been going in their attempts to accommodate the change absent any fundamental overhaul of the statute. The object of the statute has changed, and increasingly the control of combines is recognized as a sophisticated problem requiring analysis of economic data. The Canadian courts, aware of their deficiencies in the training needed for such evaluations, resist as much as possible any debate over or inquiry into economic data or theory.
>
> The considerations of 1889 which impelled the legislators to make the combines law criminal no longer obtain. The undesirability of combines no longer stems appreciably from rejection on moral grounds; nor can the Act be specific in such a way as to bring combines offences within the other general category of moral element... This is not to suggest that combines ought to be in one of the two categories; but only that, if it is not, the use of the criminal law as the appropriate control device must be seriously questioned.[31]

This theme was echoed by the Economic Council in its 1969 *Interim Report on Competition Policy*. The Council had been asked in 1966 "In light of the government's longterm economic objectives, to study and advise regarding ... combines, mergers, monopolies and restraint of trade...". It concluded that the primary goal of competition policy should be the promotion of economic efficiency. That, to the Council, also meant moving from the strictures of the criminal law to a more flexible civil law basis:

---

27. *R. v. Campbell* (1966), 58 D.L.R. (2d) 673n (S.C.C.).

28. (1964), 46 D.L.R. (2d) 83 (Ont.C.A.).

29. *A.-G. Canada v. Canadian National Transportation Limited et al.* [1983] 2 S.C.R. 206.

30. *Queen v. Shaklee Canada Inc.* [1985] 1 F.C. 593 (C.A.), appeal dismissed April 28, 1988 (S.C.C.).

31. B.C. McDonald, "Criminality and the Canadian Anti-combines Laws" (1965), 4 *Alberta Law Review* 67 at pp. 92-93.

> The basic reasons for seeking to place some of the federal government's competition policy on a civil law basis would be to improve its relevance to economic goals, its effectiveness, and its acceptability to the general public. The greater flexibility afforded by civil law is especially to be desired in those areas of the policy that do not lend themselves well to relatively unqualified prohibitions and that may in addition call for some case-by-case consideration of the likely economic effects of particular business structures or practices.[32]

Three main concerns about the use of the criminal law in the competition area are reflected in the above quotations and other similar commentary. The first is that the criminal law is not morally well adapted to the type of conduct involved. It was argued that it is difficult to brand as a criminal, a businessman who is engaging in activities such as a corporate merger which the law itself may label publicly harmful or beneficial depending on the effects or circumstances. The requirement of "*mens rea*" or "guilty mind" does not fit comfortably in this context.

The second concern related to the procedural nature of criminal law. A broad inquiry into economic effects, including the nature of foreign competition, markets, cross-elasticities, barriers to entry and efficiencies is often required in a competition law case. Many of these factors must be weighed or balanced. Particularly in merger law, a projection as to future effects may be required. Such an inquiry may not be well suited to a criminal "beyond a reasonable doubt" burden of proof or strict rules of evidence which may exclude important information. Criminal remedies, which tend to be backward-looking and punitive, are also not as flexible or creative as those that may be needed, for example, to restructure a monopolistic industry and monitor the results. Civil law makes possible the use of a specialized tribunal for adjudication with the expertise and experience to tailor its remedies to the circumstances, with more flexible evidentiary rules to receive the necessary information and with the knowledge to conduct the difficult balancing sometimes needed in these cases.

The third concern was that the criminal courts would not, or could not, enforce competition sanctions based solely on the criminal law. By the 1970's there had never been a criminal conviction in a contested case under the combines laws' merger provisions and only one under the monopoly prohibition.[33] In that decade the Supreme Court confirmed acquittals in the

---

32.   E.C.C., *Interim Report on Competition Policy* (Ottawa: Queen's Printer, 1969), p.109. See also L.A. Skeoch with B.C. McDonald, *Dynamic Change and Accountability in a Canadian Market Economy* (Ottawa: Minister of Supply and Services Canada, 1976) at pp.39-41.

33.   The contested conviction was in *Eddy Match Co. Ltd. et al. v. The Queen* (1953), 109 C.C.C. 1 (Que.Q.B.A.D.). In *R. v. Electric Reduction of Canada* (1970), 61 C.P.R. 235 the accused pleaded guilty to both monopoly and merger.

Aetna Insurance, K.C. Irving and *Atlantic Sugar*[34] cases and in the process further narrowed the existing criminal conspiracy and merger laws or placed them in doubt. This led to much commentary, including the statement that such decisions "may threaten to make Canadian competition policy ineffective or even inoperative".[35]

An overburdening concern was that the criminal law power would not constitutionally support needed amendments in the form of more flexible enforcement powers or remedial measures, such as a civil damage remedy. The Supreme Court reinforced this concern in the *MacDonald v. Vapour Canada* in 1976 when it ruled that an independent civil remedy for acts "contrary to honest industrial or commercial usage" in the *Trade Marks Act* was not supportable on the criminal law power.[36] (This view was applied to the competition law private civil damage remedy in more recent lower court decisions.)[37]

On the basis of these concerns, the view took hold among competition policy-makers that an alternative to the criminal law structure was needed. The process of achieving such a result was not to be an easy one, however. The story has been told elsewhere of this painful process of amendment.[38] There were two legislative results. The first was the passage in late 1975 of the "Stage I" amendments providing for the civil review of certain practices before the Restrictive Trade Practices Commission and also for a private civil damage remedy.[39] The second consisted of the June, 1986 *Competition Act*

34.   *Aetna Ins. Co. et al. v. The Queen* [1978] 1 S.C.R. 731; *R. v. K.C. Irving Ltd. et al.* [1978] 1 S.C.R. 408, 72 D.L.R. (3d) 82; *Atlantic Sugar Refineries Co. Ltd. et al. v. A.G. Canada* [1980] 2 S.C.R. 644, 115 D.L.R. (3d) 21.

35.   C. Green "Canadian Competition Policy at a Crossroads" (1981), 7 *Canadian Public Policy* 418, p.419; See also G.B. Reschenthaler and W.T. Stanbury, "Recent Conspiracy Decisions in Canada: New Legislation Needed" (1981), 26 *Antitrust Bulletin* 839; J.P. Cairns "Merger Policy in Canada and the Decision in K.C. Irving" (1981), 19 *Alberta Law Review* 303.

36.   *MacDonald v. Vapour Canada Ltd.* (1976), 66 D.L.R. (3rd) 1 (S.C.C.), p.25 per Laskin C.J.; see also *R. v. Zelensky* (1978), 86 D.L.R. (3d) 179 (S.C.C.).

37.   E.g., *Rocois Construction Inc. v. Quebec Ready Mix Inc. et al.* [1980] 1 F.C. 184 (F.C.T.D.); *Henuset Bros. Ltd. v. Syncrude Canada Ltd. et al.* (1980), 114 D.L.R. (3d) (Alta.Q.B.).

38.   E.g., W.T. Stanbury, *Business Interests and the Reform of Canadian Competition Policy 1971-1975* (Toronto: Carswell/Methuen, 1977); Irving Brecher, *Canada's Competition Policy Revisited* (Montreal: The Institute for Research on Public Policy, 1981).

39.   S.C. 1974-75-76, c.76. See Gordon Kaiser, "The Stage I Amendments: An Overview" in J.R.S. Prichard et al. (eds.) *Canadian Competition Policy* (Toronto: Butterworths, 1979), pp. 25-77.

and *Competition Tribunal Act*[40] which established the Competition Tribunal and placed the merger and monopoly law on a civil review basis.

Through this period, the constitutional foundation for these civil law amendments remained in doubt. In 1985, the Macdonald Commission Report reflected the frustration of the continued uncertainty over the constitutional foundation of competition law:

> Effective competition policy is essential to developing the full benefits that can occur from an economic union. Canada has not been very aggressive in encouraging competition, and one reason for this may be our constitutional situation. Canadian legislation relating to competition has found its constitutional justification almost exclusively in the federal power to make criminal law. This arrangement has resulted in limiting the policy tools and the range of remedies available, and in creating some ambiguity about the location, federal or provincial, of the power to launch prosecutions. It provides an excellent example of the tendency for the exigencies of federalism to constrain the tools and instruments through which policy is pursued.[41]

The potential for development of a non-criminal basis for competition law rested mainly on Parliament's trade and commerce power, which had remained largely unutilized since Confederation. Whether this power would provide the flexibility to support the new civil remedies had become the critical question at this stage of the history of competition law.

3.0 ORIGINS OF THE TRADE AND COMMERCE BASIS

Section 91(2) of the *Constitution Act*, 1867 gives Parliament exclusive legislative authority over "The Regulation of Trade and Commerce". The breadth of these words, read literally, has created difficulties. The courts have expressed a desire to limit the trade and commerce power "in order to preserve from serious curtailment, if not from extinction, the degree of autonomy which, as appears from the scheme of the [Constitution] Act as a whole, the Provinces were intended to possess"[42] over matters such as property and civil rights (92(13)), local works and undertakings (92(10)) and local matters (92(16)). It is not surprising that the courts have resisted the expansion of the trade and commerce power in search of the proper balance between federal power and provincial autonomy. What is perhaps surprising

---

40. S.C. 1986, c.26. See W.T. Stanbury, "The New Competition Act and Competition Tribunal Act: 'Not With a Bang, But a Whimper'," 12 *Canadian Business Law Journal* 1 (1986).

41. *Royal Commission on the Economic Union and Development Prospects for Canada* (Macdonald Commission) (Ottawa: Minister of Supply and Services Canada, 1985), Vol. III, p.168.

42. *King v. Eastern Terminal Elevator Co.* [1925] S.C.R. 434.

is that it was not until very recently that the courts have developed tests which reconcile this balance.

Under Canadian constitutional law the trade and commerce power has developed two "branches". Their source is *Citizens' Insurance v. Parsons*,[43] an 1881 decision of the Privy Council. Sir Montague Smith held that the words "the regulation of trade and commerce" included: "...political arrangements in regard to trade requiring the sanction of parliament, regulation of trade in matters of interprovincial concern, and it may be that they would include general regulation of trade affecting the whole dominion."[44] The two branches that developed from this statement are "interprovincial and international" and "general" trade and commerce. Both branches were given little content until the abolition of appeals to the Privy Council in 1949. Since that time the interprovincial/ international branch has swelled to life. The "general" power, however, upon which the constitutional hopes of competition legislation rested, was given little vitality until 1976.

The "international and interprovincial" power deals largely with the regulation of the <u>flow</u> of trade across provincial or international boundaries. Such regulation will almost always incidentally impact local trade. Initially the courts, concerned with provincial autonomy, invalidated such regulation on the grounds of its local impact.[45] In the late 1950's, it was finally held that such effects were not offensive as long as the scheme as a whole was directed at the flow of international or interprovincial trade.[46]

The scope of the "general" trade and commerce power, in contrast, is defined around the <u>static</u> subject matter under regulation. If the subject matter relates to the "general regulation of trade affecting the whole dominion", it may fall within the power. Again the courts have been quick to strike down regulatory schemes which impact on local matters. And again it was only when the Supreme Court accepted that the power, properly qualified, may incidentally apply to such matters that life was breathed into this branch. For the general power, as will be seen below, this recognition did not come until the last decade.

The early cases under general trade and commerce provided mainly a catalogue of what was <u>not</u> included in this head of power. In *Parsons* it was held by the Privy Council that it did not include the power to regulate the contracts of "a particular business or trade, such as the business of fire

---

43. (1881), 7 A.C. 96 (P.C.).

44. *Ibid.*, at p.113.

45. E.g., *Eastern Terminal, supra.*; *Natural Products Marketing Reference* [1937] A.C. 377 (P.C.).

46. *Ontario Farm Products Marketing Reference* [1957] S.C.R. 198 per Kerwin C.J. at p.265; *R. v. Klassen* (1959), 20 D.L.R. (2d) 406 (Man.C.A.), leave refused [1959] S.C.R. ix.

insurance in a single province".[47] In the 1916 *Insurance Reference* it was held that the power did not extend to the licencing of a particular trade such as insurance, even though that trade extended beyond the boundaries of a province.[48] In the 1922 *Board of Commerce* decision the Privy Council rejected trade and commerce as a basis for supporting the price-regulation power of the Board and held that the regulation of a group of industries through a series of regulatory codes offended the *Parsons* rule against regulating contracts of a particular trade within a province.[49] The Privy Council through Viscount Haldane also espoused the theory that trade and commerce was an ancillary power without independent substance. This position was, however, rejected by the same court after Viscount Haldane's death in the *P.A.T.A.* case.[50]

Only in two cases did the Privy Council (or any final appellate court prior to this year) support a scheme of federal regulation on the trade and commerce power. In the *Wharton*[51] case in 1915 it was held that the power permitted Parliament to define the scope of the powers of federally incorporated companies. In the 1937 *Dominion Trade and Industry Commission Reference*,[52] it was held that the power extended to the creation of a national trade mark. Unfortunately, neither decision defined with any precision the nature of the subject matter covered by the general trade and commerce power.

In 1959 Professor Bora Laskin (as he then was) called the Privy Council's treatment of the trade and commerce power its "saddest legacy".[53] It was only when Professor Laskin became the Chief Justice that the Supreme Court of Canada's decisions began to reflect some hope for a broader interpretation of the general power. In the 1976 *Anti-Inflation Reference*[54] the Chief Justice noted that, although it had not been argued, the wages and prices legislation might have been sustained under the trade and commerce power. It was upheld on the basis of the peace, order and good government power. In 1977, in *MacDonald v. Vapour Canada*[55] Laskin C.J. struck down section 7(e) of

47. (1881), 7 A.C. 96 at p.113.

48. *A.G. Can. v. A.G. Alta.* [1916] 1 A.C. 588 (P.C.).

49. (1920), 60 S.C.R. 456; [1922] 1 A.C. 191 (P.C.).

50. [1931] A.C. 310 (P.C.).

51. *John Deere Plow Company v. Wharton* [1915] A.C. 330 (P.C.).

52. *A.G. Ontario v. A.G. Canada* [1937] 1 D.L.R. 703 (P.C.).

53. Prof. B. Laskin, "*R. v. Klassen*, Case Comment" (1959), 38 C.B.R. 630.

54. *Re Anti-Inflation Act* [1976] 2 S.C.R. 373; (1976), 68 D.L.R. (3d) 452.

55. (1977), 66 D.L.R. (3d) 1.

the *Trade Marks Act*, which prohibited certain broadly framed unfair business practices. He rejected trade and commerce as a basis. However, the decision is of significance because in his reasons Chief Justice Laskin appeared to accept the possibility that the general trade and commerce power could be the basis for federal regulation if certain requirements were met. Most significantly, he suggested what those requirements, which will be discussed later, might be.

Despite the potential of the *Vapour* case, in the *Labatt Breweries*[56] decision in 1979 the Supreme Court returned to an approach reminiscent of the Privy Council era. At issue was a federal *Food and Drugs Act* scheme creating national standards for products, and in the particular case, light beer. It was made an offence to label, package, advertise or sell products under the standard name (i.e. "light beer") unless the product complied with regulations governing content and character. Estey J. for the majority held that the appropriate test was whether what is regulated is "a question of general interest throughout the Dominion". He stated that "what clearly is not of general national concern is the regulation of a single trade or industry"[57] and found the regulatory scheme offensive because it created a series of industry-specific regulatory codes. This preoccupation with the specific local impact of regulation rather than its broader purpose recalled the approach of the Privy Council. Neil Finkelstein, among others, took issue with the Court's approach:

> The majority in *Labatts* struck down the national product standards regulation because it formed a series of detailed codes. Why should that matter? The "codes" were insuring uniformity of generic products, not regulating industries as such. The thrust of the regulation ... was to control the composition and quality of goods on a national level, not to trench on local aspects of trade such as production, labour or contracts of sale.[58]

The Supreme Court considered the trade and commerce power again in 1979 in the *Dominion Stores* case.[59] Estey J. relied on the Privy Council precedents as the state of law and struck down a national grading system for apples.

In the aftermath of the *Dominion* and *Labatt* decisions there was a suggestion that "the deathknell has probably sounded for the second branch"

---

56. *Labatt Breweries of Canada Ltd. v. Attorney-General of Canada et al.* (1979), 110 D.L.R. (3d) 594 (S.C.C.).

57. *Ibid.*, at p.624.

58. N. Finkelstein, "Case Comment: *A.G. Canada v. C.N. Transportation*, Kripps' Pharmacy" (1984) 62 *C.B.R.* 182 at p.195. See also MacPherson, *infra*, note 60.

59. *Dominion Stores Ltd. v. The Queen* (1979), 106 D.L.R. 581 (S.C.C.).

of the trade and commerce power established in *Parsons*.[60] It was not immediately clear whether this statement was an overreaction. There followed conflicting decisions on whether the trade and commerce power could support aspects of competition legislation.[61]

One of these cases led to a decision of the Supreme Court in 1983: *Attorney-General for Canada v. Canadian National Transportation*.[62] That decision and *Vapour Canada* became the cornerstones of the Supreme Court's recent consideration of competition legislation under the trade and commerce power.

The issue in *Canadian National Transportation* was whether the criminal law power enabled Parliament to provide that the Attorney-General of Canada could prosecute a charge under section 32 (the conspiracy provision) of the *Combines Investigation Act*. The majority decided that section 32 was criminal law and confirmed that the federal government could prosecute such criminal matters, a question left open by the majority in the 1979 *Hauser*[63] case. Dickson J. (as he then was) for a minority of three judges held that section 32 was supportable on the trade and commerce power. That the section could be justified on the trade and commerce power was important for Dickson J. and the minority since they followed the narrow holding in the *Hauser* case to the effect that matters which are constitutionally supportable on a head of jurisdiction other than the criminal law power (e.g. trade and commerce) may be prosecuted by the Attorney-General of Canada.

Dickson J.'s reasons contained a detailed review of the case law and were significant in the development of the law for two reasons. First, they dealt explicitly with the issue of constitutional balance. Second, they set out a list of criteria for deciding whether matters fall within the trade and commerce power. Both of these addressed weaknesses in the earlier jurisprudence. On the first issue, Mr. Justice Dickson suggested that the difficulty in past jurisprudence was its failure to develop an approach which reconciled the trade and commerce power with provincial autonomy. He considered the test

---

60. J.C. MacPherson "Economic Regulation and the BNA Act" (1981), 5 *Canadian Business Law Journal* 172 at p.192. See also H.C. Kushner "*Dominion Stores* and *Labatt Breweries*" (1981), 9 *Osgoode Hall Law Journal* 119.

61. Holding the civil damage remedy *ultra vires*: *Seiko Canada Ltd. v. Consumers Dist. Co. Ltd.* (1980), 112 D.L.R. (3d) 30 (Ont.H.C.); aff'd. on other grounds (1981), 128 D.L.R. (3d) 767n; rev'd. on other grounds (1984), 10 D.L.R. (4th) 161 (S.C.C.); *Rocois and Henuset, supra*, note 37. Upholding the predatory pricing prohibition (s.34) on trade and commerce: *R. v. Hoffman-La Roche Ltd.* (1980), 109 D.L.R. (3d) 5; aff'd. (1981), 125 D.L.R. (3d) 607 (Ont.C.A.). Upholding misleading advertising: *P.G. du Canada v. Miracle Mart Inc.* (1982), 68 C.C.C. (2d) 242 (Que.S.C.).

62. *A.-G. Canada v. Canadian National Transportation Limited et al.* [1983] 2 S.C.R. 206, reversing (1982), 135 D.L.R. (3d) 89 (Alta.C.A.).

63. *R. v. Hauser* [1979] 1 S.C.R. 984.

based on a matter being a "question of general interest through out the Dominion" unhelpful because it swept in most economic issues. On the other hand, he found an analysis such as that of Duff J. in the *Board of Commerce* case, which focussed on the effect on local matters and contracts, too narrow:

> Every general enactment will necessarily have some local impact, and if it is true that an overly literal conception of "general interest" will endanger the very idea of the local, there are equal dangers in swinging the telescope the other way around. The forest is no less a forest for being made up of individual trees.[64]

He concluded that, while the regulation of a single trade or business would offend local autonomy, a "different situation obtains ... when what is at issue is general legislation aimed at the economy as a single integrated national unit rather than as a collection of separate local enterprises".[65] He felt the latter was not offensive because the provinces were, separately or in combination, constitutionally incapable of enacting such legislation.

This, then was the key to constitutional balance for Mr. Justice Dickson: developing a test for identifying matters beyond the practical constitutional power of the provinces. Granting jurisdiction over such matters to Parliament could not harm provincial autonomy, because the provinces could not enact such national legislation in any event. Because many economic matters could not meet such a test, the "floodgates" to a sweeping application of trade and commerce were closed. Dickson J. set out the applicable test in the following terms:

> In approaching this difficult problem of characterization it is useful to note the remarks of the Chief Justice in *MacDonald v. Vapour Canada Ltd.*, *supra*, at p.165, in which he cites as possible indicia for a valid exercise of the general trade and commerce power the presence of a national regulatory scheme, the oversight of a regulatory agency and a concern with trade in general rather than with an aspect of a particular business. To this list I would add what to my mind would be even stronger indications of valid general regulation of trade and commerce, namely (i) that the provinces jointly or severally would be constitutionally incapable of passing such an enactment and (ii) that failure to include one or more provinces or localities would jeopardize successful operation in other parts of the country.

> The above does not purport to be an exhaustive list, nor is the presence of any or all of these indicia necessarily decisive. The proper approach to the characterization is still the one suggested in *Parsons*, a careful case by case assessment. Nevertheless, the presence of such factors does at least make it far more probable that what is being addressed in a federal enactment is genuinely a national economic concern and not just a collection of local ones.[66]

---

64. [1983] 2 S.C.R. 206 at p.266.

65. *Ibid.*, p.267.

66. *Ibid.*, p.267-268.

Mr. Justice Dickson went on to apply his reasoning to the facts. He found section 32 of the *Combines Investigation Act* to be part of a national regulatory scheme concerned with "trade as a whole rather than a single business".[67] He concluded, as mentioned above, that the provinces would be incapable of enacting such a scheme of competition laws and that if competition is to be regulated at all it must be regulated federally.[68]

Although Dickson J.'s findings were not those of a majority of the Supreme Court and would be later refined, the groundwork had been laid for finding competition legislation valid under the general trade and commerce power.

4.0 THE CITY NATIONAL LEASING AND ROCOIS CONSTRUCTION DECISIONS

While *Canadian National Transportation* was being decided several other cases dealing with the constitutionality of competition legislation were working their way through the courts. Two of these were bound for the Supreme Court of Canada. The first, *Rocois Construction*, went to trial in the Federal Court in the fall of 1979.[69] The case was a private civil action under what was then section 31.1 of the *Combines Investigation Act*.[70] That section permits civil actions for damages flowing from, *inter alia*, a breach of the criminal provisions of the Act. The plaintiff claimed damages from an alleged conspiracy involving cement firms in Quebec City. Marceau J. ruled on a preliminary motion that section 31.1 was *ultra vires* Parliament's powers. He rejected the criminal law, peace order and good government and trade and commerce heads. By the time a delayed appeal of the matter was heard, it was the fall of 1985 and *Canadian National Transportation* had been decided. the Federal Court of Appeal had also decided the *BBM Bureau of Measurement*[71] case, in which the Court per Urie J. endorsed and applied Dickson J.'s reasoning in *Canadian National Transportation* in finding the civil law tied selling provision in the *Combines Investigation Act* valid under the trade and commerce power.

---

67. *Ibid.*, p.276.

68. *Ibid.*, p.278.

69. *Rocois Construction Inc. v. Quebec Ready Mix inc. et al.* [1980] 1 F.C. 184 (T.D.).

70. Now section 36 of the *Competition Act*; the sections were renumbered effective December 12, 1988.

71. *BBM Bureau of Measurement v. Director of Investigation and Research* [1985] 1 F.C. 173 (C.A.).

In the face of these precedents, the Court of Appeal in *Rocois* found section 31.1 constitutional.[72] MacGuigan J. wrote the main opinion of the Court. He adopted Mr. Justice Dickson's criteria and found the civil damage remedy "an integral part of the overall plan" of enforcement in the *Combines Investigation Act*. He found the section sufficiently connected to a scheme of regulation in the Act which itself was valid under the trade and commerce power.

City National Leasing went to trial after *Canadian National Transportation* had been decided. The case was also a civil action under section 31.1. The plaintiff, a national car leasing company, alleged General Motors was discriminating in its payment of interest rate support among different customers. Rosenberg J. in the Ontario High Court struck out certain paragraphs of the statement of claim.[73] The grounds included that section 31.1 was *ultra vires* Parliament. He ruled that because the *Combines Act* had existed for "some 75 years" without such a provision and because it was not part of the regulatory scheme in the Act, it was not "truly necessary" for the Act to be effective.

The Ontario Court of Appeal reversed this judgment, ruling that section 31.1 was constitutional.[74] The Court held it was "in agreement with the Federal Court of Appeal" in *Rocois* without further reasoning.

On appeal, *City National* and *Rocois* were set down to be heard together in the Supreme Court of Canada. The issue framed for decision in both cases was whether the *Combines Investigation Act* as a whole, and section 31.1 in particular, were valid under the federal trade and commerce power. (It is of note that the Chief Justice's framing of the issue extended to the validity of the whole Act and did not mention the peace order and good government power as a potential basis.) The Attorney General of Canada, and the Attorneys General of Quebec, British Columbia, Saskatchewan and Alberta intervened in these appeals.

The *City National* appellant's argument characterized section 31.1 as an isolated remedy dealing with property and civil rights or local matters within the province.[75] It was also argued that Dickson J.'s criteria from *Canadian National Transportation* were not satisfied because the section lacked the oversight of a regulatory agency and the character of national scope because its enforcement was left to the action of private complainants within a province.

---

72. [1985] 2 F.C. 40 (C.A.).

73. *City National Leasing Ltd. v. General Motors of Canada Ltd.* (1984), 47 O.R. (2d) 653 (Ont.H.C.).

74. (1986), 28 D.L.R. (4th) 158 (Ont.C.A.).

75. Appellant's Factum, paragraphs 15, 16, 25-37.

The Attorney General of Quebec supported the appellants.[76] Quebec directed its submissions at the conclusion of Dickson J. in *Canadian National Transportation* that because Canada is, from a competition standpoint, "one huge marketplace", competition must be regulated federally if it is to be regulated effectively. It was argued that, as a result of provincial regulatory barriers caused by such factors as marketing boards, product standards, and restrictions on the mobility of manpower, Canada is not one market but a number of distinct markets. Because Canada is not one market, Quebec argued, the federal government is not alone competent to regulate competition. It was argued that "competition" is not a separate subject matter governed by exclusive authority under the Constitution. For example, Quebec said, the Provinces already regulate business competition through laws dealing with consumer protection and other local matters. Quebec concluded that federal authority over competition matters should extend only to activities which are essentially interprovincial in nature and effect. The Quebec submission was thus more concerned with confining federal jurisdiction over competition under trade and commerce than excluding it altogether.

The Attorney General of British Columbia made the most direct plea to constrain the federal power on the grounds of constitutional balance.[77] The Dickson criteria, it was argued, did not adequately address this balance. British Columbia argued that the appropriate test should involve a comparison of the federal government's ability to act in an area with the ability of the provinces to so act. On the facts, British Columbia submitted that the federal criminal law power provided ample authority over competition matters and that further expansion of this authority was not warranted.

The argument of the respondents was that the civil damage remedy was constitutional both alone and due to its relationship with a regulatory scheme which had already been characterized as constitutional by Dickson J. in *Canadian National Transportation*, the Federal Court of Appeal, the Ontario Court of Appeal and several trial courts.[78] It was argued that, because the remedy is confined to violations of the Act and private enforcement complements public enforcement, the remedy was either "part of" or "rationally, functionally connected to" the regulatory scheme. It was pointed out that civil damages for anti-trust infractions are available in other jurisdictions including the United States, Australia and certain Western European countries.

---

76. Factum of the Intervener Attorney-General of Quebec.

77. Factum of the Intervener, Attorney-General of British Columbia, paras. 9-21. See also Factum of the Intervener, Attorney-General of Alberta.

78. Factum of the Respondent, City National Leasing Limited, para. 3.

The Attorney General of Canada supported the respondents' position, focussing on the connection between section 31.1 and the regulatory scheme.[79] Canada referred to reports and articles such as the *Interim Report on Competition Policy*[80] and the *Macdonald Commission Report*[81] which had urged a shift from the criminal law to a broadened civil law basis for competition regulation. As for constitutional balance, the Attorney General of Canada submitted that the courts had placed ample limitation through *Labatt Breweries, Parsons, Vapour Canada* and other cases which confined the scope of the federal trade and commerce power.

The Supreme Court's judgments in both cases were delivered on April 20, 1989.[82] Dickson C.J., for an unanimous court held that both section 31.1, and the *Combines Investigation Act* as a whole, were within Parliament's authority over general trade and commerce. Three significant points were made in the reasons:

1.   The Court set out an analytical approach for assessing constitutionality and dealt with the "necessarily incidental" and related tests cited in earlier cases.
2.   The Court confirmed the criteria to be used in determining whether a given subject falls within the general trade and commerce power.
3.   The Court confirmed, for the first time, a noncriminal legislative basis for competition legislation as a whole and for section 31.1 in particular.

1.   Analytical Approach: Dickson C.J. set out in his reasons a procedure for constitutional analysis. The procedure involves first focussing on the challenged section and then the scheme of the legislation to determine validity. His own words provide the best summary of the procedure:

> The steps in the analysis may be summarized as follows: First, the court must determine whether the impugned provision can be viewed as intruding on provincial powers, and if so to what extent (if it does not intrude, then the only possible issue is the validity of the act). Second, the court must establish whether the act (or a severable part of it) is valid; in cases under the second branch of section 91(2) this will normally involve finding the presence of a regulatory scheme and then ascertaining whether that scheme meets the requirements articulated in *Vapour*

---

79.   Factum of the Intervener, Attorney General of Canada, para. 8.

80.   *Supra.*, Note 32.

81.   *Supra.*, note 41.

82.   *Supra* notes 1 and 2. The main reasons for judgment of the court were given in *City National Leasing* and adopted and referred to in the *Rocois* reasons. Beetz, McIntyre, Lamer, Laforest and L'Heueux-Dube J.J. concurred in the result with Dickson C.J.; Le Dain J. took no part.

> *Canada, supra,* and in *Canadian National Transportation, supra.* If the scheme is
> not valid, that is the end of the inquiry. If the scheme of regulation is declared
> valid, the court must then determine whether the impugned provision is sufficiently
> integrated with the scheme that it can be upheld by virtue of that relationship.
> This requires considering the seriousness of the encroachment on provincial powers,
> in order to decide on the proper standard for such a relationship. If the provision
> passes this integration test, it is *intra vires* Parliament as an exercise of the general
> trade and commerce power. If the provision is not sufficiently integrated into the
> scheme of regulation, it cannot be sustained under the second branch of section
> 91(2).[83]

The question of how "integrated" the provision is within the scheme
raised the question of what test of integration (or "fit" as he put it) to use -
"necessarily incidental", "rational, functional connection", "integral part", "truly
necessary" or some other test used in previous cases. The Chief Justice held
that the test would vary, depending on the nature of the encroachment on
provincial powers; the greater the encroachment, the stricter the "fit" that
would be required.

Chief Justice Dickson's method of analysis represents a new page in the
constitutional law books concerning the assessment of the incidental impacts
of the legislation of Parliament on matters principally within the constitutional
purview of the provincial legislatures. Tests which had developed from
previous case law such as "necessarily incidental" and "rational, functional
connection"[84] have now given way to a test which is a variable one, and
depends on the extent of the apparent encroachment and the degree to which
the impugned provision is integrated into the legislative scheme.

Also of significance was the Chief Justice's statement concerning the
judicial application of such a test:

> In determining the proper test it should be remembered that in a federal system
> it is inevitable that, in pursuing valid objectives, the legislation of each level of
> government will impact occasionally in the sphere of power of the other level of
> government; overlap of legislation is to be expected and accommodated in a federal
> state. Thus a certain degree of judicial restraint in proposing strict tests which will
> result in striking down such legislation is appropriate.[85]

How times have changed from the Privy Council days! The Court
apparently is less inclined to use the division of powers as a vehicle of striking
down "undesirable" federal regulation than in the Privy Council era. It has
followed the approach to the "paramountcy" doctrine which originated with the
highway traffic cases. It has become clear since those cases and *Multiple*

---

83. *Supra,* note 1 at pp.276-277.

84. See, e.g., *Multiple Access Ltd. v. McCutcheon et al.* (1982) 138 D.L.R. (3d) 1 (S.C.C.) at
p.18; *Papp v Papp* [1970] 1 O.R. 331 (C.A.).

85. *City National Leasing, supra.,* note 1 at p.274.

Access v. McCutcheon[86] that the Supreme Court will find conflict between federal and provincial regulation giving rise to overriding federal authority only where "compliance with one is defiance of the other". Such judicial restraint facilitates giving effect to a power such as trade and commerce which, as pointed out by the courts repeatedly, inevitably involves incidental impacts on local and intra-provincial matters. Such "restraint" also gives effect to a broader federal role in national economic matters.

2.   The Criteria for the Trade and Commerce Power: Chief Justice Dickson confirmed the five criteria or "hallmarks of validity for legislation under the second branch of the trade and commerce power" in his reasons. As set out earlier in the quotation from the *Canadian National Transportation* case, these criteria are:

    1.   The impugned legislation must be part of a regulatory scheme;
    2.   The scheme must be monitored by the continuing oversight of a regulatory agency;
    3.   The legislation must be concerned with trade as a whole rather than with a particular industry;
    4.   The legislation should be a nature that the provinces jointly or severally would be constitutionally incapable or enacting; and
    5.   The failure to include one or more provinces or localities in the legislative scheme would jeopardize the successful operation of the scheme in other parts of the country.

It will be recalled that the first three criteria had originally been gleaned by Dickson J. (as he then was) in *Canadian National Transportation* from the reasons of Laskin C.J. in *Vapour Canada*.[87] In *City National* Dickson C.J. went further and stated how, in his view, the Laskin criteria aid in determining if a given matter falls within the trade and commerce power:

> Each of these requirements is evidence of a concern that federal authority under the second branch of the trade and commerce power does not encroach on provincial jurisdiction. By limiting the means which federal legislators may employ to that of a regulatory scheme overseen by a regulatory agency, and by limiting the object of federal legislation to trade as a whole, these requirements attempt to maintain a delicate balance between federal and provincial power.[88]

Chief Justice Dickson thus thought that the criteria assist in maintaining constitutional balance by screening out matters which encroach too much on

---

86.   *Supra*, note 84, at p.24. See also *OPSEU v. Attorney General of Ontario* [1987] 2 S.C.R. 2 at p.18.

87.   *MacDonald v. Vapour Canada Ltd.* (1976), 66 D.L.R. (3rd) 1 (S.C.C.) at p.26 (emphasis added).

88.   *Supra.*, note 1 at p.268.

provincial power. If this was the rationale for the criteria originally, it was not explicitly stated in *Vapour Canada*. Chief Justice Laskin had taken a more philosophical approach in employing these criteria in his search for the subject matter within federal legislative power. Nonetheless, striking the correct constitutional balance has been, as suggested earlier, the major stumbling block for the courts in their consideration of the trade and commerce power and Chief Justice Dickson's approach illustrates a practical desire to deal overtly with this critical issue.

The fourth and fifth criteria were introduced by Mr. Justice Dickson in *Canadian National Transportation* like a *deus ex machina*, with little explanation of their origin. His judgment as Chief Justice in City National provided an opportunity for further explanation. Again this explanation rested on the need for constitutional balance: "These two requirements, like Laskin C.J.'s three criteria, serve to ensure that federal legislation does not upset the balance of power between federal and provincial governments."[89] It is of interest to compare these criteria with those articulated by the Supreme Court in another recent decision which deals with the peace order and good government or "residual" power, *Crown Zellerbach*.[90] Dickson's fourth and fifth criteria show close resemblance to the "provincial inability" test employed in *Crown Zellerbach* under which the question posed in determining federal competence is whether or not "provincial failure to deal effectively with the intraprovincial aspects of the matter [in question] could have an adverse effect on extraprovincial interests". Concern with constitutional balance has arguably played an important role in the history of both powers. With the heightened visibility of that factor in the Supreme Court's recent jurisprudence it is not surprising that the test for both these broadly-based powers has apparently converged. A final point made by Dickson C.J. was that:

> ... the five factors provide a preliminary checklist of characteristics, the presence of which in legislation is an indication of validity under the trade and commerce power. These indicia do not, however, represent an exhaustive list of traits that will tend to characterize general trade and commerce legislation. Nor is the presence or absence of any of these five criteria necessarily determinative ... a careful case-by-case analysis remains appropriate.[91]

3. Application of the Criteria: (a) <u>The Act as a Whole</u>: In applying the five criteria to the *Combines Investigation Act*, Dickson C.J. had "no difficulty in finding that" the Act as a whole embodied a complex scheme of economic regulation, possessing three components: elucidation of prohibited conduct; creation of an investigatory procedure; and, the establishment of a remedial

---

89. *Ibid.*, at p.269.

90. *R. v. Crown Zellerbach Ltd.* (1988), 49 D.L.R. (4th) 161 (S.C.C.) at p.185.

91. *Supra.*, note 1, at p.269.

mechanism. It was found that "the control of the process exercised by the director [of Investigation and Research] and the [Restrictive Trade Practices] commission satisfies the requirement that there be vigilant oversight of the administration of the regulatory scheme."[92]

Dickson treated the third, fourth and fifth criteria together as "indicators that the scheme of regulation is national in scope and that local regulation would be inadequate" and found that the Act satisfied this overall test. However, his reasons do reflect consideration of evidence that appears to fit discreetly under certain of the criteria.

With respect to the third criterion, he cited the reasons of Ryan J. of the Quebec Superior Court in *R. v. Miracle Mart*[93] to the effect that the Act involves "a complete regulatory scheme aimed at eliminating commercial practices which are contrary to healthy competition <u>across the country</u>, and not in a specific place, in a specific business or industry."[94] This he found to be evidence of the regulation of trade in general rather than "concern with the regulation of a particular industry or commodity." He distinguished the scheme from that in *Labatt*, which applied to a single trade or industry.

The fourth and fifth criteria were supported by reference to Hogg and Grover's 1976 article[95] and a 1974 study by economist A.E. Safarian, both of which had been relied on by the Attorney General of Canada.[96] The passages of these reports cited by Dickson C.J. presented the view that competitive forces in Canada, as an "economic union", tend to be national or at least trans-provincial due to the mobility of labour, goods and services, the trend toward enhanced communication and transportation and the freedom of movement of corporate interests. Two arguments for national regulation of competition flowed from these factual assertions. The first was that national regulation of competition is better able to influence the efficient allocation of resources among the differently endowed regions of Canada. (The unstated assumption of this argument was apparently that parochial provincial influences might tolerate local anti-competitive conduct which would inhibit the distribution of resources.)

The second argument was that the mobility referred to would make regulation of competition by the provinces impossible, because the forces in question can adapt to, and escape, the scope of provincial authority. (Dickson C.J.'s reasons do not provide examples to flesh out this reasoning. A possible

---

92. *Ibid.*, at p.281.

93. *P.G. du Canada v. Miracle Mart Inc.* (1982), 68 C.C.C. (2d) 242, (emphasis in original).

94. *Ibid.*, at p.259.

95. Peter Hogg and Warren Grover, "The Constitutionality of the Competition Bill," 1 *Canadian Business Law Journal* 197 (1976).

96. Both these studies were carried out on behalf of the federal government.

example is a trans-provincial price fixing conspiracy. A province subject to higher prices due to a conspiracy in an out-of-province industry would have difficulty attacking such a conspiracy due to its constitutional inability to regulate interprovincial trade or business interests beyond its borders. Even several provinces acting together would have difficulty regulating practices which span more than one jurisdiction due to their constitutional inability to regulate interprovincial and international flows of capital and trade and national corporate matters. The temptation to harbour anti-competitive practices to create local jobs and trade may create a "race for the bottom" which erodes the incentive for provincial cooperation in any event.)

Dickson C.J. found that this logic answered the Quebec position that federal jurisdiction should be confined to the interprovincial dimension of competition, whatever that may be. He held that, to be effective, competition law must be national and cover intraprovincial trade. He noted that this was not inconsistent with the fact the provinces possess jurisdiction to enact, and have enacted, laws bearing on local competition such as unfair business practices laws. Nor was it inconsistent with the view expressed by the Economic Council that the provinces "could play a most useful role" in the area. He concluded:

> ... competition is not a single subject matter, any more than inflation or pollution. The provinces too, may deal with competition in the exercise of their legislative powers in such fields as consumer protection, labour relations, marketing and the like. The point is, however, that Parliament also have the constitutional power to regulate intraprovincial aspects of competition.[97]

Competition is evidently a subject to which the "double aspect" doctrine applies - the provinces may regulate it under provincial heads of jurisdiction while the federal government may regulate it under the trade and commerce and criminal law powers. The application of this doctrine has made possible the tolerance of federal authority in the face of its evident effects on local matters.

3.   Application of the Criteria: <u>Connection of Section 31.1 to the Regulatory Scheme</u>: The remaining question was the constitutional status of section 31.1. Dickson C.J. held that section 31.1 by itself involved an encroachment on provincial powers, because the creation of civil actions was generally a matter within provincial authority over property and civil rights. However, he held that three factors affected this encroachment: "the provision is a remedial one; federal encroachment in this manner [i.e. civil relief] is not unprecedented

---

97.   *Supra.*, note 1, at p.284.

and, in this case, encroachment has been limited by the restrictions of the Act."[98]

When it came to considering the connection between section 31.1 and the valid regulatory scheme, Dickson C.J. concluded that because of these factors, the section only intrudes "in a limited way" on provincial powers. Therefore, he held, a "strict" test of connection to the scheme such as "necessarily incidental" was not required. The test he chose was whether the provision was "functionally related to the general objective of the legislation".[99] He cited no specific precedent for this test, stating only that a "similar test" had been used in earlier cases. His choice of a "similar" but previously unused test may have been intended to underline that a flexible approach, adapted to the circumstances of each case, was required.

The Chief Justice concluded that section 31.1 satisfied the test as "an integral, well-conceived component of the economic regulatory strategy" in the Act. He held that even a stricter "necessarily incidental" test would have been satisfied. He provided the following reasons for this conclusion:

1.   The section is one of an "arsenal of remedies" in the Act and reinforces other sanctions such as interim injunctions and criminal remedies;

2.   The section has "no independent content" because civil actions are possible only for particular violations of provision of the Act and the section does not involve "a private right of action at large";

3.   Private enforcement coincides with the overall goal of enhancing healthy competition in the economy. It supplements public enforcement.   This function goes beyond private interests to promote the public interest in deterrence and compliance;

4.   He noted the Economic Council's conclusions that a civil law basis for competition law was desirable in order to move away from the rigidity of the criminal law; and,

5.   He took into account the fact that, in the United States, private actions have performed an important deterrent function.

The final element considered by the Chief Justice was constitutional balance. He held that section 31.1, "carefully constructed and limited by the terms" of the Act did not upset this balance. He noted that the section did not fall within the exclusions developed in cases such as *Labatt, Parsons* and *Vapour Canada*. Dickson C.J. distinguished *Vapour* on the basis that the civil remedy there was a detached provision, unlimited in its application. Section

98. *Ibid.*, at p.278.

99. *Ibid.*, at p. 285, emphasis added.

31.1, he held, was limited in its application to combines violations and consistent with the purposes of its enabling Act.

5.0 CONCLUSIONS: THE PATH AHEAD

One hundred years after it was first enacted, Canadian competition legislation has received a firm constitutional foundation outside the criminal law. This result was made possible by what might be called the "modern approach" to interpreting the federal trade and commerce power. Under this approach, it is no longer fatal that a regulatory scheme framed under this power has an impact on local matters. What matters is the character and scope of the legislation.

Perhaps the critical factor in giving effect to the general trade and commerce power has been the development of criteria which give the power content while showing respect for constitutional balance. Chief Justice Dickson has set out such criteria in the *City National* and *Rocois* decisions. The 1976 *Vapour Canada* and 1983 *Canadian National Transportation* cases were the major steps leading to these decisions. In the latter case the current Chief Justice developed the criteria. He relied in part on the factors articulated by Laskin C.J. in the former case. An additional element of this process was the inclination, expressed in such cases as *Multiple Access*[100] toward judicial tolerance of the interplay and overlap of federal and provincial powers under the "double aspect" concept. This approach makes federal jurisdiction over the regulation of competition possible without denying the potential for provincial legislation in the same area. This assists in achieving the necessary balance of constitutional authority.

It remains to consider the possible impact of the *City National* and *Rocois* decisions on the future of Canadian competition law. What follows will discuss the potential impact of the decisions on the 1986 amendment package, on further expansion or amendment to the law and on the application of competition law to provincially regulated conduct.

5.1 The 1986 Amendments

The 1986 amendment package, among other things, shifted the merger and monopoly provisions from the criminal law to a civil basis.[101] Adjudication of these provisions, along with the existing civilly reviewable practices, was placed in the hands of the newly created Competition Tribunal. The Tribunal is a hybrid court which sits in panels consisting of judges of the Federal Court Trial Division and lay members possessing knowledge of economics and business matters.

---

100. *Supra.*, note 84.

101. S.C. 1986, c.26.

Already the merger provisions of the Act have been challenged on constitutional grounds in *Alex Couture v. A.G. Canada*.[102] A trial of the constitutional issues was completed before Quebec Superior Court on November 3, 1989. The Attorney General of Canada argued that the constitutional validity of the 1986 amendments under the trade and commerce power is clear from the recent decisions of the Supreme Court of Canada. It was argued that the legislative scheme in question is virtually identical to that in the *Combines Investigation Act*, the constitutional status of which under the trade and commerce of power in general was definitively settled in the *City National Leasing* and *Rocois Construction* judgments.

The applicant and the Attorney General of Quebec (intervening) are attempting to re-examine Chief Justice Dickson's reasoning in the recent judgments, arguing that the Supreme Court was incorrect in holding that intraprovincial competition must be regulated nationally if it is to be regulated at all. Reports filed in evidence include those of American antitrust experts which cite the experience in that country under which States have developed their own laws and enforcement policies governing local antitrust issues. The Attorney General of Canada has argued that, as a matter of law, such evidence is unnecessary and irrelevant as the issue has been settled and that, in any event, the Supreme Court's reasons do not exclude the availability of provincial activity in the competition law area. Judgment has been reserved.

5.2 Further Amendments

A further issue of interest is whether certain suggested changes to competition law can be supported due to the Supreme Court's recent judgments. One possibility, discussed at length during the amendment process that began in 1969, is a class action remedy.[103]

Although class action procedures are dealt with under provincial Rules of Court, cases such as *Naken v. General Motors*[104] have proven that satisfying the requirements of such rules may be very difficult. The Supreme Court in that case, in striking down a class claim on the grounds that it would necessitate individual assessments of entitlement, expressed concern about the lack of coverage in the Ontario Rules of Court surrounding notice to interested parties, costs and determination of entitlement to damages. More detailed rules might have facilitated class actions. Provinces such as Quebec

---

102.   *Alex Couture Inc. et al. v. A.G. Canada et al.* (Que.S.C.).

103.   See, e.g., N.J. Williams and J. Whybrow, *A Proposal for Class Action Under Competition Policy Legislation* (Ottawa: Minister of Supply and Services Canada, 1976).

104.   (1983), 144 D.L.R. (3d) 385 (S.C.C.).

have passed more detailed rules,[105] but such provisions are not available across the country.

In 1977, Bills C-42 and C-13, two of the many packages of amendments presented in the process of reforming our competition laws, contained proposals which would have dealt with some of the issues raised in the *Naken* case. Although those amendments were never carried forward, a House of Commons Committee studying misleading advertising released the so-called "Collins Report" in June 1988, and rejuvenated the issue by recommending that the *Competition Act* be amended by adding a "code of procedure for regulating the commencement, maintenance and conduct of class actions".[106]

Without entering the debate on the merits of federal class action provisions, it can at least be observed that the *City National* and *Rocois* decisions would provide some support for their constitutionality. The relevant rule is that "with respect to matters coming within the enumerated heads of s.91 [of the *Constitution Act*, 1867], the Parliament of Canada may give jurisdiction to provincial courts and regulate proceedings in such courts to the fullest extent."[107] This suggests that the federal government may be competent to enact detailed procedural rules governing class actions in civil damage cases brought pursuant to section 36 of the *Competition Act*. As long as such rules are procedural and not substantive in nature, their constitutionality should derive support from the *City National* and *Rocois* finding that the civil damage action itself is valid.

Parliament could also proceed by amending the Federal Court Rules. Jurisdiction over such rules flows from the power to create the federal courts under s.101 of the *Constitution Act*, 1867. This route would avoid the need to open up the *Competition Act* to amendment, but it has certain disadvantages. First, the procedures would only apply to proceedings in the Federal Court, within its limited jurisdiction, and the Provincial Rules of Court would continue to apply elsewhere. The checkerboard of procedures across the country would continue. Second, the Rules would apply, unless expressly restricted, to all federal proceedings and the procedures in question would have to be tailored carefully to permit general application.

The provinces themselves could, of course, also act to deal with some of the procedural problems surrounding class actions. In spite of the Supreme

---

105. *An Act Respecting Class Action* L.R.Q., c.R-2.1, modified by L.Q. 1982, c.37 art. 20-25; *Quebec Code of Civil Procedure*, L.R.Q. c.C-25, art. 999.

106. *Report of the Standing Committee on Consumer and Corporate Affairs on the Subject of Misleading Advertising*, (Ottawa, June, 1988).

107. *Laskin's Constitutional Law* (3d ed.) at p.835, citing *A.G. Alta. et al. v. Atlas Lumber Co.* [1941] 1 D.L.R. 628 (S.C.C.) per Rinfret J. at p.632. See also *Valin v. Langlois* (1880), 3 S.C.R. 1; *C.N.R. v. Pszenicnzy* [1916] 54 S.C.R. 36; *Nykorak v. A.G. Can.* [1962] S.C.R. 331; *The Queen v. Hauser* 46 C.C.C. (2d) 481 (S.C.C.); *A.G. Can. v. C.N. Transp. Ltd. et al.* (1983), 3 D.L.R. (4th) 16 at p.39. See also Davis, *Constitutional Law Handbook*, pp.537-538.

Court's plea for action in *Naken* and the release of studies calling for reform such as the Ontario Law Reform Commission's 1982 *Report on Class Actions*, the pace of such reform has been glacial. Ontario has recently announced a consultation process on class action provisions but there is no indication of similar action in other jurisdictions.[108] Federal action may be the only practical way to adopt a consistent procedure across the country.

The Supreme Court's recent decisions also raise the possibility of expansion of the current civil damage remedy by way of amendment. The current remedy in section 36 is limited to the recovery of damages arising from violations of the criminal provisions of the Act and violations of orders of the Tribunal arising from the civil provisions. There is no independent right of application to the Tribunal for orders concerning merger, abuse of dominance, tied selling and other civilly reviewable practices. The Director is the "gate-keeper" of those sections as (with the exception of the specialization agreements provisions) it is only he that may make an application to the Tribunal for a remedial order. One might ask whether the *City National* and *Rocois* decisions would permit an amendment of the *Competition Act* to expand the private civil remedy to permit independent applications to the Tribunal. Such applications could extend to challenges to mergers and monopolistic situations as well as to vertical arrangements.

It can be argued that such an extension of the civil remedy would be constitutional under the trade and commerce power on the basis of the principles established by the Supreme Court. Applying Chief Justice Dickson's reasoning in *City National Leasing*, such an amendment would appear to satisfy all of the five considerations mentioned by the Chief Justice in this finding that the civil damage remedy is "functionally related to the general objective of the legislation" and therefore constitutional. The extension would add to the arsenal of remedies in the legislation; it would be limited to specific violations of the Act and not simply create a statutory tort; enforcement action by private individuals would enhance the goals of deterrence and compliance; it would reinforce the use of a non-criminal remedial process; and it would coincide with the breadth of the civil remedy in the United States, where private parties may bring private civil actions in relation to vertical practices, monopolies and mergers and where such private enforcement has performed an important enforcement function.

The consequences of the Canada-U.S. Free Trade Agreement may also provide a need for amendment to competition law. For example, the Agreement in Chapter 19 provides for a period to negotiate rules governing anti-dumping. There has been some suggestion of replacing anti-dumping law

---

108.   Hon. Ian Scott, "Statement to the Legislature on Class Actions"; Ministry of Attorney General, News Release, "Attorney General Announces Class Action Reform", June 29, 1989.

with domestic competition legislation covering predatory pricing.[109] The existing predatory pricing law is criminal in nature. The proposed change may require the creation of a civil predatory pricing regime to supplement or substitute for trade legislation. While the international trade and commerce power would be an obvious basis for a law directed solely at external trade, the general trade and commerce power may be a necessary basis were such a scheme to apply as well to domestic transactions. The private civil damage action could also feature in any scheme proposed to replace the anti-dumping laws.

5.3 Provincially Regulated Conduct

Another area that provides fertile ground for speculation concerning the impact of these decisions is the application of competition legislation to activity regulated under provincial legislation. The existing case law under the so-called "regulated conduct defense" has held that conduct which is authorized by the exercise of validly enacted provincial regulatory authority will be "deemed to be in the public interest" and therefore not within the ambit of the criminal competition law.[110] As long as the competition legislation is styled as criminal law, Estey J. held for the Supreme Court of Canada in *Jabour v. Law Society of B.C.*,[111] it will require a demonstration of conduct contrary to the public interest. Therefore, conduct authorized by provincial legislation (there, a ban on lawyers' advertising) was held to be beyond the scope of the criminal conspiracy provision.

Now that it is clear that competition legislation can be supported on constitutional authority aside from the criminal law, it is open to question whether the authorities dealing with the application of criminal law to regulated conduct should be applied to competition legislation. One might now suggest that conflict between competition law and provincial regulation should be resolved in favour of the federal legislation under the paramountcy doctrine, under which federal legislation governs where validly enacted laws of both jurisdictions apply to the same subject matter and are inconsistent. However, based on the historical judicial concern for constitutional balance, the courts will undoubtedly continue to be sensitive to the potential for federal encroachment on provincial autonomy. A sweeping application of the paramountcy doctrine in this area which could displace much provincial

---

109. See, e.g., "The Interface of Trade/Competition Law and Policy" (1987), 56 Antitrust L.J. 395; Rosenthal, "Antitrust Implications of the Canada-United States F.T.A." (1989), 10:1 *Canadian Competition Policy Record* 51.

110. E.g., Farm Products Marketing Reference [1957] S.C.R. 198 at p.220.

111. *Jabour v. Law Society of British Columbia et al.*; *A.G. Canada v. Law Society of British Columbia* [1982] 2 S.C.R. 307, 137 D.L.R. (3d) 1. More generally, see W.T. Stanbury, "Provincial Regulation and Federal Competition Policy: The *Jabour* Case" (1983) 3 *Windsor Yearbook of Access to Justice* 291.

jurisdiction over local matters, is unlikely. However, there is certainly room for the courts to place a greater onus on the provinces by holding that only conduct which is under active, specific provincial regulation will be considered to be publicly beneficial and therefore exempt from federal competition law. In the United States, such an approach developed in rubric of the "state action doctrine."[112] There, States must put in place regulations under a "clearly articulated and affirmatively expressed" policy in order for an exemption from federal anti-trust laws to apply. In addition, regulated conduct must be "actively supervised". It is not enough, for example, to simply turn the power to regulate over to the interested parties without some checks and balances to ensure the scheme operates in the manner intended.[113] It is hoped that the recent constitutional decisions in Canada will similarly reinforce the general applicability of federal competition legislation except where provinces have clearly and affirmatively satisfied a minimum onus to remove the activities from the competitive sphere through regulation.

6.0   CONCLUSION

Overall, the prognosis for an effective national competition law is much brighter now that a non-criminal basis has been confirmed by the Supreme Court of Canada. Already, for example, the merger law has enjoyed a renewed relevance in domestic commerce, even if the number of contested matters before the Competition Tribunal has not, to date, been what some had expected. The number of Competition Tribunal applications does not reflect the important role the law has played in restructuring or discouraging transactions with potentially anti-competitive effects.[114]

This renewal of the law is due in no small measure to the civil law basis, which permits among other things, a more flexible compliance process, non-contested civil consent orders and specialized injunctive relief. As markets continue to internationalize and competition legislation is required to adapt, the constitutional basis of the Canadian legislation now appears broad enough to accommodate the pressures for flexibility and change that will no doubt continue and expand as we embark upon the legislation's second century.

Postscript: After this paper was prepared, the merger[115] and conspiracy[116]

---

112.   E.g., *California Retail Liquor v. Midcal* (1980), 445 U.S. 97 at p.105.

113.   E.g., *Goldfarb v. Virginia State Bar* (1975), 421 U.S. 773.

114.   For a recent review of the enforcement record, see *Annual Report of the Director of Investigation and Research*, years ended March 31, 1990, 1989, 1988 and 1987. See also 12(1) *Canadian Competition Policy Record* (1991) at 6-9.

115.   See *Canadian Competition Policy Record*, Vol. 8(3), 1987, pp. 7-8; Vol. 8(4), 1987, pp. 7-8; Vol. 11(2), 1990, pp. 1-3 re the *Couture* case (Quebec Superior Court, April 6, 1990).

provisions were subject to constitutional challenges as was the composition of the Competition Tribunal.[117]

---

116. *R. v. Nova Scotia Pharmaceutical Society and Pharmacy Association of Nova Scotia et al.* (1990) 32 C.P.R. (3d) 259 (NSSC TD); Unreported, NSSC-Appeal Division, April 24, 1991; *Canadian Competition Policy Record*, Vol. 11(3), 1990, pp. 1-3. Generally, see Brian Facey and W.T. Stanbury, "Is the Opportunity to Cartelize a Charter Right in Canada?" (Paper presented to the Western Economics Association 66th Annual Conference, July 2, 1991, Seattle, Washington). See also *R. v. L'Association Quebecois Pharmaciens Proprietaires et al.* (Quebec Supreme Court, December 6, 1990, Unreported). See also the discussion in Howard Wetston, "Recent Developments in Competition Law: The Perspective of the Bureau of Competition Policy" (Presentation to the Law Society of Upper Canada, Toronto, April 26, 1991, mimeo).

117. See the *Couture* case *supra* note 115 and the *NutraSweet* case (1990) 32 C.P.R. (3d) 1; *Canadian Competition Policy Record*, Vol. 11(2), 1990, pp. 7-8; Vol. 12(1), 1991, p. 1; and Wetston, *ibid.*.

RELATED PUBLICATIONS

Baggaley, Carman D. (1991) "Tariffs, Combines and Politics: The Beginning of Canadian Competition Policy, 1888-1900" in R.S. Khemani and W.T. Stanbury (eds.) *Historical Perspectives on Canadian Competition Policy* (Halifax: The Institute for Research on Public Policy).

Brecher, Irving (1982) *Canada's Competition Policy Revisited: Some New Thoughts on an Old Story* (Montreal: The Institute for Research on Public Policy).

Gorecki, Paul K. and W.T. Stanbury, eds. (1979) *Perspectives on the Royal Commission on Corporate Concentration* (Toronto: Butterworths for The Institute for Research on Public Policy).

Gorecki, Paul K. and W.T. Stanbury (1984) *The Objectives of Canadian Competition Policy, 1888-1983* (Montreal: The Institute for Research on Public Policy).

Khemani, R.S., D.M. Shapiro and W.T. Stanbury, eds. (1988) *Mergers, Corporate Concentration and Power in Canada* (Montreal: The Institute for Research on Public Policy).

Khemani, R.S. and W.T. Stanbury, eds. (1991a) *Canadian Competition Law and Policy at the Centenary* (Halifax: The Institute for Research on Public Policy).

Khemani, R.S. and W.T. Stanbury, eds. (1991b) *Historical Perspectives on Canadian Competition Policy* (Halifax: The Institute for Research on Public Policy).

Rowley, J.W. and W.T. Stanbury, eds. (1978) *Competition Policy in Canada: Stage II, Bill C-13* (Montreal: The Institute for Research on Public Policy).